Nine Li

To Bob,
Thanks for your
support!
Josh Schonwald

Nine Lives of Israel

*A Nation's History through the
Lives of Its Foremost Leaders*

Jack L. Schwartzwald

McFarland & Company, Inc., Publishers
Jefferson, North Carolina, and London

Index created by Clive Pyne Indexing

LIBRARY OF CONGRESS CATALOGUING-IN-PUBLICATION DATA

Schwartzwald, Jack L., 1958–
    Nine lives of Israel : a nation's history through the lives
of its foremost leaders / Jack L. Schwartzwald.
        p.   cm.
    Includes bibliographical references and index.

    ISBN 978-0-7864-6684-9
    softcover : acid free paper ∞

    1. Israel — Biography.   2. Zionists— Israel — Biography.
3. Statesmen — Israel — Biography.   4. Prime ministers—
Israel — Biography.   5. Generals— Israel — Biography.
6. Israel — History.   I. Title.
DS126.6.A2S39 2012
956.9405092'2 — dc23   2012006528

BRITISH LIBRARY CATALOGUING DATA ARE AVAILABLE

Front cover image © 2012 Shutterstock

Manufactured in the United States of America

McFarland & Company, Inc., Publishers
    Box 611, Jefferson, North Carolina 28640
        www.mcfarlandpub.com

To my wife, Cheryl, and to our cats, Cody and Crosby — all of whom exercised extraordinary patience while it was written.

Also to the people of Israel, who have endured tribulation with every triumph, and who, despite it all, have persevered to build the Middle East's only functioning democracy while making contributions to the human endeavor out of all proportion to their numbers.

Contents

Preface

Nine Lives of Israel begins at the dawn of modern political Zionism and runs to the present day, profiling nine celebrated people who played key roles in the Jewish national revival. I have sought at every step to remain true to the factual record. Mark Twain is said to have remarked that "a lie can travel halfway around the world while the truth is putting on its shoes." Surely, in today's world, a lie can circumvent the entire globe in that amount of time. There are a great many preconceived notions about Israel in this day of instantaneous communications. It is hoped that this work will serve as an accessible resource for those who are attempting to navigate through them — whether the interested party is a general reader, a student, a perplexed media consumer or a journalist attempting to maintain objectivity while covering a complex and contentious subject.

Taking its inspiration from E. T. Bell's classic *Men of Mathematics*, which tells the story of mathematics by focusing on the lives of history's greatest mathematicians, *Nine Lives of Israel* is a unique tapestry of history and biography that balances comprehensiveness with brevity and scholarly content with informal tone. The distinctive format sets it apart from other works on a topic that — whether it inspires pride or incites passion — never ceases to fascinate.

The monograph collections at the libraries of Brown University and the University of Rhode Island were extremely useful in building a bibliography from which to research this work. It is a matter of great convenience that all of the book's main protagonists left behind one or more volumes of memoirs or diaries and that all have had multiple biographies written about them. Likewise, many fine detailed histories of Israel are available. Although many such volumes were consulted, four that were essential to the writing of this book were Howard M. Sachar's *A History of Israel from the Rise of Zionism to Our Time*, Sir Martin Gilbert's *Israel: A History*, Abba Eban's *Personal Witness*, and Conor Cruise O'Brien's *The Siege*. For primary source materials, I made extensive use of the 5th and 8th editions of Laqueur and Rubin's *The Israel-*

Arab Reader as well as Isaacs and Olitzky's *Critical Documents of Jewish History*. In researching current and very recent events, leading English language newspapers and periodicals from the U.S., the U.K. and Israel were indispensable, and one stands in awe of the labors it must have taken to utilize such sources prior to the Internet age. Two online resources that proved particularly helpful were Mitchell Bard's meticulously referenced Jewish Virtual Library, which is encyclopedic in its own right, but also provides an unparalleled reference guide, and the website of Israel's Ministry of Foreign Affairs, which contains much documentary and statistical evidence concerning the Arab-Israeli conflict.

I owe a great debt of gratitude to a great many people for their assistance with this book. My wife, Cheryl, in particular, displayed what can only be described as infinite patience while offering much-needed moral support during its writing and publication. Special thanks are extended to the Israeli Government Press Office for its gracious permission to use the collection of photographs included herein. Thanks are likewise owed to Julia Bertelsman, former editor-in-chief of *New Society*, for her kind permission to reprint extensive passages from an article entitled "Did Golda Meir Cause the Yom Kippur War?" which I originally wrote for the July 2008 issue of that journal, and to Gal Hubara at Israel's Shalem Center for her kind attention to my queries about that article. Lee Green, Karen Satz and Steven Manchester invested valuable time reading the manuscript and caught many errors in content that might otherwise have found their way into the finished book. (The responsibility for any errors that remain is my own.) My mother Frances, sister Ann, and father Joe apprehended a great number of misspellings and grammatical violations before the book went to print. Thanks are also owed to Harriett Gross of the *Texas Jewish Post* for encouraging me to enter the manuscript in the Mayborn Literary Nonfiction Competition, and to Mitch Land, George Getschow, Susannah Charleson and Sarah Whyman, whose enthusiasm as coordinators and workshop leaders at that event contributed greatly to the joy of participating. I am also greatly indebted to Sir Martin Gilbert, Edward Alexander, Efraim Karsh, Mitchell Bard and the late Elly Dlin (longtime director of the Dallas Holocaust Museum) for their gracious endorsements. It would be difficult to overestimate the motivational affect their words had on me during the publishing journey.

Introduction

May 2, 2010, passed without notice in the international community. Yet it marked an important anniversary. One hundred and fifty years earlier, Theodor Herzl, the father of modern political Zionism, was born in Pest, Hungary. Formerly a staunch advocate of Jewish assimilation, Herzl concluded amidst chants of "Death to the Jews!" during the 1895 trial of Captain Alfred Dreyfus (a Jewish officer falsely accused of treason by the French army) that Jewish assimilation, even in the most progressive of nations, could never succeed. The only hope for Jewish salvation, he declared, lay in the creation of a sovereign Jewish state, where "we shall at last live as free men on our own soil and die peacefully in our own homes. The world will be freed by our liberation, enriched by our wealth, magnified by our greatness. And whatever we attempt there to accomplish for our own welfare, will react powerfully and beneficially for the good of humanity."[1]

In a diary entry dated September 3, 1897, Herzl recorded a remarkable 50-year prediction concerning the reestablishment of Jewish statehood in Judaism's ancestral homeland. His calculations were off by a mere eight months. The modern state of Israel was proclaimed on May 14, 1948. Since that date, the Jewish state has indeed accomplished much for the benefit of humanity. "Over the last 60 years," writes Harvard law professor Alan Dershowitz,

> no nation in the world has contributed more per capita to the general welfare of the people of this planet than Israel. Israel has exported more lifesaving medical technology to the far-flung corners of the earth than any nation of comparable size. It has done more to protect the environment; to promote literature, music and the arts and sciences; and to spread agricultural advances. Its scientists and engineers have secured more patents and its high-tech entrepreneurs more new listings on NASDAQ than any but the largest nations in the world. Its academics have won more international prizes, published more papers, and achieved more technological breakthroughs than any other nation of comparable size. Its students have been accepted at more elite graduate and professional schools than those of other small countries.[2]

Dershowitz goes on to praise Israel's independent judiciary, her free press, and her dedication to fighting terrorism within the bounds of international law.[3]

Yet today, Israel is a virtual pariah among the nations. At the United Nations, 191 states are eligible to sit on the security council. Israel alone is not.[4] Antipathy to Israel has been the pretext for resurgent anti–Semitism in Europe.[5] In 2003, the British Political Cartoon Society's annual competition awarded first prize to a caricature of Ariel Sharon biting off the head of a Palestinian child.[6] In 2009, the Davis Cup tennis match between Israel and Sweden was closed to the public amidst anti–Israel street rioting in the Swedish city of Malmo.[7] Israeli government officials have been threatened with arrest as "war criminals" if they set foot on British soil,[8] and have been subjected to abuse in attempting to speak on university campuses.[9] "Israel Apartheid Week," which falsely portrays Israel as an "apartheid" state, has become an annual event at prestigious universities worldwide.

It would be sad indeed if such vilification were justified. But it is even more ominous that it is so widely countenanced when it rests on a foundation of distortion and falsehood. Israel is not a perpetrator of apartheid. Indeed, while women, gays and ethno-religious minorities face institutionalized discrimination in the surrounding Arab states, Israel's 1.2 million Arab citizens enjoy full and equal rights under Israeli law. Nor is Israel the aggressor in the Arab-Israeli conflict: within hours of Israel's declaration of independence, five superiorly-equipped Arab armies invaded the Jewish state with the avowed purpose of carrying out "a war of extermination."[10] From that day to this, the Israeli people have never known a day of secure peace. While blame for this unfortunate circumstance is frequently ascribed to Israeli actions— the "occupation" of the West Bank, the "blockade" of Gaza, "settlement" construction, the establishment of checkpoints and security barriers, etc.— the historical record shows that none of these issues is fundamentally at fault. The intractability of the conflict antedates all of them, and it persists despite the fact that each of the leaders profiled in these pages desired and sought mutually beneficial neighborly relations with the Arab peoples.

Nor may we attribute the continuing conflict to some fundamental misunderstanding between the sides that can be sorted out by the sober mediation of a third party. Indeed, as Edward Alexander put it, "In the Middle East, the two sides do not misunderstand each other at all, but rather, understand each other only too well. The Arabs do not accept a Jewish state in their midst, and the vast majority of Israelis refuse to yield up their national sovereignty."[11]

This work recounts Israel's story through the lives of nine of its leading citizens and founders. Each succeeding chapter chronicles a critical epoch in the Israeli saga and catalogs the impact made on that epoch by one of the story's nine leading protagonists. The cast, in order of appearance, includes Zionism's unlikely patriarch, Theodor Herzl — an assimilated Jew who once argued for the compulsory baptism of Jewish children as a solution to the enduring problem of European anti–Semitism. Tormented by the realization that true assimilation was a forlorn hope, Herzl penned the treatise that was to make him famous: *The Jewish State: An Attempt at a Modern Solution to the Jewish Question.* The dream of Jewish statehood ultimately consumed him. He died at 44, having literally worked himself to death in its pursuit.

Second in line is Chaim Weizmann, a chemist who solved a critical problem for the British munitions industry during World War I. Two decades later, as Zionism's unofficial ambassador to Britain, Weizmann testified before the Peel Commission (1936), saying that for Europe's six million Jews "the world is divided into places where they cannot live, and places into which they cannot enter.... There should be one place in the world, in God's wide world, where we could live and express ourselves in accordance with our character, and make our contribution towards the civilized world."[12] By the time such a place existed, the six million had perished and Weizmann had lost a son in the war against Hitlerism. Nonetheless, he persevered to play a crucial role in garnering UN and U.S. support for the establishment of Israel in 1948, and served thereafter as Israel's first president.

Third, we meet David Ben-Gurion who, despite a desperate war, extended an unambiguous olive branch to his Arab neighbors in proclaiming Israel's independence on May 14, 1948: "In the midst of wanton aggression, we yet call upon the Arab inhabitants of the State of Israel to preserve the ways of peace and play their part in the development of the State, on the basis of full and equal citizenship and due representation in all its bodies and institutions."[13] Ben-Gurion was the colossus of Israel's early history. His party, Mapai, would dominate the Israeli political scene for the first three decades of the nation's life.

The *Lives* continue with Abba Eban, Israel's longtime UN ambassador and foreign minister — an eloquent orator who helped extricate Israel from a diplomatic quagmire in the wake of her shockingly successful Sinai campaign of 1956; Moshe Dayan, the architect of that campaign, who, a decade later, elevated the spirit of the entire nation in the tense days leading up to the Six Day War; and Golda Meir, who refused arrogant demands for Israel to surrender all the gains of that war for the "privilege" of *entering into* peace negotiations with Egypt.

Finally, there is Menachem Begin — decried for decades as a warmonger and extremist — who, nonetheless, became the first of Israel's leaders to forge a peace treaty with a neighboring state; Yitzhak Rabin, the architect of Israel's decisive victory in the Six Day War, who gave his life in the quest to forge an impossible peace with Yasser Arafat and the Palestine Liberation Organization; and lastly, Ariel Sharon, who was faced with a brutal terrorist war in the wake of Israel's magnanimous peace offer to the Palestinians at Camp David, and who fought thereafter to provide his people with security — even as he demonstrated to the world that Israel was prepared to make the "painful concessions" necessary for peace.

Within the next several decades, those who personally recall the events and personalities of modern Israel's first 60 years will have passed from the scene, leaving behind generations with no such recollection. In contemplating this unhappy thought, one may take solace from the Greek historian Herodotus, who wrote his masterwork, *The Persian Wars*, "in the hope of thereby preserving from decay the remembrance of what men have done."[14] This simple phrase defines the most fundamental purpose of historical writing. Herodotus and his fellow Greeks were the first to embrace the use of rational thought and empirical evidence to distinguish right from wrong and truth from falsehood. In so doing, they founded Western civilization. By taking the Greeks as our model in an era when freedom of expression extends without limit to caricatures of Israel, yet truth itself must yield to the dictates of moral relativism and political correctness, we may yet preserve the knowledge for coming generations that behind all the caricatures of the Jewish state there stands an embattled nation with a human face.

1

Theodor Herzl and the Genesis of Modern Political Zionism

In January 1893, a Viennese journalist wrote to the Society for the Combating of Anti-Semitism, saying, "When I think of [my son's] future I am ready to admit that the pressure of his Jewishness will teach him much concerning humanity. But I ask myself whether I have the right to make life so superfluously difficult for him as it has become for me and will become in increasing measure.... That is why we must baptize Jewish children while they are still incapable of giving themselves an accounting, and while they can still feel nothing either for it or against it. We must submerge in the people."[1]

These are hardly the words one would expect to hear from the founder of modern political Zionism, but for a brief period in 1892–93 it seemed to Theodor Herzl that the compulsory baptism of Jewish children was just the antidote that anti–Semitism required. Born in Pest in 1860, he was the son of Jacob Herzl, an entrepreneur who rose to become director of the Hungarian Bank. As a child, Theodor dreamt of the Messiah leading the Jewish people back to Palestine, little realizing the relevance to his future mission. While awake, he daydreamed of building a canal across Panama. His father thought it was a worthy idea and enrolled the ten-year-old boy in technical school. Over the ensuing five years, young Theodor learned that he hadn't the foggiest notion how to build a canal. He might have continued his studies regardless, but when he was 15, his teacher announced to the class that Jews and Muslims were heathen idolaters. Stung to the quick, he transferred in mid-semester to Budapest's Evangelical High School, a Christian academy open to Jews.[2] Here, he developed a passion for writing, formed and led a literary circle, and fell in love for the first time with a girl named Madeline Kurz.

In his eighteenth year, this happy interlude came to an end. Madeline and his sister, Pauline (whom he idolized), both succumbed to disease. Unable to bear the loss, the family moved to Vienna, where Theodor entered the University of Vienna Law School. After graduating in 1884, he served briefly as a public attorney in Salzburg. Three years later, he married 19-year-old Julie Nashauer, who bore him three children — Pauline, Hans and Trude. His great love, however, was writing. He had hoped to be a playwright, and during his career he produced several plays of no mean success — including two that were published before he graduated law school.[3] To support his family, however, it was necessary to have a steady income. Consequently, he redirected his formidable literary talents to the writing of editorials and reviews for Vienna's leading newspaper, the *Neue Freie Presse*. It was as Paris correspondent for this prestigious publication that Herzl covered the sensational scandal that was to change his life: "the Dreyfus affair."

In 1894, Captain Alfred Dreyfus, a Jewish officer in the French army, was charged with espionage and court-martialed. His trial was attended by a circus of anti–Semitic hysteria. "All Israel is on the move!" declared the popular journal *La Libre Parole*. Throughout the country, Jewish businesses were boycotted. In French Algeria, there were pogroms.[4] Convicted on the basis of a spurious handwriting sample, Dreyfus was stripped of his commission in a humiliating ceremony at the French military school and exiled to the dreaded penal colony on Devil's Island. Initially, France rejoiced at the verdict, since it jibed nicely with the prevailing anti–Semitic slander claiming that Jewish financiers had caused the nation's defeat in the Franco-Prussian War of 1870–71. But if the proponents of this absurd hypothesis hoped to use Dreyfus' conviction to confirm their innate prejudices, fate had a cruel blow in store for them: Dreyfus was innocent. In 1896, Colonel George Picquart, chief of military intelligence, proved beyond reasonable doubt that the actual culprit was a disreputable non–Jewish officer named Esterhazy. Too embarrassed to reopen the case, the French high command chose instead to dismiss Picquart. For an entire decade, justice was trodden

Theodor Herzl in 1898 (courtesy of the State of Israel Government Press Office; photographer unknown).

underfoot. Only in 1906 were Dreyfus and Picquart fully absolved and rein-stated.

But Herzl's epiphany occurred long before this. He was present on January 5, 1895 — the day of Dreyfus' degradation at the military school — when Frenchmen turned out in droves to howl anti–Semitic slurs at the unjustly condemned Jewish officer. It was predictable that cries of "death to the traitor!" would fill the air, but what troubled Herzl was the accompanying cry: "death to the Jews!"[5]

For European Jewry, the nineteenth century was an era of emancipation. For centuries, Jews had been confined to ghettos across the continent and had been subjected to discriminatory laws. In Herzl's homeland, the Austro-Hungarian Empire, things had begun to change during the reign of the enlightened emperor, Joseph II (ruled 1765–90), who freed the Jews from discriminatory taxation and from the obligation of wearing the Star of David as an identity tag. Next came the French Revolution of 1789, which brought forth the notions of liberty and equality. In 1791, the French National Assembly decreed the annulment of "all adjournments, restrictions and exceptions ... affecting individuals of the Jewish persuasion, who shall take the civic oath."[6] In the ensuing years, the Revolutionary and Napoleonic wars exported the concept of egalitarianism beyond the borders of France, and one by one, the nations of western Europe abolished the edicts that had condemned Jews to second-class citizenship.

Emancipation, however, came at a price. The Jews were emancipated as individuals, but not as a people. It was expected that they would assimilate into society, severing the ties of togetherness that had helped them survive in the ghetto. As Herzl's biographer, Alex Bein, relates, "The Jew was to be made at home in the State in which he lived — but at the same time he was to die, or cease to exist, in his capacity as a member of the Jewish people."[7] Thus, for example, when Joseph II passed his reforms in 1782, he demanded in return that the Jews Germanize their names, serve in the military, and document public records in German rather than Hebrew or Yiddish. In 1807, a failed attempt to force assimilation upon the Jews of Russia (without actually emancipating them) carried with it a ban on the Yiddish language. Also in that year, Napoleon Bonaparte convoked an assembly of Jewish notables in Paris—calling it the Sanhedrin after the ancient parliamentary court of the Israelites— and put to it a series of questions to determine whether French Jews considered France their homeland and whether they felt bound to defend it. (The convocation issued a resounding "yes" on both counts.[8])

Although it entailed the rejection of their cultural heritage, many Jews— Herzl among them — enthusiastically embraced the opportunity to assimilate. It was during this period that the reform movement was initiated in the synagogues to help shape Jewish worship to secular needs. Yet, try as the Jews might to assimilate, an insurmountable obstacle stood in their path — namely, anti–Semitism. The emancipation process itself had not been free of it. It gave Jews full legal rights without giving them equality. Despite the decree emancipating them in 1812, the Jews of Prussia were banned from public office.[9] Throughout Europe, their exclusion from high-ranking positions in the army and civil bureaucracy was commonplace. No matter how patriotic a given Jew might be, society suspected him of conspiring with his fellows. In 1881, Eugen Dühring published *The Jewish Problem as a Problem of Race, Morals and Culture*, in which he argued that the Jews were a contemptible race whose integration in society via emancipation was having a pernicious influence. He concluded that emancipation must be abrogated. Three years later, Edouard Drumont alleged in his tome, *La France Juive*, that Jews were using their commercial acumen to attain global dominion. The book went through 100 editions in its first year.[10]

Thus, while emancipation allowed some Jews to fare better economically, it did not confer equality upon them. This paradox had troubled Herzl's mind for years by the time of the Dreyfus affair. If emancipation and assimilation could not answer what was already being touted as the "Jewish Question," where was the solution to be found?

The issue was not merely one of intellectual interest. As bad as anti–Semitism was in western Europe, it was far worse in Russia. The West's "enlightened" emancipation policy had made no headway in the land of the tsars, where it had been fashionable to persecute Jews since the Muscovite period. With the partial annexation of Poland in 1772, Russia acquired 900,000 new Jewish subjects. Unwilling to let them disseminate through the realm, Catherine the Great passed a decree forcing them to remain within the bounds of the annexed territory.[11] In 1835, the segregation of Russian Jewry was reaffirmed by a decree of the reactionary Tsar Nicholas I, who threatened his Jewish subjects with exile and forfeiture of citizenship if they strayed beyond the infamous Pale of Settlement — a sharply demarcated zone in western Russia where the vast majority of the realm's Jews were legally confined.[12] By 1881, more than half of world Jewry lived within the Pale as second-class citizens.[13] In March of that year, the lenient Tsar Alexander II was assassinated, and his successor, Alexander III, a vicious anti–Semite, unleashed a series of violent pogroms against the Jews. The massacres were carried out by bands of Cossacks known as the "Black Hundreds," who were allowed to rape, pillage and murder for three days at each onslaught before the authorities deigned to intercede. In desperation, masses of Jews attempted to emigrate. The luckiest got out, mostly to the United States and Great Britain, but the majority had nowhere to go, and remained at the mercy of their tormentors.

Amidst such experiences, Russian Jews gave little thought to assimilation.[14] Their emancipated brothers in the West, however, thought of little else. It was in this atmosphere that Herzl contemplated the compulsory baptism of Jewish children. But when he took his idea to the *Neue Freie Presse*, one of his editors— Moritz Benedikt — reminded him that apostasy had been an option for 2,000 years, and that Jews had borne one tragedy after another rather than accept it. It could not be done honorably, for it would render meaningless the sacrifices made by world Jewry across 100 generations.[15] Realizing the truth of this argument, Herzl discarded his plan. Still, his own experiences taught him that the problem of anti–Semitism could not be denied. His own country had spawned a major political party — the Christian Socialists— whose whole platform was anti–Semitic, and whose leader, Karl Lueger (later the Mayor of Vienna), openly referred to Budapest as "Judapest."[16] More than once on his travels through Germany and Austria, Herzl heard the medieval, anti–Semitic cry "Hep! Hep!" (an abbreviation for *Heirosolyma est perdita!*—"Jerusalem is lost!"). In 1888, a member of the audience at a Mainz concert hall directed the taunt at him, thus provoking peals of laughter.[17] In Baden one night, a soldier overheard Herzl extolling the virtues of liberalism and barked, "Shut up, dirty Jew!"[18] Less personal but more disheartening was the Panama Canal Company scandal of 1892. Founded by Ferdinand de Lesseps, the world-famous promoter of the Suez Canal, the company collapsed in ruin, provoking a national economic crisis. Although no Jews were implicated, the press saddled them with the blame. With sad resignation, Herzl accepted the truth: "There is a Jewish Question," he intoned. "Those who deny it are wrong."[19]

Through it all, Herzl had remained optimistic that some way could yet be found for Jews to gain acceptance in their adopted homelands. Dreyfus' degradation taught him otherwise. Amidst the cries of "death to the Jews!" Herzl realized that if mobs could form in the streets of a liberal western society like France, screaming for the blood of all Jews in response to falsified claims against one man, then assimilation was impossible.[20] An entirely different solution was required — and one of the nineteenth century's leading trends now gave him an idea of what that solution might be.

The trend was national self-determination. During the nineteenth century, Germany and Italy had both achieved national unification. In the same period, Greece, Bulgaria, Serbia and Romania had all attained their independence from the tottering Ottoman sultanate, while the polyglot Hapsburg Empire was virtually aflame with nationalist sentiment. In sum, national self-determination was in the air. Might it be the answer to the Jewish Question? And, if so, how might it be achieved?

Despite their dispersion, the Jewish people had never relinquished their intimate bond with their historical homeland. Ever since they had been cast into the Diaspora by Rome's destruction of the Second Temple in A.D. 70, Jews had ended their Passover prayers with the incantation "next year in Jerusalem." Traditionally, the idea had been that the Messiah would gather the Jews out of the Diaspora and lead them to Jerusalem at the End of Days—a process that was not amenable to worldly manipulation. But in the mid–1800s, two orthodox Jewish rabbis—Judah Alkalai and Zvi Hirsch Kalischer—proposed the notion that some Jews might return to Zion prior to the appearance of the Messiah in order to lay the groundwork for the redemption to come.

In point of fact, some Jews were already there. Palestine had never been totally bereft of Jews. In 1850, there were 10,000 Jews in residence—some indigenous, some recent immigrants (mostly from Poland). Out of this total, 8,000 lived in Jerusalem, giving the city a Jewish plurality. By 1880, the number of Jewish Palestinians had swelled to 25,000 (in Jerusalem, they now constituted a majority), and the ensuing pogroms in Russia led to the immigration of 25,000 more between 1880 and 1903—the era known as the First Aliyah or "Ascent."[21] During this period, the term "Zionism" was coined by Nathan Birnbaum, one of the founders of *Kadima* ("Eastward"), the first Zionist student organization in Vienna.[22] Jewish settlers formed a number of colonies—mostly agricultural—throughout Palestine with the goal of revitalizing the province, which had become a backwater after four centuries of Turkish rule. Malaria, economic hardship, and a variable degree of Arab hostility proved formidable barriers to these nascent settlements. While some achieved economic self-sufficiency, others had to rely upon charity from well-meaning Jews abroad.

In compiling a diary entitled *The Jewish Question*, Herzl thought he perceived a solution—both for the struggling colonies in Palestine and for the plague of anti–Semitism throughout the world. The Jews must seek the ultimate refuge: a state of their own. The idea had been broached before. *Rome and Jerusalem*, a little-known tract written by Moses Hess of Bonn in 1862, and *Auto-Emancipation*, a better-known treatise authored by Leo Pinsker, a Jewish doctor from Odessa in 1882, had both espoused ideas remarkably similar to the ones that Herzl was now contemplating. Herzl had never heard of them or their works, and prior to his epiphany, he would not have been interested. But now his thinking had changed, and in five frenetic days during June of 1895, he promulgated his entire theory in his diary. Eight months later, he would publish it in concise, logical prose under the title *The Jewish State: An Attempt at a Modern Solution of the Jewish Question*.[23]

In the introduction to this work, Herzl explained that Diaspora Jews had traditionally migrated to areas where they would not be persecuted, but as more Jews arrived in a given locale, anti–Semitism invariably arose. All efforts to assimilate were doomed to failure. "In vain are we loyal patriots, our loyalty in some places running to extremes; in vain do we make the same sacrifices of life and property as our fellow-citizens.... In countries where we have lived for centuries we are still cried down as strangers...." Why was this? Because the Jews were "a people — one people." Moreover, try as it might to blend in, this "people" did not wish to sacrifice its identity and disappear. "This is shown during two thousand years of appalling suffering.... Whole branches of Judaism may wither and fall, but the trunk will remain."[24]

What then was the answer? The Jews must have self-determination in a state of their own, where "we shall at last live as free men on our own soil and die peacefully in our own homes. The world will be freed by our liberation, enriched by our wealth, magnified by our greatness. And whatever we attempt there to accomplish for our own welfare, will react powerfully and beneficially for the good of humanity."[25] Anti-Semitism would be the engine that drove the Jews to their new homeland, and as they left their former countries, the anti–Semitism that had been fueled by their presence would lose its impetus and fade away.

The proposed state was to be a model society, replete with a seven-hour workday for laborers. A "relief by work" program would provide jobs for the unskilled. Instead of handing ten cents to a beggar and allowing him to remain as such, the state would put him to public employment with the goal of losing no more than ten cents when his wages were balanced against the receipts from his productivity. Ten cents would be lost either way, but instead of having a beggar on its hands, the state would have a productive worker with substantial earnings in his pocket — earnings that would fuel the economy.[26]

Herzl described the economics of the exodus, including the formation of a joint-stock company, based in London, to assist Jews with liquidating their assets in order to emigrate. Argentina was a possible destination, but far better was Palestine, the historic homeland of the Jewish people. The Turkish sultan at this time was in severe financial straits and might be convinced to relinquish Palestine to the Jews in return for Jewish assistance in solving his fiscal woes.[27]

When he first outlined these ideas in his diary, Herzl received a social call from his friend Emil Schiff, who was surprised to find the normally impeccable journalist appearing disheveled and agitated. He asked if something was wrong, or if, perhaps, Herzl had worked out the principle of the dirigible balloon. Herzl dismissed this jest and laid out his ideas in detail. It was all here in his diary, he assured Schiff. Moreover, he had prepared an excerpt entitled *An Address to the Rothschilds* and had sent it to the Chief Rabbi of Vienna with the request that the latter read it to Austria's Albert von Rothschild, from whom Herzl hoped to obtain financial backing. All that was needed now was to convince the major powers to transfer sovereignty of a suitable piece of land to the Jews and the process could get underway.

Schiff, a trained physician, listened quietly to this exposition, and then began to sob. Clearly, his friend Herzl had been under extraordinary pressure and his delicate mind had snapped. He checked Herzl's pulse. Medical attention would be essential. In the meantime, a brisk walk in the fresh air might be therapeutic. In the course of this walk, which took place the following day in the Tuileries gardens, Schiff prevailed upon Herzl to recall his letter to the Rothschilds before someone took him to a madhouse.[28]

Had matters ended there, Jewish history might have taken a different course. But Herzl was not easily discouraged. No sooner had he withdrawn his letter to the Rothschilds than he dashed off another along the same lines to Otto von Bismarck, formerly Germany's "Iron Chancellor" and Europe's premier statesman. Herzl got nowhere by taking this alarming step. His letter to Bismarck was never answered. But when he brought his ideas to the attention of the renowned men of letters Max Nordau and Israel Zangwill, he received an invitation to speak on the subject at London's Maccabaeans Club and to write a summary article for the *London Jewish Chronicle*. Then, in February 1896, at the age of 35, he published *The Jewish State*.

The book was by no means universally applauded. Religious Jews thought it blasphemous that the redemption of Israel should be contemplated in the absence of the Messiah. Many assimilated Jews saw it as a breach of their emancipation contracts, which called upon them to abandon notions of collective Judaism in return for their civic freedoms.[29] Would not the anti–Semites—who had long held that the Jews were an untrustworthy, unassimilable foreign element—have a field day with it? Some expressed hope that Herzl would be silenced, even if it required bribery or assassination.[30] Many others, however, found Herzl's ideas exhilarating: the Zionist youth groups were all for it, as were the downtrodden Jewry of eastern Europe and a number of Palestinian colonists (who saw in Herzl's ideas a new sense of purpose for their formidable labors in Palestine).[31] After reading a copy of *The Jewish State*, even the former English prime minister, William Ewart Gladstone, pronounced the topic "highly interesting."[32]

Among the most zealous proponents of the book was a half-crazed cleric named William Hechler, who appeared at Herzl's door in March 1896, proclaiming, "Here I am!" "I see that, but who are you?" Herzl had replied.[33] Hechler, the chaplain at the British embassy in Vienna, wore a beard that would have put Moses to shame and had authored a book prophesying that Palestine would be restored to the Jews by 1898. More to the point, however, he had formerly served as tutor in the household of the Grand Duke of Baden—an uncle of the German kaiser. Capitalizing on this connection, he arranged Herzl's first audience with a major political figure. After a two-hour meeting on April 23, 1896, the grand duke pronounced his verdict on the Jewish state: "I should like to see it come about. I believe it will be a blessing for many human beings."[34]

In June 1896, another intermediary, the Polish nobleman and part time rogue Philip von Nevlinski, obtained an audience for Herzl with the Turkish grand vizier in Constantinople. The Turkish government was in debt to European creditors to the tune of £100 million, and the creditors were exercising undue influence in Turkish affairs. Herzl offered a way out. If the Jewish people were given leave to establish their own state in Palestine, they would return the favor by solving the Sultan's debt crisis, thereby removing the lien on Turkish sovereignty.[35] Although they were intrigued, the Turks rejected the scheme. Refusing a request for an audience, the sultan commented, "The Turkish Empire belongs not to me, but to the Turkish people.... When my Empire is partitioned, [the Jews] may get Palestine for nothing. But only our corpse will be divided. I will not agree to vivisection."[36] Nevertheless, Herzl was awarded a medal as a token of the Turkish government's regard for his ideas. The trip, moreover, had elevated his prestige. At the train station in Sofia, Bulgaria, crowds of Jewish onlookers had greeted him with shouts of "next year in Jerusalem!"[37]

All this while, Herzl's home paper, the *Neue Freie Presse*, refused to have any truck with his ideas. So, in June 1897, Herzl founded *Die Welt*, a weekly publication dedicated to Zionism. Two months later, under Herzl's tutelage, the first World Zionist Congress convened in Basle, Switzerland. It was attended by 204 delegates[38] from 15 countries and constituted the first representative assembly of the Jewish people in 2,000 years. Standing at a podium before a white flag with two horizontal stripes and a Star of David in the blue hue of the *tallit* (i.e., the Jewish prayer shawl), Herzl opened the proceedings by announcing to delirious applause that "We are here to lay the foundation stone of the house which is to shelter the Jewish nation." By the time the congregation dispersed several days later, it had promulgated the so-called Basle program, the principal tenet of which was that "Zionism seeks to secure ... a publicly recognized, legally secured home in Palestine for the Jewish people."[39]

Over the next half-decade, Herzl presided over five annual World Zionist Congresses in pursuit of this goal. Despite the diverse viewpoints of the myriad delegates, Herzl forged a unified front dedicated to a common purpose: the creation of the Jewish homeland. At the second Congress, also held in Basle and attended by 400 delegates in 1898, Herzl oversaw the establishment of the Jewish Colonial Trust, a bank built upon private subscriptions, which would fund the activities of the Zionist organization. The fourth Congress, held in London in August 1900, gained the attention of the British press and brought Herzl into contact with some of Britain's leading political figures. Back in Basle for the fifth Congress in December 1901, the delegates put the finishing touches on the Zionist organization's guiding statutes and established a Jewish national fund dedicated to the purchase of inalienable Jewish property in Palestine.

Through it all, Herzl relentlessly pursued the missing piece: the consent of the major powers in acquiring "a publicly recognized, legally secured home in Palestine for the Jewish people." At times during this odyssey, his object would seem tantalizingly close. Invariably, it slipped away again. But Herzl was not to be deterred. After his meeting with the Turkish vizier failed to bear fruit, he pursued a new avenue. Owing to a brutal series of massacres perpetrated upon their own Armenian subjects, the Turks were in a difficult diplomatic position. The only European leader who still supported them was the German kaiser, Wilhelm II. Relying on the good offices of the Grand Duke of Baden, Herzl managed to have his program brought to the kaiser's attention. In September 1898, he learned that Wilhelm had decided to support Jewish migration to Palestine and that he wanted Herzl to organize a Jewish delegation to meet with him on an upcoming trip to Jerusalem.

At an introductory meeting in Constantinople, the kaiser explained why Zionism fascinated him so: it might, for example, rid the German principality of Hesse of its Jewish usurers. This wasn't precisely the sentiment Herzl yearned for, but by the end of their discussion the kaiser had promised to seek the sultan's permission for the establishment of "a chartered company under German protection" to promote Jewish colonization in Palestine.[40]

The two men met again on the route from Constantinople to Jerusalem, where the kaiser shook Herzl's hand and remarked that Palestine would be a fine location if it were provided with water. Afterwards, in Jerusalem itself, Herzl delivered an address to the kaiser in which he referred to Palestine as "a land suitable to colonization and cultivation" that "cries out for people to work it."[41] Unfortunately, by this time, the kaiser had already proposed the idea to the sultan and had met such a cold response that he privately decided to extricate himself from the project.[42] Hence, the initiative came to naught.

On returning to Europe, Herzl was subjected to ridicule by those hostile to his enterprise. He responded with calculated diplomacy. Had he publicized the details of his journey, he might have exposed the kaiser as a promise-breaker. In doing so, however, he would have offended the kaiser and alienated any other European leader who might consider dealing with him in the future. Consequently, he merely stated the facts: He had been offered an audience with the kaiser in Palestine, he had attended the audience, and the kaiser had been friendly throughout.[43]

Herzl's next opportunity came in May of 1901, when Arminius Vámbéry, professor of Oriental languages at the University of Budapest and former tutor to the sultan's sister, obtained an audience for him with the Turkish sultan. Having been advised by Vámbéry not to mention Zionism, Herzl raised the issue without mentioning it. After praising the sultan's kindness to the Jews,[44] he mentioned that if the sultan could make a positive statement regarding Judaism for publication at the next Zionist Congress, he (Herzl) might be able to raise funds among his followers to help the sultan with his debt problem. The sultan invited him to write up a proposal for assisting with the debt, as well as outlining what sort of concession would be required in return.[45]

Vámbéry was stunned that Herzl had achieved this much, but the plan ultimately foundered. Herzl had hoped to convince the sultan that if he allowed extensive Jewish settlement in Palestine, the Zionists would not only be able to raise funds abroad to alleviate the Turkish debt, but could provide the Ottoman government with a new tax base at home (i.e., the industrious Jewish immigrants). The sultan's underling Izzet Bey replied that mass immigration to Palestine wasn't feasible owing to domestic opposition. The best that could be offered was scattered settlement within the Empire but outside of Palestine — and the immigrants would have to become Turkish citizens. Herzl rejected the proposal, saying that Jews could already count upon similar privileges throughout Europe. What they required was not "individual" sanctuary, but "national" sanctuary.[46]

Another route had come to a dead end, but international developments now conspired to open up a new one. Between 1898 and 1900, there were anti–Semitic pogroms in Galicia and Romania. As a result, eastern European Jews began to emigrate in massive numbers. Traditionally, Britain and the United States had a liberal policy towards Jewish immigration, but the heightened scale now created a backlash. Britain convened a royal commission to study the issue and recommend a way forward. Herzl was invited to testify. On appearing in July 1902, he said that the British government had put itself in a quandary by calling the commission into being; for the commission had either to restrict immigration and sever Britain's long tradition of providing a haven to the oppressed, or leave it unrestricted. If they chose the latter, the Jews of eastern Europe would view Britain as a hospitable destination and would arrive in droves, thus intensifying the problem that the commission had been charged with alleviating.[47]

Herzl would not presume to lecture his hosts on immigration policy. But he reiterated his conviction that Jewish migration was a "world problem" of pressing import and invited the British government to take the Zionist solution under consideration.[48]

In seeking Britain's support for Zionism, Herzl knew that there was no prospect of massive Jewish settlement in Palestine in the foreseeable future. But if the British view was favorable, he had some ideas on how the outlook might be improved. There followed an interview with the British colonial secretary, Joseph Chamberlain, the master of a far-flung Empire with an unquenchable thirst for European colonists.[49] In the course of this meeting, which occurred on October 22, 1902, Herzl outlined a plan for a Jewish colony on British colonial soil — preferably in Cyprus or at El Arish in the Sinai. A vibrant settlement in such close proximity to Palestine would serve a three-fold purpose: first, it would provide an immediate haven for the suffering Jews of eastern Europe; second, by demonstrating profitability, it might soften the sultan's view toward granting concessions in Palestine itself; and third, it would let mainland Britain off the hook with regard to its immigration policy. Chamberlain protested that the Turkish and Greek inhabitants of Cyprus had sufficient trouble with each other and, thus, were unlikely to welcome the Jews, while settlement in Egypt would likely encounter similar obstacles. Herzl corrected him on the latter point. The Jews had no desire to settle in Egypt. They had already been there once, and on the whole it hadn't been a pleasant experience. He then pointed out El Arish, in the Sinai near the border with Palestine — an underdeveloped and sparsely inhabited region. If Britain would allow Jewish settlement there, said Herzl, "she would reap an increase in power and the gratitude of ten million Jews."[50]

Chamberlain was sold, but the decision was not his to make. Theoretically, Egypt was not a British colony, but a sovereign state (albeit under British occupation and nominal Turkish suzerainty). Herzl would, therefore, have to take his case to Lord Lansdowne in the foreign office. A meeting with Lansdowne was duly arranged wherein Herzl said that the El Arish region was currently "worthless and almost uninhabited," but "could be made the place of refuge, the home of the Jews hard-pressed all over the world, if England permits the establishment of a Jewish colony there."[51] Lansdowne promptly delegated Lord Cromer, the British consul general in Egypt, to determine the feasibility of colonization at El Arish. It was established at the outset, however, that any Jewish settlers would have to become Turkish subjects and abide by the laws of Egypt. In March 1903, Cromer's commission reported that El Arish was presently uninhabitable, "but if water is made available, it can be settled."[52]

Sadly, the hopes raised by this assessment were dashed to pieces in May, when the commission's irrigation specialist issued an unfavorably high estimate for the area's irrigation requirements. Water, it concluded, would have to be diverted in mass volume from the Nile, rendering the entire project impracticable. (In point of fact, the irrigation requirements were nowhere near this level, as a subsequent investigation showed. The truth was that the Egyptian government would not countenance the project, prompting Cromer to seize upon the irrigation pretext as a convenient way out.[53])

The blow was a bitter one, and the bitterness was magnified by concurrent events in Russia. During Easter of 1903, a devastating pogrom was perpetrated upon the Jewish community of Kishinev — the capital of Russian Bessarabia. A mob of rioters, shouting "Death to the Jews!" burst into Jewish homes to rape, murder and pillage. Property was carted off or smashed in pieces. Children were thrown from upper story windows or had their brains dashed out on the tenement walls. Fleeing Jews were pelted with rocks. In one of the synagogues, a temple worker was murdered while attempting to shield the Torah with his body. Police were present but did not intervene — except to arrest a group of Jewish meat carvers who had successfully resisted a crowd of attackers. (Afterwards, looted Jewish property was found in the homes of many of these same policemen.) The local governor refused to take action without instructions from St. Petersburg, but forbade the telegraph office from sending off appeals. When the violence ended, the streets were littered with corpses, broken glass and destroyed furnishings. The death toll was placed variably from 47 to 120, with up to 1,100 wounded.[54]

The fear generated by the Kishinev pogrom gave new urgency to the issue of Jewish migration. Herzl again approached the British government about settlement in Cyprus or El Arish. Chamberlain regretfully informed him that neither option could be pursued in the present atmosphere, but that there was another alternative: "Uganda."

Actually, the land in question wasn't Uganda at all, but a portion of the Kenyan highlands in what was then known as British East Africa.[55] Located in the east-central portion of the continent, it could scarcely be seen as a stepping-stone to Palestine in the way that El Arish or Cyprus had been. But the plight of eastern European Jewry was deteriorating, and on this basis alone, Herzl felt compelled to give the offer serious consideration. A colonial charter, prepared by future British prime minister David Lloyd George, christened the settlement "New Palestine."[56] For the first five years, a British governor would administer the territory. Afterwards, it would be fully autonomous.

In August 1903, Herzl placed the project before the sixth World Zionist Congress in Basle. There was an emotional ovation over the fact that Great Britain had become the first European state to officially recognize the Jews as a people, but the notion of a Jewish state in Uganda rent the Congress in two. The delegates from Russia, who had long been agitating for a cultural platform (to include the resurrection of Hebrew as a national language) to complement Herzl's political one, stormed out of the hall in the belief that the Basle program's mandate for a Jewish state *in Palestine* had been betrayed. Herzl found them distraught in an adjoining hall and explained his position: The Basle program was in no way affected. A Jewish state in Palestine would remain the ultimate and inalienable goal of the Zionist movement. Nor had Herzl ceased to work toward it. All that he was asking now was that the Congress agree *to investigate* the British government's generous offer of Uganda — nothing more. Failure to do so would be a diplomatic rebuff to Britain. Indeed, it might dissuade the British from offering further assistance. Having done what he could to heal the rift, Herzl closed the Congress with the ancient Jewish oath "If I forget thee, O Jerusalem, may my right hand forget itself."[57]

In fact, the rift had not been healed. In early December 1903, the Russian Zionists held their own conference in Kharkov and dissociated themselves from the Uganda proposal. Later in the month, a deranged Zionist fired a pistol at Herzl's longtime associate, Max Nordau, while shouting, "Death to Nordau, the East African!" Nordau escaped unscathed, but a man standing nearby was wounded.[58]

Herzl created further controversy by entering into talks with Russia's minister of the interior, Wenzel von Plehve, whom the Russian Zionists held to be culpable for the Kishinev pogrom. The stimulus for the initial meeting, held in St. Petersburg in August 1903, was Plehve's crackdown on Russian Zionism. Several Zionists had been arrested, and the Jewish Colonial Trust and National Fund's activities had been outlawed, thereby robbing the Zionist organization of a major source of subscriptions. Without the slightest suggestion of irony, Plehve pronounced the Russian government sympathetic to the notion of Zionism. The recent crackdown, he said, had been provoked by Russia's "cultural" Zionists, who were emphasizing Jewish separateness and de-emphasizing emigration. He went on to disparage the willingness of western European governments to condemn the Kishinev pogrom while refusing to accommodate those Jews who wished to emigrate from Russia.[59]

In sum, Plehve's "sympathy" toward Zionism was motivated by two concerns: his desire to see Russian Jewry emigrate and his embarrassment over the Kishinev pogrom. Ever the master of diplomacy, Herzl sought to make these facts work to the benefit of Zionism. He pointed out that Zionism was a *solution* to Jewish separateness, not a *cause* of it. The whole thrust of the movement was emigrationist. The problem was that the Jews had nowhere to go. They were like Columbus' sea-weary sailors, searching for land. Plehve's government could bring the emphasis back to emigration by removing its restrictions from the Jewish Colonial Trust and National Fund, and by issuing a statement to the Turkish sultan in support of a Jewish state in Palestine.[60] Plehve departed the meeting as something resembling a Zionist. Forthwith, he allowed the Colonial Trust and National Fund to resume their activities.

Four months later, he instructed the Russian ambassador in Constantinople to issue a favorable statement on Zionism to the sultan. Unfortunately, the ambassador declined to do so on the grounds that, in his view, it would be both provocative and futile.[61]

Meanwhile, the Uganda proposal was also foundering due to opposition from European settlers who held competing grants in the East African colony. Herzl was not unduly disturbed by this development. The important thing was that Britain was now dealing with the Jews as a people. If the British were to withdraw their offer, Herzl could honorably let the matter drop and concentrate wholly on Palestine, or perhaps reopen discussions on Cyprus or El Arish.[62]

In the meantime, he explored other avenues. In January 1904, he met with Pope Pius X and with King Victor Emmanuel III of Italy, but his efforts to win their support for Zionism were unavailing. The king's sole concession was to advise Herzl that anything was possible with the sultan if one employed enough "backsheesh" (i.e., the semi-institutionalized form of bribery prevalent at the Turkish court). The pope went one better, saying that he could not support a project to send those who had not accepted Christ to Palestine, but that he would pray for the Jews to accept Christ.[63] Then, at the end of the month (whether or not the pope's intercession had anything to do with it), the British government made a formal proposal for settlement in Uganda after all. Herzl, therefore, summoned the Zionist Congress' greater actions committee to formalize plans for an investigatory commission to cooperate in the matter.

Tragically, the frenzied pace of all this work took a toll on Herzl's health. For some years, he had been suffering from a heart ailment. Now, he became critically ill. Those who saw him were mortified by his appearance.[64] He dearly wanted to continue his work; for the Zionist enterprise had reached a delicate juncture. Without his leadership skills and diplomatic acumen, the wrong decision could throw the movement into disarray. But his doctors told him that his heart condition had taken an undeniable turn for the worse and that rest was the only thing for it. Before withdrawing, Herzl wrote to his colleague Wolffson, kidding him not to "do anything foolish while I'm dead."[65] By the end of June 1904, he was struggling for breath. Fever set in and with it the coughing of blood. He had contracted pneumonia in an age when antibiotics did not exist. His wife and eldest child were with him. He now summoned his younger children and his mother. When they arrived, he was near death, but their appearance rallied him briefly. He died at 5:00 P.M. on July 3, 1904, at the age of 44.

The Herzl saga was over, but the Zionist saga was not. In 1895, Herzl proclaimed in his diary that "the Jewish state is a world necessity."[66] He understood that far from affecting the Jews alone, anti–Semitism tormented whole nations, regardless of their respective Jewish policies. Britain was touted as having sidestepped the poison of anti–Semitism, yet the rise in Jewish immigration from anti–Semitic eastern Europe compelled her to reconsider her celebrated policy of providing a free haven to refugees. French Jews were emancipated, yet the anti–Semitism surrounding the Dreyfus trial cleaved France into opposing camps, with profound, and enduring, implications. Russia never deviated from her policy of persecution — destroying the productive potential of millions of her citizens and driving many Jewish intellectuals into the revolutionary socialist parties. In 1917, those same parties toppled the tsarist regime.

In seeking to alleviate the plight of his people, Theodor Herzl had framed the Jewish Question as "a political world-question" and had placed the notion of Jewish statehood before the family of nations.[67] He had convened the first "national" representative assembly of the Jewish people since the destruction of the Second Temple and had supervised the creation of the institutions — the Jewish Colonial Trust and National Fund — necessary for it to pursue its object. Moreover, he had held discussions with the leading statesmen of Europe, and, with the British offer of Uganda, had obtained recognition of the Jews as a "people" from a leading European state.

Fully aware that his demeanor would reflect upon his organization, he dressed impeccably and conducted himself with dignity. Toward this same end, he insisted that the delegates of the first Zionist Congress appear in frock coats and white ties. At his first audience with the sultan, he was awarded the Order of the Mejidiye, second class, but respectfully turned it down.[68] He felt (one gathers) that his people had suffered a second-class designation for far too long. (The sultan replaced the medal with the "Grand Cordon" of the Order of the Mejidiye.) In some circles, his approach was derided as "frock-coat Zionism," but it achieved its purpose: Zionism did not wither as a discreditable movement, but solemnly forged ahead.[69]

Most importantly, Herzl had shown world Jewry — and indeed the world as a whole — the visage of a Jewish leader. Chaim Weizmann, who was to become his most distinguished successor and the first president of Israel, said that Herzl arrived on the scene "like a bolt from the blue" — not because of his ideas, but because of "the personality which stood behind them...."[70] At the Sofia train station en route to Constantinople in June 1896, the crowd of onlookers had hailed him as "lord and leader in Israel." At Vilna in August 1903, a young worker toasted him as "King Herzl," and a town notable called him "the greatest son of the Jewish people." Before departing, Herzl offered a gold coin to a downtrodden man who refused it, saying that he had not come for money but "to see Herzl."[71] At his funeral in Vienna less than a year later, near mayhem erupted as 6,000 mourners pressed in upon his coffin, sobbing and wailing.[72]

Although he had not succeeded in creating a Jewish state during his lifetime, he had laid its foundation stone — and he knew as much long before he died: the first Zionist Congress had been attended by newspaper correspondents from around the world, and had thus brought the question of political Zionism onto the international stage.[73] Summing up his accomplishment in organizing it, Herzl wrote in his diary: "At Basle I founded the Jewish state. If I said this out loud today, I would be answered by universal laughter. Perhaps in five years, and certainly in fifty, everyone will know it."[74]

Had Europe been amenable to persuasion, five years might have sufficed. Tragically, by the time world leaders were ready to listen, the problem had been plumbed to its depths and European Jewry had been destroyed. Nonetheless, Herzl's proposal was on the table, and precisely 50 years after he recorded his assessment of Basle in his diary, the United Nations approved a report calling for the partition of Palestine into separate Jewish and Arab states. Statehood came the following year.

After a wait of nearly 2,000 years, the cry "next year in Jerusalem!" had become a reality. In 1949, a grateful nation paid Herzl his due: in accordance with his dying wish, his remains were brought from Vienna and buried on a crest overlooking Jerusalem. The name of the crest is Mount Herzl.

2

Chaim Weizmann and the British Mandate

At the height of the First World War, Dr. William Rintoul, a researcher at the Nobel explosive works in Ayrshire, Scotland, paid a visit to an enterprising chemist at the University of Manchester. In the course of their conversation, Dr. Rintoul's interest was piqued by the chemist's research on a fermentation process that produced acetone as a by-product. "You know," said Rintoul, "you may have the key to a very important situation in your hands."[1] Other Nobel officials were likewise impressed, and the company offered to purchase the process for a substantial sum. A contract was drawn up and signed, but before production could begin, the Ayrshire plant did what only its products were supposed to do — it exploded. With the plant out of commission, Nobel asked to be released from its obligations. The chemist agreed. It was not long, however, before he had another offer.

The "situation" to which the chemist held the key was Britain's wartime shortage of acetone. The chemical was vital to the production of the smokeless explosive cordite, which in turn was indispensable in the fabrication of rifle and artillery cartridges. Without acetone, there could be no cordite. And without cordite, the British guns could not fire — a rather large inconvenience in time of war.[2] Hitherto, acetone had been produced by wood distillation, but by the spring of 1916 domestic wood was in short supply. The chemical could be imported from the United States, but the demand was so overwhelming that American producers could not keep pace.[3] Moreover, there was the issue of transporting the chemical across the Atlantic in the dangerous environment of U-boat warfare.

Frantically searching for a solution, David Lloyd George, Britain's minister of munitions, mentioned his problem to C. P. Scott, editor of the *Manchester Guardian*, who happened to know "a very remarkable professor of chemistry in the University of Manchester" — namely, Chaim Weizmann, the very man whose fermentation process had caused such a stir at the Nobel

Company. Weizmann told Lloyd George that his fermentation process could indeed produce acetone, but only a few hundred cubic centimeters per batch. The First Lord of the Admiralty, Winston Churchill, was calling for 30,000 tons. Weizmann said that the problem of mass production would have to be studied. "How long can you give me?" he asked Lloyd George. "I cannot give you very long. It is pressing," said the latter. Weizmann assured him that he would "go at it night and day."[4] Within three weeks, he had isolated a bacterium that could convert the abundant cereal plant, maize, into acetone with a high degree of efficiency. Seven months later, the Nicholson gin factory was putting out half-ton batches.[5]

Sometime afterwards, Lloyd George told Weizmann, "You have rendered great service to the state, and I should like to ask the prime minister to recommend you to His Majesty for some honour." Weiz-

Portrait of Chaim Weizmann, painted by Sir Oswald Birley, 1938 (courtesy of the State of Israel Government Press Office).

mann insisted that he desired nothing for himself. "But is there nothing we can do as a recognition of your valuable assistance to the country?" Lloyd George asked. "Yes," answered Weizmann, "I would like you to do something for my people." "That," Lloyd George recorded in his memoirs, "was the fount and origin of the famous declaration about the National Home for the Jews in Palestine" known to history as the "Balfour Declaration."[6]

Chaim Weizmann was born in the Russian hamlet of Motol inside the Jewish Pale of Settlement on November 27, 1874. As a schoolboy in neighboring Pinsk, he became an avid Zionist, trudging door-to-door in the mud to collect kopeks for the movement. Even at this tender age, he looked to England for support. "All have decided: The Jew must die," he wrote to his schoolteacher, "but England will nevertheless have mercy upon us...."[7] Russia's anti–Semitic quota system excluded him from pursuing university studies in his native land, so at age 18, Weizmann moved to Germany where he sat for a degree in chemistry. While in Berlin, he had a chance to lay eyes on the man whom many regarded as the Gandhi of Zionism[8]: Asher Ginzberg — better known by his pen name, Ahad Ha'am (from the Hebrew, meaning "one of the people"). In Ahad Ha'am's view, Theodor Herzl's purely "political" approach to Zionism was insufficient. Jewish statehood could not be conjured in a vacuum from meetings with European princes and ministers. A critical prerequisite must first be met: The Zionists must promote a worldwide "Jewish cultural revival," with Palestine serving as a "national spiritual center."[9]

Owing to financial incapacity, Weizmann missed the inaugural World Zionist Congress in Basle in August 1897. Thereafter, he attended its annual sessions as an avid proponent of Ahad Ha'am's program of cultural Zionism. At the fifth Congress (December 1901), he played an instrumental role in the formation of the "Democratic-Zionist Fraction" — an opposition party within the Zionist movement, which sought to induce Herzl and the political Zionists to adopt the cultural program. At the next Congress (August 1903), he was among the Russian delegates who stormed out in despair over the British proposal to establish a Jewish colony in the Kenyan highlands. (By a narrow margin, the Congress voted to consider the "Ugandan" scheme, but under pressure from the cultural Zionists, the decision was overturned after Herzl's death.)

In 1906, the English Zionist, Charles Dreyfus, a staunch advocate of the Uganda proposal, introduced Weizmann to Arthur James Balfour in hopes that the latter might win the Manchester chemist as a convert. Balfour, who had been prime minister at the time of the Uganda offer in 1903, was curious to know why so many Russian Zionists had opposed it. Millions of Weizmann's Jewish brethren in the Russian Pale of Settlement were being persecuted. In Balfour's view, the practical issue was the need for an immediate refuge for these tormented souls. Why not Uganda? In reply, Weizmann said that Zionism's survival relied not on pragmatism, but on spiritual conviction, "and that this conviction had to be based on Palestine and on Palestine alone. Any deflection from Palestine was — well, a form of idolatry." He added that "if Moses had come into the sixth Zionist Congress when it was adopting the resolution in favor of the Commission for Uganda, he would surely have broken the tablets once again." The two men talked for more than an hour, but the exchange of three sentences settled the issue: "Mr. Balfour," said Weizmann, "supposing I were to offer you Paris instead of London, would you take it?" "But Dr. Weizmann," Balfour replied, "we have London." "That's true," countered Weizmann. "But we had Jerusalem when London was a marsh."[10]

Far from winning Weizmann as a convert, Balfour was himself won over. The two men did not cross paths again until Balfour succeeded Churchill as

First Lord of the Admiralty in 1916. Soon thereafter, Lloyd George became prime minister and Balfour was named foreign secretary. Weizmann thus had access to the two most powerful men in England. Just as fortuitously, it became evident that the very sincere desire of these men to help the Jewish people coincided perfectly with the strategic needs of the British Empire. The Suez Canal was the principal thoroughfare of that Empire, and Palestine comprised the canal's strategic eastern flank. In the event of an Allied victory in World War I, the long-tottering Ottoman Empire was certain to collapse. In Britain's view, it was critical that the Holy Land fall into friendly hands at that junc-ture — and many members of the government sincerely believed that it was not merely expedient, but morally right that those friendly hands should be Jewish.[11] After all, Palestine comprised only 1 percent of the largely Arab-inhabited land that the Allies stood to liberate from Turkey.[12] The British gov-ernment was dedicated to the notion of Arab nationalism in the rest, but Palestine was the historic homeland of the Jews. Moreover, during the pre-vious four centuries, the Turks and Arabs had allowed the province to lapse into a piteous state of neglect. Far from being fertile, the land outside the squalid towns was largely divided between rocky terrain, desert and swamp-land. In 1914, there were fewer than 600,000 people in residence, 85,000 of them being Jews.[13] Many of the latter were refugees from European persecu-tion. Over the preceding generation, their pioneering had played a critical role in restoring part of the land to agricultural production. Indeed, the Jews seemed to be the only part of the population who were intent on bringing the province back to life.

With many high-ranking political figures showing sympathy, the British government embarked upon a series of talks with Zionist leaders in February 1917 aimed at the possibility of reestablishing a Jewish homeland in Palestine. Perceiving Weizmann's importance in the ongoing negotiations, the English Zionist Federation appointed him its president. He, in turn, devised new and unlikely ways of generating enthusiasm for the project. David Lloyd George, for example, seems to have come away from one of their discussions with the impression that hilly Palestine was very much like his native Wales.[14]

By October, Britain had obtained the consent of her allies — France, Italy and the United States. The stage was thus set for a decisive proclamation by the British government — i.e., the Balfour Declaration. Dated November 2, 1917, and addressed to Lord Walter Rothschild, a relative of the famous Baron Edmond de Rothschild, whose philanthropy had been instrumental in the early Zionist pioneering in Palestine, its text ran as follows:

> I have much pleasure in conveying to you, on behalf of his Majesty's Govern-ment, the following declaration of sympathy with Jewish Zionist aspirations which has been submitted to, and approved by, the Cabinet.

"His Majesty's Government view with favour the establishment in Palestine of a national home for the Jewish people, and will use their best endeavours to facilitate the achievement of this object, it being clearly understood that nothing shall be done which may prejudice the civil and religious rights of existing non–Jewish communities in Palestine, or the rights and political status enjoyed by Jews in any other country."

I should be grateful if you would bring this declaration to the knowledge of the Zionist Federation — Yours sincerely, Arthur James Balfour.

Jews around the world received the Balfour Declaration with delirious enthusiasm.[15] Two days earlier, British forces under Lord Allenby had captured the stronghold of Beersheba in Palestine. Jerusalem fell on December 8, and three months later, the British government dispatched Weizmann to Palestine at the head of a Zionist advisory commission to study possible means of implementing the government's new policy. Donning a top hat — the only one he ever wore[16] — he was received by King George V before setting out for Palestine on March 9.

He was welcomed with high emotion. The Zionist agricultural colony at Rishon Le Zion held a festive dinner for him. Afterwards, he traveled to Mount Scopus where he presided over the laying of twelve foundation stones for Hebrew University — each stone commemorating one of the twelve Israelite tribes. This was a special moment for Weizmann. Since the turn of the century, he had been the heart and soul of an ongoing movement to establish a Jewish university in Palestine. On the eve of World War I, Baron Edmond de Rothschild had thrilled him by agreeing to fund the project, but the war had intervened. Now at last, the work had started. (Seven years later, in one of the most touching scenes in Zionist history, Arthur Balfour delivered an address at Hebrew University's inaugural ceremony, thus cementing his reputation as a friend and benefactor of the Jewish people. Afterwards, Balfour told his niece and biographer, Baffy Dugdale, that of all the work he had done in his 50-year public career, "I think that my work for Zionism is probably the most worth while [sic] of any of it."[17])

Also on this trip, Weizmann held his first meeting with the leading light of the pan–Arab movement, Emir Faisal. Faisal was a scion of the Hashemite clan, which traced its ancestry directly to the prophet Muhammad. His father was Hussein Ibn Ali, the sharif of Mecca and Medina — Islam's holiest sites. The Hashemites wanted to erect an Arab successor state on the ruins of the Ottoman Empire and portrayed themselves as the accepted leaders of all the Arab peoples.[18] Although this was a rather egregious overstatement, the British — still smarting from their own disastrous 1915 Gallipoli campaign against the Turks — decided to support the clan's territorial claims (Palestine excepted)[19] if the clan would foster an Arab revolt against Turkish rule. With assistance from T. E. Lawrence (a.k.a. "Lawrence of Arabia"), the "Great Arab

Revolt" was duly organized under Emir Faisal. In total, no more than 20,000 Arabs participated, while hundreds of thousands of others—including the Arabs of Palestine—continued to fight for the Turks. (The Hashemite contribution—described as "trifling" by one British commentator—was greatly overstated in Lawrence's memoir, *The Seven Pillars of Wisdom*.[20])

After a cordial meeting with Faisal, Weizmann reported to Balfour that the emir earnestly intended to foster cooperation between their respective nationalist movements. When the two men met again in London on January 3, 1919, they agreed in writing to assist one another in developing "the Arab state and Palestine" while promoting mass Jewish immigration to the latter.[21] Clearly, then, the Hashemites did not feel that the existence of a Jewish national home in Palestine would be at odds with their own pan–Arab aspirations.[22]

On returning from Palestine, Weizmann was greeted at Victoria Station by thousands of cheering Jews. But there was still serious work to be done. Britain was seeking a "mandate" over Palestine to promote the establishment of the Jewish national home. Weizmann was chosen to head the Zionist delegation to speak in its support at the Versailles peace talks. There, he made the case for Zionism, but no definite decision was taken. It was not until the Treaty of San Remo was signed with Turkey in 1920 that the Balfour Declaration was written into an international treaty. At the same conference, the League of Nations granted the Palestine Mandate to Great Britain.

By 1921, Weizmann's fame had carried him to the presidency of the World Zionist Organization despite a determined challenge from the American jurist, Louis Brandeis, the first Jew ever appointed to the U.S. Supreme Court. By now, however, there was bad news from Palestine. Although Syria had been apportioned to France by the secret Sykes-Picot agreement of 1916 and had not been included in the territories promised to the Hashemites, Emir Faisal now laid claim to it (1919). Clandestinely abetting him in this purpose was a cadre of double-dealing, anti–Zionist British officers in Palestine led by Colonel Richard Waters-Taylor (chief of staff to GOC Sir Louis Bols) and Colonel Ronald Storrs, the military governor of Jerusalem. These officers hoped to filch Syria from the French and Palestine from the Zionists, and fuse them into a Syrian kingdom beholden to Britain.[23] In short order, Faisal reneged on his agreement with Weizmann (July 1919), accepted the throne of Syria from the "Syrian National Congress" (March 1920), and claimed Palestine as part of his new patrimony. One month later, with representatives of the major powers actively debating the fate of the Balfour Declaration at San Remo, a fanatical anti–Zionist named Haj Amin al-Husseini—once again egged on by Waters-Taylor and Storrs[24]—incited a wave of pro–Faisal, anti–Semitic riots in Jerusalem's Old City, replete with plundering, rape and murder. Many of the perpetrators were actually foreign Arabs, who had come to Jerusalem as "pilgrims" for Islam's Nebi Musa festival.

At this time, Palestine was still ruled by Lord Allenby and the British army, with Storrs and Waters-Taylor enjoying leading roles. Consequently, apart from preventing the nascent Haganah[25] from coming to the Jews' defense by barring the gates to the Old City once the rioters were already inside running amok, Allenby's government did nothing. Many on both sides suspected that the regime was sympathetic to (if not complicit with) the rioters. Indeed, during the attacks, many Arabs shouted, "We will drink the blood of the Jews! Don't be afraid, the government is on our side!"[26] Afterwards, Storrs—who might have halted the violence at any time—visited the Zionist notable, Menachem Ussishkin, and disingenuously expressed his sorrow at the "saddening events" that had transpired. Ussishkin asked, "Is your Honour referring to the pogrom?" Storrs protested that the term "pogrom" was not applicable. Ussishkin assured him that it was.[27]

One year later, the Mandate succeeded Allenby's regime. At its head was former British cabinet minister Sir Herbert Samuel. Although Samuel was himself a Jew, he took care to avoid charges of favoritism. As one of his first acts, he not only amnestied Haj Amin al-Husseini, the instigator of the riots, but also appointed him Grand Mufti of Jerusalem. This made Haj Amin the "legitimate" spokesman of Palestine's Arabs—despite the fact that his candidacy had been rejected in the traditional vote of Muslim clerics. The fruit of this attempted appeasement was a second ghastly pogrom, this one in Jaffa (May 1921). Panicked by the episode, Samuel transiently halted Jewish immigration to Palestine—in effect, "punishing the victims."[28]

After touring Palestine for himself, Britain's colonial secretary, Winston Churchill, warned against allowing generations of Jewish effort in Palestine "to be brutally overturned by ... a fanatical Arab attack from outside."[29] On this same tour, however, he dealt a rather stiff blow to the Zionist cause by cleaving the British Mandate in two. By now, the French had chased Emir Faisal from the Syrian throne, and Churchill had received word that the emir's brother, Abdullah, was crossing the eastern half of the Mandate in order to renew the fight. Rather than see Abdullah stir up further trouble with the French, Churchill offered him autonomous rule over "Transjordania"—i.e., all of Palestine east of the Jordan River: fully three-quarters of the British Mandate.[30] Churchill's action was actually a breach of Article 5 of the Mandate charter, which states that, "The Mandatory shall be responsible for seeing that no Palestine territory shall be ceded or leased to, or in any way placed under the control of, the Government of any foreign Power."

To clarify its policy amidst so much wheeling and dealing, the British government issued the famous Churchill white paper of 1922, saying, among other things, that (i) on the basis of their "ancient historical connection" with the land, the Jews were in Palestine "as of right and not on sufferance," (ii) the British government did not wish "to create a wholly Jewish Palestine," but rather to promote the "development of [Palestine's] existing Jewish community," and (iii) "the Jewish community in Palestine should be able to increase its numbers by immigration," though not "to exceed whatever may be the economic capacity of the country." Furthermore, it was the government's view that this interpretation of the Balfour Declaration did "not contain or imply anything which need cause either alarm to the Arab population of Palestine or disappointment to the Jews."[31]

Though greatly disappointed, a Zionist delegation led by Weizmann signed the paper. Alarmed, an Arab delegation refused to do so.[32] And this was not the end of the trouble. With the Mandate now up for ratification in the British parliament, a "smear campaign" was launched in the British papers, calling Palestine a "morass" and denouncing Weizmann as a "foreign meddler" whose adventures had cost the British treasury hundreds of millions of pounds sterling.[33] Although Parliament approved the Mandate in May, the opposition was such that Winston Churchill felt an obligation to remind a number of wavering members of the statements they had made in favor of the Balfour Declaration prior to the Arab riots. Speaking in the House of Commons on July 4, 1922, he said it was one thing to criticize the specific means adopted by the government in fulfilling its obligations to the Zionists, but quite another to recommend overturning "a policy adopted and confirmed by this country before the whole world."[34]

Three weeks after Churchill's speech, the League of Nations issued its Mandate charter, which stated categorically that "the Mandate should be responsible for putting into effect the declaration originally made on November 2nd, 1917" (i.e., the Balfour Declaration). To assist in this process, it called upon the Zionist Organization to create a representative Jewish Agency to cooperate with the Mandate, and designated Hebrew as one of Palestine's three official languages, with English and Arabic being the other two.[35]

In the same year (1922), a British census put the Palestinian population at 650,000 Muslims, 87,000 Jews, and 73,000 Christians.[36] It might thus be argued that the Mandate's charter calling for implementation of the Balfour Declaration was ill-considered and that Palestine's fate ought to have been placed in the hands of the province's overwhelming Muslim majority.

But there were other factors to consider: for one thing, world Jewry had a competing historical claim to the land, which they had never relinquished through 1,850 years of exile and persecution. For Jews, Palestine represented the eternal homeland. For Arabs, it represented no such thing. "The centres of Arab culture," said Weizmann in 1920, "are Damascus, Baghdad, and

Mecca. And I hope that there a great and flourishing nation will again arise. But Palestine will be the national home of Israel. We must say this forthrightly and openly, both to our friends and our enemies."[37] Ninety-nine percent of the territory liberated by Britain from the Turks was already earmarked for eventual Arab self-rule (i.e., Iraq, Transjordan, Syria, Lebanon, and the Arabian Peninsula). The last 1 percent (i.e., Palestine) embodied the sole hope on the planet for Jewish self-determination in an era when "the self-determination of peoples" held special prominence (as evidenced by Wilson's Fourteen Points).[38] Moreover, prior to its liberation from Turkey, Palestine had been excluded from the territory meant for Arab self-rule by the "McMahon Letter" (1915), and had been designated as a national home for the Jewish people by the Balfour Declaration (1917). Both of these documents had had the consent of the Hashemites—i.e., the only Arabs who had rebelled against Turkish rule. The Arabs of Palestine, it should be noted, had not taken part in the "Great Arab Revolt." They had backed the Turkish regime to the last and had played no part in Palestine's liberation.[39] In contrast, the Jews of Palestine had been overwhelmingly pro–British. Many had served with distinction alongside Jews from Britain, Russia and the United States in the so-called Jewish Legion during Allenby's 1918 campaign against the Turks. Indeed, the legion's service figured significantly in the Jewish claim to a national home in Palestine — no less significantly, says one historian, than the Jewish pioneering efforts of the preceding generation, which initiated Palestine's rehabilitation after centuries of Turkish neglect and Arab indifference had allowed the province to fall into decline.[40]

Prior to World War I, the Turkish government had imposed restrictions on Jewish immigration to Palestine. With the overthrow of Turkish authority, those restrictions no longer obtained. As the new legally constituted and internationally recognized authority, the British Mandate was within its rights to promote Jewish immigration, provided that its policy did not displace or impinge upon the civil rights of the existing Arab population. In the early 1920s, an estimated 90 percent of Palestine consisted of uncultivated land. Extensive Jewish immigration might thus have taken place without any risk of crowding out the resident Arab population.[41] (Indeed, the Jews were highly sensitive to this issue. As David Ben-Gurion put it, "under no circumstances must we touch land owned by [Arab peasants] or worked by them."[42]) At the same time, the Jews of Poland, Romania and Russia were being savagely persecuted, and few countries were willing to accept them as immigrants. Jewish immigration to Palestine thus constituted a pressing humanitarian need.

Given the overall balance of factors, it was by no means unjust for the Mandate to give precedence to the establishment of the Jewish national home in Palestine, even if the Arabs were opposed to it.[43] In pursuing this aim, both the British and the Jews were aware that they were not at liberty to violate the rights of Palestine's non–Jewish population. Nor did they have any intention of doing so: speaking in New York in 1923, Weizmann said, "We do not even let it enter our minds to build Palestine at the expense of others. There is plenty of room for them and for us and for a large number of Jews who will come and bring with them an abundance of blessing and prosperity, not only for Palestine but for the whole Near East."[44] David Ben-Gurion concurred. In 1918, he had published an article citing scientific evidence to the effect that, properly irrigated, Palestine could accommodate six million citizens. "The demand of the Jewish people," he argued, "is based on the reality of unexploited economic potentials, and of unbuilt-up stretches of land that require the productive force of a progressive, cultured people.... However we must remember that such rights are also possessed by the inhabitants already living in the country — and these rights must not be infringed upon."[45] Likewise, during his tour of Palestine in 1921, Winston Churchill addressed a Zionist audience at Mount Scopus, saying that Britain's "promise was a double one. On the one hand, we promised to give our help to Zionism, and on the other, we assured the non–Jewish inhabitants that they should not suffer in consequence. Every step you take should therefore be also for normal and material benefit of all Palestinians. If you do this, Palestine will be happy and prosperous, and peace and concord will ... reign."[46] As further confirmation, the Mandate charter itself called for the "safeguarding of the civil and religious rights of all the inhabitants of Palestine, irrespective of race and religion."[47]

These pledges were redeemed in deeds as well as words. Under the Mandate's first high commissioner, Sir Herbert Samuel, the Jewish community supplied 45 percent of the Mandate's revenues, yet the bulk of the Mandate's public services redounded to the benefit of the Arab population, which grew apace.[48]

Despite the above arguments and assurances, there was a strong undercurrent of antipathy toward the aims of the Mandate amongst Palestinian Arabs.[49] Although Palestine had never been a sovereign Arab state, hitherto the Arabs had been in the majority. If the aims of the Mandate were pursued in unrestrained fashion, the Arabs stood at some future date to be a minority in an alien society. Believing that most Palestinian Arabs were not politically minded and that the opportunities created by Zionist economic development would naturally lead to cooperation and acceptance, Zionist leaders tended to minimize these concerns. The riots of 1920 and 1921, they pointed out, were the result of religious incitement and of unfounded claims that the Zionists meant to drive the Arabs from their homes.[50] Although Weizmann initially subscribed to the view that the Arabs would place economics before politics, by 1936 he had come over to the opinion "that among the Arab people, rightly or wrongly, there are fears for the future, for what will happen to them when they become a minority."[51]

Given the circumstances, it was a practical certainty that the Arabs would challenge the Mandate's policies. What they ought to have kept in mind was that, just as it was incumbent upon the British and the Jews to safeguard Arab civil and religious rights, it was incumbent upon themselves not to tread upon the rights of Palestine's non–Arab residents.[52] Their majority status gave them a strong bargaining card with the British, but too often, rather than seek redress through legal avenues, the Arabs resorted to violence (witness the deadly riots of 1920 and 1921) and fanatical religious incitement (involving, amongst other things, the distribution of postcards depicting imaginary Jewish flags atop Jerusalem's mosques[53] and the anti–Semitic slur that Jews were handing out poisoned candy to Arab children[54]). Had the British authorities demonstrated that violence and incitement would not be tolerated by taking firm action against the perpetrators, they might have averted a repetition of such incidents. Tragically, they failed to do so.

Notwithstanding these pitfalls, Palestine's Jewish community — in Hebrew, the *Yishuv*—continued to grow and prosper under the tutelage of the Jewish Agency and its president, Chaim Weizmann. Only in 1926, when an economic recession resulted in widespread impoverishment, did Jewish emigration begin to outpace immigration. To reverse the tide, Weizmann attempted to secure a loan from the British cabinet. His request was denied.[55] As a result, at the 1929 Zionist Congress, he unveiled an expanded plan for the Jewish Agency, welcoming the participation of Diaspora Jews and characterizing the Balfour Declaration as a gift to all Jews, not just to Zionists.[56] A publicity tour was undertaken in America with Albert Einstein, and hopes were high for promoting heavy Jewish investment in Palestine.

These hopes were soon dashed. By 1929, the worst of Palestine's economic crisis was over, and Jewish immigration was again on the rise. But now, the Great Depression set in everywhere else, and the prospective sources for Jewish investment ran dry. Moreover, in response to the new upsurge in Jewish immigration, Haj Amin al-Husseini incited a new wave of Arab rioting across Palestine, in which 133 Jews were murdered and hundreds more injured. In Hebron, where Judaism's heritage dates to the time of Abraham, the Jewish community was blotted out with the utmost savagery — the victims being bludgeoned and stabbed without regard to age or sex. Arriving belatedly at the scene, the local British police chief, Raymond Cafferata, apprehended one Arab rioter in the act of beheading a child and another (an Arab policeman) standing over the bloodied corpse of a young woman. He shot both men — killing one and wounding the other. Afterwards, British authorities forced the captured Arab rioters to dig a mass grave for the 65 Jewish victims. Showing reprehensible disrespect, these same Arabs disrupted the burial ceremony with loud singing.[57] Elsewhere during the riots, anti–Zionist Arabs distributed leaflets depicting Jews not just as "Christ-killers" but also as the poisoners of Muhammad. By disseminating these falsehoods to neighboring states, the perpetrators raised the specter — later fulfilled — of participation by foreign Arabs in the anti–Jewish violence.[58]

Again, the Jews looked to the Mandatory government for strong action, and again they were disappointed. In 1930, the new colonial secretary, Lord Passfield, issued a white paper that sought to appease the Grand Mufti and his murderous thugs at the expense of Zionism. Specifically, Passfield called for strict limitations on Jewish immigration and land acquisition. Leading parliamentary figures — including Stanley Baldwin, Winston Churchill, and David Lloyd George — issued strong condemnations of the report. Weizmann — who met a cool reception in London, including a query from Passfield's wife as to why the Jews were making "such a fuss over a few dozen of their people killed" when the same number died each week in London traffic[59] — resigned his presidency at the Jewish Agency in protest.

Popular disapproval of the white paper was so intense that the British prime minister, Ramsay MacDonald, was forced to issue a partial recantation in a letter to Weizmann. For many Zionists, this was not enough. For decades, Britain had been Zionism's most valued friend, and through a combination of charm, personal magnetism, and persuasive skill, Weizmann had become Zionism's leading "ambassador" to Britain. By his pursuit of modest and attainable goals and by his willingness to compromise when others would have demanded more, he had preserved British support through every crisis. But in the wake of the Passfield white paper, Zionism was in no mood for moderation. At the 17th World Zionist Congress in Basle (1931), Weizmann was assailed for refusing to demand the immediate establishment of a Jewish state. He answered that "the walls of Jericho fell to the blowing of trumpets. But I have never heard of walls having been erected by such means."[60] Although he argued eloquently against "adventurous policies, which can only lead to heartbreaking disappointments," the Congress voted him out of the presidency, consoling him with a loud ovation for his long labors.[61]

For a time, Weizmann sought to concentrate on his chemical research. Ridiculously, his request for a lab at Hebrew University was rejected owing to a petty grudge on the part of the university president. Weizmann decided, therefore, to found a research institute near his home in Rehovot. By 1935, however, the disastrous rise of Nazism in Germany mandated his return as president of the World Zionist Organization (WZO).[62]

In 1933, the Jewish population of Palestine was 235,000, accounting for some 20 percent of the population. In 1934, 42,000 Jews fled to Palestine to escape persecution in Poland, Romania and Germany. In 1935, this figure rose to 61,000. By 1936, the Yishuv numbered nearly 400,000 souls in a population of 1.35 million (i.e., approximately 30 percent).[63] The predictable result of this influx was a new outburst of Arab unrest. Calling for an immediate halt to Jewish immigration and the establishment of an Arab-ruled state, the Mufti installed himself as president of the newly formed Arab Higher Committee, which instigated a general strike of Arab workers (thereby destroying the Palestinian Arab economy) and enlisted Syrian and Iraqi fanatics to participate in new acts of violence against the Jewish community. By October, 80 Jews had been killed, numerous orchards and farms had been destroyed, and entire communities had been displaced. Additionally, violent clashes between British troops and Arab rioters had resulted in 197 Arab and 28 British deaths.[64]

Alarmed, the British government dispatched the famous Peel Commission to make a full inquiry. Weizmann testified before it, saying that the "Jewish problem" was "the problem of the homelessness of a people." Many Jews in the West, he conceded, had comfortable homes. But in Europe east of the Rhine "there were six million people doomed to be pent up where they are not wanted, and for whom the world is divided into places where they cannot live, and places into which they cannot enter.... There should be one place in the world, in God's wide world, where we could live and express ourselves in accordance with our character, and make our contribution towards the civilized world." He reminded the commission of the yearning of the Jewish people for its homeland through 2,000 years of exile; of the sweat and toil of Zionist pioneers in revitalizing the country; and how the benefits of their labors had been felt by all Palestinians, whether Jew or Arab. He spoke of how the influx of Jews had not saturated Palestine's capacity for absorption, but had increased that capacity by creating new economic opportunities. Finally, he reminded the commission of the pledge put forth in the Balfour Declaration for the establishment of a Jewish national home in Palestine and of the sincerity of the statesmen who had made that pledge.[65]

The Mufti also testified, saying that Jewish immigration must stop, that the country could not accommodate the number it now had (he would not say whether any would have to leave),[66] and that the Jews intended to demolish the Al-Aqsa Mosque and the Dome of the Rock in order to rebuild their temple.[67] During cross-examination by the commissioners, he admitted that the tax burden on Arabs was less under the Mandate than it had been under Turkish rule, that military conscription had ended, and that there were now more schools. But he maintained that the plight of the Arabs had worsened nonetheless.[68] Cross-examined in his turn, Weizmann was asked whether it was prudent to invite more Jews into Palestine if the Mandatory government could not ensure their protection. He replied that it was preferable to be in Palestine without protection than to be in Poland with it.[69]

After hearing both sides, the commission concluded that Jewish and Arab aspirations in Palestine were incompatible. Consequently, it recommended the partition of the Mandate into separate Jewish and Arab states, leaving Tel Aviv and Jerusalem (and a corridor connecting them) under Mandatory control. The amount of territory allotted to the Jewish community was perilously small, but the offer of a state was unprecedented, and Weizmann knew that it could not be turned down. In answer to outcries at the 1937 Zionist Congress in Zurich that God had promised *all* Palestine to the Jews, he replied, "Well, let us do what we can with our existing modest ... circumstances and leave God to accomplish his promise in his own time."[70]

At his bidding, the congress approved the idea of partition with the reservation that further negotiation on final boundaries would be necessary. In contrast, the Arab leadership refused the commission's recommendations outright and resorted once more to violence. A high-ranking British official was gunned down in cold blood. The British retaliated by outlawing the Arab Higher Committee and arresting its leaders. Escaping to Lebanon, the Mufti directed a new wave of terrorism — not only against the Jews and British, but also against his rivals in the Arab community, of whom 3,000 were killed.[71] Finding their troop strength inadequate, the British enlisted 3,000 Jews— all members of the Jewish "Defense Force" or *Haganah*— to serve under the pro–Zionist British officer, Orde Wingate. Wingate promptly instituted a program of night patrols to ambush Arab attackers in the darkness, either en route to their targets or while still in their dens. Finding this too restrained, the extremist splinter group, Irgun, ignored the remonstrations of the Jewish Agency and savagely repaid Arab terrorist attacks in their own coin.[72] By the time the fighting quieted down in 1939, there had been 2,400 Jewish, 3,700 Arab, and 600 British casualties.[73]

Having quashed the Arab revolt, the British government found itself assailed by protests against its Palestine policy from all over the Middle East. Meanwhile, in Europe, it had become increasingly clear that the Chamberlain government's appeasement policy toward Nazism was an abject failure. With the prospect of a European war growing more likely with each passing day, Britain could ill afford to jeopardize its Middle Eastern oil interests by alienating the entire region.[74] Consequently, the government renounced the Peel Commission's partition scheme and issued the infamous 1939 white paper, limiting Palestine's Jewish immigration quota to 15,000 annually over the next five years, after which there was to be no Jewish immigration at all without Arab consent. At ten years, the Mandate was to become an independent Arab state with the Jews forever in the minority.

Once again, the Chamberlain government had found it expedient to appease belligerence. The outcry was immediate. With so-called coffin boats full of "illegal" Jewish refugees from Europe already being turned away from Palestine's shores,[75] Churchill rose in the Commons to say, "Now, there is the breach; there is the violation of the pledge; there is the abandonment of the Balfour Declaration; there is the end of the vision, of the hope, of the dream.... It is hoped to obtain five years of easement in Palestine by this proposal; surely the consequences will be entirely the opposite. A sense of moral weakness in the mandatory Power, whose many years of vacillation and uncertainty have ... largely provoked the evils from which we suffer, will rouse all the violent elements in Palestine to the utmost degree."[76] At the 1939 World Zionist Congress in Geneva, Weizmann concurred, saying, "I am reluctantly compelled to say that the British government has gone back on its promises."[77] In fact, the British had done much more; they had violated their Mandate charter — and the Permanent Mandates Commission of the League of Nations censured them for it. Henceforth, British rule in Palestine was based not on international sanction but on force.[78]

While the Zionist Congress was still in session, it received another devastating blow: the announcement of the Ribbentrop-Molotov Pact, allying Nazi Germany and Soviet Russia. With the specter of death now hanging over eastern European Jewry and the gates of Palestine all but closed, Weizmann adjourned the session, saying, "There is darkness around us ... if, as I hope, we are spared in life and our work continues, who knows—perhaps a new light will shine upon us from the thick, bleak gloom.... May we meet again in peace."[79] Many of the delegates wept.

The rest of the story is readily told. The white paper of 1939 sounded the death knell of the Balfour Declaration and the Mandate charter — and also of European Jewry. An international conference held in Evian, France in July 1938 had effectively ruled out increased quotas for Jewish immigration anywhere in the world (with the gallant exception of the Dominican Republic). Now the hope of sanctuary in Palestine was likewise extinguished. European Jewry was trapped in a vise. The first mass killings of the Holocaust took place in 1941. Anticipating a German victory, the Mufti turned up in Berlin and plotted the extermination of Palestinian Jewry in a meeting with the fuehrer. Later, he organized a Muslim SS unit that murdered Jews, gypsies, and other "undesirables" in the former Yugoslavia. At Nuremberg, he was convicted of war crimes but was never punished.

The lone bright spot on the horizon was Churchill's accession as prime minister in 1940. After the infamous Chamberlain years, Weizmann again had an influential friend in the British government. At age 65, he became honorary chemical advisor to the Ministry of Supply and developed fermentation processes to ease the military shortages of rubber and aviation fuel.[80] With Churchill, he tried to organize the formation of a 10,000-man Jewish brigade to fight the Nazis, but opposition within the Foreign Office thwarted the project until 1944. In the meantime, droves of Palestinian Jews attempted to enlist in the British army only to be turned away owing to the army's desire to maintain "enlistment parity" with the Arabs (who volunteered in trickles).[81] Weizmann's two sons— Michael and Benjamin — enlisted in England. The former was killed flying an RAF reconnaissance mission in 1942. The latter was discharged secondary to combat fatigue and suffered from post-traumatic stress disorder for the remainder of his life.[82]

In the meantime, Weizmann did all that he could to combat the 1939 white paper and champion the cause of Zionism. In 1941, he published an article in *Foreign Affairs*, putting forth the moral case for a Jewish commonwealth in Palestine. In 1942, he attended the Biltmore Conference in New York City, which issued a definitive rebuke against the 1939 white paper, calling it "cruel and indefensible in its denial of sanctuary to Jews fleeing from Nazi persecution."[83] Addressing a "Stop Hitler Now" protest at Madison Square Garden (1943), he inveighed against the now undeniable reports of the Holocaust's horrors. The following year, he toured Palestine, where he was feted as a head of state, witnessed a parade of the newly formed Jewish Brigade, and laid the foundation stone of the Weizmann Institute of Science in Rehovot.

Prior to his departure for Palestine (November 1944), the Churchill cabinet had been on the verge of reviving the partition idea put forth by the Peel Commission. But a supreme act of folly supervened: bent on vengeance for Britain's continued refusal to grant unrestricted sanctuary to European Jewry even as the latter were being exterminated, a terrorist splinter group called the "Stern Gang" assassinated Lord Moyne, Britain's minister-resident for the Middle East. (The act was as senseless as it was odious, since Moyne had recently come to favor partition.[84]) Although the Jewish Agency denounced the assassination and cooperated with the British in suppressing extremism, Churchill temporarily postponed further action on partition. Germany's defeat in May 1945 rekindled his zeal. Unfortunately, he was defeated in that year's elections, and Ernest Bevin, the foreign secretary of the incoming government, turned out to be an implacable foe of Zionism.

After the war, most of Europe's surviving Jews were gathered into displaced persons camps established by the UN. The overwhelming majority of these detainees had no desire to resume their lives in the (still) anti–Semitic states that had rejected their right to life during the Holocaust. When asked their preference in a UN survey after months of languishing in the camps, 96 percent said they wanted to live in Palestine. Intent on maintaining the existing immigration restrictions there, Britain intercepted shiploads of these unhappy individuals and forced their return to the camps.[85] Testifying before an Anglo-American Committee of Inquiry on their plight, Weizmann argued that the quarrel between Arab and Jew must no longer be viewed in terms of absolute "right and wrong" but in terms of "the greater and lesser injustice."[86]

Meanwhile, the leadership of the Yishuv had decided to resist British policy by force of arms. For the remainder of Britain's tenure in Palestine, two old friends— Jew and Briton — would wage a bitter struggle. In the end, their relationship would very much resemble hatred. In failing health, Weizmann made an impassioned plea for restraint and cautioned against "un-Jewish methods" at the 22nd World Zionist Congress in Basle.[87] The speech was his farewell address. When his motion in favor of continued negotiation in London was narrowly defeated, he relinquished the presidency of the WZO (1946).

His work, however, was not complete. After the UN approved a new partition plan for Palestine in November 1947, Weizmann's diplomacy was crucial in maintaining the support of the United States. As Abba Eban relates, U.S. President Harry Truman was sympathetic, but had become so exasperated by what he considered "immoderate Zionist pressure" that he would no longer meet with Zionist intermediaries. Espying a statue of Andrew Jackson on the president's desk, Eddie Jacobson, Truman's longtime Jewish friend and business partner, broke the quarantine by revealing the unlikely truism that Chaim Weizmann was none other than "the Jewish Andrew Jackson."[88] Granted an audience, Weizmann played an instrumental role in anchoring Truman's support for an independent Jewish state, and in making sure that the largely empty Negev Desert was included in it.

Independence was declared on May 15, 1948. Weizmann was still in New York, and it is something of an injustice that his signature was never appended to Israel's Declaration of Independence. He was honored to learn that he had been elected to serve as the state's first president, and though he was disappointed to find that the position was mainly symbolic, he remained in office for the rest of his life. When he died after a protracted illness on November 9, 1952, a quarter of a million mourners filed past his coffin to pay tribute to him.[89]

His had been the defining career of the Zionist movement. If, in the end, the violence he deplored[90] had played its role in convincing the British to leave Palestine after their betrayal of the Mandate charter, Weizmann's diplomacy and moderation had achieved much more. His advocacy of the Jewish cause had helped bring about the Balfour Declaration and, after it, the British Mandate dedicated to the establishment of a Jewish national home in Palestine. Then, like a modern Moses, he led the Jewish people through the diplomatic vicissitudes of three decades, steering them away from the false idols of unrealistic goals and "un–Jewish" methods, until finally, at journey's end, with Israel's rebirth weighing in the balance, he was called upon to play yet another crucial part — placing the Jewish case before the UN while it considered partition, and maintaining the critical support of U.S. President Harry Truman.

Such was the career of Zionism's greatest diplomat. Today, his body rests on the campus of the Weizmann Institute in Rehovot. His grave, like that of Theodor Herzl, modern Zionism's founder, lies on a hill facing Jerusalem.

3

David Ben-Gurion and Independence

As the 22nd World Zionist Congress convened in Basle, Switzerland, on December 5, 1946, talk swirled about naming Chaim Weizmann "honorary" president of the World Zionist Organization. This would have been a fitting tribute to the man who had symbolized the Zionist movement for three decades had it not been for the fact that Weizmann was already the *actual* president of the WZO and was being offered the "honorary" title by rivals who wished to deprive him of his influence.[1] Chief among these rivals was David Ben-Gurion, chairman of both the Zionist Executive and the Jewish Agency.

The issue in this power struggle was not to be found in the aims of the protagonists, for these were the same. Rather, it was to be found in the tactics employed in achieving those aims. In the wake of the Holocaust, with a quarter million Jews languishing in displaced persons camps in Europe, a majority of the delegates felt that the time for talk had passed and that Britain's continuing restrictions on Jewish immigration to Palestine must be resisted by force. Weizmann, however, retained confidence in negotiation. "Assassination, ambush, kidnapping, the murder of innocent men are alien to the spirit of our movement," he told the assembly in his opening address. "We came to Palestine to build, not to destroy...."[2]

A ten-day debate ensued over policy, and on December 16, Weizmann mounted the rostrum to make a final plea. He was interrupted by a cry of "demagogue!" from a hostile delegate. "I — a demagogue!" he roared. "I who have borne all the ills and travails of this movement. The person who flung that word in my face ought to know that in every house and stable in Nahalal, in every little workshop in Tel Aviv or Haifa, there is a drop of my blood...."[3] As a supportive ovation issued from the assembly, Weizmann spoke on: "If you think of bringing the redemption nearer by un–Jewish methods, if you have lost faith in hard work and better days, then you are committing idolatry, and endangering what we have built."[4]

In conclusion, he proposed participation in a new set of talks in London. Ben-Gurion openly dissented, and by the narrow vote of 171–154, Weizmann's motion was defeated. The congress adjourned without reelecting him to the presidency. Indeed, it adjourned without any president at all. But there was to be no power vacuum: authority now lay with Ben-Gurion.[5]

David Ben-Gurion was born to Avigdor and Sheindel Green on October 16, 1886, in Plonsk, Poland (inside the Russian "Pale of Settlement"). At age nine, a phrenological exam of his skull performed by the local doctor foretold an extraordinary future.[6] His mother naturally assumed that he would be a rabbi. After all, he had learned Hebrew from his grandfather at age three. But destiny had a different plan: David's father was a devoted Zionist, who hosted meetings of Plonsk's *Hovevei Zion* ("Lovers of Zion")

Israeli Prime Minister David Ben-Gurion, January 24, 1959 (courtesy of the State of Israel Government Press Office; photographer David Eldan).

chapter in the family home. Hearing their discussions, David concluded that the rightful home of the Jews was Palestine, not Plonsk. In his tenth year, two events confirmed this opinion. The first was a visit to Plonsk by Theodor Herzl, the founder of political Zionism, who seemed the very picture of the Messiah with his stately beard and majestic bearing.[7] The second was the untimely death of David's mother.

Shattered by the loss, David immersed himself in his father's Zionism. His first inclination was to earn an engineering degree, thinking thus to obtain valuable skills for life in Palestine.[8] Denied the necessary education owing to the Jewish student quotas in the Pale of Settlement, he moved to Palestine in 1906 and sought work wherever he could find it: transporting buckets of manure at Petah Tikvah (where he contracted malaria),[9] stomping grapes at Rishon LeZion,[10] and working a plow in the Galilee where he helped organize a defense force — the *hashomer* or "watchmen" — to guard against raids by Arab Bedouins. (A photo shows these armed defenders clad in Arab *kaffiyeh* headdresses.)

As a member of the *Po' alei Zion* or "Workers of Zion" organization, David served as a "permanent pioneer," traveling to various locales to clear wasteland for incoming settlers. Feeling that the Yishuv (Palestine's Jewish community) lacked solidarity, he moved to Jerusalem in 1910 to work as a journalist for the Hebrew-language periodical *Ahdut* ("Unity"), which sought to promote cooperation among Palestine's Jewish workers. It was at this time that he changed his last name to "Ben-Gurion" as a tribute to a Jewish hero from the war with Rome in the first century A.D.[11]

Meanwhile, the sultan's government had fallen into the hands of the so-called Young Turks who had gained power by coup d'état in 1908. Believing the democratic, pro-minority rhetoric of the new leaders, Ben-Gurion decided to move to Constantinople and earn a law degree. He hoped thereby to gain election to the Turkish parliament and to champion the cause of Zionism from within the government.[12] Learning Turkish in three months, he donned a fez and entered the University of Constantinople.

When Turkey entered World War I, Ben-Gurion sought to rally Palestine's Jews to the Turkish banner. After the Turks arrested him and sentenced him to eternal exile, however, he reconsidered his stance.[13] He spent the war years in the United States giving Zionist speeches at the behest of *Po' alei Zion*. On his tour of the country, he acquitted himself well against non–Zionist Jewish hecklers, co-authored a book entitled *Remembrance* about the Pale of Settlement, and helped organize a Jewish youth "pioneer corps" to prepare potential immigrants for life in Palestine. The existence of segregation laws in the southern states greatly disillusioned him. In Galveston, Texas, he was nearly evicted from a local movie theatre for sitting with the segregated blacks.[14]

When the Allies announced the formation of a Jewish Legion, Ben-Gurion enlisted, but the war came to an end before he saw action. Returning to Palestine, he continued to promote labor unity — his efforts culminating in the founding of the "Federation of Jewish Labor," or *Histadrut*, in 1920. Nominally a labor union, the Histadrut was, in practice, very much more. It participated actively in preparing Jewish laborers for service in new industries, found jobs for incoming Jewish immigrants, provided education and social welfare for Palestine's Jewish community, and established a unified defense force, the Haganah, to guard Jews against Arab attacks (which had become increasingly widespread following the incorporation of the Balfour Declaration into the 1920 Treaty of San Remo).

As general-secretary of the Histadrut from 1921 to 1935, Ben-Gurion became a bona fide leader within the Zionist movement. In 1930, he brought about a merger of the Yishuv's two leading labor parties to form the "Eretz Israel Workers Party" or *Mapai*. (Mapai, and its descendant, the present-day Labor Party, would dominate Israeli politics for three decades after independence was attained in 1948.)

At the 1931 World Zionist Congress in Basle, Ben-Gurion found himself in an influential middle position between WZO President Chaim Weizmann, who favored continued moderation in negotiating with the British (an unpopular stance in the wake of the anti–Zionist Passfield white paper of 1930), and the hard-line "revisionist," Vladimir Jabotinsky, who pressed for a resolution defining the goal of Zionism as "the creation of a Jewish majority ... *on both sides* of the Jordan."[15] (The latter notion sounds extremist to the modern ear, but Jabotinsky was demanding nothing more than what had been implied in Article 5 of the League of Nations' Mandate charter — namely that it had been illegal to separate Transjordan from the Jewish national home.[16]) Although Ben-Gurion supported Weizmann, the latter lost the presidency — sealing his own fate by suggesting that a Jewish majority was not required *even in Palestine* (never mind in Transjordan) to fulfill the purpose of the national home. The congress, however, was not done: after turning out Weizmann, it rejected Jabotinsky's resolution without so much as a formal vote, and then opened the Zionist executive to all parties.[17] In the end, Mapai came away with two of the five seats — a positive coup. Two years later, at the 1933 congress, Ben-Gurion gained a seat on the executive committee, and at the next congress (1935), he was named its chairman and chosen to head the Jewish Agency. Henceforth, he was to be the Yishuv's leading domestic political figure, while Weizmann, who had regained the presidency of the WZO, resumed diplomatic leadership.[18]

Between 1933 and 1936, Ben-Gurion met with local Arab notables hoping to reach an accord that would allow unrestricted Jewish immigration. In return, he proposed that Jewish statehood in Palestine should exist within the framework of a regional Arab commonwealth in which the Arabs would hold the majority.[19] Although these negotiations had a promising beginning, the Mufti of Jerusalem, Haj Amin al-Husseini, put an end to them by inciting the 1936 riots. Ben-Gurion directed the Haganah to resist the Mufti's terror campaign, but insisted that his fighters show restraint. The Haganah was not to engage in terrorism of its own, but to behave as a legitimate defense force. The policy proved instrumental in maintaining British goodwill.

Hoping to obtain concessions on immigration from the British government, Ben-Gurion dissimulated in his testimony before the 1936–37 Peel Commission — claiming that the Yishuv was satisfied with Palestine's status as a Jewish national home and had no desire for statehood. Publicly, he maintained this posture, even after the Peel Commission recommended partition and the establishment of a Jewish state. Privately, the offer made him euphoric.[20] At the 1937 World Zionist Congress, he played an influential role in obtaining a vote in favor of partition, and was deputed to travel to London to negotiate enlarged borders for the prospective Jewish state.[21] Angered by Britain's subsequent retreat from partition and by the infamous 1939 white paper (which presaged an end to Jewish immigration and the establishment of a unitary Arab-dominated state), he testified in London that British bayonets would be required to enforce such a settlement.[22]

In promulgating the 1939 white paper, Britain turned its back on the Balfour Declaration and (just as significantly) on the Mandate charter, which was the legal basis for British rule in Palestine. Before the dust could settle from this bombshell, Hitler invaded Poland and World War II was inaugurated in Europe. Amidst these earthshaking events, Ben-Gurion summarized his war policy with the refrain, "We shall fight the War as if there were no White Paper, and the White Paper as if there were no War."[23] At the war's outset, more than 100,000 Jewish volunteers mobbed the British recruitment stations in Palestine.[24] Most of them were turned away — nominally because the Mandate authorities wanted to maintain parity between Jewish and Arab recruits, but in truth because these same authorities didn't want to be beholden to the Zionists (or have to fight a trained army of them) once the war was won. Ultimately, 30,000 Palestinian Jews served in the British army during World War II versus 9,000 Palestinian Arabs — and half of the latter deserted or were discharged.[25]

Meanwhile, behind the scenes, Weizmann and Ben-Gurion had long been at loggerheads over Zionist policy. In the ensuing years, their tussle would emerge into the light of day. At the 1942 Biltmore Conference in New York City, both men contributed to the so-called Biltmore Program calling for an end to the white paper, the recruitment of a Jewish army to fight the Nazis, and the foundation of a Jewish Commonwealth in Palestine. Ben-Gurion, however, clearly favored a more aggressive approach toward achieving these goals.

Both men deplored the Stern Gang's assassination of Lord Moyne in 1944, which effectively cost Zionism the active support of Winston Churchill (who had, by then, delivered on the promise of a Jewish Brigade and was actively considering a new partition plan for Palestine). In the aftermath of this catastrophe, Ben-Gurion cooperated with British authorities in rounding up extremists who defied his directive to desist from terrorist activities.

A year later, however, with the war won and Britain's new Labor government clinging to the white paper restrictions on Jewish immigration, the period of cooperation came to an end. In the fall of 1945, Ben-Gurion visited the displaced persons camps in Germany and promised the detainees that

Palestine would soon be their home. But the British government had no intention of supporting such a pledge. Colonial Secretary George Hall had already rebuffed Ben-Gurion's demand for the immediate issuance of 100,000 immigration certificates: the secretary would issue 2,000 certificates and then (subject to Arab approval) 1,400 per month after that.[26] In defiance of this Draconian policy, the Haganah erected an elaborate European "underground railroad" terminating on the shores of the Mediterranean, and shipped thousands of displaced persons (DPs) to Palestine "illegally."[27]

Britain struck back with rigorous countermeasures. Her occupation forces in Austria apprehended hundreds of concentration camp survivors who were attempting to reach Palestine, and confined them in former POW camps. At the same time, British naval vessels blockaded the coast of Palestine, intercepting shiploads of "illegal" immigrants from the displaced persons camps and sending the passengers to Cyprus (or, worse, back to their detention in Europe).[28] The clampdown was largely successful in the short term, but when American and European audiences saw the newsreels of hapless Holocaust survivors being turned away from Palestine's shores, their sympathies rarely lay with the British military authorities.

In Ben-Gurion's view, if the cataclysm of the Holocaust was not enough to change British policy, then armed resistance was the only answer. In October 1945, he sanctioned the merger of the Haganah, Irgun and Stern Gang into the "Hebrew Resistance Movement." As its first act, the resistance raided the detention camp in Athlit to liberate 200 Jewish "illegal" immigrants who were facing imminent deportation. An intense guerrilla campaign followed, in which British bases were attacked and railroads and communications were destroyed. The battle raged until July 1946, when the resistance came apart under the weight of two separate actions. The first occurred on "Black Sabbath"—June 29, 1946—when British troops burst into Jewish homes across Palestine, searching for weapons and carrying out mass arrests. The second was the bombing of the King David Hotel.

Initially, Ben-Gurion had agreed to the hotel bombing, but he subsequently deemed the project too risky and withdrew his support.[29] The Irgun, however, would not relent, and on July 22, 1946, a whole wing of the building, which housed Britain's administrative offices in Jerusalem, was reduced to rubble. Ninety-one persons (71 of them civilians) were killed, and scores of others were wounded. Twenty-five minutes prior to the explosion, the Irgun phoned the King David Hotel, the *Palestine Post*, and the French Consulate, warning of the intended attack and demanding the immediate evacuation of the premises. Inured to false alarms, the British went about their business. By one (contested) account, a high-ranking official curtly said that he didn't take orders from Jews.[30]

Although Ben-Gurion and Weizmann were both appalled by the deaths, the two men were now clearly on opposite sides of the strategic fence — Weizmann calling for an end to "un–Jewish methods" and a resumption of talks, Ben-Gurion bent on continued resistance. The showdown between them at the 22nd World Zionist Congress in Basle that December, as we have seen, resulted in a victory for Ben-Gurion. Weizmann blamed the British for this outcome. Had British foreign secretary Ernest Bevin offered even token support (for example, a moratorium on the deportation of "illegal" Jewish refugees), Weizmann would likely have won.[31]

Thus, owing to her own shortsightedness, Britain faced a continuation of the battle — and not just with the Jews of Palestine. In the wake of the Holocaust, the American public and its president favored increased Jewish immigration to Palestine. In May 1946, an Anglo-American commission voted unanimously for the immediate acceptance into Palestine of 100,000 Jewish refugees from the displaced persons camps, and Harry Truman had supported the decision. But Britain would not agree to it. In 1945, both Clement Atlee (the British prime minister) and Foreign Secretary Bevin had spurned the idea of moving Jews to "the head of the queue" when many non–Jews were also interned in displaced persons camps. Now, Bevin added an unfortunate remark about Americans favoring Jewish immigration to Palestine because they "did not want too many of them in New York."[32]

But Britain was not in a position to defy the United States. With the displaced persons camps standing as a continuing reminder of the humanitarian need for increased Jewish immigration to Palestine, Americans took an ill view of the Mandatory government's militarist posture. Moreover, Britain was requesting a large post-war loan from the United States, and the request was up for consideration in the U.S. Congress. Something had to give, and in the end it was Britain's hard line. In early 1947, Winston Churchill rose in the House of Commons to say, "If we cannot fulfill our promises to the Zionists we should, without delay, place our Mandate for Palestine at the feet of the United Nations, and give due notice of our impending evacuation from that country." Exhausted by the conflict, the Atlee government announced on February 18, 1947, that it would seek the UN's recommendation.[33]

In truth, however, the government had no intention of evacuating Palestine. Atlee and Bevin believed that the UN could never muster the required two-thirds majority to pass a resolution on the matter. The Muslim states and the Soviet Bloc were anti–Zionist. Together, they did not control enough votes to pass a pro–Arab resolution, but they controlled more than the necessary third to block a pro–Zionist one. Unable to act, the UN would have to hand authority back to the Mandate and grant it the freedom of action to do what it could.[34]

But Britain had not counted upon Joseph Stalin's sense of irony. The Soviet ruler wanted to undermine British influence in the Middle East in order to increase his own. And what more galling way to do it than to renounce the single Anglo-Soviet point of agreement in the region: i.e., anti–Zionism. Accordingly, in May 1947, while the UN busily assembled delegates from 11 nations to go investigate the Palestine situation (the famous UN Special Committee on Palestine or "UNSCOP"), the Soviet deputy foreign minister, Andrei Gromyko, mounted the general assembly rostrum and delivered a very serviceable pro–Zionist oration, concluding with the remark that if a single-state solution in Palestine was not feasible, Russia would favor partition of the Mandate into separate Arab and Jewish states.[35]

Soon after these remarkable words were uttered, the 11 delegates of UNSCOP arrived in Palestine (June 1947). During their stay, they saw British authorities hang three members of the militant Jewish group Irgun for bombing British installations, and saw the Irgun hang two kidnapped British sergeants (and booby-trap the execution site) in retaliation. (As a sequel, British troops ran amok in Tel Aviv, gunning down innocent Jews in a berserk Black and Tans style shooting spree.[36])

On quieter days, the delegates saw British personnel virtually confined in barbed-wired compounds—a sure sign that the Mandate was losing its grip. They saw Arab demonstrators chanting anti–Zionist slogans in all the major cities, and listened to Arab leaders from the surrounding countries vowing bloodshed if the committee recommended partition.[37] They listened to Jewish spokesmen make the case for Zionism and for the needs of the suffering Holocaust survivors in the displaced persons camps. (Weizmann spoke with characteristic eloquence about the "homelessness of a people." Ben-Gurion cited a post-war Gallup poll indicating continued anti–Semitism in Germany and said of the DPs that "the countries of their birth are a graveyard of their people. They do not wish to return there and they cannot."[38])

And finally the delegates were treated to the spectacle of the *Exodus 1947*—an old American ferryboat that arrived from France with 4,500 concentration camp survivors aboard. As it neared the Palestine coast, it was forcibly boarded by British troops. By the time the ship surrendered, three Jewish passengers were dead and a hundred wounded, while the British suffered casualties of their own. Afterwards, in Haifa harbor, four distressed UNSCOP delegates looked on as British troops forcibly prodded the refugees from the tattered ship.

But this was only the beginning of the story. With the news cameras rolling and the world watching, the British reembarked the passengers on British transport vessels and sent them back to France. Once arrived, the passengers refused to go ashore, saying that Palestine was their home. The French were willing to take them in, but had no intention of helping the British remove them from the ships by force. So the British took them to Hamburg, Germany — and when 1,500 passengers still refused to budge, the British picked them up and carried them ashore. They were then conveyed to the DP camp in Poppendorf, where the registrars asked them the standard registration questions and received the single answer *Eretz Israel* from every passenger (no matter what was asked).[39]

After visiting the DP camps for themselves, the UNSCOP delegates voted seven to three in favor of partition with one abstention. Abba Eban and David Horowitz went to give Ben-Gurion the news, but found him hopelessly absorbed with another problem. Having evoked no response from him, they left the room. Suddenly, Ben-Gurion bolted after them, shouting, "What was that you said?"[40]

UNSCOP issued its report to the UN on August 31, 1947, replete with a partition map that anticipated Crick and Watson's double helix by six years. Along the coast, the north and south were apportioned to the Arabs, and the middle to the Jews. Inland, the north and south were given to the Jews and the middle to the Arabs. Jerusalem and Bethlehem were to be incorporated into an international zone. Significantly, the largely empty Negev Desert in the south was apportioned to the Jews, giving their population room to grow without displacing Arab residents. The Jews accepted the report with reservations. The Arabs rejected it out of hand.

After a period of debate in the UN General Assembly, the matter came to a vote on November 29, 1947. Despite intense pressure from U.S. oil corporations and from his own state and defense departments (all of whom were concerned solely with U.S. oil interests in the region), Harry Truman remained staunchly pro–Zionist. The U.S. vote was thus certain. The position of France was questionable to the end, and when the French delegate voted in favor, the tense Jews in the gallery thought they saw the rays of the sun poking through the storm clouds of 2,000 years and gave a rousing cheer.[41] The final vote was 33–13 in favor with 10 abstentions. (India, Greece, Cuba and 10 Muslim states voted no. Britain abstained.)

Across Palestine, Jews danced in the streets. The following day, the minions of the Mufti (who had taken asylum in Cairo after being charged with war crimes at Nuremberg) attacked two buses near Jerusalem, killing seven Jews— among them, a 22-year-old girl who was en route to her wedding.[42] Two days after that, an Arab mob stormed into Jerusalem's New City and set Jewish shops aflame. Sir Alan Cunningham, the Mandate's high commissioner, phoned the Arab Higher Committee to demand an end to the riot, but was told that the Jews had provoked it by dancing in the streets. He seems to have regarded this as a reasonable explanation.[43] British troops and police were in the vicinity and did nothing to halt the violence. But when the Haganah tried to intervene to protect the victims, British soldiers forcibly barred them from the riot zone. Over the ensuing twelve days, 80 Jews were killed in pogroms and terrorist attacks (many of which were orchestrated in absentia by the Mufti). Arabs threw rocks at Jewish vehicles and bombs into Jewish shops. Similar violence was perpetrated against Jews living in Arab countries across the Middle East.[44]

As the Arab attacks multiplied, the Irgun and Stern Gang responded with their own brand of terrorism, which not infrequently involved the tossing of hand-held bombs into *Arab* crowds. Abhorring these tactics, the Haganah adopted a policy of "aggressive defense": After an Arab attack, the Haganah responded with lethal force, but directed it specifically against individual perpetrators or, when this was impracticable, against the Arab village that had launched the attack. At the same time, they distributed leaflets to uninvolved Arabs imploring them to drive out those who wanted war and to accept Jewish entreaties for peace.[45]

The British authorities, meanwhile, had announced that they would comply with the UN resolution of November 29, but would not participate in enforcing it. In practice, they did everything in their power to deliver the entire country into Arab hands: While British vessels continued to patrol the coast, blocking the arrival of arms and of "illegal" Jewish immigrants, the Mandate authorities turned a blind eye to the arrival of Arab fighters from Syria and Egypt.[46] Whenever a position was to be evacuated, the British informed the Arabs in advance so that the latter could seize crucial fortresses and strategic ground. British troops handed captured Haganah fighters over to Arab lynch mobs[47] and doled out weapons to Arab combatants, while the government in London equipped the armies of Iraq and Transjordan, which were laying plans to attack the Jews.[48] In Haifa and Jerusalem, British deserters who had enlisted with the Arabs detonated car bombs in crowded Jewish areas, inflicting heavy casualties. By mid–January, there were 1,069 Arab and 769 Jewish casualties in Jerusalem alone.[49]

Under the UN partition plan, Jerusalem was to be an "international" zone. Geographically, however, it was surrounded by territory allotted to the Arabs. The Haganah did its best to keep the city's 100,000 Jewish residents supplied with food and water, but Arab villages dominated the main road from Tel Aviv, and Jewish convoys had to run a gauntlet of sniper fire to reach the city. On March 22, Arab forces severed the supply road completely. The Haganah responded with its first offensive of the war in a concerted effort to reestablish a line of supply. Following the capture of Kastel in early April, a Jewish convoy safely entered Jerusalem for the first time in two weeks. On April 9, Arab troops retook Kastel, but they abandoned it again in confusion when their leader, the Mufti's kinsman Abdel Kader al-Husseini, was killed.

The supply road was open again, but it was not secure. On April 20, Ben-Gurion insisted on accompanying a large convoy bound for Jerusalem so that he could be with the city's defenders for Passover. The convoy came under heavy attack, and though Ben-Gurion ultimately arrived in one piece, the convoy did not. It sustained more than 20 fatalities and left a score of vehicles abandoned by the roadside.[50]

On April 9 (the day that Abdel Kader al-Husseini took Kastel), Jewish paramilitary forces attacked the neighboring Arab village of Deir Yassin. Owing to a chronic shortage of men and equipment, the local Haganah commander had agreed — for the first time — to let the Irgun and Stern Gang participate in the campaign to open the Jerusalem road. Although the residents of Deir Yassin had not played a direct role in the fighting, the village was strategically located and had been used as a transit point for Arab soldiers in the Kastel sector — some of whom had sallied out of the village to shoot at passing cars.[51] The village's occupation seemed like a simple matter. The plan had been to summon the inhabitants to flee by loudspeaker and to seize the hamlet once they had left.[52] Unfortunately, the vehicle upon which the loudspeaker was mounted drove into a tank ditch and could not be extricated. (There are conflicting reports as to whether any subsequent announcement was or was not heard by the populace.[53])

In any event, as soon as the Irgun/Stern force began its advance, it came under heavy fire from the town's defenders and was soon pinned down in a house-to-house fight for which it was neither trained nor equipped.[54] In the weeks preceding the attack, a force of Iraqi soldiers had garrisoned the town, securing the entryways of many of the community's stone houses with iron doors.[55] Unable to breach these obstacles, the Jewish soldiers set off demolition charges or threw hand grenades through the windows of houses from which they were taking fire.[56] The attendant destruction may be imagined, but the tactic was not decisive. The battle raged for eight hours before a contingent of Haganah soldiers entered the fray and subdued the most resilient Arab stronghold with mortar fire.[57] Of 132 Irgun and Stern fighters engaged, 4 had been killed and 37 wounded in the fighting.[58]

Things came off rather worse for the Arabs. Although the Jewish attackers left open an escape route for the village's civilian populace and a majority of the latter availed themselves of the opportunity to get away,[59] the Arab forces had opened fire from civilian houses with civilians still in them. Consequently, the civilian death toll from the battle was high, with women and children being among the dead. Moreover, amongst those who surrendered at battle's end were a number of Iraqi soldiers who had disguised themselves in women's burkas. On the point of being exposed, one of these prisoners drew a pistol and shot a Jewish officer, thereby provoking a chaotic burst of fire from the Jewish side which killed a number of those who had surrendered in earnest.[60]

Jewish authorities initially put the Arab death toll at 250 out of a total population of 400, but Arab accounts, including a study done at Bir Zeit University by Arab investigators, determined that no more than 120 had been killed (although the same study concluded that only 13 of the dead were armed combatants).[61]

At the Jewish Agency, David Ben-Gurion immediately expressed his revulsion over the attack, while the local Haganah commander, wishing to divorce himself from any culpability, issued a report accusing the Irgun and Stern Gang of acting without orders and perpetrating a premeditated massacre. (The Irgun responded by publishing the commander's letter authorizing their attack.[62]) Hoping to get the neighboring Arab states to intervene in the conflict, the Arab-controlled Palestine Broadcasting Corporation (PBC) purposefully transmitted fabricated accounts of the incident, claiming (among other things) that Arab women had been raped.[63] Such reports were as unnecessary as they were untrue. Palestine's Arab neighbors were already making ready to intervene and were only waiting for the British to withdraw (as they were scheduled to do on May 15). Moreover, the broadcasts produced an entirely unexpected result. Frightened by the propaganda, Arab civilians began fleeing Palestine en masse. By mid–May, the total number of refugees had climbed to an estimated 300,000 since the outbreak of fighting in November.[64]

Four days after the PBC broadcasts, Arab soldiers ambushed a Jewish medical convoy en route to Hadassah Hospital on Mount Scopus. In an attack lasting several hours, 76 doctors, nurses, hospital staff and medical students were murdered — many of them burnt alive in their armored vehicles. British soldiers stationed nearby might have stopped the massacre with ease, but cruelly allowed the slaughter to continue.[65] One month later, Arab forces captured Kfar Etzion near Jerusalem. When the fighting ceased, 15 Jewish soldiers surrendered. After disarming them, the Arabs gunned them down. Then, they proceeded to murder the village's surviving inhabitants.[66]

With the surrounding Arab states now champing at the bit to intervene in the conflict, the United States proposed a three-month truce, during which time there was to be a moratorium on Jewish independence. Asked by Ben-Gurion whether his forces could withstand a concerted attack by the combined Arab armies, Yigael Yadin, the Haganah chief of operations, gave a noncommittal reply, replete with several "ifs." He did not, however, say no. After hearing him out, Ben-Gurion put the U.S. proposal before his provisional council, conceding that war would be perilous, but arguing that there was danger, too, in shrinking from the struggle and leaving the fate of Jewish statehood in the hands of others. The chance to declare independence might never arise again. With five Arab armies poised to intercede against them, the council voted six to four to reject the truce offer.[67]

On May 14, 1948, one day before the last British soldiers were scheduled to depart from Palestine, David Ben-Gurion read Israel's Proclamation of Independence before a large Jewish audience at the Tel Aviv Art Museum. (The 15th was the Sabbath, so the ceremony had to take place a day early.[68]) On the wall behind the speaker's rostrum was a portrait of Theodor Herzl flanked by a pair of Israeli flags. Despite the level to which some of the fighting had descended, the proclamation included the passage: "In the midst of wanton aggression, we yet call upon the Arab inhabitants of the State of Israel to preserve the ways of peace and play their part in the development of the State, on the basis of full and equal citizenship and due representation in all its bodies and institutions...."[69] Additionally, the document extended an offer of peace to all of Israel's neighbors.

At one minute past midnight on May 15, Egyptian planes answered Ben-Gurion's olive branch by bombing Tel Aviv. At dawn, the armies of Syria, Lebanon, Transjordan, Egypt and Iraq rolled into Palestine, while Azzam Pasha, secretary-general of the Arab League, announced that the Arab states were embarking on "a war of extermination ... which will be spoken of like the Mongol massacres and the Crusades."[70]

On the bright side, the British were now gone, and Harry Truman had recognized Israel's independence a mere ten minutes after it went into effect.[71] Moreover, the Haganah — which hitherto had been fighting with small arms, a few mortars, no bona fide artillery, and an air force consisting of a few piper cubs whose pilots employed hand grenades as bombs[72] — had worked out an agreement with Czechoslovakia for the purchase of actual weapons (a good thing for Israel, since the invading Arab armies were armed to the hilt).

Ben-Gurion assumed the role of commander in chief in the new government and established his headquarters at Ramat Gan, northeast of Tel Aviv. When the position was attacked by Arab artillery, those around him insisted that he retreat to a bomb shelter, but he would do no more than don a helmet. In this garb, he served as a stretcher-bearer for a sentry who had been wounded in the shelling.[73] He had long since rejected the suggestion that isolated settlements be abandoned in order to establish defensible lines, since evacuated areas would likely be lost forever. Although his stubborn policy entailed a strategically undesirable dispersion of forces, it sometimes paid dividends: In the opening phase of the new struggle, outnumbered Israeli defenders made a valiant stand at the Yad Mordechai kibbutz, stalling Egypt's drive on Tel Aviv for a full six days. (The Egyptians had expected the settlement to fall in an hour.[74]) Out of ammunition on the last day, the defenders gathered up their wounded and stole away in the dark of night.[75]

But in the Jerusalem sector, the army of Transjordan had the upper hand — forcing the surrender of the Jewish quarter of the Old City and occupying the town of Latrun to sever the Tel Aviv–Jerusalem road. Unable to dislodge the enemy from Latrun despite several attempts, the Israelis took up shovels and pickaxes and built an alternate supply road along the course of a remote footpath, dubbing it the "Burma Road."[76]

On June 11, 1948, the UN imposed a 30-day cease-fire on the combatants, replete with an arms embargo.[77] During this interlude, a ship — the *Altalena* — put in from France with an arms cache for the Irgun. Its arrival presented Ben-Gurion with a dilemma. Contraband or not, Israel desperately needed the weapons, and the Irgun was willing to turn them over to the government in return for certain guarantees regarding their allocation. Indeed, the Irgun leader, Menachem Begin, had demonstrated his willingness to cooperate by informing the government of the ship's approach and by directing the vessel to a government-designated landing site.

From this point forward, however, the situation deteriorated. Due to a misleading assurance from one of Ben-Gurion's intermediaries, Begin believed that he had obtained partial agreement on weapons allocation and he did not hesitate to press for a full agreement that would give priority to Irgun soldiers. After a period of discussion, the government rejected Begin's conditions and informed him that it would not assist in unloading the ship. Begin therefore put his own men to the task.[78]

In Ben-Gurion's view, such independent action was unacceptable. On May 28, the prime minister had announced the formation of the IDF, or Israel Defense Force, to serve as Israel's sole legitimate army. By formal agreement, Irgun units were to be incorporated into the IDF. Rightly or wrongly, Ben-Gurion believed that Begin's decision to unload the ship without a government order represented a bid by the Irgun to create "an army within an army," thereby undermining the sovereignty of the state.[79] At an emergency cabinet session, he roared that there was only one state and only one army — and that Begin was not free to do as he pleased.[80]

On June 20, as the first crates of weaponry came ashore at Kfar Vitkin in northern Israel, IDF troops surrounded the landing site and demanded surrender of the entire weapons cache. Begin was given ten minutes to respond, and when he protested that this was not enough time, the IDF opened fire. Six Irgunists and two IDF members were killed. Weighing anchor, the ship made for Tel Aviv harbor where, despite repeated pleas from Begin, it was attacked again on June 21. As the vessel went up in flames, scores of Irgun fighters jumped into the sea. (It is reported that Begin had to be thrown

overboard to keep him from going down with the ship.[81]) Ten more Irgun
men were killed — some being cut down in the water as they sought to swim
ashore.[82] The bulk of the cargo was lost (and with it, claim many Irgun supporters, Israel's best hope for retaking Jerusalem's Old City).[83] The incident
threatened to ignite a fratricidal war. To Begin, however, the very thought of
Jews killing Jews was anathema. Hence, after lodging a sharp protest, he
ordered his men to stand down.[84]

One week later, UN mediator, Count Folke Bernadotte of Sweden, put
forward an ill-conceived peace proposal envisioning a Transjordanian-Israeli
confederacy, and calling for (i) the surrender of the Negev to Transjordan
with western Galilee going to the Israelis in compensation; (ii) the annexation
of the West Bank of the Jordan (including Jerusalem) by Transjordan; (iii)
return of all Arab refugees to their homes; and (iv) unrestricted Jewish immigration into the Jewish state for two years, with authority over immigration
then devolving upon the UN.[85] In promulgating these terms, Bernadotte seems
to have been influenced by his friends in the British Foreign Office, who
desired nothing better than to truncate and marginalize the emerging Jewish
state.[86] The Arabs, however, wanted no Jewish state at all. Moreover, they did
not see why Transjordan should reap the rewards of their collective labors.[87]
Egypt had not invaded the Negev to hand it over to King Abdullah. Thus,
both sides rejected the proposal as unsatisfactory, and on July 8, Egypt broke
the cease-fire with a new push into the southern desert.[88]

The battle now resumed for ten days, during which time the Israelis
seized the Arab towns of Ramle and Lydda — a modest enough gain in terms
of area, but strategically a major accomplishment since the centrally located
towns had imperiled Israel's east-west *and* north-south supply lines.[89]
When the guns fell silent again, the number of Arab refugees stood at a
half million. Ben-Gurion was adamant that the fate of these refugees was
not Israel's responsibility. "War is war," he insisted, "and those who have
declared war on us will have to bear the consequences after they have been
defeated."[90]

A second truce ensued, but hardly a tranquil one. On September 28,
1948, a member of the Stern Gang approached the open window of Count
Bernadotte's limousine and shot the UN negotiator to death in cold blood.
Ben-Gurion immediately cracked down once and for all on the Irgun and
Stern Gang, but worldwide anger was directed at the Jewish state.

Shortly afterwards, a revision of the Bernadotte Plan — this one leaving
Jewish immigration permanently in Jewish hands—came before the UN for
consideration. Once again, the plan called for transfer of the Negev to Transjordan. But the Negev had been promised to Israel by the UN partition resolution of November 1947, and was deemed essential to Israel's future growth

and development. Consequently, before an adverse political solution could be imposed on them, the Israelis decided to force the issue militarily.[91]

According to the existing truce terms, Israeli supply convoys were guaranteed safe passage to settlements in the Negev during certain hours of each day. Egypt, however, made a habit of firing upon them as they passed. On October 15, a large convoy of Israeli trucks made its way southward to bait the Egyptians into a new round of fighting. The Egyptians opened fire. At least one truck exploded. (There is some speculation that the Israelis blew it up themselves in order to magnify the incident.[92]) Citing this as a breach of the truce, Israel launched "Operation Ten Plagues"— an all out offensive in the Negev.

The Egyptians had invaded the Negev along two lines— one inland, extending through Beersheba to Hebron and Bethlehem, the other along the coast through Gaza. At the outset of the new offensive, the Israelis thrust south to capture Beersheba, thus forcing an Egyptian withdrawal from Hebron and Bethlehem. Then after searching for, and finding, a forgotten Roman road that IDF chief of operations Yigael Yadin had learnt about in an archaeological guide,[93] they fell upon au-Auja on the old Palestine-Egyptian border, captured it, and drove into the Sinai towards El-Arish. The capture of this coastal city would have severed the communications of Egyptian forces in Gaza. Unfortunately, the Sinai thrust roused the ire of Great Britain — so much so, that the British threatened to invoke their 1936 defense treaty with Egypt and enter the war.[94]

Ben-Gurion had not sanctioned the drive into the Sinai, and under international pressure he ordered the troops to withdraw (although one wonders why the IDF should have been barred from striking the enemy on his own turf). To verify the IDF's withdrawal, British planes flew reconnaissance patrols over the combat zone. Taking them for enemy planes, Israeli fighters shot several of them down. The threat of war loomed, but anti–British sentiment was now rife on the Arab street. Britain's help wasn't wanted. Consequently, the Atlee government sheathed its sword and announced its intention of recognizing Israel.[95]

Meanwhile, bogged down on every front, the Arab governments decided that they had had enough. Thus, between February and July 1949, Egypt, Lebanon, Transjordan and Syria all signed armistice agreements with Israel, whereby the latter was confirmed in possession of the territories she had obtained in the fighting: western Galilee, the Tel-Aviv Jerusalem corridor, and the Arab portions of the Negev (Gaza excluded).[96] On the last day of fighting with Transjordan, IDF forces occupied Um Rashrash — the site of an old Turkish police station, which was subsequently to blossom into the port of Eilat (Israel's lone outlet to the Red Sea).[97]

Although the shooting had stopped, there was to be no formal peace. Such was the hostility to the new Jewish state, that by 1951 the rulers of Syria, Transjordan and Lebanon had all been assassinated or executed simply for considering peace talks with Israel. Nonetheless, Israel had survived the war, and Ben-Gurion was the toast of his people. At home and abroad he was regarded as Israel personified — a sort of uncrowned king who had conjured his nation into being on the strength of his own willfulness.

The reality of power, however, was rather different. Israel's new government consisted of a fractious single-house legislature — the Knesset — wherein even relatively miniscule parties were represented in direct proportion to the percentage of votes they had garnered. Although Mapai was by far the most popular party in the state, it received only 36 percent of the vote in the multiparty elections that followed the war. In order to obtain a working majority, Ben-Gurion had to forge an alliance with an odd bedfellow, indeed: Israel's religious party. (Ben-Gurion, himself, had never been particularly devout.)

During his first year in office, Ben-Gurion presided over Israel's admission to the United Nations, and then provoked protests from that body by relocating Israel's capital from Tel Aviv to Jerusalem. (The UN still desired "international" status for the Holy City despite the fact that it had done nothing to uphold it as such when it came under Arab attack during the war.)

The 1939 white paper had been abolished as part of Israel's Proclamation of Independence, and to underscore this fact, Ben-Gurion championed Israel's famous "Law of Return" (1950), granting asylum to any Jew who wished to immigrate. There followed an influx of refugees, not just from Europe, but from the Arab states — many of which had begun expelling their Jews in "punishment" for Israel's victory. (In 1957, the number of Jewish refugees from Arab countries stood at 470,000. By 1972, it would climb to 820,000 — 586,000 of whom settled in Israel. In contrast, an estimated 650,000 Arab refugees fled their homes in Palestine during the war.[98]) The flood of new arrivals promptly eclipsed the capacity of Israel's existing infrastructure. Hundreds of thousands of immigrants were thus consigned to rapidly constructed huts without running water or electricity. An estimated one billion dollars was required to ease their plight. In May 1951, Ben-Gurion traveled to the U.S. on a bond tour to raise money. In two weeks, he raised $55 million,[99] but Israel needed more — and quickly.

The dilemma drove Ben-Gurion to a controversial decision: he agreed to accept one billion dollars in Holocaust reparations from the government of West Germany. The money, he was careful to point out, represented payment for property confiscated by the Nazis, and was not meant to compensate for the loss of lives — no amount of money could ever do that. Nonetheless, opposition leaders denounced the plan as a plea for "blood money." Incited by a speech to this effect from former Irgun chief, Menachem Begin (who now headed the opposition Herut party in the Knesset), an anti-reparations mob marched on the Knesset and pelted the building with rocks. In the end, the Knesset voted 61–50 to uphold Ben-Gurion's plan, and the Israeli government received a payment of more than $800 million from West Germany.[100] Thus, not only did the so-called ingathering of the exiles continue, but Israel was now able to provide them with work and housing. By the end of the decade, a "ship-to-settlement" program was in place, providing permanent homes to all immigrants upon arrival.[101]

The search for a durable peace, however, proved elusive. In 1952, a military junta toppled Egypt's King Farouk in a bloodless coup. Ben-Gurion promptly extended an olive branch to the new government, but was scornfully ignored. The following year, exhausted by the cares of office, he retired to Sdeh Boker (a kibbutz in the Negev) in order to reflect and to set an example of pioneering as he had done in his youth. For two years, he basked in the daily tasks of farming; but in 1955, he was recalled to office as defense minister to deal with the escalating provocations of Gamal Abdel Nasser, who had emerged as Egypt's new ruler. By year's end, Ben-Gurion was prime minister again. There followed (i) an arms deal with France; (ii) a secret Anglo-French-Israeli alliance against Nasser (who had angered the Western powers by nationalizing the Suez Canal); and (iii) the Sinai War of 1956. Fought almost exclusively by Israel (whose forces drove deep into the Sinai), the war roused the ire of world opinion, but put an end to Egypt's blockade of Eilat (Israel's southern port), and to the *fedayeen*[102] terrorist raids Egypt had been sponsoring. Afterwards, Ben-Gurion forged consultative ties with Iran, Turkey and Ethiopia, all of whom shared Israel's concerns about regional Soviet influence.[103]

In the 1959 Knesset elections, Mapai won its most resounding victory to date. The following March, Ben-Gurion negotiated an arms deal and a $500 million loan from West Germany. In May, Adolf Eichmann — the notorious coarchitect of the Holocaust, who had taken refuge in Argentina after World War II — was abducted by Israeli intelligence officers on Argentine soil and brought back to the Jewish state for trial. (He was subsequently executed — the only example of capital punishment in Israel's history.)

But in the midst of these triumphs, an old scandal resurfaced to poison the remainder of Ben-Gurion's tenure in office. The issue was an all but forgotten covert operation from 1954. In that year, Britain had reached an agreement with President Nasser of Egypt to withdraw her troops from the Suez Canal zone. Because the British presence there was viewed as a buffer against Egypt, Israel viewed the planned withdrawal as a strategic threat. Consequently, Benjamin Gibli, Israel's chief of intelligence, set in motion a bizarre

covert operation in which a cadre of sympathetic Egyptian Jews attempted to
bomb several British and American establishments in Cairo. Known alter-
nately as "the Lavon affair" or "the Mishap," the plot had been meant to frame
radical groups within Egypt in hopes that the British would decide that Egyptian affairs were too unstable to leave the Suez Canal undefended. It didn't
work. The Jewish perpetrators were apprehended.

Moshe Sharett (Israel's prime minister at the time) had been told nothing
of the enterprise. Aghast to find the blunder on his doorstep, he attempted
to intervene on behalf of those who had been apprehended, pleading that they
had been duped into an illegal and unsanctioned operation. But Nasser would
have none of it. Two of the detainees were executed, and two others were
given long prison terms. At the time, the blame was pinned on Sharett's
defense minister, Pinhas Lavon, who protested his innocence, but was compelled to resign nonetheless.

And so matters stood — for six years. But in 1960, Lavon learned that he
had been implicated on the basis of forged documents and demanded exon-
eration. Most of the cabinet was inclined to grant his request, but Ben-Gurion
insisted that only the courts could handle such matters. The cabinet objected
that a public judicial hearing on the topic of forged documents and half-
baked intelligence schemes would needlessly provoke a scandal. Rather than
take this risk, they designated a commission of seven cabinet members, who
promptly overstepped their authority by declaring Lavon innocent. (They
were only authorized to make a recommendation.) Ben-Gurion never forgave
this transgression.[104]

The division on the Lavon affair accentuated a growing rift between Ben-
Gurion and the Mapai "Old Guard." Hitherto, Ben-Gurion had had a pen-
chant for having things his own way. He had been rather brusque in nudging
Moshe Sharett aside upon returning to office as prime minister in 1955. Afterwards, he had shown undue favoritism toward his devoted young protégés,
Shimon Peres and Moshe Dayan, who were more inclined to do his bidding
than were his long-time Mapai colleagues. To cite one example: although
Golda Meir was his foreign minister, Ben-Gurion deputed crucial negotiations
with West Germany to Peres, thus sidestepping Meir who opposed ties with
Germany. Such actions left a trail of ruffled feathers and finally led to the
outright clash of wills over the Lavon affair.

In 1963, Ben-Gurion relinquished the prime minister's seat and returned
to Sdeh Boker. Finding the policies of his successor, Levi Eshkol, not to his
liking, he formed a new political party — Rafi— and made a bid for a come-
back. Although Moshe Dayan and Shimon Peres joined forces with him, Rafi
garnered a mere ten Knesset seats in the ensuing elections (1965). Thus,
despite the fact that Ben-Gurion remained in the Knesset until 1970, his period

of political dominance was definitely at an end. He spent his final years at Sdeh Boker, adored by the Israeli populace, but viewed with suspicion by the Israeli cabinet, whose members had been stung too frequently by his criticisms. On his 80th birthday, 10,000 admirers appeared at Sdeh Boker to wish him well, but his old Mapai colleagues were not among them. (On his 85th birthday, however, the whole cabinet thought better of the matter and took a helicopter to Sdeh Boker for his party.[105]) At Israel's 25th anniversary celebration in 1973, the government invited him to sit in the audience, but did not invite him to speak.

He was now a distant figure on the periphery of political affairs. But the story does not end on a wholly unhappy note. Deeply affected by the sudden death of his wife, Paula (1968), Ben-Gurion took a new interest in his children and grandchildren. Thus, the father of his country found joy anew as the patriarch of his family, and spent his hours recounting the adventures of his youth or yielding to unalloyed play.[106] He died on December 1, 1973, after suffering a stroke, by which time he had made amends with his surviving political rivals. At his funeral service, the cantor eulogized him as the man who had brought about "the redemption of the people of Israel in their land."[107] His body was laid to rest at Sdeh Boker alongside his wife on a rise overlooking the Negev.

4

Abba Eban and Statesmanship

On July 20, 1949, the last of the armistice agreements ending Israel's War of Independence was negotiated between Israel and Syria. It was the fourth such agreement obtained since February by Dr. Ralph Bunche, the able African-American diplomat who had succeeded Count Bernadotte as UN mediator for the conflict. In recognition of his considerable labors, Bunche received the Nobel Peace Prize. But he had not actually produced peace. Indeed, he had not been asked to: his task had been to silence the guns, while peace negotiations were left to the UN's Palestine Conciliation Commission. The Arab states had voted unanimously against the establishment of this commission in December 1948. Now that it existed, they refused to talk peace unless two preconditions were met: First, Israel must withdraw to the boundaries outlined in the UN's November 1947 partition resolution. Second, she must allow all Palestinian refugees to return to their homes.[1]

In sum, having lost a war of their own making, the Arab combatants were demanding that the results be rescinded — and none of these results has created as much longstanding controversy as the Palestinian refugee problem. A 1949 Israeli census put the number of Arabs living in Israel at 160,000. In November 1947, the number had been estimated at 809,000, suggesting that 650,000 (minus casualties) had become refugees.[2] It has been an unvarying tenet of Arab wisdom that Israel bears full responsibility for the refugee problem and must agree to 100 percent repatriation. This claim is based in part on UN Resolution 194, which states, among other things, "that refugees wishing to return to their homes and live at peace with their neighbors should be permitted to do so at the earliest practicable date...."

But the goal of 100 percent repatriation is not to have the returning refugees "live at peace" with the Israelis. It is to have them gain ascendancy in Palestine and undo Israeli statehood. Nor is this idle speculation. In 1949, the Egyptian foreign minister, Muhammad Salah al-Din, said, "It is well-known and understood that the Arabs, in demanding the return of the refugees to Palestine, mean their return as masters of the Homeland and not

Abba Eban, Israeli ambassador to the United States and UN, January 1, 1951 (courtesy of the State of Israel Government Press Office; photographer unknown).

as slaves. With a greater clarity, they mean the liquidation of the State of Israel."[3]

A second basis for the so-called Arab right of return is the allegation (authored by the Arabs themselves) that the Israelis drove the refugees from their homes in a purposeful attempt at "ethnic cleansing." The facts do not bear out this contention. To be sure, some refugees were forced to flee: fifty thousand were expelled from the strategically located towns of Lydda and Ramle in the ten days of fighting between the first and second truces,[4] and several thousand others were driven out of Galilee and from the villages dominating the Jerusalem road. But these were the exceptions, not the rule, and ethnic cleansing had nothing to do with it. The expulsions were carried out in accordance with "Plan D"—the operational orders issued by the Haganah in the spring of 1948, at a time when Jerusalem and other Jewish population centers had been cut off by Arab

forces. In order to survive, the Jewish state had to establish open and functioning supply lines.[5] Lydda and Ramle had been used as bases for Arab attacks on Jewish convoys and settlements.[6] Convoys to Jerusalem were routinely taking heavy casualties, and the situation in other isolated areas was even worse: In January, a relief force of 35 Jewish soldiers attempted to reach the isolated kibbutz of Kfar Etzion. All 35 were killed en route. In March, a convoy attempting to reach Kibbutz Yehiam was intercepted, and all 46 Jewish fighters perished.[7]

With much of the populace cut off and besieged, and with five Arab armies poised on the borders for invasion, the Haganah's chief of operations, Yigael Yadin, issued Plan D, authorizing Jewish forces to occupy any Arab village or town that imperiled Jewish supply lines, housed Arab combatants, or had high strategic significance. Where necessary, the Arab population was to be expelled.[8] In some instances, this was accomplished by employing Arabic-speaking agents to spread panic in the targeted towns; in others, brute force was employed.[9] But whatever the method, Plan D was a matter of survival, not of "ethnic cleansing." Moreover, it was only one reason among many for the Arab flight — and by no means the dominant one.

To begin with, as violence erupted in the days and weeks following the UN's 1947 partition vote, tens of thousands of wealthy Arabs fled Palestine in apprehension of the battle to come. Cognizant of the approaching storm, the laboring classes followed their example in a flight encompassing as many as 100,000 individuals by winter's end.[10] The flight accelerated as British forces withdrew from Arab areas in preparation for their May 1948 evacuation, leaving public services in disarray.[11]

In addition to these factors, there are myriad well-known examples of Arabs being encouraged to flee by their own leaders: in a bid to ruin the Jewish economy, for example, the Mufti issued a call for Arab workers to leave Jewish areas.[12] Iraqi prime minister Nuri Said boasted that Israel would be annihilated, and called upon Palestinian Arabs to "conduct their wives and children to safe areas until the fighting has died down."[13] Edward Atiyeh, secretary of London's Arab League office, who felt that the establishment of the state of Israel represented the "infliction of a grievous wrong on the Arabs," conceded nonetheless that the Arab "exodus was ... encouraged by the boasting of an unrealistic Arab press and the irresponsible utterances of some of the Arab leaders that it could be only a matter of some weeks before the Jews were defeated by the armies of the Arab States and the Palestinian Arabs enabled to re-enter and retake possession of their country."[14] Similarly, in his 1973 memoir, Syrian prime minister Haled al Azm wrote, "Since 1948 we have been demanding the return of the refugees to their homes. But we ourselves are the ones who encouraged them to leave."[15]

Nor have the refugees themselves remained silent: speaking to a Jordanian journalist in 1954, one refugee made the oft-quoted remark that "The Arab governments told us: Get out so that we can get in. So we got out, but they did not get in."[16]

In addition to calls from political leaders, whole precincts were abandoned at the orders of local Arab military commanders. In some cases, the intention had been to evacuate women and children only, but as often as not the men went, too.[17] There were also cases in which inhabitants fled because of maltreatment by Arab fighters.

The most notorious examples of Arab-induced flight occurred in the major cities. In April 1948, Jewish forces took Haifa after its Jewish inhabitants came under attack. About half of the city's Arabs fled before the Jewish forces arrived. Once in control of the city, the Jews implored the remaining Arabs to stay — in part, because continued flight at this juncture might be mistaken for expulsion by outside observers.[18] Initially, the Arabs were inclined to accept the offer. But the Mufti's spokesmen in the Arab Higher Committee informed them that they must leave the city or be counted as traitors. Thus, despite a tearful plea from the city's Jewish mayor who was desperate to prevent their departure, the populace withdrew.[19]

All told, nearly 60,000 Arabs evacuated Haifa—constituting almost 10 percent of the entire refugee population.[20] In Jaffa, a slightly higher number fled—perhaps 67,000.[21] On learning of the mass hegira, David Ben-Gurion expressed incredulity, for these Arabs were not driven out either—unless one counts those who ran for their lives when Arab mercenaries ran amok in the city, accosting inhabitants and ransacking homes.[22]

Safed, in Galilee, was home to 10,000 Arabs and 1,500 Jews. The latter were part of a religious community whose heritage in the city could be traced to the sixteenth century. In April 1948, Syrian mercenaries placed the city's Jewish Quarter under siege threatening the inhabitants with starvation. On May 6, they initiated an artillery barrage. Four days later, Jewish forces fought their way into the city. The Syrian forces fled, and the Arab populace followed on their heels. The story was similar in Tiberias: when the Haganah captured the city in April 1948, the whole Arab community (roughly 2,000 individuals) departed, despite the pleas of the Jewish city council, which promptly passed an ordinance forbidding Jews from disturbing their abandoned property.[23]

The Arab flight from Haifa, Jaffa, Tiberias and Safed precipitated a panic in the surrounding villages whose inhabitants likewise fled.[24] Another panicked flight occurred when Arab radio stations broadcast fabricated atrocity stories about the Irgun attack on Deir Yassin (see chapter 3). Finally, some Arabs left Israel in the months *after* the war simply because they did not wish to live under Jewish rule.[25]

Clearly, a variety of factors contributed to the Arab flight. But this does not mean that it is impossible to assign culpability. It is important to recall that the Jewish population of Palestine wanted peace in 1947, and that Israel's Proclamation of Independence invited the "Arab inhabitants ... to play their part in the development of the State, on the basis of full and equal citizenship and due representation in all its bodies and institutions...." In contrast, the Arab leadership openly called for a "war of extermination," in which the Jews were to be "swept into the sea."[26] The implications of these facts are clear, and no Israeli has ever stated them more succinctly than Israel's first ambassador to the United Nations, Abba Eban, who declared to the General Assembly:

> Once you admit that Arab governments launched the war, once you accept the axiom that this refugee problem arose from that war and would not have arisen without it, then you prove by the simplest laws of truth and logic that

the Arab governments bear primary responsibility for the creation of this
refugee problem. You cannot let loose a war and wash your hands of all
responsibility for its tragic consequences.... Israel bears no responsibility for a
war which it opposed, [and] which it repeatedly yearned to end. And therefore
it does not bear the responsibility for the consequences of that war — either for
the suffering inflicted by the aggressor in his attack or the defender in his
response.[27]

In sum, if the reader is determined to find an example of "ethnic cleansing" in the 1948 War, he would do better to scrutinize Arab policy rather than
Jewish. Foiled in their attempt to drive the Jews out of Palestine (which was
itself an attempt at ethnic cleansing), Israel's enemies vented their hostility
on Jews living within their own lands. At the end of the war, not one Jew
remained in the parts of Palestine controlled by the Arabs, including
Jerusalem's Old City.

In due course, the "ethnic cleansing" spread beyond the borders of Palestine: between 1948 and 1957, nearly 470,000 Jews fled their homes in the Arab
world where they were victimized by oppressive taxation, discriminatory laws,
and violent pogroms. By 1972, this number had risen to more than 800,000.
Most were forced to leave all their worldly valuables behind. The roll call makes
for depressing reading: In 1948, there were 75,000 Jews in Egypt. In 1972, 700
remained. In 1948, there were 40,000 Jews in Libya. In 1972, 40 remained. Of
Algeria's 150,000 Jews, a bare 1,000 remained in 1972. Of Syria's 45,000 Jews,
4,000 remained. Of Morocco's 300,000 Jews, 35,000 remained. Of Tunisia's
23,000, 9,000 remained. In Yemen, there were 54,000 Jews in 1948. In 1972,
there were two. Iraq had 125,000 Jews in 1948. In 1969 (when nine Iraqi Jews
were hanged in a public spectacle) there were only a few hundred.[28] In making
determinations about "ethnic cleansing," one should compare this with the
160,000 Arabs who were left to live in peace as citizens of Israel in 1949, and
whose numbers today exceed 1.2 million. (Likewise, one should remember
that the Jewish refugees from Arab lands were not culpable for events in Palestine. Nor did they start a war against anyone. They were innocents who were
expelled in protest of Israel's establishment — to serve ever after as living proof
of the indispensability of a Jewish state as a haven for persecuted Jews.)

The total number of Jewish refugees has been estimated at 820,000. Of
these, 586,000 ultimately found new homes in Israel.[29] Their arrival in mass
numbers before Israel had the means to accommodate them placed a crippling
burden on the Israeli economy, but none were turned away. In contrast, with
the exception of Transjordan, the surrounding Arab states refused to grant
citizenship to their dispossessed brothers, preferring instead to herd them
into miserable, overcrowded refugee camps to await the day of their return
to Israel on Arab terms. All attempts to ameliorate the problem were rebuffed.

When Israel told the Palestine Conciliation Commission that she was prepared to take in 100,000 refugees if the Arab states would make peace and assume responsibility for the remainder, the Arabs contemptuously rejected the offer (Lausanne 1949).[30] Likewise, when the United Nations Relief and Works Agency offered to fund public works projects to help the refugees build new lives, the Arab states refused to allow it.[31] Meanwhile, the "Arab state" envisioned under the 1947 UN Partition Plan disappeared from the map: Transjordan illegally annexed the West Bank (renaming herself the Kingdom of Jordan in the process), while Egypt seized the Gaza strip.

Given these facts, it is exceedingly difficult to take Arab protestations of concern for their refugees at face value. What then is the explanation for their behavior? The logical conclusion, agreed upon by multiple commentators, and confirmed in statements by Arab leaders, is that the refugees have been kept in hapless misery to serve as pawns in the continuing campaign against Israel.[32] As Abba Eban has put it, whereas Israel treated its Jewish refugees "as citizens [and] kinsmen," the Arab world saw its refugees

> as a political opportunity. They considered — and this prediction was borne out — that if they could keep them in squalor and misery, in a sense of frustration and desperation, so that their plight would cry out to the conscience of the world, they would thereby alienate Israel from world opinion, and create pressure for the entry of those refugees into Israel without peace — that is to say in conditions in which their entry would create a time-bomb.[33]

The above quotation, and the one preceding it, serves as an introduction to the man who was, perhaps, the most eloquent orator in Israel's history. Aubrey "Abba" Eban was the son of Avram Solomon, a merchant from Capetown, South Africa, who was active in that city's Zionist organization. Born on February 2, 1915, Aubrey spent his formative years in England where his family relocated when he was but seven months old. Within a year, his father was dead of cancer. His mother subsequently remarried, and Aubrey happily adopted the surname of her devoted second husband — a doctor named Isaac Eban.[34]

Aubrey's destiny as a Zionist was sealed by an event that occurred in November 1917 when he was still a toddler. Of necessity, his widowed mother (who had not yet remarried) took employment as a secretary at the London Zionist Office. One night, she was summoned from home to translate an important document from English into French and Russian. The document was the Balfour Declaration, which was slated for release the following day. The experience made ardent Zionists of the entire family, something Aubrey came to realize while still a boy. As he later recalled, "Something unique and exalting lit up my family's sky and the glow of it would never be lost. Zionism had conquered my inner world."[35]

At age four, Aubrey received his first Hebrew lessons from his grandfather, Eliahu, who was determined to mold the boy into a scholar of the first rank. The elder man's investment bore impressive dividends. At age 19, Aubrey matriculated at Cambridge University's Queens' College, where he gained renown for his matchless debating skills. His witticisms from the speaker's rostrum frequently found their way into the Cambridge city papers, and in 1938, he won plaudits from the *Cambridge Review* for a rousing speech against the Chamberlain government's abandonment of Czechoslovakia.[36]

All the while, he nursed a passion for Zionism. Too young to be a delegate, he attended the 1937 World Zionist Congress in Zurich as an observer — looking on as Chaim Weizmann and David Ben-Gurion spoke in favor of the Peel Commission's partition plan. The following year, Weizmann's secretary had to take an unexpected leave of absence, and after a favorable interview, Aubrey was invited to replace him. As Weizmann's protégé, he attended the 1939 Zionist Congress in Geneva when the stunning news of the Ribbentrop-Molotov Pact between Russia and Germany threw the entire Zionist movement into despair.[37]

Thanks to Weizmann's influence, Aubrey was posted to the Middle East during World War II. (The ship that brought him to Egypt was sent to the bottom by a German torpedo on its return voyage to England with loss of all hands.[38]) Fluent in Hebrew and Arabic, Eban served briefly as an army censor in Cairo before being transferred to Palestine where he helped coordinate wartime activities between the British army and the Haganah. The plan had been for the army to recruit Haganah members into an elite unit known as the *Palmach* or "shock platoons," which would assist the British if Rommel's Afrika Korps captured Egypt and pushed across the Suez.[39]

Because the Mandatory government had outlawed the Haganah, the program had to be carried out "off the books." Thus, the British army armed and trained the Jewish fighters clandestinely; the Mandatory government arrested individual fighters for illegal possession of arms; and Captain Eban, acting as liaison between the principals, bailed the fighters out of jail. The army had called for a maximum of 500 recruits, so the Haganah sent them exactly this number — although generally they weren't the same 500 men who had been there the previous week. Thus, before the program ended in early 1943 — by which time Rommel had been decisively defeated at El Alamein, thereby removing the threat to Palestine — more than 7,000 men had obtained guerrilla training under British officers. The ironic sequel to these intrigues was that within a few short years, the British and Palmach would be fighting each other.[40]

Finishing the war in Cairo with the rank of major, Eban turned down multiple offers to teach Arabic studies on the university level, and accepted a position at the Jewish Agency. Heartbroken when his mentor, Chaim Weiz-mann, lost the WZO presidency at the 1946 Zionist Congress in Basle, he con-sidered resigning, but Weizmann dissuaded him.[41] The following year, the Agency appointed him as one of two liaison officers to UNSCOP (the UN Special Committee on Palestine), which subsequently issued its landmark 1947 report in favor of partition. When Chaim Weizmann was summoned from retirement to argue the Jewish case before the UN General Assembly, Eban helped him draft his address, and found a suitable Biblical quotation with which to end it. In the weeks leading up to the November 1947 vote on the partition resolution, he practiced his oratory on eight wavering UN del-egates. All eight voted in favor.[42]

On May 1, 1948, Eban delivered his first UN speech. Three weeks later, he succeeded Moshe Shertok (later "Sharett") as Israel's UN representative. By then, Israel had proclaimed her independence, and David Ben-Gurion was encouraging his new countrymen to adopt Hebrew names. It was at this junc-ture that Eban began referring to himself by his bris name: "Abba."[43] Mean-while, five separate Arab national armies had invaded the nascent Jewish state, demanding the abrogation of Israel's independence as the prerequisite to a cease-fire. In response, Eban declared that "if the Arabs want peace with Israel they can have it. If they want war they can have that, too. But whether they want peace or war, they can have it only with the State of Israel."[44]

The following May, with the War of Independence winding down, Eban delivered a three-hour address on a motion to admit Israel to full membership in the UN. He could not help but remark on the irony of having to argue Israel's case before an audience which included the delegations of the Arab combatants: "Here sit representatives of the only states which have deliber-ately used force against the General Assembly Resolution ... posing as the dis-interested judges of their own intended victim in his efforts to secure a modest equality in the family of nations."[45] In summation, he intoned: "You will cer-tainly lose nothing and you may perhaps gain some modest asset if you join our banner to your honored company. A great wheel of history comes full circle today as Israel, renewed and established, offers itself, with all its imper-fections, but perhaps with some virtues, to the defense of the human spirit...."[46] On May 11, 1949, Israel's membership was voted, and "UN Rep-resentative" Eban became "UN Ambassador" Eban. In August of the following year, he was appointed to serve simultaneously as Israel's ambassador to the United States.

Israel now had "sovereign equality" with all other UN members. What she did not have was peace. At every opportunity, her leaders announced their readiness to pursue a final settlement, but these offers were uniformly brushed aside.[47] Unlike Israel, the Arab states did not regard the armistice as the end of hostilities, but rather as an intermission in an ongoing war.[48] Between 1949 and 1956, Arab terrorists staged incessant, small-scale raids from Gaza, the Sinai and Jordan against Israeli civilians, inflicting increasing numbers of casualties in each successive year. The Egyptian and Jordanian governments publicly disavowed these attacks, but made no concerted effort to stop them. Consequently, Israel took matters into her own hands.[49]

Although Israel's reprisals were sporadic, they were of significantly greater magnitude than the terrorist raids. Unit 101, a special operations force commanded by Colonel Ariel Sharon, carried out these operations — often with clumsy inattention to civilian casualties. For example, after a series of terrorist strikes claimed more than 100 Israeli lives in 1953,[50] Unit 101 staged two notable reprisals. The first occurred at the al-Bureij refugee camp in Gaza. The immediate provocation was an attack in Ashkelon in which an Israeli man was killed and his daughter was badly wounded by a Gazan per-petrator. In the reprisal, twenty Arab refugees were killed — twelve of them women and children.[51] Similarly, in October, following the murder of an Israeli woman and her two children, Unit 101 demolished the West Bank vil-lage of Kibya, killing nearly seventy Arab civilians, and a small number of Jordanian soldiers.[52]

Invariably, the international community reacted to the bigger attacks — censuring Israel for employing "disproportionate force" while minimizing or failing to address the terrorist provocations.[53] The predictable result was that the provocations continued, as did the Israeli reprisals (although Israel now made stringent efforts to choose non-civilian targets). Thus, in February 1955, after a series of terrorist raids in the Negev, Israeli forces retaliated against an Egyptian army base in Gaza, killing 37 Egyptian soldiers and wounding more than 20. (Eight Israelis were killed in the operation.) Then, in December 1955, after Syrian soldiers fired at Israeli fishing boats on Lake Kinneret (i.e., the Sea of Galilee), Israeli forces attacked bases inside Syria, killing 56 Syrian soldiers while sustaining six casualties of their own.

As before, the UN Security Council voted to condemn Israel for her actions while downplaying the provocations. While UN chief of staff E. L. M. Burns was willing to admit that "marauding into Israel by armed gangs is serious" (on at least one occasion he characterized it as a "war crime"[54]), he described "Israeli retaliation by armed raids" as "a dangerous remedy." The United States complained that Israel's actions were heightening tensions in the region. John Foster Dulles, the U.S. secretary of state, told Abba Eban that Israel was wrong to employ armed retaliation and should content herself with the international sympathy she received when her people were killed. Recalling these protestations years later, Eban wrote: "Whether there would really have been less tension if Israel had sat back and let its citizens be killed without 'armed retaliation' is moot. Since no such bizarre experiment in national masochism has ever been tried in any country, we shall never know the answer."[55]

Although Eban thought the prevailing UN attitude was unfair, he believed that Israel's reprisal policy was diplomatically unwise since it served to alienate world opinion. Nonetheless, the task of defending the reprisals at the UN fell to him, and he carried out his mission with aplomb. After an exemplary speech defending the Kinneret action (of which he strongly disapproved in private), he dashed off a letter to Ben-Gurion making his true feelings known. Ben-Gurion replied by cable, saying: "I myself had some doubts about the operation until I read your brilliant explanation to the Security Council which has convinced me that we were right after all. I have nothing further to add."[56] "This mischievous response," says Eban, "was the nearest that Ben-Gurion would ever come in the direction of either humor or penitence."[57]

Terrorism constituted only one component of the continuing Arab aggression against Israel. There was another of equal import: namely, economic warfare. Ever since the War of Independence, Egypt had excluded Israeli commerce from the Suez Canal. Ships traversing the waterway en route to Haifa risked confiscation of their cargoes regardless of the flag they were flying. An Egyptian "black list" singled out vessels that had been to Israel previously, and subjected them to harassment in the Canal even if they were headed elsewhere on their present journey.[58] In 1953, the blockade was extended to the Straits of Tiran,[59] thereby severing Israel's sole link with the Red Sea and Indian Ocean. These violations of international maritime law deprived Israel of trade with more than half of the globe. The Arab states also enacted boycotts against companies who traded with Israel via the Mediterranean — and in some cases against companies who did not trade with Israel, but who had Jews on their boards of directors.[60]

The introduction of Cold War politics into the region did nothing to alleviate tensions: in early 1955, the United States and Great Britain put the finishing touches on the so-called Baghdad Pact, a series of alliances that had been worked out in the preceding months between Great Britain, Turkey, Iraq, Iran and Pakistan under U.S. auspices. The pact, from which the U.S. nominally held aloof, represented a Western attempt to exclude Soviet influence from the Middle East. When Israel objected to the sale of weapons to Iraq — the sole combatant from the 1948–49 war that had refused to sign an armistice — she was told that Iraqi hostility would be tempered by participation in a Western alliance. (Eban thought this attempt at reassurance betrayed a lack of insight into the Middle East mindset.[61])

If Israel had her doubts about the pact, it was even less popular with

Egypt's pan–Arab nationalist president, Gamal Abdel Nasser, who saw it as a neocolonial venture aimed at maintaining Western hegemony in the Arab world. A veteran of the 1948–49 war, Colonel Nasser had played a leading role in the 1952 overthrow of the corrupt Egyptian monarchy, and had assumed personal control of the government in 1954. By year's end, he had achieved a stunning victory for his nationalist program by convincing Great Britain to evacuate her forces from the Suez Canal Zone. At the same time, he escalated his covert sponsorship of terrorism to such a degree that further Israeli development in the Negev became impossible.[62] It was in response to this insufferable state of affairs that Israel staged its February 1955 reprisal against the Egyptian army base in Gaza. Israel had intended, by this stinging blow, to send Nasser a message: namely, that Egypt would be held responsible for terrorist raids from Gaza whether she pretended to disavow them or not. Nasser responded by no longer disavowing them.

To be sure, this response was popular with the Egyptian masses, but there was a more tangible reason for Nasser's boldness: Russia was now offering to provide him with weaponry that would make Egypt the region's dominant military power. The offer was a logical riposte to the Baghdad Pact; for if the West's tier of alliances barred direct Soviet access to the region, an arms deal with Egypt promised admission via the backdoor.

Emboldened by the offer, Nasser drilled and equipped a 700-man throng of fedayeen, or "self-sacrificers," to carry out a new round of terrorism. In reference to this force, he announced to the world in August 1955 that "Egypt has decided to dispatch her heroes, the disciples of Pharaoh and the sons of Islam and they will cleanse the land of Palestine...."[63] The number of attacks on Israel increased — not only from Gaza, but also from the West Bank and Lebanon. In mid–September, Nasser issued a further provocation by closing the airspace over the Straits of Tiran to Israeli civilian aircraft. Then, on September 27, he put his signature to the Czech (i.e., Soviet) arms deal.[64]

David Ben-Gurion (who resumed the office of prime minister in July 1955) was fully aware that if Egypt obtained modern weaponry before Israel could identify an arms supplier, there would be no deterrent against a full-scale attack. Things looked scarcely less bleak to Abba Eban, who estimated that Israel must obtain weaponry comparable to Egypt's within six months or launch a preemptive strike.[65] Given the gravity of the situation, Israel approached the U.S. about a possible arms deal. But Anglo-American policy in the Middle East was primarily focused on oil. To preserve this interest, two things were necessary — namely, the exclusion of Soviet influence from the region, and maintenance of good relations with the Arab states. Neither purpose would be achieved by the sale of arms to Israel. Conversely, *both* might be achieved if something could be done to mollify Nasser. Hence, far from offering to redress the arms imbalance, the U.S. and Great Britain unveiled "Project Alpha"—an attempt to mediate an Israeli-Egyptian peace accord that would involve the transfer of territory in the Negev to Egypt (August–November 1955).[66] Ben-Gurion would have nothing to do with this proposal. He was happy to make peace with Egypt, and was willing to fly to Cairo to achieve it. But if *peace* was what his enemies desired, they should expect *peace* in return—not territory.[67]

Desperate to counterbalance Russia's growing influence in Egypt, the Eisenhower administration decided, next, to increase arms deliveries to its Baghdad Pact partners. Israel took no comfort from this strategy. Appearing on the CBS news program *Face the Nation* in February 1956, Abba Eban put Israel's case to the American public, asking how it could possibly be reasonable to deny Israel arms to defend itself when British arms were flowing into Jordan, American arms into Iraq, and Soviet arms into Egypt.[68]

The U.S. public's response to Eban's query was electric—the government's less so. But Nasser's tie to Moscow was growing cozier by the day, and the sale of arms to Israel might give the West some leverage. Consequently, after making a remark or two about the impropriety of foreign ambassadors appealing directly to the American people via television, U.S. Secretary of State John Foster Dulles arranged a convoluted scheme whereby American F-86 fighter jets would be sold to Israel from a factory in Canada — thus making it appear that Canada, and not the U.S., was the supplier. There was so much red tape appended to this deal, however, that by the time the Canadians were ready to deliver on the offer, Israel had found a more congenial supplier and no longer needed the jets.[69]

The "congenial supplier" was France. Troubled by the lack of headway in talks with the U.S., Ben-Gurion had dispatched his protégé, Shimon Peres, to Paris to sound out the possibility of obtaining French weapons. Quite unexpectedly, Peres struck gold. France, at this juncture, was attempting to put down a rebellion in colonial Algeria. In accordance with his pan–Arab policy, Nasser was supporting the anti–French rebels. Indeed, no sooner did Nasser obtain weapons from Czechoslovakia, before he began diverting some of them to Algeria's FLN terrorist group. Egypt had become the common enemy of France and Israel. In light of this reality, France agreed to supply Israel with up-to-date weaponry—including jet aircraft (June 1956).[70]

At the same time, Britain and the United States were making one last attempt to lure Nasser from the Russian orbit. The Egyptian leader's chief domestic aspiration was to build a massive dam at Aswan in order to harness the waters of the Nile for agriculture and energy production. The Western powers offered to fund the project through the World Bank in hopes that the resultant economic ties would moderate Nasser's behavior. For months,

Nasser remained noncommittal. In the interim, however, he alienated American opinion by continuing his chastisement of Israel, drawing closer to the USSR, and opening relations with Communist China (something the United States could not look kindly upon so soon after the Korean War). Hence, when he finally deigned to accept the offer in early July 1956, Secretary of State Dulles informed him that the proposal was no longer on the table.[71]

Nasser's response stunned the world community: on July 26, 1956, he "nationalized" the Suez Canal, declaring that the waterway's estimated $100 million in annual proceeds would be used to finance the Aswan Dam project.[72] As the leading stockholders in the Canal, Great Britain and France stood to pay the price of this usurpation. Even worse, their trade route to the oil fields of the Middle East had been delivered into the hands of a dictator who, as the reader is now aware, was not known for respecting the maritime rights of other nations.

With a cacophony of warlike words emanating from the government halls of Paris and London, Eisenhower cautioned his allies that military action was not the answer. But with a wink and a nod, Britain and France agreed that it was. Thus, when Shimon Peres returned to Paris for further arms negotiations a few days later, the French minister of defense put a curious question to him: How quickly, in theory, could Israeli forces reach the Suez Canal?[73] Although they were not yet willing to admit it, France and Great Britain were already formulating "Operation Musketeer"—a military response to Nasser's Suez usurpation.

Barely had the planning begun, however, before Britain developed cold feet. The crux of the problem, in her view, was that it was impossible to attack Nasser without rousing the ire of the Arab world. Unfazed by Britain's wavering, France pressed ahead with her attempt to enlist Israel—mentioning as an aside that rejection of the offer was not compatible with further French support for the Jewish state.[74] Britain was appalled at this development. Israeli involvement would only magnify the threat to Anglo-Arab relations. But after high-level talks with the French in mid–October, the British changed their tune: for Israel was to be cast in the role of the villain.[75]

In a nutshell, the plan called upon Israel to invade the Sinai on the pretext of her very real grievances against Nasser. As her troops approached the Suez Canal, Britain and France would express alarm for the Canal's safety, and insist that both combatants withdraw a specified distance on either side of it. Egypt would have no choice but to refuse. Both banks of the Suez would still be in her hands, and it would be inconceivable that she should retreat to the far bank at Western bidding when her soil was under attack. Upon her inevitable refusal, France and Britain would send troops into the Canal Zone on the pretext of keeping the waterway secure.[76]

The first hurdle was to obtain Israel's consent to this skewed scenario. Predictably, Ben-Gurion objected to being assigned "the role of aggressor, while the British and French appeared as the angels of peace...."[77] Moreover, Israel's air force was outmanned, and there was every danger that Egypt would bomb Tel Aviv before the Allies intervened. On the other hand, the *fedayeen* raids and the blockade of the Straits of Tiran were already intolerable; and there would be more provocations— not less— as Czech weaponry flowed into Nasser's arsenal. In short, it was bound to come to a fight. If Israel acted now, she would have allies. If she delayed, she would be on her own.[78]

The balance was tipped by Ben-Gurion's chief of staff, Moshe Dayan, who suggested that, rather than open the fight with a full-scale invasion of the Sinai, Israel might disguise her initial move as a reprisal for the ongoing *fedayeen* raids from Egypt. She could start with a paratroop drop near the Mitla Pass in the western portion of the desert. This would serve multiple purposes: first, the pass was close enough to the Canal to provide Britain and France with their desired pretext; second, it would look like a reprisal rather than war, thereby reducing the likelihood of a bombing raid on Israel's cities; third, by blocking egress from the pass, the paratroopers could cover the flank of the main operations that would follow in the north; and fourth, if Britain and France backed out for any reason, Israel could simply extricate her paratroopers and maintain that the operation had merely been a raid.[79]

Ben-Gurion was satisfied. But he raised a second objection: the attack was scheduled for the last days of October — a week before the 1956 U.S. presidential election. Surely this would forfeit U.S. support. The Allies overruled him. In their view, the U.S. would not support them anyway. It would be best to act while Eisenhower was otherwise occupied.[80]

The decision to go ahead was made between October 22 and 24, 1956, at a conference in the French town of Sèvres attended by French prime minister Guy Mollet, British foreign secretary Selwyn Lloyd, and David Ben-Gurion. During a private moment, Moshe Dayan diagrammed his attack plan for Ben-Gurion on an empty cigarette package provided by Shimon Peres.[81] Ben-Gurion did not say whether he approved, but later when Peres and Dayan handed him the cigarette package with their signatures appended, he laughed and signed it, too.[82]

The Israeli cabinet approved the final plan on October 28. The following day, low-flying Israeli planes crossed the Egyptian frontier and severed the Sinai's military phone lines with their propellers.[83] Ninety minutes later, 400 Israeli paratroopers descended upon the outlet of the Mitla Pass (some 30 miles from the Canal). Behind them, Ariel Sharon led another force of paratroopers on a 150-mile cross-country trek to reinforce them, subduing three Egyptian fortresses en route.[84] On October 30, the United States asked Israel for assurances that she would withdraw from Egyptian territory once she had dealt with the *fedayeen*. Receiving no answer, she placed a resolution before the UN Security Council calling for an immediate Israeli withdrawal to the 1949 armistice line. The British and French vetoed this motion. Hours earlier, they had issued their own prearranged "ultimatum" to the combatants. (As expected, Egypt rejected it.[85])

On October 31, Ariel Sharon arrived at the Mitla Pass, where he promptly became embroiled in a major firefight — something that he had been ordered to avoid. Having sustained 38 of Israel's 172 battlefield deaths in this single unwarranted action, he sent part of his brigade southward toward Sharm el-Sheikh. Meanwhile, three more Israeli columns pushed into the Sinai: the first advancing westward from Abu Agheila toward Ismailia; the second capturing Rafa in the Gaza Strip after a stiff fight and then marching on Kantara (taking El Arish en route); and the third advancing directly southward along the Gulf of Aqaba toward Sharm el-Sheikh. This last force reached its objective on November 4, and captured it after an intense fight the following day. With the simultaneous obliteration of the *fedayeen* in Gaza, Israel had attained all of her military objectives by November 5.

Sadly, her allies could not make the same boast. The French and British air forces had begun bombing Egypt's airfields on October 31. Most of Egypt's air force was destroyed in these raids, thus removing a potent threat to the Israeli advance. Additionally, the raids convinced Nasser to abandon several Sinai strongholds (November 1) in order to bolster his Canal defenses in expectation of an imminent Allied assault.

But here lay the glitch in the Allied war plan. Had the French and British been ready to invade on day one, their pretext for action would have been exposed as a charade. Simply put, they could not look ready prior to Egypt's rejection of their ultimatum. And when they finally could look ready, they weren't ready. Only on November 5 did their paratroopers finally descend upon Port Said (at the Mediterranean end of the Canal). Their amphibious forces did not go into action until the following day — and by then time had run out.[86]

Taken as a whole, the world viewed the Suez War with unsympathetic eyes. Outside of Israel and France, words of praise were seldom heard. If one excludes prime minister Anthony Eden and foreign secretary Selwyn Lloyd, Britain was pretty much not in favor.

Even worse was the attitude of the superpowers: Secretly, Russia was delighted, since the war deflected the world's attention from her nearly simultaneous invasion of Hungary. But she was *pretending* that she didn't like it at all — and the United States really *didn't* like it.

No one was more aware of these things than Abba Eban, who had been feeling the heat since the outbreak of the war. When U.S. assistant secretary for Middle Eastern affairs William Rountree first received written notification of the conflict, Eban was in the room describing Israel's "defensive posture." Rountree interrupted him to read the report, adding "I expect you'll want to get back to your embassy to find out what is happening in your country."[87]

The better things got militarily over the ensuing days, the worse they got politically. And ground zero for the political fallout was directly beneath Eban's shoes at the United Nations. We have seen that as early as October 30 the United States had placed a resolution before the security council calling for Israel's immediate withdrawal to the armistice line. France and Great Britain had vetoed that resolution. But their veto did not have any great effect — for the U.S. simply brought the matter before the general assembly.

UN Secretary General Dag Hammarskjöld set the tone for the ensuing debate by announcing that the entire tripartite action was illegal, and that Britain, France and Israel should not derive the slightest advantage from it. It was in this milieu that Eban took the general assembly rostrum and gave what was perhaps the most stirring speech of his career. In it, he reminded the world why war had been necessary:

> Stretching back far behind the events of this week lies the unique and somber story of a small people, subjected throughout all the years of its national existence to a furious implacable comprehensive campaign of hatred and siege, for which there is no parallel or precedent in the modern history of nations....
>
> Surrounded by hostile armies on all its land frontiers; subjected to savage and relentless hostility; exposed to penetration, raids and assaults by day and night ... embattled, blockaded, besieged, Israel alone among the nations faces a battle for its security anew with every approaching nightfall and every rising dawn....

In conclusion, he declared: "Our signpost is not backward to belligerency, but forward to peace."[88] The speech won international plaudits. The assembled delegates gave Eban a rousing ovation. Congratulatory telegrams flowed in, and within days, a recording of the speech appeared in record stores.[89] But the day after he spoke, the same delegates who had applauded him voted 64–5 to demand Israel's unconditional withdrawal from Egyptian soil. Clearly, this was going to be an uphill battle.

The first ray of hope came on November 3, when the UN's Canadian ambassador, Lester "Mike" Pearson, suggested that a UN Emergency Force (UNEF) be deployed in the Canal Zone, Gaza and Sharm el-Shiekh to ensure security and international rights as Israel's forces withdrew. Here, possibly, was the solution Eban had been hoping for. On November 5, Pearson's resolution passed the General Assembly along with a new call for Israel's withdrawal to the armistice line. Before calm could descend upon the UN, however, French paratroopers descended upon Port Said. The Allied invasion of the Canal Zone had begun that same morning. It was greeted by an international uproar. At one and the same time, the Soviet Union threatened to intervene against the transgressors with ballistic missiles, while the U.S. notified Great Britain that she would not support the latter's petition for a $1 billion International Monetary Fund loan unless there was an immediate cease-fire.[90] With both superpowers exuding hostility, the Anglo-French position became untenable. Accordingly, at midnight on November 6, their operations came to a grinding halt.

Israel failed to perceive the meaning of it all. Flush (he later said "drunk") with victory, Ben-Gurion chose this moment to deliver an obtuse address in which he declared that victorious Israel would not countenance the deployment of an international force in the territory it had conquered, and that Sharm el-Sheikh was actually rightfully Israel's. (The latter claim was based on an obscure passage he had found in the works of the sixth century Byzantine court historian, Procopius, which alluded to a Jewish kingdom on the adjacent isle of Tiran.) Ben-Gurion's declamations were badly received. On one and the same day (November 7), the U.S. State Department threatened Israel with severance of all economic assistance, President Eisenhower sent a menacing cable to Ben-Gurion, Russia intensified her missile threats, and the UN General Assembly voted 65–1 for the immediate withdrawal of all attacking forces. (Israel cast the only dissenting vote.[91])

Suddenly alert to its peril, the Israeli cabinet made terrified preparations for an unconditional withdrawal to the 1949 armistice line. Eban, however, saw a better way out. To be sure, the position outlined in Ben-Gurion's "victory speech" would have to be abandoned, but Israel's diplomatic goals need not be. In a cable to Ben-Gurion, Eban suggested that Israel announce her readiness to withdraw from all conquered territory once "satisfactory arrangements are made with the international force about to enter the Canal Zone."[92] Eban would then work to define "satisfactory arrangements" as meaning that Israel's withdrawal would require a guarantee of her rights of navigation in the Straits of Tiran and an end to the depredations of the *fedayeen*. UNEF's deployment would thus become a solution, not an imposition.

Faced with the negation of everything the army had fought for, Ben-Gurion grasped at Eban's suggestion — telling his ambassador to float the idea in U.S. government circles to see how it would be received. Taking as his starting point the fact that Egypt's blockade and sponsorship of the *fedayeen* not only had provoked Israel's attack but also were violations of international law, Eban met with influential figures in the Eisenhower administration to preach the notion that "statesmanship should correct, and not just restore, the conditions out of which the explosion had come."[93]

By degrees, Eban's reasoning bore fruit, until finally on February 11, U.S. Secretary of State Dulles stated in a memorandum that the U.S. would "support and assert Israel's right to send its own ships and cargoes without impediment through the Straits of Tiran"; would "acknowledge that if Egypt renewed its blockade Israel would be entitled to exercise its 'inherent right of self-defense under Article 51 of the UN Charter...'" and that "UN forces in Sharm el-Sheikh and Gaza" would remain in position "until such time as their removal would not lead to a renewal of belligerency." Eban was ecstatic; Ben-Gurion was not. The latter thought the guarantees were not explicit enough and said as much in his response. Dulles answered that Israel was "free to try [its] luck elsewhere" if the American offer was deemed unsatisfactory.[94]

Eban returned to Israel at once and convinced Ben-Gurion of the offer's merits. On March 1, Israeli foreign minister Golda Meir delivered an address at the UN saying that Israel would withdraw to the armistice line on the supposition that there would be free navigation in the Straits of Tiran and no resumption of *fedayeen* terrorism, and that if these suppositions were not upheld, Israel would invoke Article 51 of the UN Charter as the legal basis for acting in her own defense. Satisfied that this understanding had been accepted, Israel evacuated her troops from all occupied territory on March 15.[95]

Thus did Abba Eban preserve the diplomatic fruits of Israel's Sinai victory. His achievement was underscored by the fact that for the next decade, until the very eve of the 1967 Six Day War, Israel enjoyed quietude on her southern border and unfettered communications through the Straits of Tiran. The economic strangulation of the Negev, which had resulted from years of border terrorism and blockade, came to an end. Eilat became a bustling port-of-call for ships trading with Africa and Asia, and the development of the Negev moved forward at last. Most important of all, Israel had driven home the point of her own legitimacy. For seven years, the world had allowed Egypt to defy international law pertaining to free navigation as though the law did not apply to Israel.[96] For the same interval, it had equated Israel's reprisals against terrorism as morally equivalent to the terrorism itself. Egypt's arms agreement with the Soviet Bloc promised to render these conditions permanent. By embarking on the Sinai War, Israel forced the world to address the issue. Eban's strength of will in the ensuing political storm salvaged the opportunity, nearly lost, to end the crisis in a manner that obligated *all* sides to conform to the rule of law.

Eban continued in his dual capacity as Israeli ambassador to the UN and U.S. for two more years. When he resigned to take a position in Ben-Gurion's cabinet in 1959, a *Washington Post* editorialist summed up his work by saying that "he mobilized the English language and sent it into battle on Israel's behalf."⁹⁷ Before his departure, he received invitations to speak in several major cities as part of a farewell tour.

In the ensuing seven years, Eban served as president of the Weizmann Institute of Science in Rehovot, as minister of education and culture under Ben-Gurion, and as deputy prime minister under Levi Eshkol. After the 1966 elections, Eshkol appointed him to serve as foreign minister — a post he held until 1974. It was the pinnacle of a distinguished career, and we shall have occasion to meet Eban again in his exercise of this portfolio. Afterwards, as a member of the Knesset, he clashed with the cabinet over policy in the West Bank and Gaza. Although he blamed Arab "rejectionism" for the failure to obtain a comprehensive peace after the 1967 Six Day War, it was his heartfelt view that "permanent Israeli rule over all the populations and territories of the West Bank and Gaza was [neither] feasible [nor] desirable."⁹⁸ He retired from political life in 1988.

During his career and afterwards, he authored a number of books, including two autobiographies. Two of his works were adapted for television by PBS: *Heritage: Civilization and the Jews* and *Israel: A Nation Is Born*.⁹⁹ In 2001, he received the Israel Prize for Lifetime Contribution. His death on November 17, 2002, evoked condolences and expressions of reverence from distinguished personages around the globe.

5

Moshe Dayan and Victory

On the morning of June 7, 1967, a sound which had not been heard for 19 years emanated from the base of the Western ("Wailing") Wall, in Jerusalem's Old City. It was the trumpeting of a *shofar*—Judaism's ceremonial ram's horn. Accompanying the strain was an equally uncommon sight: a growing crowd of Israeli soldiers. Forty-eight hours earlier, Israel had stood in grave peril. During the preceding weeks, hostile armies had gathered on her borders and Arab political leaders had pledged themselves to her annihilation. In every Arab capital, fanatical mobs had staged daily demonstrations, crying out shrilly for the "stain of 1948" to be expunged in Israeli blood.

Nothing better symbolized Israel's emergence from these dangers than the return of her people to their holiest shrine after a 19-year exile.[1] Nor, it seemed, did anyone better personify the change in fortune than the familiar figure who appeared at 2 P.M. Clad in a steel helmet and military fatigues, Israeli defense minister Moshe Dayan placed a small piece of paper between two stones in the wall. Scrawled upon it was the prayer, "Let peace reign in Israel." Directly afterwards, in a radio address to the nation, he declared, "We have returned to our holiest of holy places, never to be parted from it again."[2]

Many who heard these words would have been surprised to learn that during the previous 48 hours of tense warfare, Dayan had clung tenaciously to a conservative military strategy that did not allow for the capture of the Old City. Only when subjected to intense pressure from other members of the Israeli cabinet did he finally give in to the impassioned plea of Uzi Narkiss, the commander on the scene, and sanction the attack that reunited Judaism's ancient capital.

Arguably the most recognizable individual in Israel's history, Moshe Dayan was born on May 20, 1915, at Degania — the first kibbutz in what was then Turkish Palestine. His father, Schmuel, was one of the founders of the settlement, where, in the early days, farmers and livestock were consigned to the same building.[3] At age nine months, Moshe contracted an eye infection. With no doctor in the vicinity, his mother took him on a 90-mile trek to the nearest medical station. En route, an Arab shepherd heard the boy crying and brought him some fresh goat's milk. Moshe settled down at once, whereupon the Arab offered a bottle of milk to the mother as a gift, saying that her child would live to become a hero.[4]

Desiring a private farm but unable to afford one, Moshe's father moved the family to Nahalal, where he cofounded Palestine's first "cooperative" farm or moshav in 1921. Here, as an attention-seeking schoolboy, Moshe achieved an odd trifecta — gaining notoriety as a bully, mischief-maker, and poet. At age twelve, he fought his first battle with the Arabs — shooing away a herd of cattle that were being grazed on the moshav's property by four trespassing Arab boys. For his efforts, the boys pulled him from his horse and gave him a sound thrashing.[5] Had they only paused to ask his opinion of their people, the altercation might have been avoided, for Moshe was a staunch admirer of the Arabs. Indeed, as a ten-year-old he had published a story in which he fights alongside a group of Arab boys against a common enemy, suffers a grievous wound, recovers lucidity, and offers thanks to Allah.[6] (In the real altercation, he recovered without divine intervention, and was much celebrated for his reckless bravery.)

Nahalal lacked a secondary school. Hence, after a new round of mischief-making in which he and his fellows broke a school window, Moshe

Israel Defense Forces chief of staff Moshe Dayan, July 5, 1954 (courtesy of the State of Israel Government Press Office; photographer David Eldan).

arranged a truce with the headmistress of Nahalal's newly established Agricultural School for Girls and was permitted to enroll as a student (1929).[7]

After an initial romance failed to result in marriage, Moshe began dating a young woman named Ruth Schwartz in 1934. In a peculiar episode several months later, Ruth prevailed upon nineteen-year-old Moshe to marry a German Jewish woman ten years older than he, so that the latter would not be deported back to Nazi Germany when her permit to remain in Palestine expired. Once the woman was safe, Moshe obtained a divorce, and in July 1935, Ruth and he were married. (Moshe wore khakis and sandals to the ceremony.[8])

At the outset of the 1936–39 Arab Revolt, Moshe acted as a guide for British troops guarding the Iraq-Haifa oil pipeline — a frequent target of Arab sabotage. Later, he served as a sergeant in the Mandatory's Jewish auxiliary police force, then as a deputy to Yitzhak Sadeh (commander of the Haganah) and finally as a night raider in Orde Wingate's Special Night Squads. By the end of the Arab Revolt, he had a sound command of small-scale infantry tactics. Unfortunately, the Haganah was now illegal, and, in October 1939, the British Mandatory authorities arrested Moshe and 42 others outside an illicit Haganah officer's training base.

After serving 16 unpleasant months in the horrid British prison camps at Acre and Mazra'a, Moshe obtained his freedom and a chance to help with the British war effort in World War II. On the night of June 6, 1941, he led an advance squad of 15 fighters into Vichy-controlled Lebanon on a mission to secure a pair of bridges. Finding themselves in an exposed position, the party stormed a nearby Vichy police station. Inside they found a machine gun, which they positioned on the roof. Soon, enemy snipers opened fire on them. Moshe raised his binoculars to ascertain the source of the bullets, only to be struck by one, which shattered the binoculars and sent fragments into his left eye. Those tending to the wound noted that the eye had been blown out, and suggested that he be surrendered to the Vichy forces for medical care. But Moshe's tenure as a British prisoner had not been a success, and he didn't care to try his luck with the French. He insisted that he felt okay and that he would probably live if he made it to the hospital within three hours. He then lay quietly for six hours before reinforcements arrived, and then for six more on the bumpy ride to the hospital in Haifa, where it was determined that the impact of the bullet had mangled his eye-socket, making it impossible to implant a glass eye. As a result, he donned the famous eye-patch that was to become his trademark — and which he greatly resented having to wear.[9]

At the time of his injury, Moshe was serving in the Jewish "commando platoons" or *Palmach*. By the time he was ready to return to action, Montgomery had defeated Rommel at El Alamein, and the British army had ceased its sponsorship of the Jewish force. As a result, the Palmach troops began working on kibbutzim three weeks out of the month to support their own activities.[10] Because Moshe's labor was required on the moshav at Nahalal, he was unable to meet the kibbutz obligation. Thus, in an attempt to continue his Palmach duties, he offered to pay room and board at a Palmach kibbutz for his monthly week of training while working at home the rest of the time. His offer was rejected.[11]

The outbreak of Israel's War of Independence found Moshe doing intelligence work for the Haganah. In April 1948, he sustained a tragic loss when his beloved younger brother, Zohar, was killed in a clash with Druse Arabs. (Ironically, the Druse later decided to fight alongside the Israelis.) Scarcely given time to mourn, Moshe was detailed to Haifa (which had just been occupied by the Haganah) to secure the munitions left behind by the British. Promoted to the rank of major the following month, he fought at Degania, driving off 45 Syrian tanks with a few blasts from two pre–World War I artillery pieces—the finest guns Israel then had in its arsenal.[12]

With the arrival of more up-to-date weaponry, Dayan organized the 89th Armored Brigade, which saw its first action during the truce of June-July 1948—shelling the Tel Aviv beach upon which Menachem Begin's paramilitary group, the Irgun, was attempting to land arms from the French ship, *Altalena* (see chapter 3). When the war resumed, Dayan's brigade captured Deir Tarif, a former British army camp that had been turned over to the Arab Legion. Driven from their position, the Arabs left behind an astounding prize—an upturned armored car boasting a two-pounder cannon. Forthwith, some enterprising soldiers from Dayan's brigade crept under fire across an exposed field and tied a rope to the vehicle. An Israeli tractor then towed it to safety. Restored to working order and nicknamed "the terrible tiger," the armored car led the charge as Dayan's brigade stormed through the strategic Arab towns of Lydda and Ramle, laying a thick fire on the Arab defenders.[13]

Impressed by Dayan's bravery, David Ben-Gurion promoted the 33-year-old fighter to lieutenant colonel, and placed him in command of the Jerusalem sector (July 17, 1948). As the war drew to a close, Dayan assisted in important negotiations with Jordan's King Abdullah and with the Arab Legion's Jerusalem commander, Colonel Abdullah el Tel. Because the ensuing agreement gave important concessions to Israel, el Tel refused to append his signature to it, insisting instead that a Jordanian political official do so, after which he assured Dayan that he would fulfill its terms.[14] (Dayan returned the favor by having the *Jerusalem Post* publish periodic articles complaining about how intransigent and unreasonable el Tel had been during the negotiations, thus protecting the latter's good image amongst his own people.[15])

Dayan finished the war with the rank of colonel. As Ben-Gurion's bona fide protégé, his subsequent rise was meteoric. In October 1949, he was promoted to brigadier general and placed in command of the Negev. In 1952, he was promoted to chief of operations, the second-highest position in the army. Then, in December 1953, at Ben-Gurion's insistence, he reached the top as chief of staff. Finding morale low, Dayan insisted that every officer in the IDF undergo paratroop or commando training. (He obtained his paratrooper insignia at age 39.) He also established an Israeli military college so that IDF officers would not have to seek instruction abroad.[16]

Dayan was an avid proponent of Israel's reprisal policy against terrorism during the early 1950s, and when this failed to achieve any definitive result, he played an important role in convincing Ben-Gurion to cooperate with Britain and France in the Suez War. In the lead-up to that conflict, he traveled to France with Shimon Peres for talks with the French military staff. Asked how quickly his troops could reach the Suez Canal, he replied that this would be determined by the swiftness of the vehicles with which he was supplied. Since *they* were his chief suppliers, the French officers roared with laughter. They were delighted with Dayan's confident, no-nonsense approach — finding it a welcome contrast to the hesitant attitude displayed by the British.[17]

During the war, Dayan insisted on being in the heat of the action. At El Arish, his aide was killed at his side by an enemy sniper. On another occasion, his Piper Cub was fired upon while he surveyed the field of operations from the air. At Rafa, an Egyptian shell struck the sand dune on which he was eating breakfast. Finally, towards the end of the fighting, Egyptian soldiers in retreat were stunned to see Dayan's vehicle rumble past them on the road to Sharm el-Shiekh with Moshe standing up in the back, utterly unprotected. By war's end, Dayan was a national hero, and the campaign, of which he was the architect, became a topic of study in military colleges across the globe.[18]

In 1958, Dayan resigned as chief of staff. The following year, Ben-Gurion named him minister of agriculture. His tenure in this position is best remembered for a failed attempt to introduce a new type of tomato for export, and for the massacre of a large number of chickens whose copious production of unexportable eggs had created a market crisis. "I'm sorry," he is supposed to have said, "but if the people of Israel don't like eggs, they'll just have to eat chickens."[19]

For the time being, Ben-Gurion's *Mapai* Party was at the height of its popularity, but in 1960 Pinhas Lavon reopened the dormant Lavon affair, alleging that Dayan and Shimon Peres had set him up as the fall guy for the scandal.[20] Ben-Gurion ultimately resigned over the cabinet's contentious decision to exonerate Lavon, and Dayan followed suit in 1964 after clashing with the cabinet over economic policy.

The following year, he was elected to the Knesset on the Rafi ticket as part of Ben-Gurion's failed attempt to return to power. Effectively barred from the halls of authority, he served briefly as a war correspondent in Vietnam, concluding that U.S. tactics were insufficient to bring about victory despite the army's awe-inspiring weapons arsenal. When the unit to which he was assigned came under attack during a routine patrol, Dayan calmly scaled a nearby hillock, advising the astonished unit commander to do the same if he wanted to see what was going on.[21] Returning home, he promoted a plan to offer Jordan access to Israel's ports at Ashdod and Haifa if Jordan would allow Palestininan refugees to resettle within her borders.[22]

Sadly, the atmosphere was not conducive to peacemaking. The trouble this time involved Syria. At the end of Israel's War of Independence, Syrian troops still occupied three small strips of territory on Israel's side of the old Syria-Palestine border. By terms of the 1949 cease-fire, Syria's government agreed to evacuate these forces, and Israel undertook to keep the evacuated areas demilitarized. The issue of sovereignty was not directly addressed in the agreement, but at the time of its signing, Ralph Bunche, the UN mediator, had given assurances to Israel that civilian activities would be permitted in the evacuated areas.[23]

This last point was of no minor significance. Much of the demilitarized territory abutted the Jordan River or the Sea of Galilee. Consequently, the issue of territorial sovereignty was hopelessly intertwined with a much larger issue: access to water. Exclusion from the demilitarized zones would hamper Israel's ability to carry out projects crucial to her future development — chief among them, a scheme to irrigate the Negev Desert that would allow her to accommodate as many as three million new immigrants.[24] (Needless to say, the very thought of such a project evoked cries and laments from Israel's neighbors.)

Based on Dr. Bunche's assurances, and on the fact that the demilitarized zones lay on her side of the old international border, Israel felt justified in pursuing her projects even in the absence of a definitive agreement with Syria. Syria did not agree. Indeed, by denying Israel a negotiated settlement, she hoped to stymie her development schemes indefinitely. Thus, in 1951, when Israel arranged the purchase of 100 acres of DMZ land from local Arab owners to facilitate drainage of the Hula marsh (an important land reclamation project lying outside the DMZ), Syria intervened to block the deal. Rather than acquiesce in this veto, Israel simply usurped the land. Syria answered by shelling Israel's engineering teams from the Golan Heights when they attempted to begin work. This in turn provoked Israeli air strikes against the Syrian gun emplacements. In the end, the UN forced Israel to return the confiscated real estate. (Luckily, Israel found a way to drain the Hula marsh without it.[25])

Two years later, Israel began diverting water from the Jordan River for a proposed hydroelectric plant within the DMZ. Syria immediately lodged a complaint with the United Nations Truce Supervision Organization (UNTSO) challenging the legality of the project. Pending mediation by special U.S. envoy Eric Johnston, UNTSO ordered a work stoppage. A year of deliberations ensued before Johnston determined that Israel should have access to 35 percent of the combined waters of the Jordan River and the Sea of Galilee to fulfill her national needs. Though she thought she ought to have a higher percentage, Israel accepted the ruling. Syria and Lebanon rejected it. Jordan, however, had also been awarded a large water allocation — mostly from the Yarmuk River — and when she began utilizing her share, Israel did the same.[26]

Work now began in earnest on the so-called National Water Carrier that was to bring fresh water to the parched Negev. In order to sidestep the DMZs (and to keep out of Syrian artillery range), Israel initiated the project from the Sea of Galilee instead of directly from the Jordan River — a rather large inconvenience since the Sea of Galilee lies below sea level, meaning that its water had to be pumped upwards several hundred feet in order to reach the carrier.[27]

The project was completed in 1964, and it can be argued that the lead-up to the Six Day War commences from this date. Syria, in fact, began calling for war immediately. From Egypt, President Nasser responded that the timing was not propitious— largely because his army was bogged down in an ugly civil war in Yemen, which featured, among other things, the indiscriminate murder of prisoners and the use of poison gas by the Egyptian Air Force.[28] As a temporizing measure, Nasser convened an Arab summit meeting in January 1964. The two-fold result of this convention was (i) a decision taken by Syria and Egypt to deprive Israel of water by diverting the Jordan headwaters north of Israel's border; and (ii) the enlistment of Palestinian refugees into the struggle to eradicate Israel.[29]

Within months of this summit, the Palestine Liberation Organization was founded at a conference of Palestinian Arabs in the Arab-controlled portion of Jerusalem. Finding its leadership unsatisfactory, however, Syria sponsored its own terror squad — *Fatah* or "Victory."[30] Commanded by Yasser Arafat, Fatah staged its first strike (against the National Water Carrier) on January 1, 1965. The attack failed, but more were to follow — the bulk being staged from the DMZ, Lebanon or Jordan so that Syria would have plausible deniability and would not be encumbered by Israel's inevitable retaliatory actions.[31] Hence, when Israel finally did strike back in force following a deadly wave of Fatah terrorism in the fall of 1966, her chosen target was the Jordanian village of Samua, a leading Fatah base on the outskirts of Hebron. The plan called for the destruction of 40 buildings within the town, to be preceded by loudspeaker warnings so that the populace would have time to flee. Unfortunately, a Jordanian infantry brigade caught wind of the operation, with the result that the raid blossomed into a clash of regular forces (November 13, 1966). Fifteen Jordanian troops were killed and 54 were wounded, but there were also nearly 100 civilian casualties, three of which were fatalities. (Israel lost one dead and ten wounded.[32])

The Israeli government had assumed that the West Bank populace would respond to the attack by demanding a crackdown on Fatah. Instead, the citizens rioted against their Hashemite ruler, King Hussein, for his failure to declare war on Israel. Shortly afterwards, the UN Security Council, which had reacted indifferently to Israeli complaints about Fatah's activities, condemned Israel's action in the harshest terms.[33]

Syria, meanwhile, was not content to strike at Israel vicariously through Fatah. Abundantly armed by the Soviets and possessing a mutual defense pact with Egypt, she did everything in her power to disrupt Israel's development projects—from shelling Israeli tractors in the DMZs to attempts at diverting the headwaters of the Jordan. In retaliation, Israeli tanks counter-shelled Syrian positions on the Golan Heights, and executed pinpoint strikes against Syrian bulldozers that were attempting to divert the Jordan's headwaters. The latter tactic, accurate to a distance of 2.5 miles, put a temporary halt to Syria's water diversion activities.[34]

But the shelling of Israeli tractors from the Golan Heights remained a predictable part of life — so predictable in fact, that when Syrian-sponsored Fatah attacks from Jordan accelerated in early 1967, Israeli chief of staff Yitzhak Rabin purposely sent tractors into the DMZ to draw Syrian fire so that he could shoot back at the true culprits.[35] The date was April 7, 1967. As expected, Syria took the bait and fired at Rabin's tractors. Israeli tanks moved into position and fired back. But then, the Syrians took aim at an Israeli kibbutz. This was too much. Rabin called in the air force. In the ensuing air battle, Israeli Mirage fighters of French design shot down six Soviet-built Syrian MiGs and then circled Damascus in celebration.[36]

Syria attempted to deflect blame for this embarrassment onto Egypt — calling Nasser to task for failing to enter the fray in accordance with their mutual defense pact. Still bogged down in Yemen, Nasser desired nothing less than to be dragged unprepared into a war with Israel. At some cost to his waning reputation as leader of the Arab world, he refused to activate the mutual defense pact in the absence of an actual war between Syria and Israel.

This marked the second time in a period of months that Nasser had been criticized by a neighboring Arab state. The Jordanian press had likewise castigated him for failing to confront Israel over the Samua raid. Consequently, he was now acutely sensitive to regional opinion.

No less sensitive to that opinion was the Soviet Union. Although the Soviet leaders were alarmed by Syria's provocative behavior, they were not willing to swallow the events of April 7 without doing something to show their solidarity. Direct action would run the risk of American intervention. They chose therefore to manufacture a crisis that might cause diplomatic embarrassment to Israel while bringing Egypt to Syria's defense.

On April 26, 1967, the Soviet ambassador to Israel, Dmitri Chuvakhin, angrily accused Israeli prime minister Levi Eshkol of massing troops for an imminent attack on Syria. The charge was entirely false. Eshkol offered then and there to escort Chuvakhin to the Syrian border where he could confirm with his own eyes that not a single soldier had been mobilized. Chuvakhin refused the invitation but persisted in his accusations.[37] On May 13, the Soviet Union notified Cairo that Israeli forces were present in force on the Syrian border and would attack no later than May 17. By an unhappy coincidence, Yitzhak Rabin had just issued an unauthorized statement to the press threatening unspecified measures against Syria for her ongoing provocations. The statement gave circumstantial credibility to the Soviet claim. Forthwith, Syria invoked her defense pact with Egypt. Nasser responded by dispatching his chief of staff, Muhammad Fawzi, to Damascus. Early on May 15, Fawzi reported to Cairo that there was no evidence of an Israeli build-up. Indeed, he noted, the Syrians had not even placed *their own* army on alert. The same day, General Odd Bull of Norway, the commander of UNTSO, confirmed the lack of evidence for an Israeli mobilization.[38]

May 15 was Israel's Independence Day — the traditional date for a military parade in Jewish Jerusalem. In light of the accusations against her, Israel celebrated in restrained fashion. The military parade was scaled down so as not to appear provocative. Tanks, planes and artillery were conspicuously absent. As they reviewed the marching troops, Levi Eshkol, Yitzhak Rabin and Abba Eban received a memorandum informing them that Egyptian forces were pouring into the Sinai. (Later, in support of Nasser's action, the Arab media falsely claimed that Israel's heavy equipment was absent from the Independence Day parade because it had been deployed on the Syrian border.[39])

Given that Nasser's chief of staff had already confirmed the nonexistence of an Israeli troop build-up, the most likely explanation for the Sinai deployment was the potential it offered for a low-risk propaganda victory. By moving his troops into Sinai on the false pretext provided to him by the Soviets, Nasser could claim that he had cowed the Israelis into aborting their (imaginary) preparations for an attack on Syria.[40] That Israel would not attack Syria was a virtual certainty. She had not actually massed any troops on Syria's border, and with the Soviets hurling accusations at her it was highly unlikely that she would launch so much as a small-scale raid on that front.

Thus, after suffering the opprobrium of his fellow Arabs, the Egyptian president would again stand supreme as leader of the Arab world. Likewise, the USSR would be able to congratulate itself on taking the Israelis down a notch after their April 7 air victory. And when the self-congratulations died down, Nasser could quietly withdraw his troops and resume his affairs with his reputation markedly enhanced.

This very script had been followed almost to the letter during a similar Arab-Israeli crisis in 1960.[41] But this time the situation played out differently. Standing in the way of the Egyptian Army was UNEF — the United Nations Emergency Force that had been established in 1957 to guarantee the post–Sinai War settlement. In 1960, Nasser had told UNEF to be prepared to get out of the way if fighting broke out. On this occasion, he wasn't willing to wait. On May 16, he demanded that UNEF redeploy itself outside the line of fire so that the Egyptian army could attack "Israel, in case and whenever it launches an act of aggression against any Arab country."[42] UN secretary-general U Thant answered that UNEF could not be redeployed at Egypt's whim. Nasser must either allow it to perform its duties in full or order its evacuation. The secretary general apparently thought that Nasser would not be willing to embark on the latter course.[43] He was wrong. UNEF was the very symbol of Nasser's declining stature. Various Arab leaders had chided him for "hiding behind UNEF's skirts" to avoid confrontation with Israel. In sum, his reputation in the Arab world hinged upon his answer to U Thant.[44] On May 17, he instructed UNEF to withdraw.

At the time of UNEF's establishment in 1957, then UN secretary-general Dag Hammarskjöld had assured Israel that UNEF would not be removed until it was no longer needed. If Egypt sought to force its withdrawal beforehand, the issue was to be voted upon in the UN General Assembly. If the assembly did not agree and Egypt insisted nonetheless, the UN would declare her to be in violation of the 1957 agreement. U Thant, however, did not stick to protocol. When Egypt presented its demand, he simply packed up and left without so much as referring the matter for debate. Speaking later before the UN Security Council, an exasperated Abba Eban (now Israel's foreign minister) likened UNEF's usefulness in the crisis to that of "an umbrella which is taken away as soon as it begins to rain."[45]

Had Nasser been a reflective man, he might have noticed that the easy eviction of UNEF had placed him in the horns of a dilemma. With Sharm el-Sheikh again in his hands, he must either allow Israeli ships to pass through the Straits of Tiran under his guns, or refuse such passage (as radical Arab opinion would expect him to do) and recreate the state of affairs that had led to the Sinai War of 1956. In the latter case, the entire complexion of the crisis would change: Military posturing was one thing. A blockade of the straits was quite another. Apart from constituting a violation of international law,[46] the blockade would close down Israel's access to the markets of the entire Eastern Hemisphere and sever her supply line to Iranian oil. No nation would suffer such a blow without a fight. Simply put, closure of the straits was a *casus belli*.

But this, apparently, is not how Nasser viewed the matter. At the end of Israel's War of Independence, the Arab states had signed armistice agreements with Israel, but they had not made peace. By combining this fact with a rather rare form of logic that is not to be found in any textbook on the subject, the Arab principals were able to reach a startling conclusion. As Abba Eban explains, "Cairo's theory was that the Arab states were entitled to exercise the 'rights of war' against Israel while claiming immunity from any Israeli 'acts of war' against themselves." Put another way, "the Arabs could behave as though there was war while Israel must behave as though there was peace." Under this formula, Nasser could blockade the straits "legally" since a state of war existed with Israel, but if Israel tried to protect her maritime rights, she could be labeled the aggressor.[47] Hence, once he closed the straits, the dilemma would no longer be his, it would be Israel's—for the decision to start shooting would be an Israeli one.

On May 22, Nasser put this hypothesis to the test. While awaiting a visit from U Thant to discuss the evolving crisis, the Egyptian president announced that henceforth the Straits of Tiran would be closed to Israeli shipping. In a speech on May 22, he bellowed: "We shall on no account allow the Israeli flag to pass through the Gulf of Aqaba. The Jews threaten to make war. I reply: *Ahlan wa sahalan*—'Welcome!' We are ready for war.... This water is ours."[48] Within 24 hours of this announcement, fanatical mobs took to the streets of the Arab capitals calling for Israel's destruction.[49]

Although the United States issued a statement saying that Israel would have the right to defend herself if her ships were fired upon, she quietly asked Israel not to test the blockade for at least 48 hours while a diplomatic solution was sought. The Israeli military protested that Israel must fight her own battles. If she appeared hesitant, it would invite further aggression.[50] Abba Eban countered this argument by stressing the lessons of 1956, when Israel had gone to war without the blessing of either superpower and wound up diplomatically isolated. Suppose she attacked now and won only to find that she must surrender whatever she gained militarily. Or suppose she found that no one was willing to sell her arms.[51] Eshkol likewise favored diplomacy. For one thing, Israel had been caught off guard. If it must come to a fight, Israel would need preparation time. For another, he believed that the best hope for averting war was an international declaration against the blockade. After all, Nasser's action not only violated Israel's freedom of navigation, but everyone else's, too (not to mention the guarantees made by the Western powers in 1957).[52] Accordingly, on May 24, Abba Eban embarked on a tour of Western capitals—flying first to Paris to divine the attitude of French president Charles De Gaulle.

The encounter was most unsatisfactory. De Gaulle was adamant that Israel not strike the first blow. Eban assured him that Israel would not—indeed, could not—strike such a blow since Nasser had already done that by closing the Straits of Tiran. Much to Eban's dismay, the inherent truth of this argument made no impression on De Gaulle.[53] It was beginning to appear that Nasser had wagered correctly.

Later that same day, Eban flew to London where the reception was friendlier. In a meeting with Prime Minister Harold Wilson, Eban learned of Britain's willingness to participate in an international attempt to reopen the straits.[54] In Washington two days later, U.S. president Lyndon Baines Johnson spoke of sending an international task force through the straits under naval escort. But he emphasized that Israel must do nothing precipitate in the interim—she must not strike first. "Israel will not be alone," he told Eban, "unless it decides to go alone."[55]

While Eban pursued diplomacy, Nasser withdrew his troops from Yemen—something that he had long been desperate to do—and began recruiting extranational volunteers into the Egyptian army to share in the impending triumphant march over Israel. In a speech on May 26, he made the open boast that "our basic objective will be to destroy Israel."[56] (Pope Kyrillos of Egypt's Coptic Orthodox Church added his blessing to this pronouncement by telling Nasser to "regain Palestine from those who crucified Christ."[57])

The IDF was now calling for an immediate strike before Nasser consolidated his position in Sinai. But the Israeli cabinet was divided, and despite prolonged deliberations on May 27, no consensus could be reached. The following day, messages were received from U.S. secretary of state Dean Rusk, confirming U.S. attempts to organize an international maritime demonstration, and from LBJ, reiterating that "Israel must not take preemptive military action." In deference to these communications, Eshkol and the cabinet agreed to wait on events.[58]

To many Israelis, this decision seemed like indecision. The army had been mobilized since May 20, and so many individuals were affected by the call-up that normal economic activity sputtered to a halt. Civilians were seen digging trenches and filling sandbags in preparation for an invasion. As Golda Meir later recalled, "each and every one of [us] felt personally responsible for the survival of the State of Israel and each and every one ... knew that the enemy we faced was committed to our annihilation." (It is noteworthy that while the nightly news broadcast images of fanatical Arab throngs calling for Israel's annihilation, and while Israeli rabbis consecrated city parks for use as emergency cemeteries, thousands of young American and British Jews were clamoring to enlist in the IDF. Indeed, when El Al announced that it could not accommodate all those who had come to London Airport to obtain passage, a riot broke out.[59])

As days passed without action from the government, Eshkol's leadership capacity came under fire. Following a precedent set by David Ben-Gurion, the prime minister was serving as his own minister of defense. On May 27, a cadre of soldiers' wives and mothers gathered outside his office to trumpet the popular demand that Moshe Dayan replace him in this post.[60] Criticism also came from some of the state's leading personages— among them opposition leader Menachem Begin, formerly David Ben-Gurion's political archrival, who now appealed to Eshkol to resign in favor of Ben-Gurion since the latter's proven ability to lead would rally the nation.[61]

On May 28, Eshkol decided to quiet the nation's anxieties by making a national radio address. It was a fiasco. Deprived of sleep, his vision blurred after an attempted cataract repair, Eshkol delivered a halting, uncertain rendition of a script made illegible by copious hand-scrawled corrections. If there had been any doubt as to his "ineptitude" prior to this performance, it was now dispelled. Soldiers in the Negev smashed their radios and wept.[62]

Nor was this the final blow to Eshkol's policy. Far from making progress on her proposed naval demonstration, the U.S. had asked 80 states to participate and had received an unconditional "yes" from only three.[63] For LBJ, the prospect of acting alone, or nearly alone, was insupportable. Vietnam simply weighed too heavily on the American mind to allow for any unilateral posturing in the Middle East.

The last domino fell on May 30 when Jordan's King Hussein agreed to a "defensive" pact with Nasser that placed the Jordanian army under Egyptian command. In addition, he agreed to let Iraqi forces enter his kingdom, thus magnifying the threat to Israel's cramped nine-mile "waistline" between the West Bank and the sea. If war broke out now, Israel would face combat on three fronts: the Egyptian, the Syrian and, quite unexpectedly, the Jordanian.[64] The announcement was greeted on the streets of the Arab capitals with the most delirious celebrations to date. From the mob's perspective, Israel's destruction was now assured.

If, in the midst of these goings-on, Israelis had come to regard Eshkol as indecision incarnate, they were no less convinced that they espied the embodiment of decisive action in Moshe Dayan. As one of ten Rafi members in the Knesset at the outset of the crisis, Dayan was ensconced in the political wilderness. He seemed, however, to possess powers of divination. On May

16, at a meeting of six former chiefs of staff summoned by Yitzhak Rabin, he alone predicted that Nasser would evict UNEF and close the straits.[65] On May 23, the cabinet asked his opinion on the U.S. request for a 48-hour delay in challenging the blockade. He replied that the cabinet should certainly grant 48 hours. But if the straits remained closed an hour longer, the IDF should obliterate the Egyptian army.[66] Then, while the government debated its options, Dayan toured the southern front, telling its commander, Yeshayahu Gavish, that Israel would win although the cost in casualties would be high. (Gavish later stated that Dayan was the first national figure actually to say, "you will win the war." Dani Matt, another senior officer has testified that Dayan's presence "caused a revolution in the atmosphere within the army. The army now felt capable of going to war and winning it."[67]) Recognized on the streets of Beersheba on May 24, Dayan was thronged by admirers. In Eilat on the 30th, restaurant owners insisted on allowing him to eat for free.[68] By this time, the clamor for his appointment as minister of defense had reached a crescendo. But a roadblock stood in the way: Dayan's appointment was tantamount to a decision for war, and on the 30th, there was still (fading) hope for a diplomatic solution.[69]

A day later, the same could not be said. Asked on May 31 whether the United States intended to restrain Israel from taking preemptive action, U.S. secretary of state Dean Rusk answered, "I don't think it is our business to restrain anyone."[70] Abba Eban was certain that this was America's way of notifying Israel that the international flotilla had come to naught, and that Israel was being released from her obligation to avoid a first strike. Should hostilities now erupt, the U.S. would not reflexively demand a return to the old armistice lines as she had in 1956. By staying her hand and giving diplomacy a chance to work, Israel had obtained tacit support from the Western superpower.[71]

The main obstacle to Dayan's appointment now was Eshkol. Relations had never been cordial between the two men, and if the defense ministry must be handed to a soldier, Eshkol much preferred the hero of 1948, Yigal Allon. Thinking it unlikely that Eshkol would relent, Dayan requested activation as commander of the Egyptian front. On the morning of June 1, his request was granted. But at 4 P.M., under intense popular and political pressure, Eshkol yielded and offered Dayan the defense portfolio. Menachem Begin likewise joined the cabinet, which thus became modern Israel's first "national unity" government.[72]

Dayan's appointment wrought an instantaneous change in the national mood. Doubt gave way to self-assurance. Israeli soldiers celebrated by singing songs and building bonfires. On June 2, Dayan recommended to Eshkol, Eban and Rabin that the cabinet put the issue of war to a vote no later than June

4 with the intention of initiating hostilities the following day.[73] Then, in a mesmerizing June 3 press conference, he convinced the media that there would be no war in the near term. It was too late for a military riposte to the closing of the straits and too early to assess what patient diplomacy might achieve. Persuaded by his performance — and by the fact that large numbers of soldiers had been placed on leave — many journalists flew home.[74]

In truth, with Dayan in the cabinet, Nasser had to either reopen the straits or fight. The former option was all but impossible. Nasser's prior actions had thrown the Arab world into a frenzy, making a sober approach unsustainable.[75] Across the region, there were calls for an anti–Zionist jihad "to wipe Israel off the map."[76] Fanatics spoke of "cutting the Jews' throats" and hanging "imperialist soldiers" with "Zionist entrails."[77] Palestine Liberation Organization (PLO) chief, Ahmed Shukeiry, predicted that not one Israeli would survive.[78] In this milieu, Nasser could scarcely back down. Consequently, the crisis was resolved by war.

At dawn on June 5, the traditional hour for an air strike, the skies were quiet. At 7:10 A.M. the only thing to be seen was the usual Israeli Air Force (IAF) morning patrol — nothing more. The Egyptian military confidently concluded that there would be no action that day. They were wrong: the "morning patrol" was actually a squad of antiquated training planes sent up as a decoy. Israel's real jets were speeding toward the Egyptian border — many flying at an altitude of less than 15 meters in order to evade Egyptian radar.[79] Three hours later, Egypt's air power lay in ruins with nearly 300 aircraft destroyed and a dozen airfields reduced to rubble. One hundred and eighty Israeli jets participated in the attack. A bare dozen had stayed behind to defend the home skies.[80]

Egypt attempted to conceal the catastrophe by announcing stupendous victories. Dayan made no effort to contest these claims. A major fear on the Israeli side was that Russia would insist upon a UN-mandated cease-fire before Israel could achieve her war aims. This was less likely to occur if Russia thought Egypt was winning.[81]

As the facts began to emerge the following morning, Egypt claimed that British and American jets had participated in the Israeli attack. Recognizing this as a contrived piece of nonsense, the Soviets pressed for a cease-fire in the UN Security Council. Dayan responded by ordering the immediate capture of Sharm el-Sheikh. Failure to reopen the straits by war's end would mean that Israel had been thwarted in her main purpose. The next morning (June 7) a simultaneous amphibious/airborne attack was set in motion. But when the soldiers reached their objective, they found it undefended. The Egyptian High Command had abandoned Sharm el-Sheikh on the night of June 6-7.[82]

The events of June 6 explain the Egyptian withdrawal—for the second day of the war had been as disastrous for Egypt's ground forces as the first had been for her air force. After 1956, Egypt had overhauled the formidable Abu Agheila-Um Katef fortress network in north-central Sinai. Prior to the war, Israeli intelligence had gathered detailed information on this facility and had built an exact replica in the Negev that became the focus of endless IDF training exercises.[83] On the night of June 5, Ariel Sharon's infantry stole around the flank of Um Katef while airborne troops (transported by helicopter) assaulted it from the rear. By 3 A.M., the bastion had fallen, opening a breach into central Sinai.[84] Simultaneously, in the north, another Israeli column, commanded by Israel Tal, captured Rafa and El-Arish, while a third column, under Abraham Yoffe, set off for the Mitla and Gidi Passes in an effort to sever the Egyptian line of retreat.[85]

By midnight on the second day of the war, Egypt's entire Sinai defensive structure was broken, prompting a chaotic general flight. In the absence of air cover, casualties were staggering. Egyptian officers deserted their posts, advising the marooned soldiery merely to save themselves. Advancing behind them, Israeli troops stumbled upon an entire brigade of tanks, arrayed in battle formation but empty.[86] With Egyptian forces streaming westwards, the UN Security Council sought to impose a cease-fire commencing at 10 P.M. on June 7. Nasser rejected the resolution because it did not require Israel to withdraw to the armistice line. As a result, the battle continued for another day, by which time 15,000 Egyptians soldiers had been killed, 20,000 wounded and 5,000 taken prisoner. (Rather than congest their lines of advance with a large haul of prisoners, the Israelis detained only the officers, letting the enlisted men go. In attempting to swim across a narrow stretch of the Suez Canal, some of the latter were gunned down from the far bank by their own countrymen — apparently to keep them from spreading word of the defeat.[87])

At the outset of the war, Dayan had laid down strict parameters for the campaign. Offensive action was to be confined to the Egyptian front. All attention must be riveted on this decisive theatre with the dual goal of destroying the Egyptian army and reopening the straits. The Suez Canal was pronounced off-limits. Interference with Suez shipping might provoke foreign intervention. Finally, in the event of an attack from Jordan or Syria, the northern and central commands must remain on the defensive.[88] In issuing these restrictions, Dayan had a three-fold purpose: First, he wanted to make sure Israel achieved her primary war aims; second, he wanted to avoid fighting on multiple fronts; and third, he wanted to avoid foreign intervention or premature imposition of a cease-fire.[89]

By war's end, however, events had forced him to rescind every one of his limitations. On the first day of battle, a desperate attempt was made to avoid a full-scale clash with Jordan. In the wake of the IAF's morning air strikes against Egypt, Jordanian artillery began shelling Jewish Jerusalem. At 10 A.M., King Hussein received a phone call from the UNTSO chief of staff, General Odd Bull, who forwarded an assurance from Israel that if the king silenced his guns, Jordan would not be attacked.[90] Left to his own devices, Hussein might have accepted the offer. Unfortunately, he was no longer master in his own house. His forces were under Egyptian command. Moreover, Nasser had informed him that three-quarters of the Israeli Air Force was destroyed and that victory was certain. Consequently, Hussein rejected Israel's offer, choosing instead to join Syria and Iraq in a combined air strike against Israeli targets. Israel counterattacked immediately, decimating the Syrian and Jordanian air forces and obliterating a key Iraqi air base.[91] At the same time, Israeli ground forces severed the major reinforcement routes into Arab Jerusalem by capturing two crucial positions: "French Hill" on the Old City's northeastern outskirts and Government House on the southeast. In a related attack on "Radar Hill," Israeli infantry attempted to negotiate a minefield by confining their steps to rocky outcroppings. Some were maimed, but the position was taken.[92]

With a cease-fire looming on June 7, Dayan yielded to relentless pressure from the political and military establishments and ordered the capture of the Old City. By midmorning, the Temple Mount and Wailing Wall, Judaism's holiest sites, were in Israeli hands. Within hours, Rabin and Dayan arrived on the scene. (While roaming through the city, Jewish soldiers discovered that the Jordanians had demolished all the historical synagogues and had pilfered Jewish tombstones from the Mount of Olives for use as paving stones for roads and latrines.[93]) By June 8, the entire West Bank had been cleared of Jordanian forces. That same day, Israeli troops in Sinai pressed forward to the Suez Canal in violation of Dayan's restrictions. At first, Dayan ordered them to withdraw, but by day's end he was standing alongside them with his feet in the surf.[94]

Amidst the events of June 8, a meeting took place between Abba Eban and McGeorge Bundy (LBJ's national security advisor), in which the latter noted how ironic it was that Jordan should pay in spades for a war that her king had not wanted, while Syria had caused the war and paid virtually nothing. His words were not lost on Eban, who transmitted them forthwith to the cabinet.[95] The prospect of attacking Syria weighed heavily upon Dayan. Of all the Arab states, none had closer ties to the Soviet Union, and in the event of an attack, there was no telling what the Soviets might do. Yet here was the chance to put an end to two decades of Syrian provocations (which would certainly persist if nothing were done). With a civilian deputation from upper Galilee demanding action and volunteers flocking toward the Syrian border to take part in the anticipated thrust, Dayan finally gave the green light on the morning of June 9. To obtain a footing on the Golan Heights, the Israelis had to fight an uphill hand-to-hand battle, but once they gained the road running behind the main enemy defenses, the whole Syrian position unraveled. The Israelis now pressed forward as fast as they could go.[96]

The Soviets made no secret of their displeasure. Rumors swirled that they would intervene militarily. In the Ukraine, Russian air squadrons secretly repainted their aircraft in Egyptian colors.[97] President Johnson countered this saber rattling by ordering the U.S. Sixth Fleet to take up position 50 miles from the Syrian coast. At the same time, however, he placed immense pressure on Israel to comply with a U.N. cease-fire proposal.[98] Accordingly, at 6:30 P.M. on June 10, the guns fell silent.

Russia, however, was not satisfied. She charged Israel with violating the cease-fire terms— an allegation forged from whole cloth — and cut off diplomatic relations with her. Every nation in the Eastern Bloc, save Romania, followed suit, leaving Israelis to console themselves with the fact that in a mere six days of fighting they had tripled the amount of territory under their control[99]— albeit at the sacrifice of 777 dead and 2,586 wounded.[100] (According to Levi Eshkol's biographer, two of the dead were pilots who had been captured and crucified by the Syrians.[101]) On the war's final night, Israeli audiences heard a weather report on local radio that included, for the first time, a forecast for the Golan Heights, Hebron, Gaza and Sharm el-Sheikh.[102]

Israel's astonishing victory in the Six Day War catapulted Moshe Dayan to the pinnacle of his popularity. Some have attempted to detract from his laurels by pointing out that the battle plans were drawn up long before his appointment as defense minister.[103] To a degree, this point has validity (provided one allows for the modifications that Dayan *did* make). But if good planning contributes to victory, so, too, does morale, and in this realm Dayan's contribution was undeniable.[104] Prime Minister Eshkol had postponed the fight until he was sure that he had the understanding of the United States. From a diplomatic standpoint, this courageous delay (in the face of intense popular criticism) was tremendously important. But it came at a price. To soldiers at the front watching the enemy grow stronger before their eyes, and to civilians at home watching newscasts of fanatical Arab mobs howling for their blood while hostile armies gathered on the frontiers, the government's calculated inaction looked like inept dithering. Morale plummeted and anxiety rose up in its place. Dayan's emergence restored the situation instantaneously. *Newsweek* columnist Joseph Alsop placed his return to the cabinet on a par with Winston Churchill's return to the admiralty at the outset of World War II.[105] Even Yitzhak Rabin, who didn't like Dayan very much, seemed noticeably relieved.[106]

For six years after the great victory, Dayan was the darling of the masses. But celebrity is a sword that cuts both ways. The 1973 Yom Kippur War caught the defense minister off-guard. Although Israel emerged victorious, the toll in casualties was high. An official inquiry found the intelligence community to blame and absolved Dayan of responsibility. Nevertheless, the misadventure transformed him from popular hero to popular scapegoat. War widows and demonstrators accosted him the streets with cries of "murderer!" and "minister of shame!"[107] Amidst the uproar, Prime Minister Golda Meir announced her resignation (April 1974). Dayan had little choice but to follow suit.[108]

Over the course of the next year, Dayan wrote his memoir, *The Story of My Life*. Following its successful publication in 1976, he authored a second book, entitled *Living with the Bible*. Then, in 1977, Menachem Begin succeeded to the premiership and invited him to serve as foreign minister. In this capacity, Dayan played a crucial part in the negotiations leading up to the 1979 Camp David Peace Accords with Egypt.[109] Included in the accords was a provision for eventual Palestinian self-rule in the West Bank and Gaza, which was turned down by the PLO and Jordan on the pretext that they had had no say in formulating it. Dayan thought it crucial to pursue the provision regardless, but finding Begin unreceptive once the Arab principals had turned it down, he tendered his resignation.

He now returned to private life. In previous years, two passions had ruled this domain: archaeology and women. In his spare hours, Dayan filled his home with a veritable museum's worth of artifacts that he had unearthed on his campaigns. As near as anyone can tell, his claim to these antiquities was based on proclaiming the Hebrew equivalent of "dibs" on them as he drove by in his jeep. (No other curator has ever duplicated this method, the legality of which remains uncertain to this day.) Shortly after the Six Day War, he was transiently buried alive during the collapse of a newly discovered archaeological site. Alert coworkers dug him out and saved his life.

Women were no less alluring to him than his museum pieces. Members of the fair sex found the charismatic Dayan irresistible, and sadly for Dayan's family, the feeling was mutual. Rumors of his purported womanizing prowess seem to have been so startling as to suppress the natural tendency toward censure. Indeed, an exposé, entitled *Flaming Paths* (published in 1963 by one mistress who had found out about the others) had the unintended effect of making Dayan more popular than ever.[110]

But, like archaeology, womanizing has its perils. In Dayan's case, it led to divorce from his wife, Ruth, after 36 years of marriage (1971). Eighteen months later, he married Rahel Rabinovitch, his longtime lover and soul mate. When he died, he left the bulk of his estate (valued at more than $2 million) to her, and far lesser sums to his three surviving children. The end came two years into his last retirement. After an apparently successful operation for colon cancer in 1979, Dayan's health declined. He died, aged 65, on October 16, 1981. At his request, the funeral took place in Nahalal without public commemoration.[111]

6

Golda Meir and the Yom Kippur War

On the night of May 11, 1948, a man and woman, dressed in traditional Arabic clothing, arrived by car at a house near Amman Airport in Transjordan. Inside the house, waiting to speak with them was Abdullah, the Transjordanian king. When the guests entered, Abdullah addressed himself to the woman (whose face was concealed by a veil), asking why the Jews were "in such a hurry" to declare independence in Palestine. "A people that has waited two thousand years can hardly be described as being in a hurry," came the reply.[1]

This was the second clandestine meeting between King Abdullah and the acting director of the Jewish Agency's political department, Golda Meyerson. The first had occurred the previous November on the eve of the UN partition vote. At that meeting, the two had established a *quid pro quo*: Abdullah would support the establishment of a Jewish state if the Jews would recognize his sovereignty over the Arab portions of Palestine.[2] Now, he told Meyerson, this solution was no longer possible. He had lost mastery of the situation. Five Arab armies were poised to invade Palestine within the week (one of them his own). The only chance for peace was for the Jews to drop the notion of independence and allow him to rule all of Palestine. He would treat them fairly, granting them half the seats in his cabinet and parliament.[3]

Meyerson rejected the proposal categorically. "You know all that we have done and how hard we have worked. Do you think we did all that just to be represented in a foreign parliament?" If the Jews must choose between the king's offer and having a war thrust into their laps, she continued, "We will fight and we will win."[4] The two parted cordially, but King Abdullah never forgot Meyerson's toughness. A year later, during the postwar armistice talks, he asked an Israeli official what had become of her. Informed that she had been sent to Moscow to serve as Israel's ambassador, he expressed his earnest wish that she remain there forever.[5]

When the Six Day War ended on June 10, 1967, Israel held sway over the Sinai Desert, the Gaza Strip, the West Bank and the Golan Heights. But she was not intent on keeping her new-won gains. Led by Prime Minister Levi Eshkol and Foreign Minister Abba Eban, she sought to barter the territories for a comprehensive peace. On June 19, 1967, Eban approached the American delegation at the UN with the following specific proposals: (i) Israel would return to her international boundary with Egypt in return for peace, demilitarization of the Sinai, and a guarantee of free passage in international waterways; (ii) Israel would return to her international boundary with Syria in return for peace, demilitarization of the Golan Heights, and a guarantee of Israel's fresh water rights in regional rivers; and (iii) Israel would enter into direct negotiations with Jordan regarding boundaries and peace. The American delegation forwarded these proposals to Egypt and Syria.[6]

On September 1, 1967, Israel got her answer. Led by Egyptian president Gamal Abdel Nasser, representatives of the Arab governments meeting in Khartoum promulgated the infamous "3 Nos": "no peace with Israel, no recognition of Israel, no negotiation with Israel." It is safe to assume that the annals of diplomacy do not contain a more generous peace proposal by a nation that had prevailed in war, or a more thoughtless response by combatants who had been so soundly defeated. On hearing of the Khartoum declaration, Abba Eban remarked that the Six Day War was "the first war in history in which the victor sued for peace and the loser called for unconditional surrender."[7]

In light of the impasse, the UN Security Council attempted to formulate its own peace resolution. Preliminary drafts were put forward by the United States and India, but the first was felt to be too "pro–Israel," and the second too "pro–Arab" to obtain passage. The burden of devising a more equitable formula thus fell to the British minister of state, Hugh Foot, Lord Caradon.[8]

After condemning territorial aggression in principle,

Golda Meir during her first press conference as prime minister, March 18, 1969 (courtesy of the State of Israel Government Press Office; photographer Fritz Cohen).

Lord Caradon's resolution declared that a "just and lasting peace" required *both* "withdrawal of Israeli armed forces from territories occupied in the recent conflict" *and* "termination of all claims or states of belligerency."[9] The language was carefully chosen. By linking any "withdrawal from occupied territories" to the "termination of belligerency," the resolution appeared to authorize Israel's presence on the cease-fire lines until the parties had agreed to "durable" peace terms.[10] In addition, the extent of Israel's anticipated withdrawal was not explicitly addressed. Specifically, it was not stated that Israel must withdraw from "*all* occupied territories."[11] The UN General Assembly had already rejected outcries for such a withdrawal,[12] and in the view of Lord Caradon and his government, a mandatory reversion to the prewar armistice lines would only heighten the chance of another war. In a meeting with Abba Eban, Britain's Prime Minister Harold Wilson and Foreign Secretary George Brown made it clear that a total withdrawal would set a very bad precedent — effectively teaching the Arab governments that they could provoke a war without any risk of territorial loss.[13] After an in depth discussion, Eban said that the proposal would be acceptable to Israel provided that its stated goal was the *promotion of peace* between the parties, and not the *imposition of terms* upon them.[14]

Caradon's resolution — UN Security Council Resolution 242 — was duly submitted for consideration. Predictably, there were immediate efforts to redefine its meaning: behind the scenes, Soviet premier Aleksei Kosygin pressured U.S. president Lyndon Baines Johnson to construe the resolution as calling for Israel's withdrawal from "*all* occupied territories" irrespective of what the document actually said. LBJ responded that the U.S. "would not agree to a single word beyond what was written in the British text."[15] Next, the Indian and Arab delegations attempted to wrest an informal admission from Lord Caradon that the withdrawal clause obligated Israel to withdraw from "*all* occupied territories." Caradon answered that "nothing could be read into the resolution that was not specifically stated therein."[16] On November 15, U.S. ambassador Arthur Goldberg spoke at the UN in support of the withdrawal clause *as written*, noting that the conflicting parties had never come to an agreement on borders — either before or after the war — and that they would thus need to determine these borders by negotiation. One week later, the resolution passed the UN Security Council by a unanimous vote.[17]

By this time, it had become apparent that many Israelis did not share the cabinet's views on the fate of the territories. Calling themselves the "Land of Israel Movement," a vocal minority of intellectuals and religious Zionists maintained that the territories occupied in the war had reconstituted *Eretz Israel* — the land of Israel promised to the Jews by God — and that the government did not have the authority to partition it again. Many within the movement, however, were motivated by more pragmatic concerns: given the Arab position as elucidated in the Khartoum declaration, they felt that peace with the Arab states was an unlikely prospect and that Israel would do better to keep what had been won as a strategic buffer against renewed attack.[18] Indeed, it was the Khartoum declaration that induced many Israelis to cease viewing the "occupation" as a short-term expedient pending the establishment of peace, and to start viewing it as a durable solution to the nation's security woes.[19]

In spite of these arguments, the Eshkol government continued to pursue its original policy. Abba Eban has eloquently described the cabinet's line of thinking: Israel had come into existence in 1948 largely because she had agreed to the notion of partitioning Palestine, and she would be without international support if she now adopted a policy of unilateral annexation. The Arab states would certainly not acquiesce. Thus, the expanded boundaries would not be "a guarantee of peace but an invitation to early war."[20]

Throughout the course of 1968, there was no overt showdown between the competing viewpoints. But in February 1969, Prime Minister Eshkol died in office, and the issue threatened to become divisive. Yigal Allon, the minister of labor, was pushing a plan to relinquish Arab population centers while holding on to strategic zones (i.e., the Jordan Valley and adjacent mountains, the Golan Heights and Sharm el-Sheikh). In contrast, Moshe Dayan believed that the benign administration he had imposed upon the territories would make it possible to maintain sovereignty indefinitely, even in populated areas. (His policy in the immediate aftermath of the Six Day War had been to make the occupation as inconspicuous as possible. As he told a subordinate, "I want a policy whereby an Arab can be born, live and die in the West Bank without ever seeing an Israeli official."[21]) Finally, Israel's finance minister, Pinhas Sapir, counseled near-total withdrawal before Israel confronted the problems inherent in ruling the territories' million-plus Arabs. Given the Arab birth rate, he argued, Israelis might someday wake up in an Arab-majority state.[22]

Compounding the issue was the fact that Dayan and Allon were the leading candidates to succeed Eshkol. (A popular poll showed Dayan leading Allon by 45 percent to 32 percent.) Each man headed a major wing of Israel's new Labor Party, but owing to personal animus, neither was likely to serve under the other.[23] Hence, if either of them was chosen, the other might defect from the party with his whole following, thereby precipitating a major political crisis. Desperate to prevent this scenario, Pinhas Sapir convinced the party to acquiesce in the appointment of a less-divisive candidate. Her name was Golda Meir.[24]

She was born Golda Mabovitch in Kiev, inside the Russian Pale of Settlement, on May 3, 1898. Her father, Moshe, was a carpenter — which made him more facile at boarding up the entrance to their home at pogrom time.

(Golda watched him do this when she was four. Thankfully, the expected pogrom didn't occur.[25]) In 1903, Moshe moved to Milwaukee, Wisconsin, hoping to employ his skills more profitably. The rest of the family followed him there once he had established himself (1906).

At age 14, Golda ran away from her parents—who had overruled her decision to become a schoolteacher — and went to live at her sister's house in Denver. There she met and fell in love with Morris Meyerson. Between his proposal to her and their wedding three years later, she returned to Milwaukee (1914) and became an avowed Zionist. When Yitzhak Ben-Zvi and David Ben-Gurion came to town seeking volunteers to fight in the Jewish Legion during World War I, she attempted to enlist. Her gender disqualified her. Not to be deterred, she enrolled in the local chapter of *Po'alei Zion*, and decided to spend her life in the historical homeland of the Jewish people.

In 1921, she took ship from New York with her husband, Morris (who, alas, did not possess her exuberance for the venture). On the journey, the crew mutinied, the captain's brother went insane, and the captain was murdered[26]— none of which could have brightened Morris' outlook. Determined to look forward rather than back, Golda left her U.S. passport with the authorities in Naples, Italy.[27] Immediately upon arriving in Tel Aviv, she applied for membership at Merhavia, a kibbutz in the Jezreel Valley. The kibbutzniks replied that American "girls" were too fainthearted to succeed at pioneering and turned her away. She persisted until they accepted her.

At Merhavia, Golda was as happy as her husband was miserable. She developed into a first-rate chicken coop manager and was nominated to represent Merhavia in its dealings with the Histadrut — the Yishuv's predominant labor union and political nerve center. By 1924, however, Morris had had enough. With Golda about to deliver their first child, he insisted that they return to Tel Aviv. Children, he said, were to be raised by their parents, not by a socialist collective.[28]

Reluctantly, Golda gave up the farming tasks she found so gratifying and resumed city life. For a time, she worked as a cashier, but her Zionist idealism drove her to do more with her life. In 1928, she became secretary of *Moetzet Hapoalot* (i.e., the Histadrut's Women's Labor Council), which promoted women's pioneering in Palestine. Hearing her speak at a workers' rally in London two years later, David Ben-Gurion gave her rave reviews.[29] Golda was now a rising star in the Zionist labor movement. Her career, however, was taking a toll on her family. One night, when she was hours late coming home, her children snuck into the Histadrut assembly hall, where she was putting a matter to a vote, and raised their hands in favor. (She noticed them while counting.[30]) In 1934, her indefatigable work ethic won her a seat on the Histadrut's executive committee.

Golda opposed the 1937 Peel Commission partition plan for Palestine, saying that the area allotted to the Jews was too paltry for statehood. The looming Nazi threat forced her to reconsider. Hoping to hear concrete proposals for alleviating the plight of European Jewry, she attended the 1938 Evian Conference in France as a "Jewish observer from Palestine." After watching a procession of delegates sorrowfully proclaim that their own countries could not accommodate more Jews despite what was happening in Germany, Golda bitterly told the press that she longed for the day when her people "should not need expressions of sympathy anymore."[31]

During World War II, Golda directed the Histadrut's political department, raised funds for the Haganah and helped organize the clandestine immigration of Jewish refugees from Nazi-occupied Europe. She gained notoriety in 1943 when the *Palestine Post* carried a transcription of her defiant testimony at the trial of two Jewish youths charged with stealing British weapons.[32] After the war, she organized and participated in a hunger strike to show commiseration with Holocaust survivors attempting to reach Palestine in the face of British opposition. Her subsequent testimony before the Anglo-American Commission in 1946 helped produce a recommendation for the immediate issuance of 100,000 immigration permits—a recommendation that Britain ignored. When the British left her at liberty on Black Sabbath (June 29, 1946) while arresting 3,000 others (including most of the Yishuv's leadership), she took it as a personal insult. The Jewish Agency consoled her by asking her to serve as its acting political department director until it could obtain the release of the actual director, Moshe Shertok (who *had* been arrested).

When the British refused to increase the number of immigration permits for Jews interned on Cyprus in mid–1947, Golda visited the overcrowded camps and convinced the detainees to let families with young children immigrate "out of turn."[33] Later in the year, she carried out the first of her nocturnal meetings with King Abdullah of Transjordan. In the months between this and their second meeting, she toured the United States to raise funds for Israel's independence fight. Speaking before the Council of Jewish Federations and Welfare Funds in Chicago on January 21, 1948, she said,

> You cannot decide whether we should fight or not. We will. The Jewish community in Palestine will raise no white flag for the mufti. That decision is taken. Nobody can change it. You can only decide one thing: whether we shall be victorious ... or whether the mufti will be victorious....
>
> And I beg you—don't be too late. Don't be bitterly sorry three months from now for what you failed to do today. The time is now.[34]

She returned to Palestine in March with $50 million in donations—an unprecedented sum, without which the Jewish war effort might have foundered. For her efforts, Ben-Gurion hailed her as the "woman who saved the state."[35]

In August of the same year, Ben-Gurion appointed Golda as Israel's ambassador to the Soviet Union. Visiting Moscow's Great Synagogue on Rosh Hashanah in October, she was engulfed by 50,000 Jewish admirers. "Thank you for having remained Jews!" she exclaimed, acknowledging the precariousness of Jewish life under Stalin. Her words were scarcely audible amidst the throng, but members of the crowd repeated what she said until all had heard.[36] Later, she met Ivy Molotov, the wife of Soviet foreign minister Vyacheslav Molotov, who revealed in Yiddish that she, too, was Jewish. When the conversation turned to collective ownership on Israeli kibbutzim, Ivy interrupted, saying in an alarmed tone, "That's not a good idea. People don't like sharing everything. Even Stalin is against that."[37]

Back in Israel in the spring of 1949, Golda served as minister of labor in Israel's first elected government. With immigrants flowing into the nascent state at the rate of 1,000 per day, jobs and housing became her chief obsession. Her "golden roads" public works initiative helped develop the nation's infrastructure while providing widespread employment opportunities.[38]

By the time of the 1956 Suez War, she had graduated to the post of foreign minister and had changed her last name to "Meir" (meaning "to illuminate" in Hebrew).[39] In her new role, she delivered the March 1957 UN address whereby Israel agreed to evacuate the Sinai — making clear her expectation that UNEF would prevent *fedayeen* raids from the Gaza Strip and safeguard Israel's maritime rights in the Straits of Tiran.[40] Repeatedly upstaged by Ben-Gurion's creature, Shimon Peres (the director-general of defense), she found her tenure in the foreign office exasperating. In one aspect alone did she find satisfaction: her travels in Africa. As foreign minister, she crisscrossed the continent — freely offering Israel's aid and expertise on regional development projects. Informed during a visit to Rhodesia that the black African officials traveling with her would not be able to leave their bus to view the resplendent Victoria Falls, she announced that she would not view them either. No wonder that within a few short years, she was among the most beloved figures on the continent. By the end of her term, the number of Israeli embassies in Africa had skyrocketed from one to thirty.[41]

Despite her admiration for Ben-Gurion, she opposed his decision to accept reparations from West Germany in the 1950s. A decade later, she broke with him completely when the resurgent Lavon affair degenerated into a power struggle between Ben-Gurion's protégés and the Mapai "Old Guard" (of which she was a predominant member). After Ben-Gurion resigned in 1963, Golda stayed on as Levi Eshkol's foreign minister until 1965 when an unpublicized bout with lymphoma contributed to her decision to step down.

After a short retirement, she accepted the position of secretary-general of Mapai. From this influential post, she opposed Moshe Dayan's appointment as defense minister on the eve of the Six Day War. (In her view, the army was in good hands and could fight perfectly well without a Rafi member in charge of defense.[42]) When the IDF took Jerusalem, she visited the Wailing Wall and received a spontaneous hug from an emotionally overwhelmed soldier who apparently mistook her for a random elderly woman.[43] Continuing in her role as secretary-general after the cease-fire, she oversaw the merger of Mapai with two other parties (Rafi and Ahdut Avoda) to form Israel's new Labor Party in 1968. Shortly thereafter, she retired again — for good, as she thought — only to be called to the premiership eight months later.

On her first day in office, Meir declared that her government was "prepared to discuss peace with our neighbors, any day and on all matters."[44] Nasser replied with his trademark bellicosity, saying that "what was lost in war must be restored by war."[45] By month's end, his shelling of Israeli positions in the Suez Canal Zone had made a mockery of the 1967 cease-fire and had initiated the so-called War of Attrition (March 1969–August 1970). Israel responded by bombarding Ismailia, one of the Egyptian canal cities.

Three months into the fighting, Meir offered to fly to Egypt to negotiate a settlement. In reply, the Arab press ridiculed her as "behaving like a grandmother telling bedtime stories to her grandchildren...."[46] Nasser ignored her offer and stepped up his attacks. Israel retaliated with bombing raids so deep into Egypt that the explosions were audible in Cairo. As she later testified, Meir wanted to make it clear to the Egyptian people "that they couldn't have it both ways: war for us, and peace for themselves."[47]

Whether or not her approach was the right one, it would be fair to say that the international community was less than delighted with it. And what was worse, Israel didn't necessarily get the better of the fighting. Egypt obtained antiaircraft technology from Russia, and the toll on the Israeli Air Force was such that Israel had to obtain new planes from the United States.[48]

Meanwhile, Russian pilots had begun guarding Egyptian airspace to the rear of the Canal Zone. Hoping to steer clear of them, Israel confined her bombing runs to forward targets. Nevertheless, in July 1970, there were two altercations involving Israeli and Russian pilots. In the first, there were no casualties, but in the second, Israeli fighters shot down four MiGs and got away unscathed.[49]

Anxious to avoid any escalation in the conflict that might directly involve the superpowers, the Nixon administration proposed a cease-fire agreement that included a joint commitment by Egypt, Jordan, and Israel to press forward with UN Resolution 242. Nasser accepted the plan on July 23. At first, Golda was taken aback. She doubted Nasser's sincerity — believing that he would use the truce to improve his military position[50]—and she resented the U.S. decision to publish the proposal without providing advance notice to Israel (in violation of a prior U.S. pledge). The U.S., however, offered Israel some excellent incentives to follow the Egyptian lead: (i) the U.S. would continue to supply weapons to Israel despite the fact that the shooting had stopped; (ii) Israel would not have to remove any troops from occupied territories in the absence of a durable peace settlement; (iii) Israel would not be expected to solve the refugee problem in a way that would jeopardize her sovereignty; and (iv) the U.S. would exercise its veto power in the UN Security Council to protect Israel from being bullied into concessions.[51] After obtaining guarantees that Egypt would not take advantage of the cease-fire to smuggle antiaircraft missiles into the Canal Zone, Israel embraced these terms, and in August 1970 the War of Attrition came to an end. With stunning promptness, Nasser confirmed Golda's initial hesitations by advancing his missiles into the cease-fire area in direct violation of the agreement.[52] Matters might have deteriorated, but Nasser died of a heart attack the following month. His successor was Egyptian vice president Anwar Sadat.

Sadat was widely held to be a man of straw who would slavishly adhere to the Nasserist line. Indeed, while alive, Nasser had complained in exasperation that it would be less grating on his nerves if the vice president "would occasionally vary his way of expressing agreement instead of forever saying 'Yes, sir!'"[53] On assuming office, however, Sadat shattered expectations by purging the government of Nasser's cronies and embarking on his own course.

At about this time, Israeli defense minister Moshe Dayan was advocating the idea of an interim settlement with Egypt that would call upon the parties to withdraw militarily from the banks of the Suez Canal. A key source of Egyptian revenue, the canal had been closed since the Six Day War. With a comprehensive peace seemingly beyond attainment, Dayan had come to believe that an agreement calling upon both sides to retreat beyond artillery range of the canal might serve the dual purpose of reducing the chance of renewed hostilities, while allowing commercial traffic to resume in the Middle East's most important waterway.[54]

Sadat was anxious to have the canal open again. Deprived of Suez revenues, Egypt had become increasingly dependent on funding from her allies, thereby impeding her freedom of action. Hence, on February 4, 1971, Sadat addressed the Egyptian parliament, saying (according to his memoirs) "that if Israel withdrew her forces in Sinai to the Passes, I would be willing to reopen the Suez Canal; to have my forces cross to the East Bank; to extend the Rogers Plan cease-fire by six, rather than three, months ... and to sign a peace agreement with Israel...."[55]

This was not exactly what Dayan had envisioned. (For one thing, he could do without the Egyptian troops on the east bank of the canal.) Yet it might have been the basis for talks if the plan had not been derailed by a new United Nations initiative put forth by Gunnar Jarring, the UN's special representative to the Middle East. Jarring's proposal called upon Israel to withdraw to the June 4th armistice line on the Egyptian front in return for an Egyptian pledge of peace.[56]

Jarring's opinion was that the proposal should be accepted without amendment. But it had long been a clearly and publicly stated tenet of Israeli policy that border issues would have to be resolved by negotiation and that territorial exchange would require a formal peace treaty. Jarring's initiative called upon Israel to surrender 100 percent of its gains on the Egyptian front before the parties had even reached the negotiating table. Rather than "promoting agreement," as promised by UN Resolution 242, Jarring seemed to be imposing a settlement. After considering the matter, the Israeli cabinet answered that it welcomed Sadat's interest in peace and remained committed to the withdrawal clause of Resolution 242, but that the position of final borders would have to be negotiated.[57] Also included in the reply was a phrase favored by Meir spelling out that Israel *would not withdraw to the June 4th line*. In June 1967, the Eshkol government had been willing to do so, but in the interim, Egypt had waged an 18-month attrition war against Israel, inflicting 3,000 casualties (including 720 deaths), and Meir—who insisted on receiving the latest Israeli casualty reports immediately, even if she was sleeping[58]—presumably felt that rewarding such behavior would set a bad precedent. Abba Eban disagreed. With many years of distinguished service as a diplomat, he felt that the June 4th stipulation was superfluous. Israel was already saying that the border would have to be negotiated. By ruling out a full withdrawal before negotiations even began, Meir might provoke charges of Israeli intransigence when the cabinet was merely adhering to its longstanding position that decisions on borders had to be reached by negotiation, not by imposition. Despite these arguments, the phrase was retained.[59]

Jarring received Israel's answer as though it had been the Khartoum declaration in reverse. He ceased his initiative forthwith—an unwarranted response given that Israel had clearly expressed her willingness to negotiate. (Indeed, if anyone was refusing to budge from his position, it was Jarring himself.[60]) Moreover, it is enlightening to note that Jarring seemed untroubled by the amendments *Egypt* wanted to append to his proposal. Indeed, he seems to have agreed with them,[61] even though they were far more demanding. To be sure, Sadat was willing to talk peace, but he had a number of preconditions: Israel must agree *in advance* to (i) withdraw her forces from all occupied territories on all fronts; (ii) resolve the refugee issue "in accordance with United Nations resolutions" (as interpreted by Egypt); and (iii) accept demilitarized zones of equal size on both sides of the Egyptian-Israeli border.[62] Such max-imalist demands were not worthy of serious consideration — never mind acceptance. Nevertheless, just as Abba Eban had foreseen, many of Golda Meir's detractors, at home and abroad, sought to saddle her with responsibility for the failure of Jarring's mission.[63] Recalling these negotiations years later, Meir said, "'Intransigent' was to become my middle name."[64]

Unwilling to enter discussions wherein the issue had already been decided against her, Meir reconsidered Dayan's idea for an interim Israeli-Egyptian agreement. Dayan's plan called for a 30-kilometer withdrawal of forces by each party and the reopening of the canal to international shipping. But Meir and the majority of the cabinet insisted upon a lesser drawback — 10 kilometers — so that Israel could push back to the canal in an emergency. A disengagement of 10 kilometers, however, did not suit the purpose of Dayan's proposal: At 30 kilometers, the combatants would have been beyond each other's artillery range and the canal could be traversed with a sense of security. At 10 kilometers, the opposite would have been true, making it very unlikely that Egypt would accept. Eban, therefore, offered his support to Dayan if the latter would press for the greater withdrawal. Sadly, there was a history of antipathy between the two men, and rather than side with Eban against Meir, Dayan preferred not to pursue the matter (May 1971).[65]

The final nail in the coffin, however, was Sadat's response: he would approve a bilateral withdrawal from the canal in order to restore his Suez rev-enues, but only if Israel agreed in advance that it was a preliminary step in the fulfillment of all clauses of UN Resolution 242 (again as interpreted by Egypt — meaning withdrawal from "*all* occupied territories," etc.). Once again, Sadat was seeking maximalist commitments in the absence of face-to-face negotiations— something that Meir's cabinet would not abide.[66]

Thus, by the latter half of 1971, matters had reached an impasse. Golda Meir was unwilling to cede territory in the absence of negotiations. Sadat was not willing to negotiate unless Israel accepted his far-flung preconditions. In this setting, Israel felt confident that the existing cease-fire lines guaranteed her security and that the Arab states had no choice but to accept the present situation or come to the negotiating table. Nor did events in Egypt do any-thing to alter this estimate — for an unexpected twist in Egyptian foreign pol-icy was now to make the chance of war seem exceedingly unlikely.

The Soviet Union had been Egypt's chief arms supplier since the 1950s. As late as May 1971, there was no indication that this situation would change. Indeed, Sadat signed a new Soviet arms accord that very month and began speaking of 1971 as "a year of decision" in which the humiliating verdict of 1967 would be overturned.

But then, matters suddenly deteriorated: the Soviets failed to deliver much of the promised weaponry, and when Sadat questioned them on the matter, they would not be pinned down. Moreover, the Soviet "advisors" who had been stationed in Egypt during Nasser's tenure were conducting themselves as though Egypt was nothing more than a Soviet puppet state. Incensed by these developments, Sadat ordered the "advisors" to get out (July 1972).[67]

In the opinion of Henry Kissinger (U.S. president Richard M. Nixon's national security advisor), this was a grand opportunity — one that must not be missed. In Kissinger's view, Israel's insistence on direct negotiation was "as seemingly reasonable as it was unfulfillable," since in essence Israel was asking "for recognition as a precondition of negotiation."[68] On the other hand, there was no sense in pressuring Israel to moderate her approach while the Arab states clung to their pro–Soviet policy and maximalist demands. The best course was to weather the impasse until one or more Arab states broke with the Soviet Union and assumed a more reasonable demeanor. "*Then*," believed Kissinger, "would come the moment for a major American initiative, if necessary urging new approaches on our Israeli friends."[69]

It certainly appeared as if Kissinger's moment had arrived. By evicting his Soviet advisors, Sadat had apparently dismissed his chief arms supplier. An Egyptian offensive no longer seemed feasible.

But the truth was rather more complicated: the Soviet Union had consistently failed to supply Egypt with the very weapons — particularly missile-firing jets — that were required for an offensive war. In effect, the Soviets were controlling Egyptian policy by depriving her of the means to act. By dismissing them, Sadat had freed his hands to make his own decisions. While it might not have been clear to Kissinger — or to most Israelis — war was actually *more* likely with the Soviets gone.[70]

Convinced that diplomacy was Sadat's only option, Kissinger arranged a secret meeting with Egyptian national security advisor Hafez Ismail. Owing to America's preoccupation with the Vietnam War, the talks were delayed until February 1973. As soon as they opened, Ismail made it clear that Israel must accept a return to the pre–1967 lines "with some margin, perhaps, for adjustment on the West Bank" before any negotiations could take place. Moreover, Israel would have to agree to bilateral demilitarized zones on either side of the Israeli-Egyptian border. In return, Egypt would end her belligerency with Israel and guarantee Israel's right of passage in international waterways. But there would be no formal peace treaty until Israel had negotiated an agreement with Syria and the Palestinians. Thus, said Kissinger, "The price paid for the return to the prewar borders was not peace, but the end of belligerency, not easy to distinguish from the existing cease-fire."[71]

It was exceedingly unlikely that Israel would negotiate on these terms. Most Israelis regarded the post–Six Day War boundaries as unassailable.

When Golda Meir met with Nixon and Kissinger in Washington in March 1973, the Israeli premier gave voice to the prevailing sentiment, saying of her nation's security, "We never had it so good."[72] The bellwether of this "smug"[73] mindset seems to have been the immensely popular Moshe Dayan. One of the defense minister's favorite refrains from this period — "I prefer Sharm el-Sheikh without peace to peace without Sharm el-Sheikh"[74] — has an admittedly catchy ring to it (although it is difficult to regard it as original in light of Yigal Allon's antecedent, "We prefer secure borders that are not agreed to, to agreed borders which are not secure.")[75] In addition to his duties as defense minister, Dayan was responsible for the administration of the occupied territories, and in this realm, his ideas — particularly regarding the West Bank — tended increasingly toward annexation: "I do believe Israel should stay for ever and ever and ever and ever in the West Bank," he declared in a BBC interview, "because this is Judaea and Samaria. This is our homeland."[76] In Abba Eban's view, this vision was "dark with false images."[77] But in the short term, there was a much bigger problem: Dayan's preoccupation with governing the territories (and the aura of overconfidence that he had done so much to create) was distracting him from his primary role of keeping the nation in a state of readiness.[78]

Meanwhile, in an April 1973 *Newsweek* interview, Anwar Sadat had made some choice remarks of his own, saying, "For the first time, we see total and complete agreement between the U.S. and Israel on Middle Eastern Policy.... I want a final peace agreement with Israel. But there was no response from the U.S. or Israel — except to supply Israel with more Phantoms [i.e., fighter jets].... Everything in this country [i.e., Egypt] is now being mobilized in earnest for the resumption of the battle — which is now inevitable."[79]

Out of someone else's mouth, such words might have provoked alarm. But coming from Sadat, they had all too familiar a ring. In May 1972, he had pronounced war "inevitable," and as nearly as anyone could tell, he had not meant it. Nor had he fulfilled his pledge to make 1971 the "year of decision."

Sadat's next move came in May, when he mobilized the Egyptian army. At great expense, Israel did the same. When nothing came of it, the government was assailed for "overreacting" to a dubious threat.[80] It was an article of faith in the Israeli intelligence community that Egypt could not launch an attack unless she obtained a bomber fleet with which to cast a blow at the IAF's airfields, and that Syria would not attack unless Egypt did.[81] Thus, at the end of September, when the Egyptian and Syrian armies began massing troops on their respective borders with Israel, the Israelis concluded that it was another bluff and did not follow suit.[82]

But in the intervening months, a number of changes had taken place: In June, Sadat finalized plans with Syria for a joint attack on Israel. In August, he obtained a promise from the Saudis that they would impose an oil embargo on the West if his proposed military action against Israel proved unsuccessful. In September, Jordan's King Hussein agreed to keep troops near the Israeli border (as a decoy) in hopes of inducing Israel to do the same.[83] And in the midst of these developments, the Soviet Union renewed arms shipments to Egypt on a mammoth scale in an evident attempt to salvage her regional influence. Included in these deliveries were "SCUD" ground-to-ground missiles capable of reaching targets within Israel (thereby making Israel think twice about deep air strikes into Egypt), and enough new "SAM" surface-to-air missiles to provide the Egyptian army with protection against air attack.[84]

These warning signs were either missed or misinterpreted. The result was disaster. The first reports of Arab troop concentrations came during the last week of September. On September 26, King Hussein (who did not want war) secretly flew to Tel Aviv to warn Golda Meir that, in his view, Syria and Egypt were preparing to attack. The general consensus was that he was wrong.[85] On October 3, Meir's military advisors assured her that there was nothing to fear, but by now she was complaining privately that "there's a contradiction between the signs on the ground and what the experts are saying."[86] On October 4, it was learned that the Soviets were evacuating their advisors' families from Egypt and Syria. On October 6, 1973 — Yom Kippur, the holiest day on the Jewish calendar — Egypt and Syria launched a combined surprise attack against Israel. Made aware of the impending strike at 4:00 A.M. that morning, Defense Minister Moshe Dayan and Chief of Staff David Elazar sparred over the proper course of action. Fearful that a full mobilization would lend the false impression that Israel was the aggressor, Dayan argued that only those reserves essential for defense should be activated.[87] Elazar did not think this was sufficient. He wanted a "full" mobilization and a preemptive air strike — the best chance, he said, of saving Israeli lives. Golda Meir decided between them — authorizing Elazar's mobilization plan, but rejecting the preemptive strike. Israel could not afford to alienate world opinion, lest the state find itself at war with no arms supplier. "I would like to say yes because I know what it would mean," Golda told Elazar, "but with a heavy heart I am going to say no."[88]

At 2:00 P.M., air raid sirens blared in Jerusalem for the first time since June 1967.[89] In the opening minute of the onslaught, more than 10,000 Egyptian shells slammed into the Bar-Lev Line on the east bank of the Suez Canal, where a grand total of 436 inexperienced IDF reservists were guarding a 110-mile front.[90] Alarmed citizens tuning into their radios heard nothing at first. The broadcasting stations were closed for Yom Kippur. At 2:30, there was a terse bulletin informing the public that the "sirens are not a false alarm." By late afternoon, it was known that Egypt and Syria had attacked, and that the

Egyptians were across the canal.[91] At 6:00 P.M., Golda spoke to the nation, saying, "I have no doubt that no one will give in to panic.... We must be prepared for any burden and sacrifice demanded for the defense of our very existence." Three hours later, Moshe Dayan delivered a television address. To one foreign observer, he sounded confident, but didn't look it.[92]

Simultaneous with the Egyptian attack, Syrian heli-troopers captured the Israeli radar station on Mount Hermon from which they could see, in full panorama, the undermanned condition of the Golan Heights. Eight hundred Syrian tanks now swept onto the plateau, where a mere 177 Israeli tanks awaited them — most of these being stationed far to the rear.[93] After viewing the combat zones, a dejected Moshe Dayan advised a withdrawal on both fronts. When Golda asked him what to do if the UN called for a cease-fire, Dayan said to accept. When he departed, Golda burst into tears, believing (momentarily) that she was about to preside over the demise of Israel.[94]

On October 8, the IDF counterattacked in the Sinai only to have its armor stopped cold by infantry-borne, armor-piercing antitank missiles (called "Saggers"), which blasted shrapnel in all directions upon penetrating the target.[95] Similarly, the IAF sustained heavy losses at the hands of Egypt's new antiaircraft technology.

Unable to make headway on the Egyptian front, Golda accepted Elazar's advice and opted for a holding action in Sinai while concentrating the army's resources against Syria (where the fighting was much closer to Israel's population centers).[96] The ensuing attack, on October 9, brought the first good news of the war. By the 10th, the IDF had recovered the entire Golan Heights. Elazar wanted to press on into Syria. Dayan counseled against it, saying that it might provoke Soviet intervention. Golda sided with Elazar, and on October 11, the IDF entered Syrian territory. The Soviets responded with a massive airlift of weaponry to the Arab combatants.[97]

Meanwhile, Israel had lost so much military hardware in the first six days of fighting that she could not continue the offensive without obtaining replacements of her own. At one point, Golda called Simcha Dinitz (Israel's ambassador to the U.S.) at 3:00 A.M. Washington time and told him to press Henry Kissinger for new supplies as soon as they got off the phone. When Dinitz protested that he could not wake Kissinger at that hour of the night, Golda shot back that Kissinger could sleep as long as he liked when the war was over.[98] By October 12, the arms shortage was so menacing that Golda announced Israel's willingness to accept a cease-fire on the existing lines. Had Sadat agreed, the war would have ended as a tactical victory for Egypt. But calculating that he could achieve more, he rejected the offer.[99]

There is a heated debate as to whether Secretary of State Kissinger was really working in Israel's interest to this point in the war or whether he was seeking his own Machiavellian ends.[100] Whatever the truth, the Soviet weapons airlift and Sadat's rejection of Israel's cease-fire offer placed him squarely in Israel's camp. Believing that it would be nothing short of "geopolitical disaster" to allow Soviet weaponry to inflict a defeat upon Israel, he assured Abba Eban that there would be no cease-fire until the attackers withdrew to their start lines. Meanwhile, declaring that "Israel must be saved," President Nixon ordered an airlift to counter that begun by the Soviets. The Pentagon was inclined to restrict this operation to three of the U.S.'s massive C5 "galaxy" supply planes, citing concerns that robust assistance would trigger an Arab oil embargo. Nixon rejected this suggestion, saying, "We have twenty-five; send them all at once — everything that can fly. As for the Arabs, I'll have to pay the same political price for three as for twenty-five."[101]

Kissinger now worked frenetically to get the planes in the air. By October 13, they were on their way; but unlike the Russian transports, which could fly nonstop from bases in southern Russia, Yugoslavia and Hungary, the American "galaxies" had to refuel en route. Of the nations of Europe, Portugal alone allowed them to do so. America's other NATO allies refused, thinking thus to avert an Arab oil embargo (which was subsequently imposed upon them anyway).[102]

The next day (October 14), over the protests of his chief of staff, Anwar Sadat moved Egypt's reserve tank divisions across the canal and launched a new offensive toward the Mitla and Gidi passes in an effort to lessen the stress on Syria. But unlike Egypt's initial onslaught, this one took place beyond the range of her surface-to-air missiles. Consequently, the Israeli Air Force enjoyed much greater freedom of action. For Egypt, the result was catastrophic. In a single day of fighting, she lost more than 250 tanks while Israel lost less than a dozen.[103] The next day, Ariel Sharon pushed through a gap in the Egyptian lines in a bold attempt to cross the canal and cut off the Egyptian Third Army in the southern Sinai. While widening the gap into a viable artery, his attack force took heavy casualties, and it was not until the 18th that it got across in strength. But, with few enemy tanks left on that side of the canal to intervene, the Israelis swept north and south along the western bank, knocking out the Egyptian SAMs so that the Israeli Air Force could assist with further operations.

In a panic, Sadat asked the Soviets to press for a cease-fire. Accordingly, Soviet Communist Party chairman Leonid Brezhnev invited Henry Kissinger to Moscow to discuss terms. The resulting agreement was to become UN Resolution 338, which called for the parties to cease hostilities and to *negotiate* a durable and lasting peace on the basis of UN Resolution 242. Hoping to stall for time while Israel consolidated her gains, Kissinger told Brezhnev that he would take the proposal back to Washington for approval. Much to his discomfiture, Brezhnev produced a message from President Nixon saying that the secretary of state possessed full powers to conclude an agreement on the spot. Kissinger had not been aware of this communication, but had no choice but to shrug his shoulders and complete the negotiation.[104]

As on previous occasions, Golda Meir resented the idea of an imposed settlement, particularly when Israel was on the verge of a decisive victory. But Abba Eban pointed out that the proposal committed the parties to negotiation, thereby constituting a clear diplomatic triumph for Israel.[105] The cabinet subsequently agreed to a cease-fire effective at 6:00 P.M. on October 22. But by this time, Israel had so nearly encircled the Third Army that Egypt violated the agreement six hours after it took effect in an effort to reestablish a supply line.[106] Israel struck back with a fury, driving southward to the Gulf of Suez to complete the Third Army's encirclement. At this, the USSR accused Israel of violating the cease-fire and informed Washington that, if necessary, it would intervene directly to force the Israelis back to the cease-fire line. In order to stay the Soviet hand, Nixon placed the U.S. armed forces on DEFCON 3 alert status. At the same time, however, Kissinger told the Israelis that this was as far as the U.S. would go. If Israel destroyed the Egyptian Third Army and the Soviets intervened as a consequence, Israel would be on her own.[107] Israel acquiesced, and at 4:00 A.M. on October 26 the war came to an end.

Hardly had the fighting stopped before the recriminations began. Israel had suffered 5,500 casualties — 2,552 of them deaths. Soldiers returning from the front blamed it all on military unpreparedness. Although Golda and the cabinet won a solid victory in the ensuing elections (December 1973), growing public clamor for an inquiry had already led to the formation of an investigatory commission headed by Shimon Agranat, president of the Israeli Supreme Court. While the commission listened to testimony and deliberated, disgruntled Israelis protested in the streets, howling for Moshe Dayan's ouster. Dayan offered to resign. Golda refused to let him. The Agranat Commission had not issued its findings, she said. Moreover, there were still Israeli soldiers in Arab hands, and the armies had not yet worked out a disengagement agreement.[108] When Dayan announced that he would not serve when Golda's new cabinet took office, she made her own service contingent upon his. Under pressure from the party, he agreed to stay on (March 1974).[109]

On April 2, the Agranat Commission announced its preliminary findings, exonerating Golda and Dayan on the grounds that they had been given misleading intelligence. Golda, in fact, was said to have "decided wisely ... in favor of ... full mobilization [i.e., on Yom Kippur morning] ... despite weighty political considerations, thereby performing a most important service for the defense of the state."[110] Chief of Staff David Elazar, who had advised that mobilization, fared far less well. The commission castigated him for failing to consider the possibility of a surprise attack in deploying his forces prior to the war. Elazar, who had steadied the ship almost single-handedly during the early panicked days of the war, promptly resigned. Golda thought that if Dayan had resigned, too, as a show of support for Elazar, he might have saved his own reputation. But when Dayan came to ask her advice, she didn't offer any.[111] Instead, seeing the public's displeasure with the commission's verdict, she decided to step down herself. She announced her decision on April 10, and left office on June 4 (just after the separation of forces agreements ending the Yom Kippur War were completed).

Golda was to live just four more years—time enough to publish her memoirs and act as Israel's elder stateswoman. Despite her grandmotherly persona, she had been a no-nonsense politician. Her detractors have criticized her for this—describing her as a harsh, and sometimes inconsiderate, taskmaster. She could be exceedingly difficult to please: when Abba Eban reported to her that Henry Kissinger had been able to fulfill "only" 10 of 11 requests made to him by Israel, Golda answered in dismay, "Why has Henry betrayed us?"[112] She was also a grudge-holder of Olympian proportions: in 1967, when Shimon Peres tried to tell her that David Ben-Gurion had always admired her, she scoffed and reeled off a list of Ben-Gurion's transgressions against her—some dating back to 1948.[113] Technically speaking, any or all of these factors are fair game in judging Golda. But to dwell on them as many of her detractors have done seems discriminatory when male politicians are not held to the same standard.

At the other end of the spectrum, Golda found it humorous that she was regarded in feminist circles as something of an icon owing to her political success. When, at a New York bookstore, she found a poster-size image of herself being sworn in as Israel's prime minister with the corresponding inscription "but can she type?" (a commentary on the era's male chauvinism), she quipped to those around her that indeed she could not.[114] Her career had not been aimed at striking a blow for feminism, but at pursuing her ideals.

Of all the indictments hurled against Meir, the most unjust is the ongoing attempt by her critics to saddle her with responsibility for the Yom Kippur War. The accusation first rose to prominence in the aftermath of Anwar Sadat's historic visit to Israel in November 1977. (Golda was among the Israeli dignitaries present to greet him on the Ben-Gurion Airport tarmac on that occasion.) As the peace talks progressed, it was alleged that Golda, by her intransigence, had squandered the chance to pursue similar negotiations between 1971 and 1973.[115] The charge is patently untrue. To suggest that Sadat was willing to negotiate his way to peace in those years is to misread his intentions. In his 1978 autobiography, the Egyptian leader declared that on his accession to the presidency in late 1970, "the key to everything ... was to wipe out the disgrace and humiliation that followed from the 1967 defeat. I reckoned it would be 1,000 times more honorable for us— 40,000 of my sons in the armed forces and myself— to be buried crossing the Canal than to accept such disgrace and humiliation. Posterity would say we had died honorably on the battlefield ... and posterity would carry on the struggle."[116]

Long after the war, Sadat confessed to Henry Kissinger that the restoration of Egyptian honor remained his primary purpose right up to the outbreak of the fighting, and that he had no enthusiasm for a peaceful settlement. In Kissinger's words, "If I had been able in mid–1973 to guarantee [Sadat] the 1967 borders without his having to make peace, he would have accepted it — *though with reluctance, as he later told me,* since it would have done little for Egyptian pride."[117]

Sadat did not want peace in the years prior to 1973. He wanted war to wipe out the perceived "stain" of 1967. In contrast, Golda *did* want peace. But she was not willing to let Israel's enemies impose terms upon her. Territorial disputes would have to be resolved by direct negotiation between the parties, and Israel would only withdraw to new boundaries when a durable peace agreement had been drawn up and signed. For her insistence on this dignified approach, she has been castigated as "intransigent." But if this is our starting point, one wonders what the appropriate term might be for the authors of the Khartoum declaration or for a leader who refuses to "negotiate" until every one of his maximalist demands has been met. In any case, the point is moot: even if Golda had been willing to jettison her principles (and Israel's security) by handing back every inch of occupied territory without so much as asking for a peace accord, Sadat would only have accepted "with reluctance" — not a very reassuring trade-off, and certainly not one that Israel could safely endorse. (In 1987, Sadat's wife, Jehan, confirmed that the Egyptian leader wanted war, saying, "I do not agree ... that Sadat tried to achieve a real peace before 1973. [He] needed one more war in order to win and enter into negotiations from a position of equality."[118])

Much aggrieved by the charges leveled against her, Golda began gathering documents to show that she had been willing to negotiate, while Sadat had imposed prohibitive preconditions. But in October 1978, her lymphoma resurfaced with metastases to her bones and liver. She spent her last two months in the hospital, jaundiced and in pain, before expiring on December 8 at the age of 80. On the morning of her funeral, 100,000 admirers filed past her casket to pay their respects. She was laid to rest on Mount Herzl on December 12, 1978, in a funeral attended by notables from around the world.

7

Menachem Begin and Camp David

The Yom Kippur War was the most traumatic event Israel had yet been through. Apart from exacting a heavy toll in casualties, the conflict had shattered the nation's confidence. Despite the treachery of the Arab attack, Israel received virtually no sympathy from the world community. Panicked by the oil embargo imposed during the last week of fighting, the nations of Europe, Africa and Asia adopted a pro–Arab line. Although the U.S. remained friendly, it had its own agenda for the postwar Middle East — namely, the exclusion of the Soviet Union. Toward this end, it would be necessary to mollify the Arabs, not the Israelis — a feat that could best be achieved by demonstrating that the United States alone had clout with Israel, and that if the Arabs wanted to recover lost territory, only the United States could deliver it.[1]

Hence, even though Israel had won the war, she was called upon to cede territory on both fronts. By terms of the so-called First Sinai Accord, signed in January 1974, Egypt came away with a foothold five kilometers wide on the east bank of the Suez Canal. Her troop strength in the recovered territory was limited to 7,500 men and 32 tanks — levels that constituted "virtual demilitarization" since they were too few for offensive action.[2] Further east, the Israelis established a belt of equal width with equivalent troop levels — the combatants being separated by a UN-monitored buffer zone. Finally, Egypt agreed to mitigate the chance of renewed warfare by reopening the Suez Canal and restoring civilian life to the adjacent cities.[3]

Negotiations with Syria took much longer. The agreement, signed on May 31, 1974, involved Israel's cession of the ruins of Kunietra at the eastern end of the Golan Heights. Unlike Egypt, Syria concealed the names of captured Israelis until an accord was reached, leaving the families of Israel's MIAs in agonized suspense to the bitter end. Eventually, 65 half-starved Israeli soldiers returned home. The Red Cross determined that 53 others had died — 42 of them having been cut down in cold blood at the time of capture.[4] Three days after the accord was signed, Golda Meir yielded the prime minister's

Israeli Prime Minister Menachem Begin (facing camera) is greeted by Nobel Prize Committee Chairman Aasse Lionaes at Akershus Castle in Oslo, Norway, on the occasion of his 1978 Nobel Peace Prize, December 10, 1978 (courtesy of the State of Israel Government Press Office; photographer Moshe Milner).

post to former chief of staff Yitzhak Rabin, who had narrowly outpolled his primary rival, Shimon Peres, in an intraparty ballot.

Many Israelis resented having concessions imposed upon them when they had won the war, but in the view of Abba Eban, Israel gained far more than she lost. A vast reduction in Soviet influence and a redoubling of U.S. goodwill were advantages of no mean significance. Additionally, Israel was finally able to demobilize her citizen army and resume a normal national life. In light of these benefits, Eban reserved high praise for U.S. secretary of state Henry Kissinger who had shuttled back and forth between Israel, Egypt and Syria to negotiate the respective agreements.[5]

An opposing interpretation, however, was put forward by the former diplomat Conor Cruise O'Brien, who accused Kissinger of choreographing an elaborate charade: according to this version, Kissinger's "shuttle diplomacy" was pure stagecraft, employed to create the illusion that he alone could affect progress in the negotiations. When the Israeli-Egyptian disengagement showed signs of succeeding without him, Kissinger allegedly hastened to the scene to apply the brakes. All Israeli concessions had to have the appearance of resulting from his relentless pressure on an "intransigent" ally. The result was that Israel was forced to vacate hard-won territory so that (i) Egypt and Syria could boast, in a most irritating way, that they had won a war in which they had been defeated (adding that their "victory" would have been total had it not been for the American airlift); and (ii) the U.S. could reestablish official discourse with Cairo and Damascus (severed since 1967), thereby undermining the regional stature of the Soviet Union.[6] In sum, others had reaped where Israel had sown.

Regardless of the merits of these arguments, Israel's surrender of land had done nothing to render her enemies more tractable in the quest for peace. At an Arab summit in Rabat (October 1974), the Arab combatants declared the Palestine Liberation Organization to be the "sole legitimate representative" of the Palestinian people. Any negotiation with, or recognition of, Israel was now to be contingent upon Israel reaching a satisfactory settlement with a terrorist organization whose founding covenant called for Israel's destruction.[7] The following month, the UN General Assembly endorsed this decision by allowing PLO chairman, Yasser Arafat, to address its session.

In the meantime, Henry Kissinger was pushing for a second interim accord between Israel and Egypt as part of a "step-by-step" process toward peace. Having been repaid poorly for her previous concessions, Israel demurred. In response, U.S. president Gerald R. Ford announced that the U.S. would have to "reassess" its Middle East policy. (While it did so, it ceased weapons deliveries to Israel.[8]) Kissinger, meanwhile, made a public show of seeking advice from various foreign policy specialists— Robert McNamara, Dean Rusk, Cyrus Vance and others— all of whom favored a "comprehensive" approach to peace, including the participation of the PLO.[9] Faced with this alternative to Kissinger's "gradualism," Israel toed the line. In September 1975, Prime Minister Rabin signed the "Sinai II" accord, which mandated an Israeli pullback beyond the Sinai passes in return for $2 billion in American aid and assurances that the U.S. would not recognize the PLO unless it accepted UN Resolution 242 and acknowledged Israel's right to exist. (Noticeably absent was any tangible concession on the part of Egypt.[10]) Two months later, the UN General Assembly passed a resolution condemning Zionism as "racism" by a vote of 72–35.

None of this redounded to the benefit of Israel's ruling Labor Party, which was beset simultaneously by domestic crises. The costs of the war, compounded by a postwar regional arms race, drove Israel's inflation rate to 40 percent.[11] Additionally, there was a lack of consensus on the fate of the territories. In June 1974, a fundamentalist religious faction, *Gush Emunim* or "Bloc of the Faithful," established an unauthorized settlement at Sebastia, near the

Arab town of Nablus in the West Bank. Hitherto, Jewish settlements in the occupied territories had been established on the basis of security needs and had been located away from Arab population centers. Likewise — with the notable exception of Kiryat Arba, outside Hebron — they had been government sanctioned. But Gush Emunim declared that the redemption of *Eretz Israel* (literally, the "land of Israel") was biblically ordained, giving them the right to settle anywhere they wished.[12] Prime Minister Rabin promptly vowed to evict the group and close the settlement, but his own defense minister, Shimon Peres, opposed him, as did a fair percentage of the population. After months of acrimonious debate, a controversial compromise (December 1975) left the settlers in place at Elon Moreh, a few kilometers from their original site, with the result that similar settlements were to spring up later throughout the West Bank.[13]

In December of the following year, the arrival of three F-15 fighter jets from the United States sparked a new crisis. Normally, the procurement of state-of-the-art fighters would have been cause for celebration in Israel. Unfortunately, the jets in question arrived late on a Friday afternoon, and the military ceremony arranged to welcome them extended past sundown, thereby violating the Sabbath. The upshot was an ugly "no confidence" vote in the Knesset that in turn led to a break between the Labor Party and its ally, the National Religious Party — meaning that Rabin's government no longer enjoyed a parliamentary majority. To sort it all out, new elections were set for May 17, 1977. Before they could take place, however, financial scandal supervened, resulting in the suicide of one prominent Labor official and the imprisonment of two others on corruption charges.

With so much domestic turmoil, Rabin opted for a change of venue — traveling to the United States for talks with new U.S. president, Jimmy Carter. The results could not have been less satisfying. Carter positively shocked Rabin by calling publicly for Israel's withdrawal to the pre–Six Day War borders (apart from mutually acceptable "minor modifications"). Furthermore, he announced his support for the establishment of a "Palestinian homeland" — the first time an American president had ever said such a thing. At almost the same moment, the story broke in Israel that Rabin's wife possessed two illegal bank accounts in the United States totaling $23,000. The accounts dated to her husband's tenure as ambassador to Washington. By law, they ought to have been closed when the couple returned to Israel. Rabin compounded the problem by falsely contending that there was only one account with a paltry $2,000 in it. When the truth came out, he attempted to resign (April 7, 1977). Thwarted by a legal technicality, he settled for a leave of absence. Shimon Peres replaced him as head of the party.[14]

In spite of these travails, it was an accepted "fact" that the Labor Party would win the upcoming election just as it (or its predecessor, Mapai) had won all the preceding ones. Consequently, it came as a great shock when Israel's premier news anchorman, Haim Yavin, announced to a disbelieving national television audience that the man who had lost the nation's previous eight elections was being forecast as the winner of this one by a comfortable margin. At that moment, the man in question, former Irgun leader, Menachem Begin, was trying to enjoy a quiet cup of tea.[15] For the rest of the night, his apartment at 1 Rosenbaum Street in Tel Aviv was anything but quiet. When he emerged from the building at 1:00 A.M., the entire neighborhood was teeming with reporters, well-wishers and security police. Taken by car to Independence Hall on King George Street, he addressed a crowd of the party faithful with a quote from Abraham Lincoln: "With malice towards none; with charity for all; with firmness in the right ... let us strive on to finish the work we are in; to bind up the nation's wounds...."[16]

Menachem Begin was born in Brest-Litovsk in the Russian Pale of Settlement on August 16, 1913. At the end of World War I, the city had been given over to Polish sovereignty, but as far as the Jews were concerned, this was no great improvement. Subjected to anti–Semitism from his earliest schooldays, Begin resolved to meet the challenge head-on. When one of his teachers threatened to fail him if he did not take a Latin exam on the Sabbath (when observant Jews must refrain from writing), he ignored the mockery of his non–Jewish classmates and stuck to his religious principles.[17]

In the first foreshadowing of his future as an orator, he stood atop a picnic table at age nine and delivered an address honoring Simon Bar Kochba who led the last Jewish revolt against Rome (A.D. 135).[18] In spite of his smallish stature, he never shrank from fisticuffs against anti–Semitic bullies, and he encouraged his Jewish schoolmates to emulate his example.[19] At 15, he joined *Betar*, a Zionist youth organization named for the fortress where Bar Kochba perished.[20] Founded by Ze'ev (Vladimir) Jabotinsky (1880–1940), who preached a self-assured and assertive form of Zionism, Betar issued uniforms to its members and trained them in the use of weapons for self-defense. Traditional labor Zionists denounced such methods as "fascist," but in Poland, Betar's membership grew to the tens of thousands; and owing to its activism, violence against Jewish youths decreased sharply.[21]

The heart and soul of the movement was Jabotinsky himself. Born in the Black Sea port of Odessa in 1880, he became the driving force behind the establishment of the Jewish Legion in World War I. After the war, he founded and briefly commanded the Haganah. For the crime of attempting (unsuccessfully) to bring this force to the defense of Jewish civilians during the 1920 Nebi Musa riots in Jerusalem, he was sentenced to 15 years' hard labor by the anti–Zionist British military regime then ruling Palestine. (The same sentence was meted out to an Arab convicted of raping two Jewish women during the pogrom.[22]) When the military regime was replaced by the Mandate, Jabotinsky was pardoned along with Haj Amin al-Husseini, the virulent anti–Semite who had incited the riots. The Arab rapist was likewise pardoned. Refusing to be amnestied alongside violent criminals when his own actions had been defensive, Jabotinsky demanded that the whole proceeding against him be expunged from the record (a request that was afterwards granted).[23] On regaining his freedom, he served briefly on the executive committee of the World Zionist Organization, but finding the mainstream Zionist approach too docile, he resigned. Shortly thereafter, he founded Betar (1923) and the League of Zionist-Revisionists (1925).

Jabotinsky's program, known as "Revisionist Zionism," called for the establishment of the Jewish national home on both sides of the Jordan River encompassing all of the original Mandate territory, including Transjordan. In order to create a Jewish majority, Jews were to immigrate without restriction, on a scale of at least 40,000 per year for 25 years. Based on his experience in the Arab riots of 1920–21 (in which Arab policemen joined the rioters and the British military did nothing to protect the victims), Jabotinsky concluded that the only way to safeguard Jewish lives was to place the Jews in charge of their own defense. An armed Jewish Legion would, therefore, be reconstituted to perform this service. Finally, Jabotinsky had no desire to dispossess the Arab populace: he thought it natural that the local Arabs should prefer that Palestine be added to the list of Arab states. But the Arab people already possessed territories stretching from the Near East to furthest North Africa, encompassing 200 times the land mass of Palestine, while the Jewish people were dispersed, persecuted and living in danger. Hence, when juxtaposed, the competing claims were "like the claims of appetite versus the claims of starvation."[24]

Given that the establishment of the Jewish national home was the Mandate's *raison d'être* and that his own territorial views seemed to conform to Articles 5–6 of the Mandate charter,[25] Jabotinsky hoped he could convince Britain to support his maximalist blueprint. The British answered his hopes by banishing him from Palestine forever (1930). Angered by his exile, the supporters he left behind in Palestine became increasingly radicalized. In their view, the 1917 Balfour Declaration had been framed with noble intentions, but had been implemented by self-seeking opportunists. According to the text of the document, Palestine was not to be given to the Jews as a national home — the Jews were to be given a national home *in Palestine*. But what did this mean? To Balfour, it meant that the Jews would have self-determination in their historic homeland. To the cynical implementers, however, it meant that the British would have a convenient pretext for continuing their dominance in the region of the Suez Canal. Toward this end, they desired that only a modest number of Jews should immigrate to the national home—never enough to gain a majority, but enough to claim minority rights and to require British protection from the Arabs for an indefinite period. British rule in the form of the Mandate would thus be legitimized in perpetuity.[26]

The Mandate, then, was not a potential partner in state building, but an obstacle to be removed so that the lofty purpose of the Balfour Declaration—i.e., the establishment of a true Jewish national home—could be brought to fruition along revisionist lines. In the ensuing years, this philosophy gave birth to the *Irgun Z'vai Leumi* ("National Military Organization," also known as the IZL or *Etzel*) and its offshoot, *Lehi* (the Stern Gang)—organizations that revered Jabotinsky's person but adhered to their own recipe for Jewish independence, which did not exclude the use of terrorism (a tactic that Jabotinsky abhorred).

The exiled Jabotinsky, meanwhile, was making waves of his own. When the WZO refused to adopt a hard line against the Mandate at the 1931 congress, he leaped atop his chair and shredded his membership card in front of the entire assembly.[27] In 1935, he formed the rival NZO or "New Zionist Organization." The election of delegates to its first congress (held in Vienna that same year) garnered 713,000 votes—78,000 more than were cast for the delegates of the 1935 World Zionist Congress in Lucerne.[28]

From its inception, the NZO was torn by internal strife. As the 1930s wore on, the Irgun leadership in Palestine attempted to spread its philosophy of armed revolt amongst the Betar youth groups in Europe. Jabotinsky insisted that a militarist program could not succeed. Even if joined by the whole of Betar, the Irgun would still be no match for the British Empire. Immigration (the "illegal" form of which he hoped to make the "national sport" of Palestine[29]) and steady political pressure were the only viable weapons in the NZO arsenal.

While all this transpired, Menachem Begin slowly ascended through the ranks of Betar in Poland, assisted by a flair for oratory and an austere dedication to the revisionist mission. Sent to Prague to spread the doctrine, he willingly slept on a park bench while subsisting on a single daily meal.[30] Above all, he stood in awe of Jabotinsky. Only once did he challenge his mentor: At the Third Betar Conference in Warsaw (1938), he came out in favor of militant Zionism—not an immediate rebellion as favored by the Irgun, but an acknowledgement that military action would ultimately be necessary. In reply, Jabotinsky issued a stern rebuke, likening Begin's suggestion to the useless squeaking of a door hinge.[31] A year later, however, Jabotinsky elevated his loyal protégé to the office of high commissioner of Betar in Poland.

In his new role, Begin led a demonstration in Warsaw against Britain's

1939 white paper. Apprehended for casting stones at the British embassy, he spent three weeks in jail.[32] On reemerging, he married Aliza Arnold. (Jabotinsky traveled from Paris to Drohobycz, Poland, to attend the ceremony in which the happy couple substituted Betar uniforms for the traditional tuxedo and wedding gown.[33]) When the Nazis invaded Poland three months later, Begin's associates offered him passports to take his wife to Palestine. But Begin refused, hoping instead to form a Jewish legion to fight the invaders. Turned away by the Polish army, he escaped to Vilna, Lithuania, with the intention of assisting Jews who had fled from the Nazis. Scarcely had he arrived, however, when Soviet troops occupied the Baltic states and declared Zionist activities illegal. Lithuanian agents intruded upon Begin while he was playing chess. Conceding the game to his friend, he offered the agents tea, donned his best suit and accompanied them to Lukishki Prison.[34]

At Lukishki, Begin's interrogator worked night and day to wrest a confession from him. Begin defended himself with impeccable logic, even quoting paragraph 129 of Stalin's Soviet Constitution to prove that he had been arrested illegally when he ought to have been offered asylum. (The clause in question promises sanctuary to any foreigner who is persecuted while striving for national liberation.[35]) The interrogator bombarded him with accusations. Begin calmly pointed out the flaws in his reasoning. The interrogator resorted to sleep deprivation—forcing Begin to stare at a point on the wall for hours on end. But when the breaking point was finally reached, it was the interrogator who crumpled. Driven to distraction by Begin's tenacity, he drew up a confession that Begin was proud to sign. It read simply: "I acknowledge that I was high commissioner of Betar in Poland." When Begin appended his signature, the exasperated interrogator told him to get out of his sight forever.[36]

Begin's "confession" served as a one-way ticket to eight years' hard labor in a Siberian prison camp that was located so far to the north that the sun was shining at 2:00 A.M. when his train pulled in. For a period of months, backbreaking work, starvation and lice were the main staples of his existence.[37] Then, suddenly, he was set free. Hitler had invaded Russia (June 1941), and the Polish government in exile had signed an alliance with Stalin providing for the liberation of all Polish prisoners.

Begin enlisted in the Polish army in exile, which was mobilized, fortuitously enough, to the Middle East. In May 1942, his unit arrived in Palestine. By this time, Jabotinsky had met a natural death (1940), while David Raziel (leader of the Irgun) and Raziel's erstwhile comrade, Avraham Stern (founder of what became the Stern Gang or Lehi), had met unnatural ones: In response to the 1939 white paper, the Irgun had begun a bombing campaign against the Mandate's government offices. But the outbreak of World War II brought an immediate halt to these acts. The Irgun agreed to cooperate with the British in the fight against the Nazis, and Raziel was killed while carrying out an espionage operation for the British in Iraq.[38] Stern, who remained an implacable enemy of Britain, naïvely sought an alliance with the Nazis in order to overthrow the Mandate. After a career of terrorism, he was cornered in one of his hideouts, where a British intelligence officer discovered him in a closet and shot him dead even though he was unarmed (1942).[39] For two years, the Irgun languished. But in 1943, Begin finagled his release from the Polish army and offered his services to the organization. With his rise to leadership, the Jewish Revolt began in earnest (1944).

Owing to its methods, the Irgun is commonly dismissed as an extremist organization. But from Begin's perspective, a far heftier indictment can be leveled at the British. By passing the 1939 white paper, Britain had abandoned the fundamental purpose of the Mandate (i.e., the establishment of the Jewish national home), thus terminating the legal basis of its rule. By keeping the gates of Palestine closed while six million Jews (Begin's parents and older brother among them) perished in the Holocaust, Britain plummeted into the moral abyss: "One cannot say that those who shaped British Middle East policy at that time did not want to save the Jews," says Begin in his memoir of the period, entitled *The Revolt.* "It would be more correct to say that they very eagerly wanted the Jews not to be saved. The average Englishman was probably as indifferent to Jewish lives as any other non–Jew in the world. But those who ruled Palestine and the Middle east were not in the least 'indifferent.' They were highly interested in achieving the maximum reduction in the number of Jews liable to seek to enter the land of Israel.... The aim was to maintain the British government's control over Eretz Israel with a number of 'protected Jews' in the midst of an Arab sea, whose waves would be ruled by the traditional rulers of the waves."[40]

What Britain ultimately intended by its Palestine policy may be open to debate. What seems irrefutable, however, is that when it came to a choice between saving their reputation with the Arabs and saving Jewish lives, the British authorities unhesitatingly chose the former. Perceiving this, the Irgun declared that "a national war of liberation is a just war,"[41] and unleashed a wave of bombing attacks against the Mandate beginning in February 1944. Their first strike demolished three immigration offices, obliterating a fair share of the Mandate's files on fugitive illegal immigrants.[42] For the duration of the war, the Mandate's police fortresses and supply lines were the main objectives, but afterwards, the Anglo-Iraq oil pipeline and British military installations were targeted as well.[43] Begin left the tactical planning to others. He excelled as an inspirational leader, not as a military man.[44] Fired by his rhetoric, Irgun fighters cast a "barrel" bomb into the British "security zone" in Haifa. They raided the airfields at Lydda and Kastina, blowing up 30 British planes (including a number of 4-engine Halifax bombers). In the guise of British paratroopers, they drove into Sarafand (the main British billet in Palestine), loaded their truck with weapons from the barracks armory, and fought their way back out. They repeated the trick at the Ramat Gan police fortress, this time dressed as Arab prisoners under "British" military escort.[45]

Denounced as terrorists, the Irgunists retorted that their actions had greater legality than those of the Mandatory government. Captured fighters defiantly maintained that British military courts were not fit to try them since an illegitimate regime cannot confer legitimacy upon its judiciary. Those condemned to the gallows replied to their verdicts by singing the *Hatikvah* (the Hebrew anthem celebrating the hoped-for return of the Jewish people to Eretz Israel). When the British sentenced two Jewish youths to be flogged for illegal possession of arms, the Irgun posted broadsheets declaring that equal treatment would be meted out to British officers. The first youth was flogged on December 27, 1946. Two days later, the Irgun applied the same number of lashes to a captured British major and three NCOs. The second Jewish youth was reprieved, and the episode received worldwide attention.[46]

In the eyes of the Mandate, Begin was public enemy number one. Alas for British intelligence, the photograph it possessed didn't look a thing like him, and several unfortunates were hauled in for questioning because they resembled the image in the picture more than Begin did himself.[47] Although the Irgun called itself an "underground" organization, its members did not necessarily stay out of view. Most lived "normal" lives within the community, protecting themselves not by carrying concealed weapons and hiding in the shadows, but with well-ordered identity papers, replete with aliases and mundane employment information.[48]

Begin enjoyed no such luxury, but he had an advantage that many Irgunists lacked: Since he was new to Palestine, the British had never laid eyes on him. (Nor for that matter had most of his own followers.[49]) The British conjectured that he had employed plastic surgery to alter his appearance, but they were wrong — he was merely incognito. For a time, he posed as "Israel Halperin," a Polish immigrant studying to take the Palestine Law Boards — a charade made all the more convincing by the open law books strewn conspicuously about his home near Petah Tikvah. When a credulous member of the community came to him for legal advice during this period, Begin obliged him at no charge.[50] Later, as "Israel Sassover" in Tel Aviv, he sported a very orthodox-looking beard (which made him a great favorite at the local synagogue) and inherited a dog, named Roxy, who had an inconvenient habit of barking at British policemen. Finally, he became the tubercular Dr. Yonah Koenigshoffer, whom no one, including the police, had any interest in questioning. Through it all, his confused son, Benny, had no clue as to what he actually did for a living, which is probably just as well since Begin once overheard the boy telling a playmate that his favorite underground organization was Lehi (i.e., the Stern Gang).[51]

For the most part, the Jewish Agency and Haganah viewed the Irgun with hostility. When the Stern Gang murdered Lord Moyne in 1944, David Ben-Gurion declared open season upon those who refused to abstain from terrorist activities. Ironically, the Stern Gang complied with the ban and got off scot-free, while the Irgun, which had not been involved in the murder, became the Haganah's prime target. Despite the ruthlessness of the crackdown, there was no civil war: Begin refused to let his men fight back against fellow Jews.[52]

When Britain continued to enforce the white paper restrictions on Jewish immigration at the end of World War II, Ben-Gurion abandoned the open season, and directed the Haganah to join hands with the Irgun and the Stern Gang in an anti–British assault force known as the "Hebrew Resistance Movement." But the excessive casualties inflicted by the Irgun in the July 1946 King David Hotel bombing (see chapter 3) brought an end to this collaboration, and the manhunt for Begin became so intense that he had to hide in a secret compartment in the ceiling of his home for nearly four days without food or water while British troops searched the neighborhood.[53]

Despite the collapse of the Hebrew Resistance Movement, the Irgun continued its attacks. Indeed, Begin would have us believe that the group drove the British out of Palestine single-handedly. In February 1947, British foreign minister Ernest Bevin announced Britain's intention to refer the matter of Palestine to the UN, but added that preliminary talks would not be held until September. The Irgun responded to this delay tactic by carrying out a flurry of attacks over a two-day period (March 1–2, 1947)—the most galling of which was the bombing of the British Officer's Club in Jerusalem. Bevin subsequently advanced the talks to April 28, but in the interim, the British authorities sought to demonstrate that they were still in control of the situation by hanging four captured Irgunists in the Acre fortress-prison (April 17). In reprisal, the Irgun broke into the self-same prison on May 4—freeing 251 prisoners (among them a number of their own companions). Three Irgunists were captured in the attack. The British hanged them on July 29, despite the protests of UNSCOP (which was then in Palestine looking into the question of partition) and despite warnings from the Irgun that the hangings would be repaid in kind. The following day, the Irgun hanged two captured British sergeants and booby-trapped the execution site. There was no shortage of outrage in Britain over this cold act, but the main public outcry was for the immediate evacuation of British forces from Palestine. On September 12, the British government declared that, barring a UN solution agreeable to both Jews and Arabs, it would indeed withdraw its troops. Eight months later (May 1948), the Mandate came to an end. "The revolt," Begin concludes, "was victorious."[54]

While it would be folly to discount the effect of the revolt, it was not the lone consideration in the British decision to depart. Most authorities cite a host of factors. These have been covered elsewhere (see chapter 3), along with an account of the Irgun's controversial role in Israel's War of Independence, including the attack on Deir Yassin and the sinking of the Irgun ship, *Altalena*. (The latter episode put an end to the Irgun's existence as an independent fighting force. The only alternative was a Jewish civil war — a course that Begin categorically rejected in a tearful radio address on the night of the sinking.[55])

After the war, Begin founded a new political party — *Herut* or "Freedom" (which was also the name of the Irgun's defunct underground newspaper). The party's platform promoted minority rights, nationalized healthcare and the right to work and education — the eminent reasonability of which was somewhat overmatched by the party's primary demand: continuation of the fight until the Jewish state encompassed both banks of the Jordan in accordance with Jabotinsky's old revisionist map.[56] In Israel's first election, the party gained 14 seats in the 120-seat Knesset against Mapai's 46 — enough to qualify as the main opposition on the right. As Begin walked towards the Knesset on the first day of the session, many in the crowd lining the streets shouted, "Begin! Begin!" In some places, the police had to restrain them as they pressed forward to catch a glimpse of him.[57]

Inside the Knesset building, it was a different story. David Ben-Gurion scorned Begin and his new party. Rather than utter Begin's name when addressing the assembly, Ben-Gurion referred to him as "that man sitting next to Knesset Member Bader." Additionally, he refused to acknowledge former Irgun or Lehi fighters as legitimate soldiers, thereby denying them veterans' benefits.[58] In his less dignified moments, Begin returned the favor with inflammatory histrionics. The best example occurred in 1952, when he led the opposition to Ben-Gurion's 1952 reparations deal with West Germany. Addressing 15,000 opponents of the measure (many of them Holocaust survivors) in Jerusalem's Zion Square on the day of the Knesset vote (January 7, 1952), Begin likened the agreement to the acceptance of "blood money." In this opinion, he was certainly not alone. But then, brandishing a scrap of paper, he told the crowd: "I have not come to inflame you, but this note has just been handed to me. It says that the police have grenades that contain gas made in Germany, the same gas used to kill your fathers and mothers."[59] The result of these words was that the crowd gathered up rocks and hurled them at the Knesset building. (The measure passed nonetheless.)

In the lead-up to the 1956 Sinai Campaign, it was Begin's Herut Party that first explored the possibility of obtaining weapons from France. Likewise, Begin anticipated Ben-Gurion and Mapai in calling for a preventive campaign against Egypt.[60] His prescience, however, did him little good at the polls, where Herut continued to lose one election after another. Consequently, in 1965, Begin forged a merger between Herut and Israel's Liberal Party. The new alliance, *Gahal*, obtained 26 seats in the ensuing elections—a respectable number, but a defeat nonetheless. Sick of losing, some of the Herut rank and file challenged Begin's leadership.[61] Although this made for an unruly party convention (June 1966), Begin weathered the storm.

One year later, in the crisis preceding the Six Day War, Begin cast party politics aside and called for the formation of a national unity government under his old nemesis, David Ben-Gurion. Prime Minister Eshkol refused the suggestion, saying that he and Ben-Gurion were a pair of horses who could no longer haul the same wagon.[62] Yet Begin's notion of a unity government did come to fruition with the appointment of Moshe Dayan as defense minister and Begin himself as minister without portfolio. On the first day of the war, he was sworn in as a cabinet member in Jerusalem to the sound of Jordanian mortars.[63] Listening to BBC radio before dawn on the war's third day, he was startled to hear that the UN Security Council intended to impose an early cease-fire. He immediately informed Levi Eshkol of the report, thereby precipitating the decision to capture Jerusalem's Old City before outside pressures forced a halt to the fighting.[64]

In essence, the Six Day War fulfilled Herut's old territorial aspirations, minus Transjordan (which Herut no longer claimed). In Begin's view, security and historical-religious considerations now made territorial compromise unthinkable, particularly with regard to the West Bank — the historic Judea and Samaria — which Begin, and a growing number of Israelis, viewed as an integral part of Eretz Israel.[65] After serving in the unity government for three years, Begin resigned over this very issue when the cabinet voted to accept the U.S.-sponsored Rogers cease-fire proposal (August 1970). Rogers' proposal, which ended the 1969–70 War of Attrition, called upon Israel to negotiate with Egypt *and Jordan* in pursuance of the "withdrawal from occupied territories" clause of UN Resolution 242. (The inclusion of Jordan implied that Israel was expected to negotiate the return of all or part of the West Bank.[66])

Relegated once more to the opposition, Begin played a major part in the international "Let My People Go" campaign, which placed worldwide pressure on the Soviet Union to allow Jews to emigrate from Russia.[67] At the same time, he continued to broaden the base of his party. On the eve of the Yom Kippur War, he found himself at the head of a new coalition consisting of

Herut, the Liberal Party, the Land of Israel Movement, the State List (consisting of ex–Rafi members), and the Free Center Party (an offshoot of Herut). The new party, called *Likud* ("Unity") was the brainchild of the popular war hero Ariel Sharon, an ambitious newcomer to politics who wanted to unite the parties of the right and center in order to mount a real challenge to the rule of the Labor Party.[68] Bolstered by growing unrest over Labor's perceived mishandling of the Yom Kippur War, Likud garnered 39 Knesset seats in the December 1973 elections. It appeared, however, that the new coalition had reached its zenith. Sharon did not like his role as an opposition member of the Knesset, and accepted the post of security advisor to Prime Minister Rabin.

Begin, meanwhile retained the chairmanship of the Likud, and decided to make one last electoral run. His 1977 campaign got off to a shaky start when he suffered a heart attack that landed him in the hospital for several weeks. Ezer Weizman, a former air force chief of staff, ran the campaign — downplaying Begin's hawkish political views while stressing his honesty, integrity and austere way of life. (The contrast with the Labor Party and its corruption scandals was difficult to miss.) Two days before the election, Begin took part in a televised debate with Shimon Peres, thereby dispelling concerns about his health.[69] Brimming with confidence, he campaigned right through Election Day.

No one thought he would win.

When the results were tabulated, Likud had 43 seats — an increase of 4 seats over the 1973 election. But Labor declined by an astounding 19 seats, dropping from 51 to 32. A new party, the Democratic Movement for Change, headed by famed archaeologist and former IDF chief of staff Yigael Yadin, tallied 15 seats, mainly from voters who desired an alternative to Labor but had no desire to vote for Likud.[70] The other key factor had been the Sephardic vote. The *Sephardim* — Jews from Arab countries, comprising nearly half the electorate — continued to lag behind their European (*Ashkenazi*) counterparts in educational and professional advancement despite a generation under Labor's tutelage. Tired of feeling like outsiders, they voted for Begin — the perennial outsider — by a heavy margin.[71] Thus, for the first time in its history, Israel had a non–Labor, non–Mapai prime minister.

In order to obtain the necessary 61 seats for a Knesset majority, Begin invited three smaller parties, including the National Religious Party and Ariel Sharon's new *Shlomzion* ("Peace for Zion") Party to join the Likud government. He then recruited Moshe Dayan as foreign minister — a move that provoked cries of protest from Dayan's detractors at home but enhanced the new government's stature abroad.

Begin's top priority on assuming office was to respond to President

Carter's "comprehensive" approach to peace, in which the latter called for a near-total withdrawal from the territories obtained in 1967 and the creation of a Palestinian homeland. On a visit to the U.S. in July, Begin all but ruled out the latter — driving the point home by sanctioning three new West Bank settlements soon after returning to Israel. Denouncing such settlement projects as "illegal, unilateral acts,"[72] Carter called for a new Geneva Conference — to include Russian (and Palestinian) participation. His intended message was that if Israel didn't like *his* approach, she could see what the Russians had to offer. When Moshe Dayan traveled to the U.S. to discuss the matter, he was given a dressing down by Vice President Walter Mondale, which he received in stony silence. Much to the administration's chagrin, however, the conference idea aroused a bipartisan outcry among U.S. political leaders — some being avid supporters of Israel, others being aghast that the Soviets were being invited to resume their pernicious influence in the Middle East after Henry Kissinger had taken such pains to debar them.[73]

Nor did the plan appeal to Egyptian president Anwar Sadat. He had embarked on the Yom Kippur War in order to restore Egyptian "honor" after the devastating defeat of 1967. A corollary of this motivation was his desire to show Israel that continued occupation of the Sinai was not a guarantee of security. Having achieved his object, Sadat was ready to pursue the next phase: regaining what Nasser had lost — the Sinai. For this purpose, Carter's stance was a positive roadblock. Sadat had no desire for further dealings with the Soviets, and the stipulation that an agreement must await Palestinian approval could delay recovery of the Sinai until the end of time.[74]

To get back on course, Sadat appeared before the Egyptian parliament and pronounced his willingness to go to the Knesset itself in the pursuit of peace. At first, many Israelis were skeptical, but within days, Begin had extended an invitation to the Egyptian leader, and the latter had accepted. On debarking from his plane at Ben-Gurion Airport on November 19, 1977, Sadat was greeted by a who's who of Israeli dignitaries. Later, throngs of Israelis, waving Egyptian flags, cheered him in the streets of Jerusalem. On November 20, after praying at the al-Aqsa mosque and visiting Israel's Yad Vashem Holocaust Memorial, Sadat addressed the Knesset, essentially verifying Carter's position that in return for peace Israel must withdraw to the 1967 borders and pursue an acceptable solution for the Palestinians. Many in the assembly grimaced at these words, but Begin knew that the truth lay between the lines. If Sadat didn't have something more flexible in mind, he would not have come. Thus, in his reply, Begin made no bones about Sadat's speech (which had drawn enthusiastic applause), concentrating instead on the Egyptian leader's courage in making his historic visit.[75]

As we shall see, Sadat was indeed willing to be flexible — but only within limits: when Begin proposed a formula for Egyptian sovereignty in the Sinai that would allow Israel to retain her settlements and airbases there until the year 2000, Sadat was outraged. Was it for this that he had placed his reputation on the line?[76] In response, he dug in his heels. When Begin arrived in Egypt for further discussions amidst a total absence of fanfare (December 25, 1977), Sadat reiterated his demands for Palestinian self-determination and an Israeli withdrawal to the pre–Six Day War borders.

The talks subsequently languished for nine months before President Carter took a diplomatic gamble and invited both sides to continue their negotiations at the presidential retreat in Camp David, Maryland. It was presumed that the wooded setting would provide a relaxed and serene atmosphere. To get into the spirit, Begin sat down to a game of chess with Carter's national security advisor, Zbigniew Brzezinski. As the latter prepared for his first move, Begin grasped his arm and told him in dramatic tones that he had last played chess at the time of his arrest in Vilna in 1939. Brzezinski reacted with proper solemnity until Begin's wife, Aliza, happened by and said that Menachem simply loved the game and played at every opportunity.[77]

The Camp David talks lasted for 13 exhausting days (September 3–17, 1978). On day three, a stormy confrontation nearly cut them short, with Sadat laying out a variation of the maximalist demands he had made in Jerusalem, and Begin protesting that they sounded like terms dictated by a victor to the vanquished. Thereafter, the two men refused to sit in the same room. Indeed, the only member of the Israeli delegation whom Sadat trusted was the defense minister, Ezer Weizman, whom he referred to, mistakenly, as "Ezra."[78]

Despite such obstacles, the talks culminated in two separate accords. Of these, one comprised a framework for peace between Israel and Egypt encompassing a total Israeli withdrawal from the Sinai — settlements and airbases included.[79] Begin had refused these conditions until the eleventh hour. Only when the U.S. promised to erect two state-of-the-art airbases in the Negev to compensate for those left behind in the Sinai did Begin reluctantly acquiesce.[80]

When the matter was put to the Knesset, many of Begin's staunchest adherents withheld their support, arguing that the commitment to vacate settlements in the Sinai augured ill for settlements elsewhere.[81] Likewise, many Israelis resented the fact that, apart from surrendering territory, Israel was to incur much of the treaty's economic burden: in addition to the estimated $3.8 billion it would cost to relocate civilian settlements and airfields to the Negev (only a fraction of which was to be covered by U.S. grants— the rest being financed through low-interest loans), billions of dollars worth of infrastructure was to be abandoned.[82] Nevertheless, on September 27, 1978, the Knesset approved the accord by a vote of 84–19 with 17 abstentions. Two months later, Begin and Sadat received the 1978 Nobel Peace Prize. By then, however, the agreement was in jeopardy: after leaving Camp David, both sides had attempted to interject new conditions, and it required a desperate round of shuttle diplomacy by Carter before Begin and Sadat finally put their signatures to a formal peace treaty.[83]

The signing ceremony took place on the White House lawn on March 26, 1979. It was accompanied by a demonstrative three-way handshake between the signatories: Sadat, Carter and Begin. In his speech to the assembled dignitaries, Begin declared that the time had come "to proclaim to our peoples, and to others: no more war, no more bloodshed, no more bereavement — peace unto you, Shalom, Salaam —forever."[84] A week later, he attended a state dinner in Cairo and toured the Giza pyramids, which he had always wanted to see. ("After all," he was quoted as saying, "our ancestors built them."[85])

It is fitting to leave our discussion of Menachem Begin's life at this, the moment of his greatest achievement. The rest of his tenure, which lasted until August 1983, is the story of his effort to solve the Palestinian issue in a manner that would leave the West Bank and Gaza under Israeli sovereignty. Toward this end, he became embroiled in a war against the PLO in Lebanon — allowing himself to be drawn ever further into a military quagmire in pursuit of illusory political ends. The details of this struggle are best left to the next chapter, where they can be placed in the historical context of the Israeli-Palestinian conflict. Suffice it to say here that the war's disappointment and tragedy, combined with the untimely death of his beloved wife and confidante, Aliza, ultimately broke Begin's will. He withdrew from the public eye and began to exhibit overt signs of clinical depression. A close friend who saw him at this time after a prolonged absence described him as "an exhausted, ill, aged man," who "had lost much weight ... and seemed despondent."[86]

On August 28, 1983, Begin informed his cabinet that he was unable to continue in office. For the next nine years, he lived in retirement. It is frequently said that he was a recluse during this period, but this is not strictly true. After several months of seclusion, he initiated an enjoyable tradition of having his friends over on Saturday evenings. He spent part of each morning answering letters from well-wishers, and on his birthday each year surviving comrades from Betar and the Irgun gathered in his home to sing old battle songs. His days as a public figure, however, were at an end. He never ventured from his apartment (except to attend Aliza's annual memorial service), made no political speeches and left no memoirs. He died after a major heart attack on March 9, 1992, and was buried that same day on the Mount of Olives in Jerusalem's Old City. Seventy-five thousand mourners were in attendance.[87]

Perhaps he did not realize that history would remember him for his great triumph rather than for the tribulations of his second term. Among those who delivered eulogies at his funeral were Jimmy Carter, George H. W. Bush, Yitzhak Rabin and Jehan Sadat[88]— all of whom lavished praise on him for his role as a peacemaker. As of this writing, the peace between Israel and Egypt has held firm. True, a comprehensive regional solution remains elusive, but neither has there been another general war.

The Camp David Accords opened avenues hitherto forbidden in the Arab-Israeli conflict. In the intervening years, Israel has made peace with Jordan, and has carried out face-to-face negotiations with Syrian, Lebanese and Palestinian interlocutors.

None of it would have been possible were it not for the fateful plunge taken by the alleged warmonger Begin and the visionary Sadat in 1979.

8

Yitzhak Rabin and Oslo

On June 27, 1976, Palestinian and German terrorists hijacked a civilian airliner en route from Athens to Paris. After stopping in Libya to refuel, the airliner proceeded to Entebbe Airport in Uganda, where the plane's non–Jewish hostages were set free — purportedly at the behest of Uganda's bloodthirsty president, Idi Amin, who was masquerading as "mediator" for the crisis. Aided and abetted by Amin, the terrorists issued an ultimatum: either 53 incarcerated "freedom fighters" (40 in Israel, 8 in Europe, 5 in Kenya[1]) must be released or the flight's Jewish hostages would be killed. After a weeklong standoff, it appeared that the involved governments must acquiesce. Unbeknownst to the Europeans and Kenyans, however (and, indeed, to much of the Israeli cabinet), another solution to the impasse had already been set in motion.

Acting, in part, on information obtained from released hostages, the Israeli military built a mock-up of the Entebbe air terminal in the Sinai desert and trained an elite force of IDF commandos for a daring rescue operation. When the planning was complete, Defense Minister Shimon Peres found Moshe Dayan in a local restaurant and asked his opinion. Dayan pronounced it "a beauty of a plan!"[2] By the time the matter was put to a vote in the cabinet, the rescue forces were already airborne. Israel's prime minister, Yitzhak Rabin, had approved the takeoff on his own authority. If the cabinet overruled him, he would abort the mission. The cabinet voted in favor. Taken into the prime minister's confidence, opposition leader Menachem Begin ardently approved, saying, "This is not a matter for debate.... We support the government's position, and we'll make our views known."[3]

Seven hours later, in the dead of night, the first of four IDF Hercules transport planes landed on the Entebbe runway, 2,600 miles away. Avoiding radar detection by tailgating a scheduled British freight plane, the Hercules taxied away from the lighted runway and offloaded three vehicles identical to those used by Idi Amin and his retinue. Each vehicle carried Israeli paratroopers.[4] Led by this vanguard, the commando force stormed the terminal,

Yitzhak Rabin (left) receives a visit from former U.S. ambassador to the UN Daniel Patrick Moynihan on July 5, 1976 — one day after Israel's successful Entebbe rescue operation (courtesy of the State of Israel Government Press Office; photographer Yaacov Saar).

gunned down the terrorists and their Ugandan accomplices, destroyed the Ugandan air force on the ground and got away with only four casualties— three hostages who had been hit by stray fire, and Lieutenant Colonel Yonatan Netanyahu, a Harvard scholar, and one of the IDF's bravest sons.[5] (Another hostage, Dora Bloch, had been taken, acutely ill, to a Ugandan hospital prior to the raid. She was never heard from again.) After refueling in Nairobi with the permission of Kenyan president Jomo Kenyatta,[6] the planes returned safely to Israel. The next morning, July 4, 1976, America's bicentennial, the world awoke and marveled at Israel's brave blow against international terrorism. The raid was the crowning achievement of Yitzhak Rabin's first term as prime minister, and went far to restore Israeli pride following the Yom Kippur War.[7]

Terrorism against Israeli civilians was nothing new. It had been ongoing since the time of Israel's independence. Egyptian president Gamal Abdel Nasser had sponsored it in the form of *fedayeen* raids during the 1950s. In 1964, the Palestine Liberation Organization was established with the avowed purpose of eradicating Israel from the map of the Middle East. Terror was its weapon, and following the catastrophic Arab defeat in the Six Day War, the

Arab states found in the PLO a convenient tool for striking at Israel without the risk of another direct military confrontation. Massively funded by the Arab oil-producing states, the organization carried out terrorist attacks on civilian targets, both in Israel and internationally, while the Arab states disavowed any responsibility for them. The international operations, frequently staged in western Europe, had the dual advantage of being beyond reach of Israeli security, and of undermining support for Israel among the involved states, which above all desired immunity to such incidents.[8]

Until 1968, the PLO was comprised of several fractious groups, the most formidable being Yasser Arafat's Fatah, which staged its first assault on January 1, 1965 — botching a sabotage operation against Israel's water supply.[9] In March of 1968, during a retaliatory strike against Fatah in Jordan, the IDF clashed with Jordanian troops as well as Fatah guerrillas. By the time its mission was complete, 21 IDF soldiers had been killed. Although Fatah had been defeated and he himself had taken to his heels, Arafat portrayed the clash as his own great victory.[10]

Subsequently, Fatah had no trouble finding recruits. Languishing in refugee camps sponsored by the United Nations Relief and Works Agency (UNRWA), whose perpetual funding allowed the Palestinians to become the first refugee population in world history to pass down their refugee status from generation to generation,[11] young Palestinians flocked to Arafat's standard. By June 1968, Fatah controlled half the seats in the PLO's Palestine National Council. The PLO charter was amended to state that "Armed struggle is the only way to liberate Palestine," that "claims of historical or religious ties of Jews with Palestine are incompatible with the facts of history," and that "the Arab Palestinian people ... reject all solutions which are substitutes for the total liberation of Palestine...."[12] The last stipulation meant that neither Jordanian rule nor the establishment of a Palestinian state in the West Bank and Gaza were acceptable. The only remedy was Israel's obliteration.[13] In February 1969, Arafat was elected PLO chairman.

Until 1970, the organization's headquarters was in Jordan, where its lawless activities threatened the security of the Hashemite monarchy. Operating from impenetrable, self-ruled enclaves, the PLO terrorized native Jordanians and clashed repeatedly with government troops. (In one case, they decapitated a soldier and used his head as a soccer ball.) King Hussein attempted to negotiate, but Arafat broke every agreement.[14] Finally, after the PLO hijacked three commercial airliners and blew them up on Jordanian soil, the king put his foot down. During what the PLO called "Black September" (September 1970), Hussein attacked PLO bases throughout the country, killing thousands of fighters and civilians, and forcing 150,000 others to depart Jordan for Syria.[15] Syria intervened in the conflict on behalf of the PLO, but the Jordanian army stood its ground, and when IAF jets appeared in the skies above Syria's tank formations, the latter withdrew.

Since the Syrian government's support fell short of actually playing host to the PLO's destabilizing activities, the Palestinian fugitives and their families were shuttled directly from Syria into neighboring Lebanon. Lebanon had no desire to take them, but had no means of resisting the combined pressure of the entire Arab world, which employed economic boycotts in order to force her hand. Welcome nowhere else, the PLO and its minions poured into Lebanon — 50,000 settling in West Beirut, while 100,000 others established themselves in the south along the Israeli border.[16] The PLO immediately used its new positions to stage raids into Israel. The Lebanese government sought to intervene, but chastised by the other Arab states, it was unable to do so. Consequently, in 1973, it signed the so-called Melkhart Agreement, granting the PLO a virtual "state within a state."[17]

While establishing its infrastructure in Lebanon, the PLO focused on international terrorism. The most notorious of its actions was the 1972 Munich Massacre, in which PLO terrorists, calling themselves "Black September," infiltrated the quarters of the Israeli Olympic Team during the Munich Olympic Games, killing two and taking nine others hostage. After a prolonged standoff, watched on television by the entire world, all nine athletes and five terrorists were killed in a badly mishandled rescue attempt by German police at Munich Airport. Three terrorists were taken alive, but were later set free in exchange for the release of a hijacked German airliner.[18] They were transported to safe haven in Algeria, where the international press shamelessly clamored for interviews.

Far from marginalizing the PLO, such acts won it recognition as the "sole legitimate representative" of the Palestinian people at the 1974 Arab Summit in Rabat. The following month, Arafat appeared before the UN General Assembly wearing a holster and gave a speech that, in Abba Eban's words, "would have disgraced a patient in a psychiatric clinic."[19] In the same year, the PLO issued its infamous "phased plan" for the establishment of a "Palestinian authority" in the West Bank and Gaza, which would then serve as a base for the destruction of Israel and the return of the 1948 refugees to their homes throughout "Palestine."[20]

By now the Palestinian "state within a state" was well established in Lebanon, thereby cementing the collapse of that nation's stability. At the time of its independence in 1943, Lebanon had a Christian majority. By 1974, the demographics had changed — in part owing to the arrival of 240,000 Palestinian refugees after Israel's 1948 War of Independence. The PLO influx of 1970 greatly exacerbated the difficulties of this demographic metamorphosis. Until now, Muslim pressure for a greater role in government had consisted largely of nonviolent political agitation. But the PLO ingratiated themselves with the native Muslim population and convinced them that violence could achieve very much more.[21] On April 13, 1975, unidentified assailants drove past a church in a Christian neighborhood of Beirut and unleashed a hail of bullets in the general direction of Pierre Gemayel, the head of one of the country's most influential Christian families. Moments later, a bus filled with PLO fighters firing their guns in the air drove through the same neighborhood. Christian militia opened fire on the bus, killing its occupants. In the ensuing days, the neighborhood became a war zone with significant loss of life and property. Deciding to take the battle to the enemy's turf, Christian forces attacked a nearby PLO refugee camp, killing hundreds—many of them civilians. In retribution, the PLO and its native Muslim allies attacked the Christian town of Damour, slaughtering 10,000 inhabitants and expelling the 30,000 who survived.[22]

So began the Lebanese Civil War of 1975–76, which resulted in over 300,000 casualties—a quarter of them deaths. Syria, which hoped one day to swallow Lebanon whole, and which had no interest in seeing it become a militarized PLO bastion that could defy Syrian will, intervened in the contest to separate the combatants, with the result that Lebanon was transformed into a patchwork of armed fiefdoms. The PLO was left in virtual control of the coastline from Beirut southwards through Sidon and Tyre, as well as most of the inland territory between the Litani River and the Israeli border.[23]

With the matter settled, the PLO returned to its primary purpose: murdering Israeli civilians—or as the PLO and its fellow travelers liked to call it, "freedom fighting." Between 1971 and 1982, 250 Israeli civilians were murdered and 1,628 others maimed.[24] Two examples will set the tone: The first occurred in May 1974, when terrorists from the PLO splinter group "DFLP" (Democratic Front for the Liberation of Palestine), stormed into a school in Ma'alot and took 90 Israeli schoolchildren hostage. In the ensuing IDF rescue attempt, the terrorists opened fire on the children, killing 22 and wounding many more. The second attack came on March 11, 1978. While peace talks were ongoing between Egypt and Israel, 11 PLO terrorists debarked from rubber dinghies on the Israeli shore south of Haifa. Gunning down a female nature photographer, they hijacked a civilian bus and forced the driver to make for Tel Aviv while they shot at passenger cars from the bus windows. Halted by an Israeli roadblock, the terrorists employed bullets and grenades against the innocent hostages. Thirty-five Israelis (all but two of them civilians) were killed, and seventy-one wounded. Nine of the eleven terrorists were killed. Interrogation of the two survivors confirmed that they were members of the PLO. Accordingly, on March 14, the IDF crossed into southern Lebanon.[25] Within five days, they reached the Litani River, destroying the

PLO's military infrastructure en route, although most of the PLO fighters were able to withdraw northwards in civilian guise.

As per protocol, journalists worldwide condemned "Operation Litani" as a "disproportionate Israeli response." Why so angry over 35 dead and 71 wounded? Subjected to international pressure, the Begin government agreed to withdraw its troops from Lebanon in favor of a special UN force — "UNIFIL" — which was given a mandate to prevent further terrorist incursions. As soon as the Israelis left, however, PLO fighters infiltrated the UNIFIL zone and set up shop in a region known as the "Iron Triangle." After suffering a dozen or so casualties, UNIFIL abandoned its mandate and agreed to steer clear of the PLO positions. If, by chance, PLO fighters wound up in UNIFIL custody, UNIFIL undertook to turn them over to PLO officials in Tyre (who invariably let them go). A particularly outrageous result of this policy was that PLO terrorists were able to carry out raids into Israel, flee back to Lebanon with IDF troops on their heels, and then surrender to UNIFIL, which would give them immunity and safe passage to Tyre. (Sixty-nine such raids were launched between June and December 1980.[26]) Meanwhile, the local Lebanese population suffered ill treatment at the hands of brutal PLO interlopers, who appropriated houses, cars and other property for their own use.[27]

Largely insulated from these events since 1967 were the Palestinians of the West Bank and Gaza. In 1980, their fate was not bound up with the operations of the PLO, but with the terms of the Camp David Accords. Besides providing for peace between Israel and Egypt, the Camp David Accords had produced a framework for "autonomy" for those Arabs who had come under Israeli rule by virtue of the Six Day War. According to the agreement, the West Bank and Gaza were to enter a transitional period of up to five years, heralded by the election of a "self-governing [i.e., Palestinian] authority," the dismantling of the Israeli military regime and the withdrawal of Israeli troops to predetermined security zones. The maintenance of civil order would devolve upon a local police force bolstered by joint Israeli-Jordanian military patrols. At the end of the transitional period, a committee of Palestinians, Egyptians, Jordanians and Israelis would determine the final status of the territories.

As Abba Eban has noted, if all of this had come to fruition, the chance that a committee with a 3 to 1 Arab majority would have voted for perpetual Israeli sovereignty was infinitesimally remote. Outside Egypt, however, the Arab world held the Camp David Accords in contempt. Jordan and the PLO flatly repudiated them, prompting Eban to repeat a refrain he had employed frequently over the years, to wit, "the Palestinians have never lost a chance of missing an opportunity."[28] (Arafat's telling response to the Camp David offer was "this is a lousy deal. We want Palestine. We're not interested in bits of Palestine."[29] Toward this end, he vowed "to fuel ... the revolution with rivers of blood until the whole of the occupied land is liberated ... not just part of it."[30])

At first glance, it may seem startling that a hard-liner like Menachem Begin would have accepted the Camp David agreement on Palestinian autonomy. Indeed, when the Israeli-Egyptian peace negotiations began in November 1977, it was generally held that Begin intended to be generous in pursuing peace with Egypt so that he could *avoid* concessions in the West Bank and Gaza. If this is an accurate appraisal, the text of the accord cannot be counted a success.[31] Nonetheless, irrespective of anything that he might have signed, Begin never ceased to view the West Bank and Gaza as inalienable components of Eretz Israel. In his lexicon, the proper name for the West Bank was "Judea and Samaria," and these historic lands had not been "occupied," but "liberated." Capitalizing on the ambiguous wording of the Camp David agreement, he set about making Palestinian "autonomy" conform to his own conception — replete with unrestricted Jewish settlement and Israeli jurisdiction over defense, water supplies and public land. The "self-governing authority" envisioned in the accord would be nothing more than an "administrative council." It would not possess legislative powers.[32]

Among other things, Begin's interpretation marked a definite shift away from the unobtrusive West Bank policy instituted by Moshe Dayan in 1967.[33] Under previous administrations, most Jewish settlements had been located in strategic zones at a distance from Arab towns and villages. Under Begin they were increasingly placed adjacent to these communities. Moshe Dayan objected to this policy, which he viewed as an attempt to impose functional Israeli sovereignty on a hostile population. What he proposed instead was neither to surrender sovereignty nor to impose it: Israel should restrict its settlements to largely uninhabited strategic areas, where they could serve the needs of the IDF while the latter concentrated on defending the borders. By giving a civilian face to the IDF presence, Dayan hoped the settlements might foster Israeli-Palestinian coexistence. Moreover, since the settlements were to be geographically separate, they would not hinder the evolving autonomy of the Palestinians.[34] Excluded from the decision-making process, Dayan tendered his resignation in October 1979. In May 1980, Defense Minister Ezer Weizman did the same. Both were convinced that the path taken by Begin would increase friction with the local Arabs without leading to a durable settlement.

The departure of Begin's two highest-profile cabinet ministers, combined with an inflation rate of 130 percent, eroded the government's popularity. So, too, did the ongoing withdrawal from Sinai, since many Israelis feared that Egypt would betray the peace once the withdrawal was complete.[35] As the

1981 elections approached, pollsters predicted that Likud would be turned out of office. But at 3:00 P.M. on Sunday June 7, 1981, a squadron of Israeli F-15s and F-16s took off from southern Israel and made for Tuwaitha, Iraq. In a raid lasting two minutes, the squadron scored 16 direct hits on its target — Iraq's concrete-domed Osirak nuclear reactor. Not a single Israeli plane was lost, while Iraq's evolving capacity to manufacture nuclear weapons was utterly destroyed. The raid provoked international condemnation, but at home, it was enormously popular. New polls showed an immediate shift in favor of Likud.[36]

Because the elections were only three weeks away, Begin's detractors insisted that the raid had been an electoral ploy from start to finish. But there is an alternative explanation. In Begin's view, a nuclear-armed Iraq was the harbinger of a second holocaust against the Jewish people. With the Labor Party leading in the polls and officially opposed to a military strike, Begin seems to have feared that if he did not act, no one would, leaving Israel's very existence in jeopardy.[37] By a narrow margin, the electorate agreed with him, and on June 30, 1981, Likud won 48 Knesset seats against Labor's 47.

By joining hands with the religious parties, Begin was able to muster a slender majority in the Knesset. His second coalition leaned distinctly further to the right than its predecessor. The defense portfolio in the new government was given to Ariel Sharon, who had served as minister of agriculture during Begin's first term. In his former capacity, says Israeli journalist Amos Perlmutter, Sharon planted a great number of Jewish settlements and very little else.[38] Now, as defense minister, he would sew a whole new field of controversy.

On June 3, 1982, a Palestinian terrorist attempted to assassinate Shlomo Argov, Israel's ambassador to England. (Argov was paralyzed in the attack.) Although the gunman was a follower of Abu Nidal — a rival of Yasser Arafat[39] — Israel retaliated with air strikes against Arafat's PLO in Lebanon. In response, the PLO shelled civilian areas in Galilee. It is frequently alleged that, until this moment, Arafat had adhered assiduously to a yearlong cease-fire agreement with Israel. The truth, however, is that between July 1981, when the cease-fire went into effect, and June of the following year, the PLO launched scores of terrorist attacks, killing 29 Israelis and wounding 271 others.[40] Since most of these attacks were launched from bases outside Lebanon, Arafat maintained that they were beyond the pale of the cease-fire.[41] But Israel had not agreed to a cease-fire on the understanding that the PLO could continue to kill and maim its citizens from outside Lebanon. Moreover, the PLO had used the "cease-fire" to augment its artillery and rocket strength in southern Lebanon. Hostage to this arsenal and tired of rushing to underground shelters every time a resumption of hostilities threatened, many Galilee residents had simply packed up and left. In economic and psychological terms alone, the situation was unsustainable.[42] Israel's inevitable response came in the guise of "Operation Peace for Galilee"—a full-scale invasion of south Lebanon.

The war opened on June 6, 1982, with IDF forces crossing the border in three columns. Their mission, as described to the cabinet by Begin and Sharon, was to push 25 miles into Lebanon over the course of 48 hours in order to destroy the PLO's fighting capacity in all territory within artillery range of Galilee. It was specifically stated that there was to be no altercation with Syrian forces and no advance on Beirut.[43]

Privately, Ariel Sharon did not believe that the campaign's scope was sufficient to provide Israel's northern border with definitive security. Inevitably, Israel would have to withdraw her forces—just as she had done after Operation Litani in 1978—and, just as inevitably, the PLO would take up its former positions, thereby renewing the threat to Galilee. Seizing upon a series of military pretexts, Sharon transformed the campaign from Operation Peace for Galilee (i.e., the plan outlined to the cabinet by Begin and Sharon) into the preconceived and much more ambitious "Operation Big Pines," which envisioned (i) the wholesale eviction of PLO and Syrian forces from the whole of Lebanon; (ii) the election of Israel's Christian Maronite ally, Bashir Gemayel, to the Lebanese presidency, thereby paving the way for a durable peace treaty between Israel and Lebanon; and (iii) the obliteration of PLO influence (and with it Palestinian nationalist sentiment) in the West Bank and Gaza.[44]

The military objectives of "Big Pines" were within the realm of possibility; the political objectives (upon which consolidation of the campaign's military gains depended) were utterly visionary. Five days into the fighting, the Israeli Air Force obtained uncontested control of the skies by obliterating 17 of Syria's 19 "SAM" (surface-to-air missile) installations in the Beka'a Valley. Sharon hailed the action as "the turning point of the war."[45] By June 25, Israel had isolated the PLO in West Beirut,[46] had cut the Beirut-Damascus supply highway, and had forced the Syrians into retreat.

But the result was inconclusive. Owing to the terrain, which precluded the type of mobile warfare Israel was best prepared to fight, the IDF had sustained far more casualties than anticipated, while most of the PLO's fighters had successfully withdrawn to the capital.[47]

In sum, the campaign was incomplete. Hoping to finish it, Sharon placed West Beirut under siege. From July 1 to August 22, the IDF bombarded carefully chosen PLO positions in West Beirut from the land, sea and air. Much to Israel's detriment, images of the destruction appeared on the nightly news across the world. The image created was one of "indiscriminate" shelling by the IDF.[48] This was a highly misleading characterization: throughout the war, the IDF consistently attempted to avert civilian casualties. At Tyre and Sidon, on the road to Beirut, the IDF airdropped maps delineating its intended route of ingress and charting safe zones where the populace could find sanctuary.[49] Stiff restrictions were placed on the use of airpower, explosives and artillery in these cities. Likewise, IDF soldiers were instructed to view all civilians as hostages of the PLO, and never to shoot unless fired upon. The cost of this approach included both a slowing of the IDF advance and excess casualties among its soldiery.[50]

In the siege of downtown Beirut, the IAF employed optically guided missiles and confirmed precise hits on military targets photographically. In southern Beirut, where PLO fighters conducted operations in the midst of their own civilian camps, such precision proved impossible, and the civilian death toll was higher. (In several instances, Israeli pilots refused to strike their targets because of the risk to noncombatants.) On the ground, tanks were brought up for close-in strikes against enemy strongholds.[51] In contrast, Palestinian fighters converted their own populace into human shields by taking up position in apartment buildings and other civilian structures, where their fire provoked IDF artillery shelling in return. These gunnery exchanges accounted for most of the harm done to civilians and to nonmilitary property.[52]

Despite the IDF's sensitivity to collateral damage, the siege of Beirut resulted in an estimated 5,000 civilian fatalities attributable to the operations of all combatants.[53] For a fleeting moment, it also created the illusion that Ariel Sharon's political scheme might come to fruition: on August 23, Bashir Gemayel gained election as president of Lebanon, and over the next two weeks, Yasser Arafat withdrew from the country with the bulk of his fighters. (Beirut's Christian residents serenaded them with catcalls as they embarked.[54]) This, however, was the high point of Operation Big Pines. In a September 1 meeting with Begin and Sharon, Gemayel rejected a peace treaty with Israel, saying that he would be branded a collaborator and overthrown.[55] Next, Syrian agents literally dropped a bombshell on the proceedings by blowing up Gemayel's party headquarters in East Beirut along with Gemayel himself (September 14). Although the game was now up, Sharon hoped to salvage something by taking control of West Beirut. Reticent to send the IDF into Sabra and Shatila — the city's Palestinian refugee camps — he delegated the task to Gemayel's Christian Phalangist militia.

It was a fateful decision. The Phalangists were in no mood to carry out a disciplined military action. They had been fighting the PLO since 1975 and were now livid over the assassination of their leader. Even worse, the battalion that entered the camps came from the town of Damour (site of the 1976 massacre perpetrated by the PLO).[56] Hence, instead of fulfilling their mission, the Phalangists settled old (and new) scores — murdering 750 unarmed refugees in three days without regard to age or gender (September 16–18). Menachem Begin had no idea that a massacre was occurring until the 18th, when he heard a report of it on BBC radio. There followed a domestic and international outcry of deafening proportions. In the Knesset, opposition leader Shimon Peres demanded to know "who were the fools who let the Phalangists into the refugee camps?"[57]

Initially, Begin refused to impart any responsibility to the IDF, but when 400,000 Israelis staged a mass protest in Tel Aviv, he agreed to convoke the Kahan Commission of Inquiry (so-called after its chairman, Israeli Supreme Court president Yitzhak Kahan). After hearing all sides, the commission issued its report on February 7, 1983, declaring that direct responsibility for the massacre lay with the Phalangists who had carried it out. However, given the common knowledge that "various atrocities against the noncombatant population had been widespread in Lebanon since 1975," it strongly censured Sharon and the IDF leadership for employing the Phalangists "without ... concrete and effective supervision and scrutiny of them."[58] In addition, it concluded that Prime Minister Begin's "lack of involvement in the entire matter casts on him a certain degree of responsibility."[59]

Meanwhile, the situation in Lebanon showed no sign of stabilizing, obliging Israel to continue its occupation in the face of mounting casualties, domestic discontent and international censure.[60] Coupled with the death of his beloved wife, the confluence of factors proved too much for Begin to bear, and in August 1983, he resigned from office. Yitzhak Shamir, his defense minister, succeeded him.

Despite a faltering economy and runaway inflation, Shamir refused to alter the existing Lebanon policy. Consequently, on April 4, a no-confidence vote in the Knesset forced new elections. The outcome was a stalemate: Labor won 44 seats to Likud's 41, but neither party could find enough partners to obtain a Knesset majority. The result was something entirely new in Israeli politics: a national unity government in which the premiership would be held by turns. For the first two years, Labor leader Shimon Peres would serve as prime minister, with Shamir serving as deputy prime minister and foreign minister. The leaders would then exchange posts for the remainder of the term.

As a first step toward solving the nation's economic woes, Peres thought it necessary to end the Lebanon War. In order to accomplish this in a manner that would leave Israel's security intact, he enlisted his bitter political rival, Yitzhak Rabin, the former premier and IDF chief of staff, to serve as minister of defense.

Born in Jerusalem on March 1, 1922, Yitzhak Rabin was the son of Nehemiah Rabin[61] and Rosa Cohen. His parents had met in the Old City two years earlier, during the Nebi Musa riots of 1920. They allegedly quarreled so violently on that occasion that British soldiers had to intervene[62] (the only definite record of British intervention on behalf of Jews during the entire pogrom). In 1925, the happily married couple moved their family to Tel Aviv, where Rosa took a job as an accountant in the same construction company where Golda Meir worked as a cashier.[63] Afterwards, Rosa became a well-known figure in Tel Aviv. For years after her premature death from heart disease and cancer in 1937, young Yitzhak was known as "Rosa Cohen's son."[64]

His military training began early. By age 13, he could fire a pistol, and during the Arab Revolt of 1936–39, he learned infantry tactics from Yigal Allon. At the outbreak of World War II, he turned down a scholarship to study engineering at the University of California, Berkeley so that he could be available for military duty in Palestine. The following year, a Palmach officer sought to recruit him for a mission against Vichy forces in Lebanon. When Yitzhak confessed that he could neither work a machine gun nor drive a vehicle, the officer — Moshe Dayan — said, "All right, you'll do."[65] On the ensuing mission, Yitzhak was assigned the task of severing enemy telephone lines. Cutting his first wire proved easy enough, but Yitzhak had no time to rejoice. The telephone pole had been held in position by the taut wire. As soon as Yitzhak cut it, the pole tilted violently and threw him to the ground.[66]

By 1943, the 21-year-old Rabin had risen to the rank of platoon commander in the Palmach. When the war ended two years later, he was lieutenant commander of a whole battalion. In this capacity, he played a major role in the October 1945 raid on the Athlit detention camp, where British authorities had detained 200 Holocaust survivors on a charge of entering Palestine illegally. After a successful breakout under Rabin's leadership, the escapees made their way to Bet Oren, a neighboring kibbutz. The British prepared to round them up again; but before they could do so, 15,000 Jewish civilians arrived from Haifa to inundate the kibbutz so that the authorities could no longer tell who was who. The raid was a complete success, and Yitzhak Rabin became famous throughout Mandatory Palestine.[67]

Eight months later, he fractured his leg in a motorcycle collision. Taken unconscious to Haifa's Rothschild Hospital, he awoke to the teasing of a friend, who informed him, "We found your left ankle. It was just by your knee."[68] On crutches, he was no match for the fleet-footed British. They caught up with him on June 29, 1946, during their "Black Sabbath" mass arrest campaign, and imprisoned him for five months. He spent the time productively — rehabilitating his leg. Restored to freedom in good health, he obtained command of the newly formed Harel Brigade, which participated in the fight for Jerusalem during Israel's War of Independence. In the campaign's opening weeks, the unit lost a third of its strength in dead and wounded; but for Rabin, the worst experience was watching from nearby Mount Zion on May 28, 1948, as the marooned Jews of Jerusalem's Old City sent a delegation of surrender to Jordan's Arab Legion. In the ensuing weeks, Rabin commanded IDF troops in the attack on the Irgun ship, *Altalena*, in Tel Aviv harbor and participated in the expulsion of the Arab populations of Lydda and Ramle. Although the latter operation was a necessity (since Arab fighters had been using the towns as bases for attacks on Jewish villages and supply lines), Yitzhak was tormented by the experience. For many years, it was falsely claimed that the Arabs had left the towns voluntarily. The truth ultimately came out, but when Rabin attempted to recount the events in his 1979 memoir, a cabinet committee censored the passage as too inflammatory.[69]

Shortly afterwards, during the war's second truce, Yitzhak married Leah Schlossberg, who had formerly served under him in the Palmach — one of the few times (he liked to jest) that he outranked her. When the rabbi showed up late for the ceremony, the nervous Rabin quipped that he would never get married again. True to his word, he stayed married to Leah until his death.[70]

When the fighting resumed in October, Rabin served as deputy to Yigal Allon in the victorious Negev campaign of 1948–49. At war's end, he was court-martialed for attending a farewell gathering for the outlawed Palmach. Let off with a reprimand, he obtained a series of promotions: in 1951, he became head of the operations division of the general staff; in 1953, head of the training branch; and in 1956, commander of the Syrian front. For a time, there was no prospect for further advancement, and Rabin thought of resigning. Then came another rapid ascent: in 1959, he became chief of operations; in 1961, deputy chief of staff; and finally, on January 1, 1964, he succeeded to the top post — IDF chief of staff.

By the outbreak of the Six Day War in June 1967, Rabin had used his new position to equip the IDF with advanced American weaponry and hone it into a meticulously trained, mobile force. Nevertheless, the "waiting period" (in Hebrew, *Hamtana*) leading up to that war played deeply upon his anxieties. The decision for war is a political decision. Rabin's job was to be ready with a plan of attack — which he was. (In fact, he had two.) But the Eshkol cabinet would not decide, and when Rabin sought advice from David Ben-Gurion and Moshe Dayan (Eshkol's political rivals), he received only partisan criticism. Increasingly on edge with each passing day, he took solace in chain-smoking, and looked like a man bearing the weight of the world on his shoulders. For 36 hours, commencing on the evening of May 23, he was not seen at command headquarters. According to Ezer Weizman, he had suffered a transient nervous collapse; by Rabin's account, it was "nicotine poisoning." In either case, he did not regain his composure until an army physician prescribed a sedative that put him to sleep until noon on May 24.[71] Thereafter, he was himself again. Indeed, one of the war's most poignant images is the June 7 photograph showing Rabin, Uzi Narkiss and Moshe Dayan, clad in steel helmets, as they pass the Lion's Gate into the newly liberated Old City of Jerusalem en route to the Western Wall.

By war's end, Rabin was a national hero. Levi Eshkol rewarded him by giving in to his unexpected request for assignment as ambassador to the United States. Over the next five years, Rabin cultivated close ties with top figures in the Nixon administration, including Henry Kissinger. But he was no master of subtlety, and his diplomatic assessments were sometimes incorrect: during Israel's War of Attrition with Egypt, for example, he pressed the Israeli government to pursue a campaign of deep bombing raids into Egypt after reaching the erroneous conclusion that the United States would not object to an intensification of the conflict.[72] In 1972, the *Washington Post* dubbed him "Israel's undiplomatic diplomat" after he all but publicly endorsed Richard Nixon in the latter's presidential campaign against George McGovern.[73]

He returned to Israel in March 1973, but played no formal role in the Yom Kippur War — a fact that worked to his advantage politically. While other leaders were being castigated for perceived blunders in the weeks leading up to that war, Rabin narrowly edged out Shimon Peres to emerge as the head of the Labor Party. In June 1974, he replaced Golda Meir as prime minister of Israel — the first *Sabra* (i.e., native born Israeli) to attain that office.

Rabin's first tenure as prime minister was chronicled in the preceding chapter. Despite the setbacks and scandals that forced his resignation, it is best remembered for the daring rescue operation at Entebbe. Moreover, the public admired the dignified manner in which he left office: Because his wife had made all the withdrawals from their illegal U.S. bank account, she alone was summoned to stand trial. Protesting that the onus was shared, Rabin relinquished his nomination for reelection as prime minister and effectively resigned.[74] Days later, at a Tel Aviv soccer game, the crowd acknowledged his presence with a standing ovation.[75]

Months after leaving office, Rabin was among the throng of Israeli dignitaries who welcomed Egyptian president Anwar Sadat at Ben-Gurion Airport on the latter's historic 1977 visit to Israel. Two years later, he attended the signing ceremony of the 1979 Israeli-Egyptian peace treaty. (Menachem Begin had invited Rabin both because he was a former prime minister and because he had contributed to the process by signing the 1975 Sinai II accord with Egypt.) Nevertheless, Rabin had descended from the height of power into the political no man's land — and the publication of his memoirs in 1979 (in which he fired broadsides at party rival Shimon Peres) did nothing to remedy the situation: in 1980, Peres defeated him handily in a new competition for the party chairmanship. For the next four years, Rabin was virtually invisible as a politician, but when Likud and Labor formed their national unity government in 1984, he was rescued from oblivion and given the defense portfolio.

It had been two years since Israel won the war to destroy the PLO's state-within-a-state in Lebanon. In the interim, however, the war to create a PLO-free, Syria-free, Christian-dominated Lebanon in alliance with Israel had ended in a fruitless occupation of that country at great expense in blood, treasure and morale. The time had come to abandon goals that were beyond achievement. Under Peres and Rabin, Israel carried out a phased withdrawal, leaving intact a slender security belt in southern Lebanon, patrolled by IDF troops in conjunction with a local Christian militia force known as the South Lebanese Army (1985).

The following year, Yitzhak Shamir took over as prime minister, and Peres took over the foreign ministry. In secret talks with Jordan's King Hussein, Peres forged the so-called "London Agreement," which envisioned a comprehensive Middle East peace anchored on UN resolutions 242 and 338 (April 1987). Left in the dark until the document was complete, Shamir angrily disavowed the initiative.

Then, in December 1987, came the outbreak of the first *intifada* — a mass uprising against Israel's presence in the West Bank and Gaza. In the twenty years since the Six Day War, the Arabs of the territories had generally cooperated with Israeli rule, with the results that (i) improved healthcare lowered the Palestinian infant mortality rate by 75 percent and raised Palestinian life expectancy from 48 to 72 (four years higher than elsewhere in the Arab world); (ii) average per capita income rose from $165 under Jordanian rule to $1,715 under Israeli (higher than the average in Egypt or Turkey); (iii) the number of homes with running water and electricity rose from roughly 20 percent to 85 percent; and (iv) improved education lowered the illiteracy rate to 14 percent among Palestinians aged 15 or older (compared, for example, with 61 percent in Egypt).[76] Among the things these young Palestinians were learning, however, was a disdain for authority and a desire for self-determination — something the PLO had manifestly failed to provide to them, and for which, alas, Israel's military presence, cumbersome bureaucracy and Likudist settlement policy was a poor substitute.[77]

Such was the backdrop of the upheaval that began with a chance motor vehicle accident on December 8, 1987, when an Israeli truck collided with a car at the border crossing with Gaza, killing four Arab workers. An Arabic newspaper called it "murder," falsely alleging that the truck driver was the cousin of an Israeli who had been murdered in Gaza on December 6. As a result, the funeral procession for the four Arabs evolved into a riot, with angry demonstrators marching on a nearby Israeli military installation, chanting, "*Jihad!*"[78] Thereafter, Palestinian youths participated in relentless demonstrations, throwing stones (and the occasional Molotov cocktail) at Jewish soldiers and settlers. West Bank schools became indoctrination centers for the intifada, where "teachers" disseminated a "curriculum" consisting of direct participation in the riots.[79]

In short order, the territories became ungovernable, and the duty of doing something about it fell to Defense Minister Rabin. In the ensuing altercations, Israeli soldiers fired tear gas, rubber or plastic bullets, and — when mortal danger threatened — live ammunition, at rock-throwing Palestinian teens. Not infrequently, the clashes resulted in Arab deaths— or, in intifada parlance, "martyrdom." In the next year, 150 Palestinians were killed and more than 1,100 wounded.[80] Chaperoned by agitated throngs, funeral processions degenerated into fresh outbursts of violence. When Israeli soldiers sought to subdue the agitators, the images were televised, creating a public-relations nightmare. If Israel showed restraint, the demonstrators increased their provocations until restraint ceased to be an alternative.[81] Seeking a way out of the conundrum, Rabin ordered his troops to replace their guns with riot batons, but the scenes thus produced only compounded the negative image.[82] In the midst of it all, the radical Islamic fundamentalist group, Hamas, took root in Gaza, calling for Israel's destruction while waging a campaign of terror against Israelis and Palestinian moderates alike.

In the shadow of the insurrection, Israel's 1988 elections gave Likud 40 seats versus Labor's 39. Yitzhak Shamir remained prime minister at the head of a unity government with Peres at finance and Rabin at defense. In an effort to end the intifada, Rabin proposed offering increased autonomy to the Arabs of the West Bank and Gaza. In his view, the intifada had marginalized the PLO, presenting an opportunity to promote local Palestinian elections and deal with the leadership that emerged (leaving the PLO on the sidelines).[83] On May 14, Shamir and the cabinet endorsed the proposal. In answer, the leaders of the intifada circulated a pamphlet saying that there would be no elections until the "occupation" was terminated and instructing their followers to avenge the death of every "martyr" with the blood of an Israeli settler or soldier.[84] Shamir, who had had limited enthusiasm for Rabin's initiative to begin with, found in this response a very good reason not to pursue it. Frustrated by his unwillingness to proceed, Shimon Peres withdrew Labor's support from the unity government. The move backfired: invited by Israeli president Chaim Herzog to form a Labor government pending new elections, Peres was unable to garner a majority in the Knesset. As the deadline approached, the right-wing religious parties joined Shamir, who promptly turned the tables on Peres by forging a majority without Labor's participation.

In the wake of this setback, Rabin mounted a new challenge to Peres' party leadership (1990). Among Israeli voters, Rabin was the more popular figure. Not so among the Labor Party elite: in a vote of the central committee, Rabin was defeated. But the blow was offset by the central committee's simultaneous decision to substitute U.S.-style primaries for its own cronyism, beginning with the next election cycle. Henceforth, party leaders would be chosen by popular ballot, with voting open to all registered party members.[85]

When the first primary took place in February 1992, Rabin narrowly outpolled his rivals, taking 40.6 percent of the vote. (Had he gained less than 40 percent, he would have faced a runoff against Peres. The conventional wisdom was that he would have lost, since most of the third-place candidate's votes would have gone to Peres.[86]) He entered the 1992 national election campaign on the slogan "Israel is waiting for Rabin!" Enthusiastic crowds greeted him everywhere.

In the meantime, Shamir's Likud government had been through a stormy two years. Between August 1990 and February 1991, Iraq invaded Kuwait and was driven out again by a coalition of U.S., European, and Arab nations (1990–91). Israel was politely instructed to remain on the sidelines during this conflict, lest her participation offend the Arab coalition members. Iraqi president Saddam Hussein promptly fired scud missiles into Israeli cities with impunity, injuring hundreds of civilians and destroying thousands of dwellings. In the West Bank, where the intifada was still ongoing, there were reports of Arabs cheering the missiles as they passed overhead.[87] Fearing an imminent chemical attack, the Israeli government distributed gas masks to its citizens. Shamir's forbearance in this trying period wrought closer ties with the U.S., but owing to his hard-line stance at the Madrid peace talks (convened in October 1991) and to his continued promotion of settlements in the West Bank, he soon forfeited the advantage. Hence, when he requested $10 billion in U.S. loan guarantees to help resettle Soviet Jews as they streamed into Israel in the wake of the Soviet Union's collapse, President George H. W. Bush spurned his solicitations.

On the domestic front, the government's inability to end the intifada undermined Shamir's popularity — as did a national unemployment rate exceeding 10 percent.[88] Rabin offered a new approach. Like Shamir, he rejected the notion of a Palestinian state, saying that the leaders of such an entity would seek Israel's destruction. Likewise, he insisted that Jerusalem remain undivided and that there be no return to the pre-1967 armistice lines. On the other hand, he argued, there was room for territorial compromise, provided that peace and security were achieved by it. In an effort to cut government expenditures, he promised to restrict spending in the territories to enterprises that directly affected Israeli security. (Given the overall state of the economy, Shamir was accused, in some circles, of being too lavish in his expenditures there.)

On June 23, amidst wild rejoicing at party headquarters, Labor gained 44 seats against Likud's 32. Yitzhak Rabin had returned as prime minister of Israel. It was Labor's first clear-cut victory since the elections of December 1973.[89] True to his promise, Rabin reduced projects in the West Bank in order to concentrate on economic rehabilitation for Israel as a whole. Despite deadly attacks by Hamas and Hezbollah, he continued to pursue the "Madrid" talks, which had now moved to Washington. But the talks made little progress, and after the 1992 abduction and murder of Nissim Toledano, a 29-year-old Israeli policeman, Rabin ordered the deportation of 415 Hamas operatives to Lebanon. After subsequent terrorist attacks, he launched air strikes against the Iranian-backed terrorist organization Hezbollah in Lebanon and closed the border with the West Bank. The latter move provoked outcries from Palestinians who commuted to Israel to earn their daily living.[90]

By this time, the PLO had lost much of its international stock. After his 1982 expulsion, Yasser Arafat had attempted to return to Lebanon via the northern port of Tripoli only to be driven back out by the Syrians. Possessing no base from which to stage cross-border attacks against Israel, he tried his luck with Jordan again—convening the 1984 PLO National Council meeting in Amman and inviting King Hussein to speak. But Hussein wanted to co-opt the PLO as part of a "land for peace" deal with Israel that would return the West Bank to Jordanian or joint Jordanian-Palestinian control. The PLO rejected this approach as inconsistent with the total obliteration of Israel. Moreover, Arafat was unwilling to act as a tool of Jordanian policy.[91] The talks came to nothing.

For Arafat, the 1987 intifada was another fumbled opportunity. After a year of fighting, the intifadists were convinced that their uprising could not oust the Israeli regime. A political settlement would be necessary. In 1988, they turned to Arafat, insisting that the PLO leader negotiate an end to Israeli rule in the territories *in return for peace.*[92] Through intermediaries, Ronald Reagan's national security advisor, Colin Powell, and secretary of state, George Schultz, informed Arafat that if he recognized Israel, renounced terror, and embraced UN Resolution 242 as the basis for peace, the U.S. would "open a dialogue" with him. For Arafat this was a tremendous opportunity. At a press conference in December 1988, he seemed to meet the U.S. criteria and was rewarded with the promised "dialogue." But over the ensuing 18 months, Arafat squandered the initiative. In public speeches, PLO spokesmen spoke ambiguously of "land for peace" in English, and unambiguously of the 1974 "phased plan" for Israel's destruction in Arabic. Far from starting the Palestinian masses on the road to reconciliation with Israel, Arafat bade them not to give an inch, since the day of victory was near.[93] Worst of all, there was no halt to the terrorism, and after Arafat refused to condemn a particularly egregious attempt to murder Israelis on a Tel Aviv beach, the U.S. reluctantly abandoned its PLO "dialogue" on June 20, 1990.[94]

Even this was not the low point: Arafat's pro–Iraq vitriol during the 1991 Gulf War alienated not just the U.S., but also many Arab regimes—with the result that Saudi Arabia and Kuwait withheld funding from the PLO. Moreover, Kuwait expelled over 300,000 Palestinian refugees who had come there for work, thereby erasing the estimated $200 million they sent to the West Bank in annual taxes and family support.[95] Meanwhile, the end of the Cold War rendered appeasement of the PLO by Washington less urgent. (Stunned into transient lucidity, the UN General Assembly even annulled its 1975 "Zionism is racism" resolution.[96])

Seemingly oblivious to the need for concessions, Arafat publicly compared Israel with Nazi Germany. (Fatah chimed in by issuing a pamphlet referring to Jews as the "descendants of monkeys and pigs."[97]) But the economic situation in the West Bank and Gaza was critical, and Arafat began to worry that the West Bank representatives at the Madrid talks might obtain an autonomy agreement with Israel without direct PLO participation. By coincidence, Yitzhak Rabin had reached precisely the reverse conclusion: fearing that Iran or Iraq might emerge as new regional threats to Israel over the next decade,[98] he was anxious to achieve peace with his immediate neighbors—including the Palestinians. Hitherto, he had spurned any contact with the PLO. But a year of fruitless wrangling with "non–PLO" interlocutors at the Madrid-Washington talks led him increasingly to the conclusion that there was no viable alternative to the terrorist organization.[99] These chance calculations (or miscalculations) drove both men to entertain choices that they had previously rejected.

Thus, when Shimon Peres divulged the existence of "back channel" talks with PLO members in Oslo, Norway (February 1993), Rabin tacitly sanctioned the negotiations, which were illegal under Israeli law. (Initially, even Peres had been unaware of these contacts, which were carried out under the auspices of his deputy foreign minister, Yossi Beilin—a proponent of Israel's large "Peace Now" movement, which held that the Palestinians and their leaders desired peace no less than Israelis did, and that if Israel simply made the requisite concessions, peace would result.[100]) On August 17, 1993, the final details were worked out in a phone conversation between Norwegian intermediary Terje Larsen and PLO "finance minister" Abu Ala'a. Listening in with Larsen was Shimon Peres, who could hear Abu Ala'a and Arafat alter-nately sobbing with joy and shouting in exultation when the last issue was resolved.[101]

The result was a document entitled the "Declaration of Principles," which obliged Israel to withdraw her forces from Gaza and Jericho—handing over authority to "authorized" Palestinians. It was to be the first step toward the establishment of Palestinian autonomy in Gaza and most of the West Bank. Israel would retain control of defense, foreign relations, and Jewish settlements in the territories. Over the next 5 years, the extent and pace of Israeli withdrawals would be negotiated, as would final status decisions on Jerusalem and Jewish settlements. The document was completed on August 20, 1993. It was followed by a letter from Yasser Arafat to Yitzhak Rabin stating that the PLO (i) recognized Israel's right to exist; (ii) abjured terror; and (iii) accepted UN resolutions 242 and 338 as the basis for a durable peace settlement. Offensive references to the need for Israel's destruction in the PLO covenant were deemed "no longer operative." Rabin responded with a letter extending recognition to the PLO.

Many Israelis were alarmed that the government would confer legitimacy on a terrorist organization. On September 7, tens of thousands of concerned citizens converged on Jerusalem — some of them denouncing Rabin as a traitor. At a New York synagogue five days later, angry congregation members cast tomatoes at Israel's ambassador to the U.S.[102] Nonetheless, on September 13, 1993, the Declaration of Principles was signed on the White House lawn.

It may be said that the omens were not good. The event called for a handshake between Rabin and Arafat. In complying, Rabin showed visible reluctance — a reflection of his inner turmoil over embracing the hand of a man responsible for deadly attacks on Israeli innocents. In his speech, Rabin issued a plaintive summons for an end to violence, declaring, "Enough of blood and tears. Enough!"[103] It was expected that Arafat would reciprocate with a statement denouncing terrorism. At several points in the latter's address, Israeli journalist Ehud Ya'ari, who was covering the event for Israeli television, assured his audience that the PLO leader would soon speak the historic words. Then, realizing that Arafat had no such intention, he sadly told his listeners that "he is not saying it."[104]

The worst, however, was yet to come. On the very day of the White House ceremony, Jordan's King Hussein sent Rabin a message, telling him that Arafat couldn't be trusted.[105] Proof of this assertion came within hours, when Arafat appeared on Jordanian television — not to proclaim a new era of peace, but to inform the Palestinian people that the declaration he had signed constituted the inaugural step in the long-awaited 1974 "phased plan" for Israel's elimination.[106] In the ensuing weeks, he would invoke the "phased plan" in public statements more than twelve times.[107] Likewise, he compared the Oslo agreement with the Treaty of Hudaibiya, whereby the prophet Mohammad negotiated peace with his rivals in A.D. 628, only to betray his word and attack them when better circumstances arose.[108]

Back at home, the Likud Party's new leader, Benjamin Netanyahu, warned that the Oslo agreement would lead to a PLO state dedicated to Israel's destruction. Settlers and their supporters marched in protest, hurling vitriol at Rabin. The majority of Israeli voters, however, favored the attempt at peace, and the declaration passed the Knesset by the narrow margin of 61–50. The PLO ruling council likewise voted in favor.

Still, the terrorism did not cease. Flatly rejecting the peace initiative, the Islamic fundamentalist groups Hamas and Islamic Jihad continued their deadly attacks, claiming 27 Israeli lives between September 1993 and February 1994. For appearances sake, Arafat ordered a few arrests, but the suspects were generally set free within days. (Some later obtained jobs as Palestinian Authority "policemen."[109]) Beyond this, Arafat made no substantive effort to punish the perpetrators. To do so, he claimed, would provoke a Palestinian civil war.[110]

Then, on February 25, 1994, came a rare atrocity from the Jewish side. Baruch Goldstein, a Jewish settler from Kiryat Arba, entered the Tomb of the Patriarchs in Hebron and gunned down 29 innocent Muslim worshippers in cold blood. He was still shooting when members of the congregation took up iron bars and beat him to death.[111] Israelis universally denounced this perverse attack. In contrast, there was no such outcry from the Arab side when a Palestinian suicide bomber blew himself up on a Tel Aviv bus, killing 22 and wounding 47 (October 1994).[112] After a similar blast killed twenty IDF soldiers and one civilian at a bus stop in January 1995, Israeli president Ezer Weizman announced that he would not support the road to peace if it was to be paved with Jewish corpses.[113]

Nevertheless, Yitzhak Rabin stood his ground, exclaiming, "We shall fight the terror as if there were no peace talks, and we will conduct the peace talks as if there were no terror."[114] Thus far, his efforts had not been entirely fruitless: In May 1994, he had reached a comprehensive agreement on security with the PLO. In October, he shared the 1994 Nobel Peace Prize with Peres and Arafat — a clear indication of the international community's support. Finally, on October 26, came the signing of a peace treaty between Israel and Jordan. The Knesset approved this welcome agreement by a stunning 105–3 margin, leaving Rabin more determined than ever to stay the course.

Amidst continuing acts of terror, however, his constituents were losing faith in the peace process. A March 1995 poll indicated that nearly two-thirds of Israelis were dissatisfied with the course of events and felt less secure than when the process began.[115] Nor did it help matters that Yasser Arafat refused to amend offensive articles in the PLO covenant; that he attributed ongoing terrorism to "Israeli agents"[116]; or that he told an Arab audience in May 1995 that "We should be honest with ourselves and admit that Israel is the principal enemy of the Palestinian people. It was the enemy in the past, it is the enemy in the present, and will continue to be the enemy in the future."[117]

Despite these warning signals, Rabin pressed ahead. In September 1995, he forged the Oslo II Accord with Arafat, establishing three gradations of sovereignty within the West Bank: the largest Arab cities, comprising 3 percent of the West Bank territorially and 26 percent of its population, were to be wholly administered by Palestinian authorities; the Arab villages, comprising 24 percent of the territory and 70 percent of the population, would have full autonomy except in security matters (which would remain in Israeli hands); finally, the remaining 73 percent of the land (mostly uninhabited), would be administered by Israel until a final status agreement was reached on borders.[118] Hence, although the accord entailed the interim transfer of just 27 percent of the West Bank to the Palestinians, 96 percent of the West Bank population would now be under Palestinian jurisdiction.[119] In the Knesset, Rabin garnered a bare 61–59 majority for the agreement, with the assembly's five Arab delegates being among those voting in favor.

Enraged that the government would reward unceasing terror by granting new concessions, right wing rioters demolished Rabin's car outside the Knesset building. In a speech in Jerusalem on October 5, Benjamin Netanyahu had to instruct the crowd to stop howling "traitors!" in reference to Rabin and his supporters. Street demonstrators held up placards portraying Rabin in Nazi garb. At one of Netanyahu's rallies they posted a banner saying, "Death to Arafat!" directly beneath his balcony. At another they passed around a fake coffin for Rabin.[120] Some have attributed these disturbances to *agents provocateurs* hired by the government to discredit valid, peaceful opposition to the peace process[121]— but, as events were soon to prove, some of the radicalism was only too real.

With polls showing his support on the wane, the prime minister attended a peace rally at Tel Aviv's Kings of Israel Square on November 4, 1995. After giving a spirited speech to the 100,000 assembled peace demonstrators, Rabin led them in singing the popular "Song of Peace." When the rally broke up, he said his goodbyes to the other participants, remarking that it was the happiest day of his life. He then proceeded to his limousine, which was parked behind the stage. As he approached the vehicle, three shots rang out — and with them the cry. "They're not real bullets! They're blanks!"[122]

Some thought the words were uttered by the assassin, Yigal Amir — a 25-year-old Israeli law student and narcissistic religious zealot, who believed God had commanded him to kill the man who was attempting to hand part of Eretz Israel to the Arabs. At police headquarters, he admitted his guilt for the assassination, but denied shouting anything about blanks.[123] The limousine, meanwhile, sped off to Tel Aviv's Ichilov Hospital. In the back seat, shot in both lungs with destructive "dumdum" bullets, Yitzhak Rabin lapsed into a coma. The journey to the hospital would have taken less than a minute on a normal night, but owing to the crowds departing from the rally, it took closer to two minutes. Hospital physicians attempted to revive the stricken prime minister for nearly an hour, resorting to all heroic measures, but to no avail. Shortly after 11:00 P.M., Rabin's speechwriter and close associate, Eitan Haber, announced to a distraught crowd outside the hospital that Yitzhak Rabin was dead — the victim of assassination.[124]

Thousands of mourners lined the route to pay their respects as Rabin's body was taken from Tel Aviv to Jerusalem on November 5. A million more sojourned to the Knesset building to view his coffin — the line stretching into the distance even in the black of night. Rabin was buried on Mount Herzl, in a grave dug by weeping gravediggers, very near the burial sites of Golda Meir and Levi Eshkol. At his funeral, attended by dignitaries from around the globe, Jordan's King Hussein hailed Rabin as "a soldier for peace;" Eitan Haber read the "Song of Peace" from the bloodstained copy found in the stricken prime minister's coat pocket; and, in the ceremony's most emotional address, Rabin's 17-year-old granddaughter, Noa, eulogized the loving *saba* (grandfather) she would never see again. Last to speak, Bill Clinton closed the proceedings with the words "*Shalom, haver*— Peace, my friend."[125]

In response to the assassination, mourners throughout Israel held candlelight vigils. Along the nation's roadways, signboards appeared bearing the legend, "In his death, he commanded us to seek peace."[126] But a lack of peace seeking by Israel had never been the issue. While it is true that at least two Israelis— Baruch Goldstein and Yigal Amir — were violently deranged, and that a somewhat larger number were inflexibly opposed to any cession of territory in the West Bank and Gaza as going against the dictates of God, the vast majority of those who opposed the Oslo initiative were neither religious zealots nor perpetrators of violence, neither assassins nor enemies of peace. They simply recognized that the Oslo vision of a valid accord with Yasser Arafat was a chimerical dream resting upon wishful and credulous thinking. Although Arafat reportedly "wept" on hearing of Rabin's assassination, saying, "I have lost my partner,"[127] he revealed further evidence of his true intentions on January 30, 1996, when he told a gathering of Arab diplomats in Stockholm: "We will make life unbearable for Jews by psychological warfare and population explosion.... Within five years we will have six to seven million Arabs living on the West Bank and Jerusalem. All Palestinian Arabs will be welcomed by us."[128] Such utterances were not a call to peace but an incitement to war. It was this that gave rise to protests and vitriol within the Israeli community.

There is, of course, something missing from the picture. How is it possible that Rabin and much of the Israeli populace pressed ahead with the Oslo initiative when there was abundant and repeated evidence that Arafat was not cooperating in the venture?

In his monumental study, *The Oslo Syndrome: Delusions of a People Under Siege*, Harvard psychiatrist Kenneth Levin provides a plausible explanation based in psychoanalytic theory. Levin takes the example of children subjected to abuse by their parents. Such children have either to accept the fact that they are "victims of circumstances entirely beyond their control and endure the hopelessness that would flow from that insight," or they can internalize the cruel narrative of their abusive parents— which states that their own "misbehavior" has caused the mistreatment — and "thereby sustain an illusion of control, a hope that by reforming, by becoming 'good,' they can elicit an end to the abuse."[129] (An analogous case might be made for the trapped, battered wife who concludes that her brutish husband is "right" to abuse her.)

Subjected to an endless violent Arab assault over which they had no control — and (significantly) finding no sympathy for their plight from the world community — large swaths of the Israeli community, in Levin's view, adopted a similar defense mechanism. They embraced the false indictment authored by their enemies that the cause of the Arab-Israeli conflict is not existential Arab rejection of the Jewish state, but supposed Israeli "crimes" and "aggression" against the Arabs. In so doing, they made possible the comforting delusion "that the right self-abnegations by Israel, the right mix of territorial and spiritual retreat, can win Israel the peace it desires no matter how much the objective evidence of words and deeds by the other side indicates otherwise."[130]

Rabin ought to have seen the flaw in this approach. Keeping Israel safe had been the object of his life. But for him, peace with the Palestinians had special urgency. His motivation went beyond fatigue with an endless siege to encompass the prescient belief that new forces— most notably, Iran — would one day enter the conflict to tip the balance toward Israel's enemies (or, worse, to employ weapons of mass destruction against the Jewish state).[131] This concern drove him to seek lasting security for Israel where it did not exist. He invested himself root and branch in what he incorrectly deemed to be the completion of his life's work as steward of Israel's security: an agreement with Yasser Arafat and the PLO.

Unfortunately, such an agreement was impossible, since the latter had no intention of implementing it. In pursuit of a mirage, Yitzhak Rabin died a tragic death —"a soldier for peace," an Israeli hero, and a man of noble intentions.

9

Ariel Sharon and Disengagement

The Temple Mount in Jerusalem is the holiest site in Judaism. In 1930, the city's Supreme Muslim Council published a *Brief Guide to al-Haram al-Sharif* in which the Temple Mount's "identity with the site of Solomon's Temple" is said to be "beyond dispute."[1] The site has been sacred to Jews for more than 3,000 years. It is here that God is said to have tested Abraham's willingness to sacrifice his son, Isaac. The first Jewish Temple stood here for four centuries, and after the Babylonians razed it in 586 B.C., the Jews returned to build a second one, which remained for another six centuries before the Romans destroyed it, too, at the end of the great Jewish Revolt catalogued by Josephus.[2]

But, as a recent book on Jerusalem notes, much has changed since the time of the Romans. Atop the site now are three mosques. The oldest of these, dating respectively to the seventh and eighth centuries A.D., are the Dome of the Rock—from which, according to Muslim tradition, Muhammad ascended to heaven in a dream—and the al-Aksa mosque.[3] The third was built in 1996 and occupies the underground rooms formerly known as "Solomon's Stables."

From 1948 until 1967, when the Old City was under Jordanian rule, Jews were banned from visiting the Temple Mount and the adjacent Western Wall. Following their emotional return during the Six Day War, the Israelis constructed a pavilion in front of the Western Wall where Jews the world over come to pray. The Temple Mount remains under Muslim civil custodianship, but Israel guarantees access to the site to people of all faiths (though non–Muslim visitors are not allowed to enter the mosques or partake in prayer).[4]

Matters have remained thus since 1967, but in 2000 a historic peace summit was held at Camp David during which Israeli prime minister Ehud Barak and Palestinian Authority chairman Yasser Arafat discussed the possible division of Jerusalem and the transfer of Temple Mount sovereignty to the Palestinian Authority (PA). Although the deal was not consummated, the very notions of redividing Israel's capital or surrendering sovereignty over the

Israeli Prime Minister Ariel Sharon speaking during a tour of the Ashkelon desalination plant construction site, February 3, 2004 (courtesy of the State of Israel Government Press Office; photographer Moshe Milner).

Temple Mount alarmed many Israelis. Nor did it assuage their reservations when Yasser Arafat contentiously remarked to Bill Clinton that the Mount had never been home to a Jewish Temple.

When talk of concessions continued despite the failure of the summit — and despite claims by Israeli archeologists (later verified) that, on the pretext of building a second exit to the "Solomon's Stables" mosque, Palestinian excavators had illegally bulldozed 6,000 tons of earth beneath the Temple Mount surface, thereby demolishing unspecified quantities of priceless Judaic artifacts[5]— opposition leader Ariel Sharon decided that the moment had come for a dramatic gesture: he would visit the Temple Mount, thereby embodying the Jewish people's eternal right of access to its holiest site. Receiving clearance from the Barak government and from Jabril Rajoub, the PA's chief of security (who merely requested confirmation that Sharon would not attempt to enter the mosques), Sharon arrived at 8:00 A.M. on September 28, 2000, telling accompanying reporters that he had come in peace.[6] With 1,500 Israeli policemen on duty to maintain security, Sharon remained for half an hour. It has been noted that he arrived during normal tourism hours and refrained from approaching the mosques.[7] It may be added that, unlike the Arab rioters who took to the streets later in the day, he didn't throw any rocks at anyone.

On November 22, 1995 — 18 days after the assassination of Yitzhak Rabin — Shimon Peres assumed office as prime minister of Israel. Determined to press ahead with the peace process, Peres not only sought to implement the Oslo II Accord but also pursued talks with Syria aimed at forging a comprehensive Middle East peace.[8] In late December, Israeli-Syrian negotiations began under U.S. auspices at Maryland's Wye Plantation, near Washington, D.C.

Days later (January 5, 1996), in response to ongoing terrorism, Israeli agents killed Hamas' leading bomb designer, Yahya Ayyash (whose handiwork had killed 67 Israelis and wounded 400)[9] by rigging his cell phone to explode as he spoke into it.[10] Hamas countered by accelerating its suicide bombing campaign. On February 25, one Hamas suicide bomber blew up a Jerusalem bus, killing 25, while another killed a 20-year-old Israeli girl at a bus stop. In early March, two more suicide bombings claimed an additional 31 Israeli lives. In response, Israel restricted crossings from the territories to isolated checkpoints. The Palestinian Council immediately denounced the act without making any reference to the suicide bombings that had provoked it.[11] Seeing the Israeli mood shift against further concessions, Arafat, who had visited Ayyash's family to offer his condolences,[12] and who had done nothing to prevent the new wave of bombings, finally took action. PA police clashed with Hamas and Islamic Jihad and arrested their leaders.[13] For the time being, the suicide bombings came to a halt.

Israelis were in shock. In the wake of the attacks, Peres could not possibly move forward on the Oslo track, and when Syria failed to condemn the terrorism, he also had to suspend the Wye talks.[14] Within weeks, Syria's Lebanese terrorist proxy, Hezbollah, began shelling northern Israel with Katyusha rockets. With his security credentials unraveling, Peres initiated "Operation Grapes of Wrath" consisting of artillery and air strikes against Hezbollah positions in south Lebanon. Unfortunately, in addition to inflicting casualties on Hezbollah, a number of innocents were accidentally killed, including more than 100 in a civilian shelter that was struck unintentionally by Israeli artillery fire.[15] A cease-fire halted the fighting on April 27, 1996.

One month later, Israel went to the polls. In the three years since the Declaration of Principles, almost 300 Israelis had fallen victim to terror — twice the number of the preceding six years (i.e., the period of the intifada).[16] Although Arafat had stepped in after the fact to put a halt to the suicide bombings, he was still dragging his feet on implementing his Oslo obligations. Indeed, Palestinian school curricula, religious sermons and media routinely taught that the ultimate goal of the Palestinian movement was Israel's obliteration. (In contrast, Israel's schools had rewritten their curricula to extol peace and cultivate awareness of the Palestinian plight.[17]) Despite rising disaffection among Israeli voters, Peres hoped that the 1996 elections would provide him with a mandate to proceed with the peace process. Opposing him was Likud Party leader, Benjamin Netanyahu, who ran on a platform of "peace with security," while running TV ads showing pictures of charred Israeli buses coupled with pictures of Peres shaking hands with his supposed Arab "peace" partners.[18]

In accordance with a new election law, Israeli voters cast the traditional ballot for their preferred political party and a separate ballot for prime minister. The law was meant to strengthen the prime minister by providing him with a direct mandate from the people. Instead, it broke Israel's already fractionated democracy into smaller fractions. In choosing a prime minister, voters looked to Labor and Likud. In choosing a party, they looked to their own narrow interests. Consequently, the two main political parties each lost roughly 20 percent of their Knesset seats while lesser parties gained.[19] The final tally was intensely close, with Netanyahu defeating Peres by 50.4 percent to 49.5 percent in the prime ministerial race and Labor outpolling Likud 34 seats to 32 in the party vote. By allying with the right wing and religious parties, Netanyahu was able to forge a majority coalition.

On taking office, Netanyahu vowed to abide by Israel's prior Oslo commitments, but refused to pursue further concessions until Arafat and the Palestinian Authority fulfilled their own obligations. Ignoring the fact that the PA had, indeed, not fulfilled its obligations — and that the consequences had been lethal — the international and domestic media accused the prime minister of seeking to derail the Oslo process.[20] Under immense pressure from the U.S. not to let the peace process stall, Netanyahu was forced to climb down. He agreed to open a back channel with Arafat so that negotiations could continue behind the scenes. At the same time, he sought to conciliate the right wing members of his own coalition by reinstating economic incentives (previously annulled by Rabin) for existing West Bank settlements and approving new West Bank housing projects.[21] In addition, he reiterated positions, formerly enunciated by Rabin, that the Oslo process would not lead to the establishment of a Palestinian state and that Jerusalem would remain undivided under Jewish sovereignty.[22] Then, on September 23, 1996, he sanctioned the creation of an exit to the ancient Hasmonean Tunnel in Jerusalem.

The construction of the tunnel exit has been depicted as a unilateral Israeli action undertaken in the dark of night despite well-known objections on the Palestinian side.[23] The truth, however, is that in January 1996, the responsible Muslim administrative body (known as the *waqf*), had reached an informal agreement with the Israeli government, whereby the former would gain access to "Solomon's Stables," a collection of sealed underground rooms beneath the Temple Mount (affording pious Muslims with a sheltered area in which to pray during the busy — and sometimes rainy — festival season of Ramadan). In exchange, Israel would gain the *waqf's* approval to open an exit to the Hasmonean Tunnel—a tourist attraction boasting many archae-ological curiosities (including a marker delineating a point beneath the ancient Holy of Holies).[24] Hitherto, visitors to the tunnel had had to enter and exit the 1,600-foot passageway through the same opening, meaning that they had to backtrack to get out. Israel proposed to build an exit at the far end—in the Old City's Muslim Quarter near the Arab-owned tourist district on the Via Dolorosa. The alteration would enhance tourism, both in the tun-nel and in the Arab shops. Although the *waqf* publicly denied the existence of this secret compact, it immediately began converting Solomon's Stables into a self-contained mosque in preparation for Ramadan (taking great lib-erties with the terms of the agreement in the process). By September 1996, this work was well advanced, indicating that, regardless of what it said in public, the *waqf* considered the informal agreement operative. It was in this setting that Netanyahu approved the opening of the tunnel exit.[25]

Whatever may be said of Netanyahu's decision, two things are certain: it did not constitute a direct violation of the Oslo Accords,[26] and it did not involve bloodshed. In contrast, Arafat's response did both. Indeed, Arafat had been violating the accords right along. In the months prior to the opening of the tunnel exit, for example, Arafat and other PA officials repeatedly threat-ened a resumption of "the armed struggle"—a violation of the Oslo II Accords, which call upon the parties to "abstain from incitement, including hostile propaganda," and to settle disputes by negotiation or arbitration.[27] In public statements, Arafat absurdly accused Israel of being behind terrorist attacks on her own people, referred to Yahya Ayyash as a "martyr" and to Israel as a "demon," incited his minions to employ "all means" in the struggle against Israel, and bellowed: "If Israel rejects our demands there will be a reaction and we have a 30,000-man armed force" (a curious boast given that the Oslo Accords strictly limited the PA police force to 24,000 men).[28]

Using the tunnel exit as a pretext, Arafat now redoubled his incitement, falsely alleging that Israel's tunneling would destabilize the Temple Mount and cause the Al-Aksa Mosque to cave-in.[29] (Saeb Erekat, a member of Arafat's Oslo negotiating team, embellished this fiction by telling CNN's Wal-ter Rodgers that Israel's ultimate aim in building the tunnel exit was to replace the Al-Aksa Mosque with a new Jewish Temple.[30]) In truth, the tunnel is not *under* the Temple Mount but *adjacent* to it. Moreover, it had already been excavated. All Netanyahu had done was to allow completion of an exit in the Muslim Quarter (a half-mile from the Al-Aksa Mosque). Undeterred, Arafat exhorted the faithful to "defend" the Muslim holy places. Heeding his call, Jerusalem's Arabs rioted, inflicting dozens of casualties and suffering hun-dreds as Israeli troops were called in to restore order. The next 72 hours wit-nessed the so-called Tunnel War, in which Palestinian police, armed with weapons supplied by Israel in accordance with the Oslo Accords, sniped at Israeli soldiers, killing 15.[31]

With the situation spiraling out of control, Bill Clinton invited Arafat and Netanyahu to the White House for an urgent meeting on October 2. The violence came to a halt, and during the next three months, Clinton's chief Middle East negotiator, Dennis Ross, engaged the parties in intensive negotiations aimed at jumpstarting the moribund peace process. Although the talks were difficult,[32] Ross eventually managed to forge the Hebron Protocol between Israel and the PA. The agreement provided for the withdrawal of Israeli forces from 80 percent of Hebron — the last major West Bank city to be evacuated. The residual 20 percent of the city remained in Israeli hands in order to meet the security needs of the small Jewish enclave that had been reestablished in the city after the Six Day War. The agreement also confirmed bilateral commitment to the Oslo II Accord, which called for three further IDF "redeployments" to be carried out on the basis of reciprocal fulfillment of obligations by Arafat and the PA (i.e., to combat terror, halt incitement and revise the Palestinian charter, which still called for Israel's destruction despite a 1993 pledge to remove the offending passages).

The Knesset approved the protocol on January 16 and Israel withdrew her forces from the designated 80 percent of Hebron that very day. Young Palestinians celebrated in the streets— some holding aloft outlawed Kalashnikov assault rifles.[33] In the ensuing weeks, Palestinian Hebronites staged riots in which they threw rocks and firebombs at the city's Jewish residents and IDF protectors.[34] Nevertheless, on March 7, Israel informed the PA that it would redeploy from an additional 9.1 percent of the West Bank to satisfy the first of its three Oslo II redeployment obligations.[35] As matters stood, the West Bank was divided into three zones: three percent was wholly in Arab hands; another 24 percent was under Arab civil jurisdiction with Israel in charge of security; and the rest (housing just 4 percent of the population) was administered by Israel. Israel proposed moving 2.1 percent from the third category into the second, and 7 percent from the second into the first. (The U.S. had recommended a 10 percent transfer, consisting of 5 percent from the third to the second, and 5 percent from the second to the first.) Arafat refused Israel's offer, demanding an inflated 30 percent.[36]

Eleven days later, in another move to appease the right-wing members of his coalition, who were unhappy with the government's continuing concessions, Netanyahu broke ground on a new 6,500-unit housing development beyond the old Green Line in Jerusalem. Situated at Har Homa, in the southeastern part of the city, the project would interpose a Jewish community between the Arab neighborhoods of southern Jerusalem and the neighboring Arab town of Bethlehem.[37] According to Article XXXI, paragraphs 5–7 of the

Oslo II Accord, the issue of Jerusalem was to be deferred until "final status" negotiations took place at the end of the peace process. To some, the new Har Homa project appeared to be a case of establishing "facts on the ground," thus prejudicing those negotiations before they began.[38] In an effort to soften the blow, Netanyahu announced that 3,500 Arab housing units would be approved in Jerusalem as part of the same package. U.S. negotiator Dennis Ross cautioned him that the addition of Arab housing would not placate Arafat, and advised him not to proceed — but to no avail.[39]

Har Homa is frequently cited as a prime example of Netanyahu's "unrestrained" unilateralism.[40] It would be difficult, however, to award the moral high ground to Arafat. Far from seeking to resolve the matter through negotiation as called for in the Oslo Accords, the Palestinian leader determined that Israel's new housing project was an intolerable *casus belli*.[41] Refusing to be "Israel's policeman" in the face of such unilateral acts,[42] he announced a "national reconciliation" with Hamas and Islamic Jihad, and freed a number of terrorists he had detained in his prisons.[43] The result was a suicide-bombing spree, the likes of which had not been seen since before the 1996 election. In the next four months, 24 Israelis were killed and 407 were wounded in Palestinian attacks targeting crowded Israeli markets. The implication for the Oslo process was clear. As long as Israel continued making concessions (which it was expected to do even in the setting of Palestinian noncompliance), Arafat would make a show of keeping the peace. Any perceived misstep on Israel's part, however, and the hounds of hell would be unleashed.[44] Despite this obviously flawed approach to "peacemaking," no one was inclined to point fingers at Arafat. In discussing the matter shortly after the first suicide attack, Clinton's national security advisor, Sandy Berger, and secretary of state, Madeline Albright, asked not whether it was feasible to deal with Arafat, but whether the U.S. should refuse to deal with Netanyahu.[45]

Meanwhile, in response to the new wave of terrorism, Netanyahu withheld promised financial support from the Palestinian Authority and closed crossing points, saying through a spokesman that "Israel will no longer pay with dead lying in the streets and while the Palestinian Authority does not fight terror or prevent it from being committed."[46] At the same time, the prime minister approved yet another building project — this one in the Etzion bloc, near Jerusalem — thereby drawing sharp criticism from the Palestinian Authority and from Madeline Albright (although the latter was careful to add that "there is no moral equivalency between suicide bombers and bulldozers...").[47]

It was at this delicate juncture that Mossad, the Israeli intelligence service, stepped in with its own blunder. In September 1997, an Arab gunman shot two security officers at the Israeli embassy in Amman, Jordan. In retaliation, two Mossad agents managed to inject poison into the ear of Khalid Mashaal (Hamas' representative in Amman). The agents failed in their escape, however, and wound up in the custody of Jordanian police. In order to secure their release, Israel dispatched a physician to Jordan to administer the antidote to Mashaal (who survived).[48] In addition, it paroled the imprisoned "Sheikh" Ahmed Yassin, Hamas' quadriplegic "spiritual leader" and the "spiritual father" of suicide bombing. Yassin was greeted by cheering throngs in Gaza, while Netanyahu's visage appeared on the cover of the October 11–17 edition of *The Economist*, next to the legend "Israel's Serial Bungler."[49]

For the next year, there was no substantive progress in the peace talks. Although the Israeli Ministry of Foreign Affairs documented multiple PA violations of the January 1997 Hebron Protocol during this period — including, but not limited to, the recruitment into the PA "police" force of 23 terrorists wanted by Israel for murder, failure to reduce the size of that force to specified levels, failure to confiscate illegal stockpiled weaponry, active involvement by PA "police" in anti–Israel terrorism, and failure to demolish terrorist infrastructure[50] — blame was illogically apportioned to Netanyahu for his "unilateral" house-building and his alleged "stinginess" with concessions.

Subjected to unrelenting pressure to forge ahead with the peace process, the Israeli leader ultimately signed the Wye River Memorandum (October 1998). The new agreement increased Israel's West Bank "redeployment" offer from an additional 9.1 percent to an additional 13 percent of the West Bank. After a heated debate, the Israeli cabinet approved the memorandum. But Netanyahu's decision to violate, yet again, his own principle of refusing further concessions until the PA met its prior commitments caused his coalition to crumble from within. With a no-confidence vote looming in the Knesset (December 1998), Netanyahu called for early elections, to take place the following May.

He didn't win. In the May 1999 elections, Labor candidate Ehud Barak polled 56 percent of the vote against Netanyahu's 44 percent. A former IDF chief of staff with an ironclad reputation on security (no soldier in IDF history had garnered more decorations), Barak was determined to pursue peace with all of Israel's neighbors.[51] Within ten months of taking office, he had offered to withdraw completely from the Golan Heights to the old 1923 Anglo-French border. The offer proved insufficient. Syria rejected Israel's demands for an early warning system on Mount Hermon and for the partial demilitarization of the Golan when it reverted to Syrian hands.[52] Likewise, they objected to the 1923 frontier — demanding instead a return to the pre-1967 line, including a foothold on the northeastern shoreline of the Sea of Galilee. Seeing this as a threat to Israel's water supply, Barak demurred.[53] The negotiations broke off in March 2000, by which time Syrian president Hafez Assad was terminally ill and no longer interested in pursuing a domestically unpopular agreement that might jeopardize the succession of his son.[54]

Two months later, the prime minister tried a different tack — unilaterally withdrawing IDF forces from the security zone in south Lebanon, hoping thus to improve relations with Lebanon and Syria. Unfortunately, most Arabs perceived the move as a sign of weakness, and this perception was greatly enhanced when a jubilant Hezbollah brushed aside Israel's ally, the South Lebanese Army, and moved its own "victorious" forces into the evacuated security zone.[55] Although the UN Security Council verified Israel's full compliance with Resolution 425 calling for the IDF's complete withdrawal from Lebanon, Hezbollah promptly claimed that the Sheba'a Farms (which Israel had taken from Syria during clashes with the PLO after the Six Day War) were actually part of Lebanon, and that the jihad against Israel must, therefore, continue.[56]

Barak now had but one peace card to play: in September 1999, he had concluded an agreement with Yasser Arafat at Sharm el-Sheikh, whereby Israel undertook to carry out the three Wye "redeployments" and to release several hundred Palestinian prisoners as a prelude to embarking on "final status" negotiations (to be completed not later than February 2000).[57] The February deadline was not met, but on July 5, Bill Clinton announced that the talks would commence in one week at Camp David. Although the summit meeting was Barak's idea, the announcement threw Israel's government into crisis. Believing that Barak intended to make concessions that would jeopardize Israel's security, several cabinet ministers resigned, and Barak only narrowly survived a no-confidence vote in the Knesset.[58] Arafat, meanwhile, attempted to beg out of the conference, claiming that he had not been given time to prepare.

Despite these omens, the Camp David summit kicked off as scheduled on July 11. In the ensuing 14 days, Barak offered statehood to the Palestinians — the first time this had been done in the Oslo context — and made creative efforts to resolve all outstanding issues between the parties. When Arafat rejected sovereignty over 100 percent of Gaza and 85 percent of the West Bank, Barak upped the latter offer to 92 percent and agreed to the division of Jerusalem, the unity of which he had pledged to uphold during his electoral campaign,[59] and which hitherto had been nonnegotiable. According to an official Palestinian synopsis of the talks, Barak undertook to abandon 63 West Bank settlements, to evacuate Hebron, and, after an interim period not to exceed 12 years, to withdraw from the strategic Jordan Valley. Attempts were also made to reach a compromise on the Temple Mount — including one plan whereby the Palestinians would hold sovereignty over its surface while Israel maintained sway over the Temple ruins which lay beneath.[60]

Given the unprecedented nature of the Israeli offer, Clinton and Barak expected, at the very least, to hear a constructive counterproposal from Arafat. Far from producing one, Arafat simply rejected every formulation, while insisting that Israel (i) accept "political, legal and moral responsibility for the [Palestinian] refugee problem"[61] and (ii) include a "right of return" clause in the peace accord, giving Palestinian refugees the option of "returning to their homes" inside Israel. (The latter was a hackneyed euphemism implying a Palestinian "right" to destroy Israel by overwhelming it demographically with waves of returning refugees and their progeny.[62]) For good measure, Arafat insulted the whole of Judaism by claiming that there had never been a Jewish Temple on the Temple Mount.[63]

After two weeks of exhaustive deliberations, it had become clear that there would be no agreement. Consequently, the summit was terminated. Couching his comments in diplomatic language, a disappointed Bill Clinton told a White House press gathering that, "it would be safe to say ... that the prime minister moved forward more from his initial position than Chairman Arafat.... I would be making a mistake not to praise Barak because I think he took a big risk."[64] (During the negotiations, the president had been more direct, telling Arafat, "You have been here for fourteen days and said no to everything. These things have consequences; failure will mean the end of the peace process."[65])

Arafat's apologists were to claim later that Barak had exhibited a cold demeanor, or that he had not made clear what he was offering, or even that the Israeli offer would have divided the West Bank into cantons.[66] These allegations are belied by the same Palestinian report alluded to above, which recounted Barak's offers in minute detail and dismissed the notion of cantonization.[67] U.S. negotiator Dennis Ross confirmed that the West Bank offer was "contiguous," not cantonized. He believed that the summit failed because, as a lifelong "revolutionary," Arafat was "defined" by the conflict and thus incapable of ending it.[68] (A simpler explanation, however, is that Arafat had never changed his mind from the days of the 1978 Camp David Accords, when he said, "We want *Palestine*. We're not interested *in bits of Palestine*,"[69] and that "Peace for us means the destruction of Israel."[70]) In any event, Arafat returned to cheering crowds in Gaza, while Barak, on his return, could scarcely muster 30 supporters in the Knesset.[71]

With the summit behind him, Arafat attempted to canvass support for a unilateral declaration of Palestinian independence. Finding, however, that the world held him to account for the failure of the Camp David talks and would not support a unilateral move, he decided to provoke a violent confrontation with Israel, and to use the resultant casualties among his own populace to reclaim world sympathy.[72] As early as March 2000, an Israel Ministry of Foreign Affairs report had noted a sharp increase in the level of incitement against Israel in Palestinian media and schools. An article in the *New York Times* noted that Palestinian teens attending "summer camp" were receiving instruction in terrorist tactics and guerilla warfare.[73] Following Camp David, it was noted that Arafat had released known terrorists from his prisons, had begun intensive Fatah military drills, and was stockpiling weapons, food, petrol and medicines.[74] All that was needed now was a pretext. On September 28, it arrived in the person of Ariel Sharon.

Ariel "Arik" Sharon was born Ariel Scheinerman in British Mandatory Palestine on February 27, 1928. His pedigree included a paternal grandfather who attended the inaugural World Zionist Congress in Basle as a delegate (1897), a grandmother who was midwife at the birth of Menachem Begin, and a father who headed the *Po'alei Zion* (Workers of Zion) chapter in the Soviet Republic of Georgia. Immigrating to Palestine during the Third Aliyah,[75] Arik's parents, Samuel and Vera, settled at Kfar Malal, a moshav just north of Tel Aviv.

As was typical of moshav residents elsewhere, the people of Kfar Malal took immense pride in the "semi-collective" nature of their communal settlement. Samuel Scheinerman, however, preferred to emphasize its "semi-noncollective" nature: Intent on retaining a degree of privacy and independence beyond the norm for such a community, Samuel fenced off his plot of land and refused to participate in Kfar Malal's collective marketing of foodstuffs.[76] To keep children away from his fruit trees, Samuel equipped six-year-old Arik with a club and sent him forth to patrol the perimeter of the property. By age ten, Arik had exported the tactic to other venues. At local meetings of the Zionist Youth Movement, for example, the group leader had to ask him to refrain from rapping other children on the head for talking out of turn.[77]

One result of these experiences was that Arik didn't attract many friends. Another was that he developed the underpinnings of a tough, no-nonsense soldier. At age 14, he enlisted in the Haganah, swearing the traditional oath holding a Bible and revolver.[78] As a member of his high school's paramilitary corps, *Gadna*, during World War II, he excelled in hand-to-hand battle drills—inflicting a great number of bruises on those unlucky enough to be pitted against him.[79]

Despite his unsociable childhood, he matured into a natural leader of men. A master of night actions with an uncanny sense of direction, bold in attack and unhesitating in his decisions, he became an admired platoon leader in the Haganah's Alexandroni Brigade during Israel's War of Independence.[80] In the battle for the Jerusalem road, however, the brigade was thrown into an ill-planned attack on Latrun. Through no fault of his own, Arik and his platoon were pinned down by Arab artillery and machine-gun fire with no open escape route. Seeking to keep up the spirits of his men, Arik declared, "Look, I've gotten you out of a lot of tight places before. I'll get you out of this one, too."[81] But the promise was beyond fulfillment. Hit in the abdomen and thigh, Arik only narrowly made it to safety, helped by a wounded fellow soldier while Arab Legionnaires and peasants roamed the field shooting incapacitated IDF soldiers and robbing the corpses. At multiple points in the hours-long trek to safety, Arik ordered his brother-in-arms to save his own life, but the soldier refused to abandon him.[82] Most of the platoon was not so lucky, and thoughts of the men left behind tormented Arik during his long hospital recovery.[83] Henceforth, he was determined never to leave men in the field.[84]

Serving as an IDF intelligence officer after the war, Arik harshly criticized the army's lack of initiative in combating Arab terrorism. In June 1953, he was given permission to carry out a reprisal raid, but his men were not adequately trained and the sortie accomplished little. To do the job properly, he insisted, the IDF needed a professional commando squad.[85] Impressed by his brashness, Chief of Staff Mordechai Maklef appointed him to head up just such a force — "Unit 101." In its first mission, the 101st chased off a band of Bedouin squatters. In its second — a reprisal raid against *fedayeen* guerrillas operating from Gaza's al-Bureij refugee camp — it created controversy by inflicting three dozen casualties, many of them civilian (September 1953).[86] The following month, after Arab terrorists hurled a grenade into a home in Kfar Yehuda, killing a young mother and her two toddlers, Unit 101 struck back against Kibya — the Jordanian village from which the attackers had come. After a brief firefight on the approach road, Arik and his men entered what appeared to be a deserted town. Entering some of the buildings, they fired their guns at the ceiling and shouted for the occupants to get out. Satisfied that the structures were empty, they laid explosive charges and left the hamlet in smoking ruins. Unfortunately, they had not done an adequate search. It turned out that scores of villagers had simply hidden, and in the ensuing explosions nearly 70 innocents were killed.[87] A storm of protest issued from the international community, including a reprimand from the UN Security Council. Taken aback by the reports, David Ben-Gurion made a transparent attempt to disavow the attack in a national radio address. Behind the scenes, he asked whether Unit 101 might be composed of ex–Lehi and ex–Irgun men. Reassured in a private interview with Arik that this was not the case, the prime minister decided that the tragedy and the world community's reaction to it would have to be weighed against the fact that a strong message had been delivered to Israel's terrorist enemies. He closed the interview by conferring a Hebrew surname on the unit's young commander: "Sharon" (denoting the region in Israel where Arik was born).[88] But the matter was not quite closed:

sobered by the nature of the casualties in the Kibya operation, the IDF high command issued an order restricting future reprisal raids to military targets.[89]

Wounded on a subsequent mission, Sharon was promoted to the rank of lieutenant colonel and given command of "Unit 202"—a combined commando-paratrooper force. Between 1954 and 1956, the new unit embarked on a series of aggressive retaliatory operations against military and terrorist targets in Jordan, Egypt and Syria. The most celebrated of these attacks were the February 1955 strike against Egypt's main army base in Gaza (in which 37 Egyptian soldiers were killed) and the December 1955 attack on Kinneret in Syria (which claimed the lives of 56 Syrian soldiers). Both attacks were internationally condemned, while the murders that provoked them were virtually ignored.[90]

Sharon was now a highly controversial figure, loved by his soldiers, but reviled by many in the upper echelons of the IDF, who simultaneously resented the favoritism shown to him by Ben-Gurion and objected to his habit of turning small operations into much larger ones.[91] During the Sinai Campaign of 1956, Sharon led the push to reinforce the paratroopers who had descended near the Mitla Pass in the war's opening hours. Charged with blocking the outlet of the pass, Sharon decided instead to capture it, in direct defiance of orders. A reconnaissance team advanced blindly into the Mitla Valley only to be ambushed on both flanks. Sharon dispatched reinforcements to their support. (His junior officers later called him to account for not leading them himself, saying that he was more daring with their lives than with his own.[92]) Ultimately, his beleaguered men prevailed, securing the pass at a cost of 38 dead — nearly a quarter of the Israeli total for the entire war. But the operation had been unnecessary. The pass played no further role in the war, and was soon abandoned.

Sharon's breach of discipline drew the wrath of Moshe Dayan and threw his career into eclipse. After a stint at the Royal Staff College in England, he was placed in command of infantry training, only to be dismissed amid charges of lying to a superior.[93] Next, he was given command of the infantry school (1958). There he languished until 1961, when he decided to pursue formal training in the armor branch.

His new commanders found his approach to be innovative to the point of genius, and daring to the point of recklessness.[94] Sharon's mastery of tank tactics culminated in one of the Six Day War's most brilliant ground operations—the storming and capture of Egypt's main fortification complex in Sinai. Across the globe, military college students marveled at his tactical methods.[95] By now, his military prowess had earned him the rank of major general. Nevertheless, the 1960s were a decade of profound personal tragedy for him. In 1962, Margalit, his wife of nine years, died in a car accident. (When she and Ariel were teens, her school had abutted the Scheinerman property in Kfar Malal, and Arik had been so anxious to meet her that he cut a hole in the schoolyard fence in order to do so.[96]) Needing help with his five-year-old son, Gur, Ariel enlisted the support of Margalit's sister, Lily. Within a year, Ariel and Lily had fallen in love. They married in 1963, and remained together until her death from lung cancer in 2000. But Sharon's personal tribulations were not over: On Rosh Hashanah in 1967, Gur and a friend discovered an antique gun that Ariel kept in the home. Hearing the weapon discharge, Ariel came running and found his son lying motionless, wounded in the face. His wife had taken the car, so he had to hail a passing vehicle for transport to the hospital. Gur died en route.[97]

Heartbroken, Sharon threw himself into his work, only to quarrel with IDF chief of staff Chaim Bar-Lev, who was intent on building a line of fortresses on the Suez Canal waterline. Sharon likened the idea to France's ill-fated Maginot Line, which had proven useless during World War II.[98] When it came time for Sharon to reenlist the following year, Bar-Lev initially sought to prohibit him, but afterwards relented and gave him command of the southern front. One of Sharon's new responsibilities was to quash terrorism emanating from Gaza, which he accomplished by dividing the strip into a checkerboard grid and subjecting each square to a rigorous search. It was whispered that he possessed a roster of terrorists, and that each time one was killed, he struck out his name. The number of terrorist attacks promptly fell from 445 in 1971 to 60 in 1972.[99] Learning that there were no further promotions in store for him, Sharon retired to his farm in May 1973. Within months, however, he had laid the groundwork for a new career by masterminding the amalgamation of Israel's right and center political parties into a single electoral bloc capable of challenging the Labor Party. He was campaigning for a Knesset seat on the Likud ("Unity") ticket when the Yom Kippur War broke out and the IDF called him back to duty.

Sharon was the first Israeli commander in the Yom Kippur War to espouse the theory that Egypt could not push beyond her Suez Canal-line missile umbrella without risking the destruction of her forces.[100] He also came within a hair's breadth of being dismissed for insubordination — more than once. His chief aspiration was to strike back across the canal, and by pressing forward (in defiance of orders) he discovered a gap in the Egyptian lines where this might be accomplished.[101] But his superiors refused to let him make the attempt, fearing that any Israeli bridgehead would be swept aside by the two reserve tank divisions that Egypt still possessed on the canal's west bank. In time, Sadat ordered these divisions to cross into the Sinai, and the counterstroke was approved. Sharon was ordered to secure the crossing site. When, after several tries, a bulldozer failed to knock down a brick wall blocking the approach, Sharon took the driver's seat, smashed into the barrier shouting, "Like that!" and then returned the vehicle to its operator who completed the task a few minutes later.[102] As D-day approached, Sharon's superiors told him that he would not be first to cross. Asked on the phone by his immediate commander, Shmuel Gonen, if he understood his instructions, the reply was vintage Sharon: "I hear you. No problem here. I can also cross. No problem." When Gonen pressed him, saying, "I'm ordering Bren [General Avrham Adan] to cross," Sharon replied, "He can cross first. He can cross second. It's not important."[103] Gonen may be forgiven if he found this answer maddening. In the event, Adan crossed first, with Sharon "supervising."

Directing the operation under heavy Egyptian fire, Sharon sustained a scalp laceration. Afterwards, he continued his duties with his head wrapped in a bloodstained white bandage. As the catalyst for Israel's successful counterstroke — which would have produced a crushingly decisive victory if political considerations had not supervened — Sharon became an object of reverence to his men, many of whom painted the slogan "Arik, King of Israel," on the sides of their military vehicles. After the war, Sharon lambasted his superiors for their hesitancy in embarking upon the crossing and for their subsequent failure to exploit it to the full. In answer to these very public musings, the IDF brass stripped him of his commission.[104]

In the December 1973 elections, Sharon obtained a Knesset seat on the Likud list. Finding, however, that his fellow Knesset members were not as adept at taking orders as his soldiers had been, he resigned his seat a year into his term. In June 1975, he became special military advisor to Prime Minister Yitzhak Rabin. But after eight months, he quit that post, too, and formed his own political party: *Shlomzion* ("Peace for Zion").

Following the election of Menachem Begin in 1977, Sharon returned to the Likud fold as minister of agriculture, from which post he set in train an aggressive and controversial program of settlement building in the West Bank. His goal was threefold: (i) to establish Israeli control over the strategic hills beyond the June 4 lines; (ii) to secure Israel's claim to the whole of Jerusalem by encircling the city with Jewish settlements; and (iii) to solidify Israel's hold on the strategic Jordan Valley. He also sought to strengthen Israel's presence in the part of Sinai adjacent to Gaza. Within four years, he erected 64 settlements, earning the moniker "bulldozer."[105] His policy led to friction during the 1978 Begin-Sadat Camp David talks, but at the crucial moment, Sharon did his part for peace by advising Begin to surrender Israel's Sinai settlements if they represented the only obstacle to an accord.[106]

Later, as minister of defense in Begin's second term, he attracted the ire of the settler movement by presiding over the forced evacuation and bulldozing of Yamit, Israel's signature Sinai settlement. Likewise, he was intensely criticized for his handling of Israel's 1982 Lebanon War — his detractors charging (not without justification) that he had brazenly misled the cabinet and public in pursuit of his own operational blueprint. The defining moment came when the Kahan Commission declared him negligent for allowing the Christian Phalangist militia to enter Beirut's Sabra and Shatila refugee camps— a ruling that led to his ouster as minister of defense (February 1983). But Sharon was not the "butcher of Sabra and Shatila," as his vitriolic detractors liked to caricature him,[107] and when *Time* magazine published a shoddily researched article insinuating that he had given prior consent to the massacres, Sharon successfully sued the magazine for defamation and mischaracterization of the facts.[108]

Nevertheless, following the Kahan Commission report, Sharon could scarcely go out in public without being jeered by hostile protestors. For a time, it appeared that his political career was over. But his security credentials kept him popular with the Israeli right, and in 1984, he obtained the industry and trade portfolio in the Shamir-Peres national unity government. In his new incarnation, he became Israel's highest-profile hardliner — purchasing a home in the Muslim Quarter of the Old City to symbolize his dedication to an undivided Jerusalem and bitterly criticizing Defense Minister Rabin for his failure to put down the 1987 intifada. Appointed minister of housing and infrastructure after the fall of the unity government in 1990, he publicly castigated Prime Minister Shamir for failing to answer Saddam Hussein's scud missile attacks during the Gulf War, and for participating in the 1991 Madrid peace talks without demanding an end to the intifada as a precondition. After U.S. secretary of state James Baker withheld $10 billion in loan guarantees to dissuade Israel from further building projects in the West Bank, Sharon greeted every Baker tour of the Middle East with the authorization of a new settlement.[109]

Out of office following the 1992 election of Yitzhak Rabin, Sharon bitterly opposed the Oslo Accords, arguing that Jordan was the "Palestinian state," and that Arafat, regardless of his rhetoric, was still committed to Israel's annihilation.[110] As the Oslo process gained momentum, Sharon's influence reached a nadir. When he went on an eight-day hunger strike to protest the agreements, scarcely anyone noticed. But then, in 1996, he helped engineer Benjamin Netanyahu's victorious prime ministerial campaign, and his fortunes began to change. He was rewarded with the post of minister of national infrastructure.

The new government was wracked by competing ambitions— not the least of them being Sharon's. He voted against the 1997 Hebron Protocol. Needing his support for the 1998 Wye Accord, Netanyahu appointed him foreign minister and gave him a role in the negotiations. In the ensuing talks, Sharon made a point of telling Arafat that he wouldn't get anything if he didn't fulfill his obligations (which were specifically spelled out in the agreement).[111] Despite these stern words, the Wye Accord provoked a crisis in Netanyahu's cabinet, thereby forcing the early elections that brought Ehud Barak to power. Badly mauled in the voting, Netanyahu resigned his party chairmanship and his Knesset seat. Sharon succeeded him as Likud chairman.

Thus, 16 years after his Kahan Commission disgrace, Ariel Sharon had risen to the top post in the Likud. Unfortunately, his wife and confidante, Lily, was now terminally ill with lung cancer. Though she bade him continue his work and run for prime minister, he spent endless hours at her bedside. Her death in March 2000 came as a bitter blow. He was roused back to action, however, by reports of Ehud Barak's willingness to compromise on Jerusalem and the Temple Mount at Camp David. Determined to drive home the point that Judaism's holiest site was not a mere "bargaining chip,"[112] he embarked on his symbolic visit to the Temple Mount on the morning of September 28, telling reporters, "I have come with a message of peace. Jews have the right to visit here."[113] Later that day — incited by untrue Palestinian radio reports claiming that the Al-Aksa Mosque was in danger — Palestinian protestors began to throw rocks at Israeli police. Twenty-eight policemen and four rioters were injured.[114]

On the morrow, 22,000 Muslims congregated on the Temple Mount for Friday prayer services. Below them, at the Western Wall, Jews were gathering for the beginning of Rosh Hashanah (the Jewish New Year). During the Muslim sermon, the imam slanderously accused the Jews of plotting the destruction of the Dome of the Rock and the Al-Aksa Mosque so that they could rebuild the Jewish Temple.[115] Egged on by his words (and by the goading of covert Palestinian operatives within the crowd), some of the faithful took up rocks— which had been brought to the site beforehand[116]— and began hurling them at the peaceful crowd of Jewish worshippers below. The Western Wall pavilion was hurriedly evacuated, and in the ensuing clashes with Israeli police, four Palestinians were killed and more than 160 injured.[117]

Ever since these opening salvos of Arafat's "terrorist war" (euphemistically called the "second" or "Al-Aksa" intifada), Sharon's detractors have attempted to paint the Arab violence as the inevitable result of his high-profile visit to the Temple Mount. On October 3, the editorial page of the *New York Times* consecrated this view, declaring that the war's "precipitating incident was a provocative and irresponsible visit by the Likud leader, Ariel Sharon...."[118]

This assertion is at odds with the facts. Incitement and preparation for war had been ongoing for months prior to Sharon's visit. As Palestinian communications minister Imad Faluji subsequently admitted, the "Al-Aksa" intifada "had been planned since Chairman Arafat's return from Camp David, when he turned the tables on the ... U.S. president and rejected the American conditions."[119] Mamduh Nofal, another Arafat advisor, told a Beirut journal that "the intifada was neither a mass movement detached from the PA nor an instinctive popular uprising.... Yasser Arafat viewed the visit as a flashpoint that could inflame not only the Palestinian land but also the situation beyond Palestine's [sic] borders."[120]

After investigating the matter, an independent commission chaired by former U.S. senator George Mitchell likewise concluded that "the Sharon visit did not cause the 'Al-Aksa *Intifada.*'"[121] But, as Stephanie Gutmann has noted in her book *The Other War*, the uprising was a two-front conflict: One battlefield was on the ground, where the people of Israel were being victimized in a preplanned terrorist onslaught. The second — in which the truth had only a bit part — was in the mainstream media, where the conflict was depicted as a Palestinian "freedom fight" against supposed Israeli oppression.[122] The tone of the media's coverage was set within 48 hours of the outbreak of hostilities: On September 29, Tuvia Grossman, a young American Jewish student, was forcibly removed from a taxicab by a gang of Palestinian hooligans who proceeded to brutalize him until he escaped and fled to a nearby Israeli police station. Seeking to protect him, an alert policeman angrily shook his baton at the pursuing Palestinians, who promptly took to their heels. Without making any inquiries, news photographers snapped photos of the scene, which were subsequently published in numerous newspapers across the world. Thus, the next day, readers of the *New York Times* were treated to the image of a baton-wielding, angry, uniformed Israeli, standing over a helpless, bleeding youth, with the caption, "A Palestinian and an Israeli soldier on the Temple Mount." Inaccurate in every detail — the "Palestinian" was a Jew, the "soldier" was a policeman, and the scene was not "on the Temple Mount"— the caption falsely implied an act of Israeli brutality at Jerusalem's holiest site. After repeated complaints, Grossman managed to wring a retraction, even a small news story, from the *Times* and the Associated Press, but the imagery had already done its defamatory work. Retractions were a poor substitute for getting the story straight from the beginning.[123]

Vastly surpassing this episode in impact was a film clip broadcast that same day by the French television station France 2, purportedly showing a Palestinian father and son caught in cross fire between Israeli soldiers and Palestinian gunmen.[124] In the voice-over to the 55-second scene, newscaster Charles Enderlin told his viewers that Israeli troops had purposely directed their fire at the two; that the boy, Mohammed Al Dura, had been killed and the father wounded; and that the fatal images, which he possessed, were too ghastly to show. The scene, which was soon immortalized on postage stamps and other media, became an instant monument to Israeli "inhumanity." A subsequent IDF investigation proving that there was no line of sight between the Israeli position at Gaza's Netzarim Junction (where the Israelis had come under unprovoked fire that morning) and the position of the Al Duras was ignored.[125] So, too, was an independent documentary from German ARD television, which confirmed this conclusion.

Despite mounting pressure, France 2 refused to release the raw footage from which the report was taken; but three journalists who attended a restricted screening reported that it included unrelated scenes that were obviously staged, and that there was no evidence of the child being hit or killed by gunfire. In June 2003, *Atlantic Monthly* featured an article by James Fallows, who concluded that "whatever happened to [Mohammed Al Dura], he was not shot by the Israeli soldiers who were known to be involved in the day's fighting...."

In November 2002, media blogger Philippe Karsenty publicly accused France 2 of perpetrating a hoax. France 2 promptly sued him for defamation, and though the public prosecutor argued in Karsenty's favor (which should have settled the matter), the court adjudged him guilty, refusing his request for the release of the France 2 raw footage. When Karsenty appealed the ruling, the appellate court subpoenaed the film footage, but France 2 defied the court order by releasing only 18 of the 27 minutes it possessed. In the end, the court found Karsenty not guilty of defamation—citing among other things, Enderlin's "imprudent claim that he edited out the images of the child's [death] agony." (The footage, in fact, showed the boy moving his arm to look at the camera after Enderlin announced his death.) The court, however, did not go so far as to rule that the episode was staged.[126]

In addition to what they say about journalistic integrity, these flawed media portrayals contributed to the milieu of Arab furor that was already being stoked by the Palestinian Authority's baseless campaign of anti–Israel incitement. To gauge the effect of this milieu, we must fast forward to October 11, 2000 (two weeks after Enderlin's initial report), when PA police illegally detained two Israeli reservists, Vadim Nourezitz and Yosef Avrahami, who had gotten lost en route to their West Bank base. Taken to the Ramallah police station, the two were set upon and lynched by a frenzied Palestinian mob. In the midst of this heinous act, Nourezitz's cell phone rang. It was his wife. Answering the call, one of the killers informed her that her husband was in the process of being murdered, and held up the phone so she could listen.[127] Outside the police station, an Italian film crew caught the incident on video. The film shows a violent struggle inside the station. Moments later, a jubilant murderer appears at the window, holding up his bloody hands to the cheers of those in the street below. Finally, one of the victims is thrown out the window to the eager crowd, some of whom begin pummeling and kicking his hapless corpse with unrestrained violence. (After the footage was broadcast, Italy's RTI TV had to withdraw its correspondents from PA-controlled areas owing to death threats from Palestinian Arabs.[128])

The violence, however, had begun well before this. On September 30, the day of the "Al Dura" report, the Palestinian Authority declared an official "protest day"—exempting all Palestinian schoolchildren from class so that they could enlist with the growing throngs of demonstrators.[129] In an effort to contain the uprising, Israel closed the territories, erected roadblocks,[130] and exchanged fire with Palestinian gunmen who shot at them from crowds of rock-throwing teens.[131] Attempts by Bill Clinton to arrange a cease-fire in Paris (October 4) and Sharm el-Sheikh (October 17) were nullified when Arab leaders issued a statement in Cairo on October 22 expressing support for the uprising. On November 1, Ehud Barak dispatched Shimon Peres to the Gaza border to negotiate a truce. Arafat agreed to one, but did not enforce it.[132]

By this point, Barak was willing to concede Palestinian statehood in exchange for an interim accord.[133] But his initiative got nowhere, and opinion polls now indicated that he would lose in a head-to-head contest against Benjamin Netanyahu. Because Netanyahu was not currently a member of the Knesset, he was not eligible to run. In a calculated move, Barak announced his resignation on December 9, 2000, thereby forcing new elections before Netanyahu regained his eligibility. The Knesset turned the tables with a special amendment making Netanyahu eligible. But the latter declined to run: there were only 19 Likudists in the Knesset, and he preferred to await the next legislative elections so that he might command a stronger base. This meant that Barak's opponent would be Ariel Sharon, a man Barak was certain he could beat.[134]

Prior to the election, Bill Clinton offered a final Oslo bridging proposal whereby Israel would (i) annex up to 6 percent of the West Bank (encompassing its major settlement blocs) in exchange for 1–3 percent of its own territory; (ii) cede a safe-passage corridor between Gaza and the West Bank to the new Palestinian state; (iii) withdraw from the Jordan Valley within six years while maintaining three early warning stations indefinitely; (iv) assist in international efforts to ameliorate the Palestinian plight; and (v) surrender sovereignty over the surface of the Temple Mount and the Arab neighborhoods in Jerusalem. In return, the PA was to (i) accept a territorially contiguous, but demilitarized, state; (ii) acknowledge Israeli sovereignty over Jewish neighborhoods in Jerusalem and over the archaeological ruins beneath the surface of the Temple Mount; and (iii) surrender its claim of a Palestinian "right of return" to Israel. The parties were told to approve or reject the proposal without amendment. Agreement would signify that all terms had been accepted, that there were no outstanding claims, and that the conflict was terminated. The Israeli cabinet approved. Arafat never gave a definitive answer, thereby sounding the death knell of Oslo.[135]

Meanwhile, employing the slogan "Only Sharon Will Bring Peace," Ariel Sharon kicked off his campaign.[136] Unlike Barak who had continued to negotiate in the midst of the uprising, Sharon declared that there would be no further discussion until the violence ceased. Likewise, he stated that the Oslo process was defunct, and that any new negotiations would not be bound by it.[137] In February 2001, he won a resounding victory, garnering an unprecedented 62 percent of the vote. On taking office, he called for the formation of a broad-based unity government to restore security to the nation's citizens. The result was a coalition commanding 73 Knesset seats. In his inaugural address, he confirmed that Jerusalem would remain Israel's undivided capital. He also vowed to "conduct negotiations with the Palestinians to achieve political agreements— but not under pressure of terror and violence.... If our Palestinian neighbors choose the path of peace, reconciliation and good neighborly relations, they will find that I and the government I lead are honest and faithful partners."[138] To underscore his commitment to a reasonable settlement, he appointed the dovish Shimon Peres as foreign minister, mitigated economic constraints on the Palestinians (despite ongoing terrorism), and declared that a seven-day respite in attacks on Israeli civilians would suffice for the resumption of negotiations.[139]

Israel received no such respite. To cite but a few examples of the ubiquitous violence: In March 2001, a Palestinian sniper shot a ten-month-old Israeli infant in the arms of its mother.[140] In April, mortar shells from Gaza began to rain down on the Israeli city of Sderot. On June 2, a suicide bomber detonated himself outside a Tel Aviv nightclub, killing 21 youths who were waiting in line to get in. (This, apparently, was a "reprisal" for the death of the popular Palestinian spokesperson, Faisal al-Husseini. The fact that al-Husseini had died of a heart attack did not prevent tens of thousands of mourners from "vowing revenge" at his funeral.[141]) In August, the target was a popular Jerusalem pizzeria. Fifteen were killed and 120 wounded.

By now, Israeli tourism had ground to a halt and the economy was in a tailspin. There were calls for Sharon's replacement by Benjamin Netanyahu.[142] Nevertheless, the U.S. pressed Sharon to show restraint — pressure that intensified after September 11, when Al Qaeda flew hijacked passenger planes into the World Trade Center and Pentagon. On hearing of the attacks, crowds of Palestinians danced in the streets. (After submitting a video of one such celebration in Nablus, the photographer called his AP bosses with the odd request that the tape be destroyed: armed Palestinians, he explained, were literally holding a pair of guns to his head.[143]) The U.S. response was counterintuitive: on October 2, in a move calculated to appease Arab sentiment in preparation for a U.S.-led invasion of Afghanistan, President George W. Bush made an unprecedented speech in support of Palestinian statehood. Taken aback, Ariel Sharon called upon the U.S. "not to repeat the terrible mistake of 1938 when the enlightened democracies of Europe decided to sacrifice Czechoslovakia for a temporary solution."[144] (The poignant remark was not well received in the Oval Office.)

Bush's call for statehood did nothing to forestall terrorism. On October 17, Palestinian gunmen shot down Israel's minister of tourism in Jerusalem. On December 1, a pair of suicide bombers struck the capital, killing 11 and wounding 180. Under U.S. pressure, the PA agreed to act on Israeli intelligence to apprehend terrorists en route to their targets. On December 12, Israel gave the PA the names of specific Palestinian terrorists who were poised for an imminent strike. (Their target was unknown.) The PA made no effort to apprehend the named individuals. At 6:00 P.M., the terrorists bombed a civilian bus, killing 11 and wounding 27.[145]

Despite the sentiments of his U.S. ally, Sharon could scarcely stay his hand. Since September 2000, Palestinian terrorism had claimed hundreds of Israeli lives. Declaring that the PA had not only failed to suppress terrorism, but was actively engaged in it, Sharon retaliated by closing the territories, launching helicopter strikes against PA police installations, blockading Arafat in his Ramallah headquarters, initiating targeted killings of leading terrorists, bulldozing the homes of suicide bombers, and shelling the PA's official radio station for its incessant incitements.[146] In characteristic fashion, the international community accused Israel of using "disproportionate force"—claiming that the territorial closures and antiriot measures instituted by Sharon constituted a form of "collective punishment," and portraying the IDF's targeted killings as "extrajudicial assassinations" that contributed to a "cycle of violence."[147]

On December 12, 2001, the Israeli cabinet announced that, "Arafat is no longer relevant from Israel's point of view, and there will be no more communication with him."[148] Four days into his irrelevancy, Arafat declared a cease-fire. His motive, however, was merely to obtain a respite in which to rearm — as became apparent three weeks later, when the IDF intercepted the *Karine-A*, a freighter bound for Gaza carrying 50 tons of outlawed weaponry from Iran. Seeing that there would be no effort on Arafat's part to contain terrorism, Israel decided to take security matters into her own hands, even in so-called "A" areas (i.e., zones controlled wholly by the PA). Between February 27 and March 18, 2002, the IDF carried out major operations in the

West Bank and Gaza to bring terrorism to heel. No sooner had they with-drawn, however, than the Palestinians unleashed the most concentrated string of suicide bombings to date. The culminating attack occurred at a Passover Seder in Netanya's Park Hotel, leaving 30 attendees dead—many of them Holocaust survivors—and 140 wounded (March 27, 2002).[149]

On March 29, the IDF responded with Operation Defensive Shield, occu-pying major West Bank population centers in an effort to apprehend terrorists and demolish terrorist infrastructure. Although the operation brought a prompt halt to the suicide bombing, it spawned a public relations debacle: In Jenin—which the PA itself had dubbed the "martyr's capital" (i.e., the capital of suicide bomber recruitment)—the IDF sought to minimize civilian casualties by conducting a house-to-house search. In passing from one house to another across a narrow alleyway, a squad of soldiers stumbled into a booby trap. Moments later, Palestinian gunmen began firing on them from the alley's upper story windows, killing 14. The Israelis brought in armored bulldozers to knock down the last terrorist strongholds.[150] Taking advantage of the fact that Israel refused to let reporters into the area during the resultant firefight with Palestinian guerillas, the Palestinians claimed that Israeli troops had gunned down hundreds of civilians and bulldozed the bodies into mass graves. Despite the outlandish nature of this slander, the media disseminated it as their top story of the day.[151] On CNN, Saeb Erekat informed the world that 500 civilians were known to be dead, with another 1,600 missing. Around the world, the "Jenin Massacre" was on everyone's lips. Visiting the area shortly afterwards, however, U.S. secretary of state Colin Powell could find nothing to support the Palestinian claims. Under pressure, Israel submitted to investigations by the UN, the European Union and Human Rights Watch. All came to the same conclusion: there was no massacre. In the end, a Pales-tinian review board placed the Jenin death toll at 56 Palestinians—34 of them combatants. Many of the 22 civilians who died had been employed as human shields by the terrorists, who fired on Israeli troops from multiple illicit sanc-tuaries, including a mosque and a girl's school.[152] Twenty-three IDF troops were killed. Despite the official findings, propagandists still speak of a "mas-sacre."

In Bethlehem, Palestinian gunmen seized the venerated Church of the Nativity. The Israelis studiously avoided hostilities in the vicinity of this struc-ture and ultimately agreed to let the gunmen escape. But the episode was another limited public relations victory for the Palestinians, since it resulted in television images of Israeli tanks taking up position around what is tradi-tionally regarded as Jesus' birthplace. In Ramallah, the IDF took control of Arafat's compound, confining him to his rooms. A search of the premises uncovered abundant evidence of Arafat's direct complicity in terrorism.[153]

Operation Defensive Shield delivered a powerful blow to terrorist operations in the West Bank, but when IDF troops drew back under American and European pressure, terrorism again reared its head. On June 18, a suicide bomber blew up an Israeli bus filled with schoolchildren, killing 19 and wounding 50.[154] Israel retaliated with further ground operations and targeted killings. On June 23, the IAF killed Hamas' leading terrorist, Salah Shehadeh, by destroying his home with a one-ton bomb. Shehadeh's wife and son were also killed along with 13 others.[155]

Meanwhile, the Israeli domestic situation was also in turmoil. In October 2002, economic stagnation caused Sharon's coalition to unravel. Unable to reestablish a majority on acceptable terms, he called new elections. On January 28, 2003, the electorate returned Likud to power with 38 Knesset seats against 19 for Labor. When Labor refused Sharon's invitation to form a new unity government, the prime minister forged a Knesset majority in alignment with the centrist Shinui Party and rightist National Religious Party. The new government took office in March 2003, with Sharon declaring that Israel desired peace and was willing to make "painful concessions" in order to achieve it.[156]

By this time, the United States was poised to invade Iraq. This decision, which was carried into effect on March 20, 2003, was internationally unpopular, particularly in the Arab world. In an effort to mitigate this opposition,[157] President Bush unveiled the so-called "Road Map to Peace"—an outline for achieving a lasting settlement between Israel and the Palestinians. Supported by a "Quartet" of powers including the U.S., the European Union, Russia and the UN, the plan envisioned an end to terrorism and the establishment of an independent, democratic and peaceful Palestinian state by 2005. The terms (which called for concessions far more painful than those envisioned by Sharon) were unveiled on April 30. The previous day, under Anglo-American pressure, Yasser Arafat had installed Mahmoud Abbas as PA prime minister—thereby nominally addressing Israel's refusal to have further relations with Arafat himself.[158]

Although Abbas promptly accepted the Road Map and spoke out against terrorism, the initiative was immediately derailed by a flurry of Palestinian suicide bombings. The first occurred on Abbas' first day in office, when a suicide bomber immolated himself outside a Tel Aviv nightclub, killing and injuring scores of Israelis. Between May 17 and May 19, Palestinian terrorists perpetrated five additional suicide bombings. Abbas did nothing to quell the violence, citing the fact that Sharon had not yet endorsed the Road Map (meaning that Israel had to commit itself to the establishment of a Palestinian state before Abbas would act).[159] Sharon had already decided to do so, but was in the process of submitting a list of 14 reservations to the U.S. government. When the latter promised to attend to these during the implementation phase, Sharon attended a summit in Aqaba, Jordan, and accepted the Road Map (June 4, 2003). Despite virulent rightwing protests, the Israeli cabinet approved the plan by a 12–7 vote.[160] (When Abbas subsequently claimed that he could not possibly act against terrorism without provoking a Palestinian civil war, the Bush Administration pressed Sharon to offer a few concessions in order to bolster Abbas' standing — a violation of the Road Map's terms, which specifically called upon the PA to dismantle all terrorist organizations as the initial step in the process.[161])

In acceding to the notion of a Palestinian state, Sharon remarked that Israel could not leave 3.5 million Palestinians under Israeli "occupation" indefinitely.[162] Hamas, Islamic Jihad and the Al-Aksa Martyr's Brigade greeted these conciliatory words with further deadly acts of terrorism. In retaliation, Sharon renewed his campaign of targeted killings. Although several leading terrorists were eliminated, the terrorism did not abate. In one of the worst attacks, a suicide bomber clad in the garb of an orthodox Jew detonated himself on a bus carrying Jewish families home from prayer at the Western Wall. Twenty-three were killed. Blaming Arafat, Sharon cut off all communication with the PA. Two weeks later, on September 6, 2003, Mahmoud Abbas resigned, citing Arafat's incessant meddling.[163]

With no prospect of a negotiated settlement and terrorism running rampant, Sharon took the podium on December 18, 2003, and made a startling announcement: If there was to be no progress on the Road Map (which he termed a "clear and reasonable plan") and if the Palestinian Authority would not fulfill its pledge to fight terrorism, then Israel would take unilateral action to bring about disengagement between Israelis and Palestinians.[164] Although he did not announce the details until February 2004, his plan called for a partial Israeli withdrawal on the West Bank behind a 425-mile security barrier (then under construction), and a total Israeli withdrawal from Gaza.

Many theories have been put forward to explain Sharon's revolutionary change in strategy. The least flattering is that it was all a ploy to distract attention from reports that he might be indicted for financial impropriety dating to his 2000 electoral campaign. (There were, in fact, three investigations pending — one of which resulted in the conviction of Sharon's son, Omri, for illegal campaign financing. In June 2004, however, Israel's attorney general ruled that there was no basis for an indictment against Sharon himself.[165]) Another theory holds that the hoopla around the so-called Geneva Initiative, negotiated without governmental sanction by former Oslo negotiator Yossi Beilin and PA representative Yasser Abed Rabbo (December 2003), had opened Sharon's eyes to the possibility of getting something worse than the Road Map if he did not act.[166] Indeed, in a September 2004 interview, Sharon claimed that "without an initiative on my part, Israel would have had to enter into negotiations that would have ended in an agreement imposed on us from the outside."[167] Finally, there is the demographic argument, which contends that given the extraordinary Arab birthrate, Sharon feared that Jews would soon constitute a minority between the Jordan River and the Mediterranean Sea, and that by cutting ties with Gaza's 1.1 million Arabs, he hoped to reduce the urgency of the threat.[168]

Regardless of such considerations, however, Sharon was convinced that disengagement was Israel's only viable alternative: Toppling the PA and reinstating Israel's authority over 3.5 million Palestinians was a recipe for mayhem. Forging ahead blindly with "final status" negotiations in the hope that a pair of signatures "will produce security out of thin air" constituted a dangerous pipe dream. And doing nothing at all would leave the citizens of Israel vulnerable to continued terrorism.[169]

Faced with resistance within his own party, Sharon announced that he would submit his "Disengagement Plan" to a referendum of registered Likud voters. On April 14, he traveled to Washington to present his plan to President Bush. In a show of support, Bush made several key concessions to Israel, saying that the "right of return" would apply to the Palestinian state only (the refugees could not resettle in Israel), and that there could be no return to the pre-1967 boundaries (since that would entail the unrealistic mass relocation of 235,000 Israelis living beyond the pre-1967 lines). Bush also gave tacit consent to the West Bank security barrier.[170] These concessions were delivered in the form of a presidential letter from Bush to Sharon, the text of which was subsequently approved by overwhelming majorities in both houses of Congress (407–9 in the House and 95–3 in the Senate) in June 2004.[171]

The Palestinians were not nearly so supportive. The PA rejected Sharon's plan out of hand, insisting that unilateral solutions were not acceptable. Intent on obstructing all Israeli efforts toward peace and security, Hamas and the other terrorist groups multiplied their attacks. On March 22, Israel struck back, killing Hamas' terrorist mastermind, the quadriplegic "Sheikh" Ahmed Yassin.[172] Three weeks later, Yassin's successor, Abdel Aziz al-Rantisi, followed him to the grave.

On the morning of the Likud referendum (May 2), the polls were too close to call. But in the opening hours of voting, Hamas gunmen murdered a pregnant Israeli mother, Tali Hatuel, and her four daughters in Gaza — shooting at their car until it crashed, and then finishing off the victims with point-blank automatic weapons fire. Horrified by this act of barbarism, 60 percent of the Likud rank-and-file voted against Sharon's plan.[173] Certain that the nation as a whole favored disengagement — an April poll showed that 73 percent of Israelis approved[174] — Sharon refused to back down. On October

25, 2004, he brought the matter before the Knesset. Amidst demonstrations and counterdemonstrations in the streets, the measure passed by a vote of 67–44.[175] Two and a half weeks later, Yasser Arafat succumbed to an unidentified illness in a French hospital.

The last hurdles were overcome in February 2005, when the Knesset voted 59–40 to approve a compensation package for those Gaza and West Bank settlers who stood to be removed from their homes. Four days later, the cabinet added its approval by a 17–5 vote. (Prominent among the naysayers were Natan Sharansky, who promptly resigned, and Benjamin Netanyahu, who left the cabinet on August 7, ten days before the settlers were slated to be evacuated.) In all, 24 settlements were to be dismantled — 20 in Gaza and 4 in the West Bank. The settlers themselves were in a state of disbelief that Ariel Sharon (of all people) intended to remove them.

The IDF, which had been training since February to carry out the operation in the least traumatic way, began its work on August 17. The ensuing scenes were heartrending as settlers pleaded with the soldiers not to carry out their orders. Many refused to go willingly and had to be dragged or carried from their homes by the sympathetic soldiery. The closest approximation to violent resistance came at Kfar Darom, where residents climbed onto their rooftops and spattered the soldiers with blue paint as they approached.[176] Addressing the UN General Assembly on September 15, Sharon said: "The right of the Jewish people to the Land of Israel does not mean disregarding the rights of others in the land. The Palestinians will always be our neighbors. We respect them, and have no aspirations to rule over them. They are also entitled to freedom, and to a national, sovereign existence in a state of their own."[177]

Once deplored — unjustly — as the "butcher of Sabra and Shatila," Ariel Sharon had demonstrated to the world that he could lead Israel through the "painful concessions" necessary for peace. At the same time, he had followed through on his promise to provide security to Israeli civilians by pressing ahead with construction of the West Bank security barrier. Begun in 2002, the barrier spawned immediate controversy. Because its route dipped into the West Bank at various points in order to encompass Israeli settlement blocs, detractors argued that it was meant to serve as a de facto border, and constituted an "illegal usurpation" of "Palestinian" land.[178] Proponents answered that if peaceful conditions supervened, the barrier could always be altered to conform to the border established in any final status settlement.[179] (Indeed, in June 2004, when Israel's Supreme Court ordered the barrier rerouted to minimize hardship on Palestinians who had to pass through a checkpoint to get to their farms and schools, Sharon promptly complied with the ruling.)

The barrier's effectiveness speaks for itself: Between the beginning of

Arafat's Terrorist War in September 2000 and the completion of the first section of the barrier in August 2003, terrorists from Samaria — the northern half of the West Bank, abutting the main Israeli population centers — staged 73 attacks, killing 293 Israelis and maiming nearly 2,000. In the ensuing 11 months, the number of successful attacks fell to three.[180] Conversely, of the 121 casualties (including 19 deaths) caused by West Bank terrorists between January 1 and June 30, 2004, 100 percent occurred in areas where the barrier had yet to be constructed.[181] The barrier not only saved Israeli lives, but also greatly reduced the need for IDF countermeasures that would, inevitably, have claimed numerous Palestinian lives.

Despite this success story, all was not well in Sharon's own Likud Party. In an attempt to forestall further territorial concessions on the West Bank, the party hierarchy was attempting to force early elections. When Sharon sought to address the party's central committee, someone shut off his microphone.[182] (He had intended to say, "Everyone knows that when we come down to it, not all of the [West Bank] will remain in our hands. We have a dream, and it is good and it is just, but there is also reality, and it is harsh and demanding. We cannot maintain a Jewish and democratic state while holding on to all of the land of Israel."[183])

The Likud's effort to force early elections came to naught. But no sooner did Sharon dodge the attempt than his Labor coalition partners announced that they would resign from the government over differences on social issues, leaving the prime minister without a Knesset majority. Sharon would have to face early elections after all. Surveying the field, he saw his own Likud compatriots maneuvering to block further action on his disengagement plan for the West Bank. Labor would support disengagement, but Sharon disagreed with them on almost everything else. Caught between a rock and a hard place, he responded with his boldest initiative to date. On November 21, he unleashed the "Big Bang"— announcing that he would form a new party: *Kadima* ("Forward"). On November 30, Shimon Peres, who had recently been unseated as Labor Party chairman, agreed to join Sharon's new creation, as did 13 Likud Knesset members. (The number rose to 27 the following week.[184]) Elections were set for March 2006, and early polling predicted a solid Kadima victory. The public was electrified.[185]

We will never know what Sharon might have accomplished at the head of his new party. On December 18, after a day of endless political meetings, he experienced vertigo, confusion and difficulty speaking. At Hadassah University Medical Center in Ein Kerem, he was diagnosed with a mild stroke. Improving over the next 24 hours, he was released on blood thinning medication (to prevent recurrence) and was scheduled to undergo an outpatient cardiac catheterization. On January 4, the eve of the procedure, he complained of chest pains at his home. During the ensuing ambulance ride to the hospital, his condition suddenly worsened. Doctors determined that he had sustained a hemorrhagic stroke, and took him for emergency brain surgery. Age 77 at the time, he never regained consciousness.[186] He was the last prime minister from the generation of 1948.

10

"More than any army in the history of warfare"

As a goodwill gesture at the time of the Gaza disengagement, Jewish philanthropists in the United States raised millions of dollars to purchase Israel's profitable Gaza greenhouses so that they could be turned over intact to the Palestinians. Palestinian vandals promptly ran amok through these structures, rendering them worthless.[1] Two months later, just prior to forming Kadima, Ariel Sharon addressed the question of freedom of movement for Gazans wishing to enter Egypt, Israel or the West Bank. He had hoped to maintain security installations on the border with Egypt to prevent arms smuggling by Hamas, but Arafat's successor, Mahmoud Abbas, categorically refused his consent. Prodded by U.S. secretary of state Condoleezza Rice and the "Quartet's" special envoy, James Wolfensohn, Sharon settled for the installation of closed-circuit security cameras at crossings manned by the PA. He also agreed to the establishment of a bus service between Gaza and the West Bank and to the daily entry into Israel of a specified number of commercial trucks from Gaza.[2] These measures underscored Sharon's willingness to cultivate peaceful relations with the Palestinians— and he agreed to them despite the fact that Gazan terrorists had begun to fire rockets into Israeli civilian areas 12 days after the Israeli withdrawal.[3]

Sharon had also hoped that his transit measures would alleviate financial misery in the West Bank and Gaza, thereby bolstering support for Mahmoud Abbas in time for the upcoming Palestinian legislative elections.[4] On January 25, 2006, however, (by which time Sharon had been in a coma for three weeks), the Palestinian electorate handed a landslide victory to Hamas— giving 76 seats (versus 43 for Fatah) to the terrorist organization that had murdered more Israeli civilians than all other terrorist groups taken together, and which was openly committed to destroying Israel and establishing an Islamic state in its stead.[5] At his inauguration, the new Palestinian prime minister, Ismail Haniyeh, announced that he would neither recognize nor negotiate

191

with Israel, and that he would take no action to prevent anti–Israeli terrorism (which he characterized as "legitimate self-defense").[6] The "Quartet" duly announced that it would not support the Palestinian economy unless the Hamas government renounced these purposes and abided by prior agreements. When its demands were rejected, the "Quartet" cut off all nonhumanitarian aid. Likewise, Israel withheld tax revenues earmarked for the PA.[7]

All the while, Hamas terrorists continued to fire missiles into the Israeli town of Sderot. On June 25, they tunneled into Israeli territory, murdered two IDF soldiers and kidnapped a third, 19-year-old Gilad Shalit, who remained a hostage for five years. Not to be outdone, Hezbollah terrorists violated Israeli territory from Lebanon on July 12, killing eight IDF troops and taking two others—Ohad Goldwasser and Elad Regev—hostage. (The two men were subsequently murdered.[8]) There ensued a full-scale war that turned out most unsatisfactorily both for Lebanon and for Israel. In order to deprive Hezbollah of Iranian arms deliveries, the IAF bombed Lebanon's transportation infrastructure, including the roads leading to and from Syria and the runways at Beirut Airport (which were evacuated in response to Israeli warnings prior to the strike). Meanwhile, Hezbollah fired thousands of rockets into northern Israel (many of them supplied by Iran), killing 44 civilians and chasing an estimated one million others into bomb shelters.[9] Israel also lost 117 soldiers killed in action, many of whom were waylaid in sophisticated ambushes as they tried to press into Lebanon.[10]

Initially, Hezbollah placed its death toll at 68, while claiming that more than 1,000 Lebanese civilians had been killed. However, when confronted with the fact that Hezbollah's own funeral notices in various newspapers added up to a far higher number,[11] the group changed its estimated death toll to 250.[12] In contrast, the UN estimated that 500 Hezbollah guerillas had been killed, while Israel put the number at 700—identifying 440 of them by name and address.[13] With Lebanese officials claiming a total fatality count between 1,100 and 1,191, this still leaves 400 to 691 civilians among the victims—a tragic consequence of Hezbollah's decision to operate from populated areas in civilian disguise. (In some instances, the guerillas placed rocket launchers in Christian neighborhoods so that any return fire would endanger innocent, uninvolved Christians rather than innocent, uninvolved Muslims.[14])

A UN-brokered cease-fire ended the conflict on August 14, 2006. Under its terms, peace was to be guaranteed by a 15,000-man UNIFIL force bolstered by an equal number of Lebanese army troops. Unfortunately, the promised UN troop levels were not achieved, and those "peace-keepers" who were deployed made no effort to disarm Hezbollah, leaving the group's rocket capability partially intact. (The group has since more than replenished its stores while reoccupying strategic ground.[15])

The perception across the Middle East was that Hezbollah had humbled mighty Israel.[16] In fact, Israel had inflicted enough damage to prompt an admission from Hezbollah chief Hassan Nasrallah (who has referred to Israelis as "the grandsons of apes and pigs") that he erred in instigating the war.[17] Nevertheless, the mood at home was downcast. After a five-month investigation, Israel's Winograd Commission concluded that Prime Minister Ehud Olmert (Sharon's successor) had shown "a serious failure in ... judgment, responsibility and prudence" in his handling of the war and his choice of war aims.[18]

Just months prior to the war, the nation had elected Olmert in the expectation that he would devise and implement a unilateral West Bank disengagement plan that would enhance Israel's security. The debacles in Lebanon and Gaza (from which Israel had unilaterally disengaged in 2000 and 2005, respectively) now convinced most Israelis, including the prime minister, that such a strategy was sheer folly.[19] Hamas, meanwhile, continued to smuggle weapons into Gaza via tunnels from Egypt and to fire missiles into Israel. In 2007, terrorists fired 2,000 such rockets.[20] In June of that same year, Hamas violently usurped authority in Gaza from the PA. Israel promptly imposed a blockade on Gaza in an effort to deny the terrorists access to materials for rocket manufacture. It was hoped that the continuing missile barrage from Gaza might thus be halted without resorting to direct military action.[21] Falling short of success, the government stiffened the blockade in January 2008. In response, Hamas broke down part of Egypt's security fence on the Sinai border and sent throngs of civilians into Egypt where they purchased, among other things, equipment for weapons manufacture.[22]

Despite the blockade, Israel consistently allowed food, medicines, fuel and limited construction materials into Gaza in an effort to ease the plight of the Gazan populace. Unfortunately, the Hamas regime routinely pilfered these items for its own use — particularly in the case of fuel — claiming falsely that Israel was denying such supplies. Hamas staged sham energy blackouts in order to garner media coverage.[23]

In the West Bank, conditions evolved very differently. In retaliation for Hamas' June 2007 Gaza usurpation, PA president Mahmoud Abbas suspended the Hamas legislature and formed an emergency government in the West Bank without Hamas' participation. To strengthen his position, the U.S., European Union and Israel resumed funding to the PA.[24] Five months later, Israeli prime minister Ehud Olmert (whose popularity ratings had tumbled into the single digits) accepted a U.S. invitation to Annapolis, where he embarked upon new Oslo-style negotiations with President Abbas with the expressed aim of bringing a Palestinian state into existence by the end of 2008.[25] By the time these talks ended, Prime Minister Olmert had offered to withdraw from 93.5 percent of the West Bank and to compensate the Palestinians for the other 6.5 percent by ceding land from pre-1967 Israel on a "meter-for-meter" basis. A "safe-passage corridor" between Gaza and the West Bank was to be included in this transfer in order to ensure the contiguity of Palestinian lands. Abbas (whose reputation as a "moderate" does not correlate with high precision to his curriculum vitae[26]) never responded to the offer.[27]

Soon thereafter, Olmert resigned from office amidst allegations of financial misdeeds. But when his successor, Tzipi Livni, was unable to forge a Knesset majority, Olmert was forced to resume office pending new elections slated for February 2009.

Meanwhile, the number of Hamas rockets fired into Israel from Gaza since the 2005 disengagement topped the 6,000 mark. By December 2008, the range of this missile arsenal was up to 40 kilometers— enough to strike Beersheba, Ashdod and Ashkelon and to disrupt the lives of an estimated 800,000 Israelis. In Sderot (the Israeli city most frequently targeted by Hamas rocket attacks), more than 75 percent of children were now suffering one or more symptoms of posttraumatic stress disorder.[28] Consequently, on December 27, after a ten-day surge in Hamas missile fire,[29] Olmert initiated "Operation Cast Lead"— an effort to cripple Hamas' ability to launch further strikes.

For the first week, operations were conducted from the air. On January 3, 2009, IDF ground forces joined in the assault. To minimize civilian casualties, the IDF employed leaflet, loudspeaker and telephone warnings,[30] and sent 20,000 tons of humanitarian provisions into Gaza.[31] In contrast, Hamas set up its headquarters in a bunker below Gaza's main hospital, clad its "soldiers" in civilian garb, stored weapons in private homes, mosques and schools— sometimes directing civilians to climb onto the roofs of these structures to deter Israeli air strikes[32]— and purposely fired rockets and mortars from civilian areas so that any noncombatant deaths from retaliatory fire would be blamed on the IDF.[33] The result of these Geneva Convention violations was that Hamas' own kinsmen, the citizens of Gaza, were transformed into a collective human shield. In total, between 1,166 and 1,338 Gazans were killed. Hamas claimed that all but 49 were civilians, but after reviewing the names, occupations and "circumstances of death" of 1,004 of the fatalities, the IDF's Gaza Coordination and Liaison Administration determined that 709 were combatants.[34] Nearly two years later, in October 2010, Hamas admitted that as many as 700 of the dead were militants.[35] Lamentably, at least 295 others (including 49 women and 89 children) were civilians, whose deaths were made tragically inevitable by Hamas' provocation of the war and choice of tactics.[36]

Gazan civilians, however, weren't the only ones at risk of life and limb. Throughout the crisis, the residents of southern Israel spent their days racing into bomb shelters as Hamas peppered civilian areas with rockets. Two such weapons struck kindergartens in Beersheba and Ashdod. (Luckily, both schools had been evacuated owing to the ongoing missile fire.[37]) Meanwhile, in Europe, the Gaza fighting was used as a pretext by anti–Semitic extremists to attack innocent European Jews. England's Community Security Trust noted more than 20 such attacks in the week beginning December 29.[38] In Denmark, several school principals refused to allow Jewish children to attend class out of concern for their safety. In France, Sweden, Belgium and Greece, synagogues came under attack, while the continent played host to intimidating demonstrations in which the cry. "Jews to the gas chambers!" and other expressions of bigotry were heard. French president Nicolas Sarkozy issued a firm condemnation of this upsurge in violent anti–Semitism, but most European leaders remained discouragingly silent. In Belgium, nine members of parliament actually participated in an anti–Israel march in which Hamas, Islamic Jihad and Hezbollah flags were proudly displayed alongside anti–Semitic placards.[39]

On January 17, after three weeks of fighting, the Israeli cabinet declared a unilateral cease-fire. After launching a last rocket salvo, Hamas reciprocated with a cease-fire of its own. Ten days later, a roadside bomb killed three Israelis on security duty near the Gaza border.[40] Hamas praised the attack, but did not claim credit.

In the midst of the fighting, a letter coauthored by a cadre of intellectuals appeared in *The Sunday Times* (U.K.) accusing Israel of "prima facie war crimes," and declaring that the 6,000-plus rockets fired by Hamas into Israel's cities prior to the war did "not, in terms of scale and effect amount to an armed attack entitling Israel to rely on self-defense."[41] Amongst the signatories was Professor Christine Chinkin of the London School of Economics. Three months later, the UN Human Rights Council (UNHRC) appointed Ms. Chinkin to a four-member commission charged with investigating allegations of war crimes in Operation Cast Lead. The other three commissioners— Richard Goldstone of South Africa (who chaired the commission), Hina Jilani of Pakistan and Desmond Travers of Ireland — had all signed a different letter prior to their respective appointments, declaring that "the events in Gaza have shocked us to the core."[42]

Israel was invited to testify at the inquiry, but could scarcely have done so without conferring legitimacy on a hostile jury, all of whose members would have been disqualified from sitting in judgment in a court of law. Unwilling to place trust in a jury of its accusers, Israel rejected the commission's invitation. Hence, after gathering testimony from, among others, a "credible and reliable" Gazan family that provided 12 separate versions of the same incident, and a Human Rights Watch "weapons analyst" who collects

Nazi memorabilia during his spare time,[43] the so-called Goldstone Commission concluded in a 575-page report that Israel had "committed actions amounting to war crimes, and possibly crimes against humanity." In a *New York Times* editorial defending these findings, Commission chairman Richard Goldstone declared that "repeatedly, the Israel Defense Forces failed to adequately distinguish between combatants and civilians, as the laws of war strictly require."[44]

In the hearings that ensued at the UNHRC, Colonel Richard Kemp, the former commander of British forces in Afghanistan, testified that based on his extensive field service and knowledge of military history, he could confidently make the following statement: "During Operation Cast Lead, the Israeli Defense Forces did more to safeguard the rights of civilians in a combat zone than any other army in the history of warfare."[45] The UNHRC received these words in grim silence. Three weeks later the UN General Assembly approved the Goldstone Report by a vote of 114–18 with 44 abstentions (Great Britain among them).

Over the next 18 months, Israel's detractors liberally cited the report as a means of impugning the reputation of Israel and the IDF. On April 1, 2011, however, Richard Goldstone suddenly disavowed the report's main findings, stating in a *Washington Post* editorial that "if I had known then what I know now, the Goldstone Report would have been a different document," and that, in contrast to Hamas' tactics, "civilians were not intentionally targeted" by Israel.[46]

Meanwhile, to prevent Hamas from replenishing its munitions stores in the aftermath of Operation Cast Lead, Israel kept its blockade of Gaza intact. Simultaneously, however, it sought to ease the plight of the Gazan populace by dispatching large amounts of humanitarian assistance. Indeed, in the 16 months following the war, Israel delivered more than a million tons of food, fuel, medicine, clothing, educational materials and building supplies to Gaza — an average of 15,000 tons per week — and provided Gaza's citizenry with 70 percent of its electricity needs. (The other 30 percent was imported from Egypt or generated locally.[47]) Further stimulus to the Gazan economy arrived in the form of a $900 million assistance pledge from the U.S., and from a robust traffic in black market consumer items arriving via tunnels from Egypt. Writing for the *Financial Times* on May 24, 2010, Tobias Buck declared that "shops all over Gaza are bursting with goods."[48] Ten days later, a report in the *Washington Post* announced that Gazan "grocery stores are stocked wall-to-wall."[49]

It would be a useless exercise to argue that Gaza had been transformed into the envy of the Western world by virtue of this aid and illicit commerce. But it would be equally untruthful to argue that Gaza was in the throes of a humanitarian crisis. The goal of Israel's blockade was to reduce Hamas' ability to attack Israeli civilians by interdicting the organization's access to weaponry — a purpose that is entirely legal and has many precedents under international law. Indeed, it is tantamount to an act of war to interfere with such a blockade.[50] Nevertheless, in the last week of May 2010, a self-described "Freedom Flotilla," consisting of six vessels, purportedly carrying humanitarian aid, sought to do just that. As the ships steamed toward Gaza, the Israeli government informed them that they would not be allowed to proceed but invited them to offload their "humanitarian supplies" at the Israeli port of Ashdod for inspection and overland transport to Gaza.[51] With their offer being ignored, the IDF moved to intercept the ships in international waters on May 31, 2010.

Five of the six ships surrendered without incident. But as helicopter-borne IDF soldiers descended by rope onto the deck of the sixth, they were set upon by a mob of Turkish "activists" who accosted them with metal clubs, knives and tear gas.[52] One soldier was thrown from the top deck to a lower one, 30 feet below, sustaining a skull fracture.[53] Another was shot in the stomach with a gun wrested from his own holster. Two more jumped overboard out of fear of being lynched. By the time the IDF got the upper hand, nine of the "activists" — eight of them Turks — had been killed, and seven Israeli soldiers wounded.[54]

Israel was immediately subjected to international opprobrium. Turkey recalled its ambassador,[55] while the Turkish prime minister, Recep Tayyip Erdogan, termed the Israeli action a "bloody massacre."[56]

Far from perpetrating a massacre, however, the Israeli soldiers had come aboard wholly unprepared. Their only live-ammunition weapons were holstered pistols, and they were under strict orders to keep them holstered unless their lives were threatened.[57] Otherwise, they were to rely on riot-control paintball guns (which, in the circumstances, proved wholly ineffectual).

It was soon revealed that the involved ship — the *Mavi Marmara* — had no humanitarian supplies onboard.[58] When it departed Turkish waters, its passengers were singing songs of martyrdom. Indeed, three of those who were subsequently killed had told family and friends of their unabashed desire for a "martyr's" death prior to boarding the ship.[59] After the raid, a review of the ship's security cameras showed groups of passengers wielding metal clubs before any IDF members had come aboard.[60] In a subsequent interview, the ship's captain confirmed that the Turkish violence had been premeditated.[61] Further investigation revealed that fifty of the "activists" were actually mercenaries, paid and recruited by elements within the Turkish government.[62]

In spite of these revelations, Turkey demanded an apology from Israel, while the UN Human Rights Council chimed in with another of its world-class "fact-finding" missions, which concluded that the Israeli raid — and, indeed, its Gaza blockade —violated international human rights law. Israel dismissed the report as being no less "biased" and "distorted" than the Goldstone Report had been. Turkey heartily embraced it.[63] After due consideration, U.S. envoy Eileen Chamberlain informed the UNHRC that the United States was "concerned with the [report's] tone, content and conclusions," while the U.S. State Department advised against its implementation.[64]

11

Prospects for Peace: Stuck Between Two Paradoxes

In order to cross a room from one wall to the other, one must first traverse half the length of the room. Having done so one must traverse half of the second half of the room, then half of what is left, and half again of what is left after that. Consequently, it is impossible to cross a room from one wall to the other, since no matter how far one has come, half the remaining distance must still be traversed — ad infinitum — before the far wall can be reached. — Zeno's Dichotomy Paradox[1]

You [cannot] meet halfway those who do not want to meet you. — Jabotinsky's Paradox[2]

At the end of his encyclopedic *A History of Israel from the Rise of Zionism to Our Time*, Howard M. Sachar, professor emeritus of history at George Washington University, concludes that Israelis and Palestinians will never "accept a compromise formula for mutual quietude" unless it is imposed upon them by "uncompromising and unrelenting Great Power pressure."[3] This conclusion from a highly-regarded historian is not only pessimistic, but deeply flawed; for it implies that both sides are equally unwilling to compromise in the name of peace and that they are in equal need of prodding. Such a contention flies in the face of the historical record. Each of the Israeli leaders profiled in this book consistently spoke of the desire for a peaceful settlement with Israel's Arab neighbors and of Israel's willingness to compromise in order to reach such an agreement. The Israeli side accepted the notion of partition put forward by the Peel Commission in 1937, accepted the UN partition plan of 1947, sweated out the tense days leading up to the Six Day War hoping that a peaceful resolution might be found, made territorial concessions after a war that it had won in 1973, abandoned its Sinai settlements and military bases in order to make peace with Egypt in 1979, offered autonomy to the Palestinians as part of the Egyptian peace agreement, made repeated concessions to the Palestinians during the Oslo period (even when it should have

been evident that Yasser Arafat had no intention of fulfilling his own obligations), offered statehood to the Palestinians in 2000–2001, withdrew unilaterally from Lebanon in 2000 and from Gaza in 2005, accepted the "Quartet's"
Roadmap to Peace in 2003, and offered statehood to the Palestinians anew at
Annapolis in 2007–08.

On November 25, 2009, Israeli prime minister Benjamin Netanyahu
announced the institution of a ten-month construction freeze within existing
West Bank settlements. This unprecedented gesture was calculated to bring
the Palestinians back to the negotiating table at a time when the peace process
appeared moribund. The Palestinian leadership promptly declared the gesture
inadequate.[4] Only after nine of the ten months had elapsed did they agree to
participate in new talks— and then they stormed out again when Israeli deputy
foreign minister Danny Ayalon pressed Palestinian prime minister Salam
Fayyad to agree that the endpoint of negotiations was not simply to be "two
states," but "two states for two peoples— Jewish and Palestinian."[5]

When the construction freeze expired, the Palestinian leadership
announced that peace talks could not possibly resume unless it was extended.[6]
Netanyahu offered such an extension in return for Palestinian acknowledgement that Israel is the national state of the Jewish people, saying, "Just as the
Palestinians expect us to recognize their state, we expect reciprocal treatment.
This is not a condition, but a trust-building step which would create wide-
ranging trust among the Israeli people, who have lost trust in the Palestinian
will for peace over the last ten years."

A spokesman for Mahmoud Abbas rejected this summons, maintaining
that "the issue of the Jewishness of the state has nothing to do with the matter."[7] In the ensuing weeks, the chief Palestinian negotiator, Saeb Erekat,
wrote an opinion piece for the *Guardian* reiterating the inviolability of the
Palestinian "right of return,"[8] while the Palestinian Authority published a
"study" concluding that Judaism has no historical tie with the Temple Mount
or Western Wall.[9]

Hence, despite Israel's persistent willingness over the years to meet the
Palestinians halfway, and despite repeated unreciprocated concessions
demonstrating this willingness, the fundamental positions of its supposed
"peace partner" are (i) a refusal to recognize Israel as the national state of the
Jewish people; (ii) a denial of the historical connection between the Jewish
people and the land of Israel; and (iii) the immutable insistence that any
"peace deal" with Israel must include the seeds of Israel's demographic
destruction in the form of the Palestinian "right of return."

Not so long ago, the UN infamously equated "Zionism" with "racism."
In fact, the two terms have nothing in common. Zionism — the dream of Jewish self-determination in Judaism's historical homeland — was conceived as

a means of liberating the Jews (and thereby the entire world) from the scourge of anti–Semitism. It did not seek to subject others to discrimination.

Let us contrast this with what might be termed "Palestinianism"—i.e., the movement encapsulated in the Palestinian positions outlined above. Fundamentally, this movement has never been about "self-determination in an ancestral homeland," for if it had been it would have been brought to fruition long ago. If the Arabs of Palestine had desired statehood above all else, they could have had it when the Peel Commission offered it to them in 1937 or when the UN offered it to them in 1947. They could have demanded it from their Arab brethren in Jordan and Egypt at anytime between 1948 and 1967 (when the latter states controlled the West Bank and Gaza). They could have pursued it in accordance with the 1979 framework for Palestinian autonomy or during the Oslo years or more recently at Camp David and Taba or with the Bush Roadmap or with the Annapolis talks or in the subsequent Abbas-Netanyahu talks.

Offered statehood time and again in return for peace and an end to the conflict, Palestinian leaders have chosen instead to cling to positions that negate the possibility of a peaceful two-state solution. When one considers that they have done so at the price of allowing their own kinsmen to continue languishing in squalor as refugees, the only plausible conclusion is that what the Palestinian leadership desires above all else is not Palestinian self-determination in a putative Palestinian "ancestral homeland," but *the eradication of Jewish self-determination in Judaism's ancestral homeland.*[10]

If such is the case, then the goals of Zionism and "Palestinianism" are mutually exclusive. The desire for Jewish self-determination in Judaism's historical homeland and the desire to destroy that self-determination cannot be reconciled. There is no halfway point between them. Rather there is an infinite chasm.

And this brings us back to the two paradoxes in the preface to this chapter.

Let us begin with Zeno's dichotomy paradox: When dealing with finite distances—as in crossing a room from one wall to the other—Zeno's argument is patently absurd. The fact that a given distance can be infinitely subdivided doesn't mean that the distance itself is infinite. The distance from one wall to the other in any room that has ever existed is finite and measurable—and whether Zeno likes it or not, finite distances can be crossed. As postulated above, however, our problem boils down not to a finite distance but to an infinite one—and it is here that Zeno's paradox becomes an insurmountable problem. For to approach an infinitely distant goal, one would first have to get halfway there, and infinity has no halfway point. Nor does it have a quarter-way point or an eighth-way or a sixteenth-way point. Indeed, in attempting to approach an infinitely distant goal by traversing finite distances, one can make no progress at all.

But one *can* get into a great deal of trouble in the attempt. And this brings us to our second paradox, to wit: "*You* [cannot] *meet halfway those who do not want to meet you.*" The origin of this paradox is a single sentence in an article entitled, *The Ethics of the Iron Wall*, published in 1923 by Vladimir Jabotinsky — Menachem Begin's mentor and the forefather of Israel's Likud Party. His actual quote was: "You *must not* 'meet halfway' those who do not want to meet you," and Jabotinsky characterized it not as a paradox, but as a timeless "rule of life," familiar even to the compilers of the Talmud (the written compendium of all Jewish religious law). Indeed, it is from the Talmud that Jabotinsky cites a relevant parable of two men who find a piece of cloth in the road: One obstinately insists that he saw the cloth first and that it belongs to him. In an effort to be reasonable, the second man concedes that both parties have a claim to the cloth and states that he will settle for half. The case comes to court, and the judge renders the following verdict on the basis of Talmudic scholarship: Since the reasonable fellow has already conceded that half of the cloth is not his, the judge cuts the cloth in half and hands the "uncontested" half to the obstinate man. Next, he cuts the remaining half in two and hands one of the "contested" pieces to each of the contending parties.

Thus, says Jabotinsky, "the obstinate claimant gets three-quarters of the cloth, while the 'gentleman' has only one quarter, [which] serves him right. It is a very fine thing to be a gentleman, but it is no reason for being an idiot. Our ancestors knew that. But we have forgotten it."[11]

Of course, the conflict need not have ended where it did, for the obstinate man could have protested that he had a claim on the quarter of the cloth that had been given to the gentleman. And given half of that, he could have protested that he had a claim on the remaining eighth, and so on ad infinitum. This is nothing other than Zeno's dichotomy paradox played out in practical terms, and it shows that the present paradigm for achieving peace between Israelis and Palestinians — which calls upon Israel to make repeated, unreciprocated concessions in an effort to meet halfway a "peace partner" that never concedes anything — is hopelessly flawed. For meeting a man halfway, who doesn't want to meet you at all, gets you either nowhere or somewhere very much worse — as the world ought to have learned at Munich in 1938.

This is not to say that an agreement between Israelis and Palestinians is impossible. Jabotinsky himself argued to the contrary. But he also argued that no voluntary agreement would be forthcoming from the Palestinian side in the absence of a figurative "iron wall" — an ironclad demonstration that the Jewish people have returned to their ancestral homeland and that they have come to stay. In his own words:

As long as the Arabs feel that there is the least hope of getting rid of us, they will refuse to give up this hope in return for either kind words or for bread and butter, because they are not a rabble, but a living people. And when a living people yields in matters of such a vital character it is only when there is no longer any hope of getting rid of us.... Not until then will they drop their extremist leaders, whose watchword is "Never!" And the leadership will pass to the moderate groups, who will approach us with a proposal that we should both agree to mutual concessions....

"And when that happens, I am convinced that we Jews will be found ready to give them satisfactory guarantees, so that both peoples can live together in peace, like good neighbors."[12]

This, alas, is not the situation that obtains today. The PLO founding charter states that "claims of historical or religious ties of Jews with Palestine are incompatible with the facts of history," and that Zionism is "organically associated with international imperialism" and "colonial in its aims."[13] Nearly a half-century later, such sentiments dominate the discourse in Palestinian media, mosques and schools. Hence, Palestinians have never ceased to believe them.

A dissection of the historical record, however, will show that the Palestinian position is demonstrably false: For even the mighty British —formerly the possessors of the modern era's greatest empire —cannot dig in Boston or Bombay and find evidence of their own civilization antedating their colonial experience. Israelis, in contrast, can dig almost anywhere between the Jordan and the Mediterranean and find evidence of Jewish civilization dating as far back as 4,000 years. Jerusalem boasts the Western Wall dating to the reign of Herod the Great. Hebron is home to the Tomb of the patriarchs, Bethlehem to Rachel's tomb, and Nablus to Joseph's tomb. Israeli archaeologists have uncovered Masada, the Dead Sea Scrolls, and coins and other relics from the Bar Kochba Revolt of A.D. 135. And if the Arab world would ever let them, they would excavate the 3,000-year-old City of King David in eastern Jerusalem and artifacts from the First and Second Temples beneath the Temple Mount.

What does it all mean? It means that unlike the British in their heyday, the Israelis aren't colonists. When a Jewish man (or woman) can dig into the earth beneath him and find the fortress where a brave band of Jews made their final stand against the legions of Rome in A.D. 70, or walk into a cave along the Dead Sea and discover 2,000-year-old scrolls written in Hebrew, he is not a colonist, but someone who has returned to his ancestral homeland.

In a phrase, he is in Israel "as of right and not on sufferance."

In a word, he is *home.*

On May 4, 2011, Mahmoud Abbas' Fatah organization signed a reconciliation agreement with Hamas, whose founding charter states that "there is no solution to the Palestinian problem except by Jihad."[14] Israeli prime minister Benjamin Netanyahu characterized the agreement as "a mortal blow to peace and a big prize for terror."[15] Speaking before a joint session of the U.S. Congress on May 24, 2011, Netanyahu called upon Abbas to abrogate the Hamas accord and make peace with Israel, vowing that "if you do, I promise you this: Israel will not be the last country to welcome a Palestinan state as a new member of the United Nations. It will be the first to do so."

Responsibility for solving the Arab-Israeli conflict cannot be borne on the shoulders of Israel alone. The world community must also do its part — not by exerting "uncompromising and unrelenting Great Power pressure" on both parties when they are separated by an infinite abyss, but by forthrightly identifying aggressors as aggressors and victims as victims; not by appeasing extremism with Goldstone Commissions and Israel Apartheid Weeks, but by demonstrating that the community of nations will not seek or accept a solution that grants "Palestinian" self-determination in a putative Palestinian "ancestral" homeland *at the expense of* Jewish self-determination in Judaism's ancestral homeland.

Only when the world has committed itself to a just solution, rather than to appeasement, only when it ceases to apologize for — and, indeed, to finance — leaders committed to incitement and violence against Israel, only when the Jewish presence in the land of Israel is deemed unassailable — protected, as it were, by an "iron will" (for which Jabotinsky's "iron wall" served only as metaphor) — will the Arab side put forward moderate leaders who are willing to compromise. And at that moment, a problem of seemingly infinite scope will be reduced to a problem that is finite — and finite problems can be solved, because when the distance between contending parties is measurable rather than endless, the parties can meet halfway. Indeed, they can find solutions that allow both sides to come away feeling like winners— as they will be if true peace is achieved.

So, if one day, a Palestinian toddler can tune-in to the Palestinian Authority's version of "children's" television and learn in genuine earnestness that Tel Aviv is an "Israeli" city, instead of a "Palestinian" one (as he is told today), or that Eilat and Haifa are "Israeli" rather than "Palestinian" ports,[16] a truly moderate Palestinian leadership will more than likely find an Israeli hand still extended in compromise ... and "two states for two peoples" will be the result — with or without "uncompromising and unrelenting Great Power pressure."

Chapter Notes

Introduction

1. Herzl, *Jewish State*, 95.
2. Dershowitz, *Enemies*, 2.
3. Ibid., 2–3.
4. Donald Macintyre, "Israel seeks seat on Security Council," *Independent*, September 22, 2005, http://www.independent.co.uk/news/world/middle-east/israel-seeks-seat-on-security-council-507827.html (accessed 4/25/11); American Jewish Committee, "Countries eligible to sit on the United Nations Security Council," AJC advertisement in *New York Times*, September 23, 1997, http://www.ajcarchives.org/AJC_DATA/Files/211.pdf (accessed 4/25/11).
5. Daniel Schwammenthal, "Europe Reimports Jew Hatred," *Wall Street Journal*, January 13, 2009, http://online.wsj.com/article/SB123180033807075069.html (accessed 4/25/11).
6. Haaretz Service, "Cartoon of naked Sharon devouring infant wins top U.K. prize," *Haaretz*, November 26, 2003, http://www.haaretz.com/cartoon-of-naked-sharon-devouring-infant-wins-top-u-k-prize-1.106892 (accessed 4/15/11).
7. Karl Ritter, "Sweden-Israel Davis Cup to go ahead without public," *New York Times*, February 24, 2009, http://www.nytimes.com/2009/02/24/sports/24iht-tennisdavis24.20403874.html (accessed 4/25/11); Associated Press, "Sweden takes 2–1 lead after doubles," ESPN, March 7, 2009, http://sports.espn.go.com/sports/tennis/news/story?id=3960144 (accessed 4/25/11); Tommie Ullman, "Malmo decision to ban fans from Israel-Sweden Davis Cup match irks locals," *Haaretz*, March 5, 2009, http://www.haaretz.com/jewish-world/news/malmo-decision-to-ban-fans-from-israel-sweden-davis-cup-match-irks-locals-1.271486 (accessed 4/25/11).
8. Ian Black and Ian Cobain, "Israeli minister Ehud Barak faces war crimes arrest threat during UK visit," *Guardian*, September 29, 2009, http://www.guardian.co.uk/world/2009/sep/29/ehud-barak-war-crimes-israel (accessed 4/25/11); James Hider, "General Moshe Yaalon cancels London trip after arrest fear over Gaza bombing," *Times* (U.K.), October 6, 2009, http://www.timesonline.co.uk/tol/news/uk/article6862322.ece (accessed 4/25/11); Ian Black, "Tzipi Livni arrest warrant prompts Israeli government travel 'ban,'" *Guardian*, December 15, 2009, http://www.guardian.co.uk/world/2009/dec/15/tzipi-livni-arrest-warrant-israeli (accessed 4/25/11); Leigh Phillips, "Israeli foreign minister accused of apartheid in attempted citizen's arrest," *Guardian*, February 22, 2011, http://www.guardian.co.uk/world/2011/feb/22/israel-minister-avigdor-lieberman-citizens-arrest (accessed 4/2/11).
9. Natasha Mozgovaya and Haaretz Service, "Muslim students scream 'killer' during Israel envoy speech in L.A.," *Haaretz*, February 9, 2010, http://www.haaretz.com/news/muslim-students-scream-killer-during-israel-envoy-speech-in-l-a-1.265933 (accessed 4/25/11); Associated Press, "Netanyahu Cancels Speeches in Bay Area After Protest," *Los Angeles Times*, November 30, 2000, http://articles.latimes.com/2000/nov/30/news/mn-59373 (accessed 4/25/11); Daniel Pipes, "The War on Campus," *New York Post*, September 17, 2002, http://www.danielpipes.org/465/the-war-on-campus (accessed 2/16/11); Deborah Passner, "Film Review: Confrontation @ Concordia," CAMERA.org, 2003, http://www.camera.org/index.asp?x_context=46&x_review=9 (accessed 4/25/11).
10. The words are those of Abdul Rahmen Azzam Pasha, secretary general of the Arab League (Goldston, 230; Sachar, 333).
11. Edward Alexander, "No, an Exercise in Jewish Self-Debasement." *Middle East Quarterly* 5, no. 4 (December 1998): 28–30, http://www.meforum.org/134/no-an-exercise-in-jewish-self-debasement (accessed 4/14/05).
12. Statement by Dr. Weizmann made before The Palestine Royal Commission in

Jerusalem, on November 25, 1936, quoted in Weisgal, 305–6, 310; Blumberg, 150–53.

13. State of Israel Proclamation of Independence, quoted in Laqueur and Rubin, eds., p. 109.

14. Herodotus, vol. 1, 27.

Chapter 1

1. Bein, 91.
2. Chouraqui, 11–12; Cohen, 22.
3. Chouraqui, 24–25.
4. Ibid., 69–70.
5. Bein, 115.
6. Quoted in Eban, *Heritage*, 226.
7. Bein, p. 510.
8. Eban, *Heritage*, 231–34; Gilbert, *Atlas*, 149.
9. Eban, *Heritage*, 235.
10. Bein, 36–37, 80–81; Tuchman, *Bible*, 283.
11. Gilbert, *Atlas*, 149; Eban, *Heritage*, 239–40.
12. Eban, *Heritage*, 242. (The final boundaries of the Pale had been set in 1812.)
13. Bein, 173.
14. The aforementioned attempt to force it upon them during the reign of Alexander I (ruled 1801–25) had failed. Ninety years later, 97 percent of the Jews in the Pale of Settlement still spoke Yiddish (Eban, *Heritage*, 241; Gilbert, *Atlas*, 151) and clung to their cultural ties, which included praying three times a day for the Messiah to lead them back to Jerusalem (Sachar, 5–6).
15. Bein, 95.
16. Chouraqui, 13.
17. Cohen, 63; Bein, 59–60; Chouraqui, 58–59.
18. Chouraqui, 66.
19. Chouraqui, 60–61; Bein, 92–94.
20. Bein, 115–16; Chouraqui, 81; Cohen, 65–67.
21. Gilbert, *Israel*, 3–5; Sachar, 23–27; Curtis, et al., 24.
22. Bein, 185.
23. Bein, 138, 159–60.
24. Direct quotes are from Herzl, *Jewish State*, 7–12; see also Bein, 161–2.
25. Herzl, *Jewish State*, 95.
26. Herzl, *Jewish State*, 40.
27. Herzl, *Jewish State*, 28.
28. Bein, 140–41; Chouraqui, 95–97; Elon, 149–51; Cohen, 73.
29. Eban, *Heritage*, 250.
30. Chouraqui, 103–4.
31. Bein, 183–84.
32. Herzl. *Complete Diaries*, vol. 1, 360; Cohen, 99.

33. Bein, 191; Chouraqui, 106.
34. Herzl, *Complete Diaries*, vol. 1, 340; see also Chouraqui, 108; Cohen, 108.
35. Bein, 199–200.
36. Herzl, *Complete Diaries*, vol. 1, 378; see also Chouraqui, 112; Cohen, 113.
37. Bein, 201; Herzl, *Complete Diaries*, vol. 1, 368; Chouriqui, 111; Cohen, 112.
38. Sachar, 44. At the opening gavel, 197 delegates were present (Bein, 229).
39. Bein, 229–39.
40. Herzl, *Complete Diaries*, vol. 2, 728–34; Cohen, 190–91; Bein, 294–96.
41. Herzl, *Complete Diaries*, vol. 2, 720; Bein, 300–304.
42. Bein, 308–9; Cohen, 200–201.
43. Bein, 310–11.
44. The sultan had recently accepted 1,500 Jewish refugees from pogrom-ridden Romania into the Turkish Empire.
45. Bein, 354–59, 364; Cohen, 242–46.
46. Bein, 378–79; Cohen, 260–61.
47. Bein, 388–89.
48. Bein, 389; Cohen, 273–74.
49. Tuchman, *Bible*, 296–97.
50. Herzl, *Complete Diaries*, vol. 4, 1361–63; Bein, 414–18; Cohen, 287.
51. Herzl, *Complete Diaries*, vol. 4, 1365; Bein, 422; Cohen, 288.
52. Herzl, *Diaries*, vol. 4, p. 1450; Bein, 433–34; Cohen, 298.
53. Bein, 437–42; Cohen, 298–301.
54. Singer, 1–31; "Jewish Massacres Denounced," *New York Times*, April 28, 1903; Tuchman, *Bible*, 304; Cohen, 302–3; Bein, 438.
55. Sachar, 59; Tuchman, *Bible*, 303.
56. Bein, 443.
57. Bein, 454–55, 460–64; Chouraqui, 247–50; Cohen, 324–33.
58. Bein, 485–86; Cohen, 343.
59. Sachar, 60; Bein, 448–49.
60. Bein, 448–49, 490; Sachar, 60; Laqueur, 123–25; Cohen, 308–12.
61. Bein, 490; Chouraqui, 253–54.
62. Bein, 483–84.
63. Chouraqui, 264–68.
64. Sachar, 63.
65. Bein, 499–500; see also Chouraqui, 271; Tuchman, *Bible*, 308.
66. Herzl, *Complete Diaries*, vol. 1, 106.
67. Herzl, *Jewish State*, 8.
68. Herzl, *Complete Diaries*, vol. 3, 1112; Bein, 354; Laqueur, 115.
69. Johnson, 400.
70. Weizmann, vol. 1, 43.
71. Bein, 201, 451–52; see also Herzl, *Complete Diaries*, vol. 1, 368 and vol. 4, 1544.
72. Sachar, 63.
73. Laqueur, 107.
74. Herzl, *Complete Diaries*, vol. 1, 581.

Chapter 2

1. Weizmann, vol. 1, 172.
2. Tuchman, *Bible*, 331.
3. Lloyd George, vol. 2, 47–48.
4. Lloyd George, vol. 2, 49; Tuchman, *Bible*, 332.
5. Weizmann, vol. 1, 173.
6. Lloyd George, vol. 2, 50; Tuchman, *Bible*, 318; Bar-Zohar, 30.
7. The letter was actually written to a teacher in Motol. Blumberg, 15; see also Greenfield, 59.
8. Or, perhaps, the "Mazzini" of Zionism (Weizmann, vol. 1, 37; Blumberg, 19).
9. Sachar, 56–57; Tuchman, *Bible*, 307.
10. Weizmann, vol. 1, 109–11; Tuchman, *Bible*, 314–15.
11. Tuchman, *Bible*, 330–31, 335–36.
12. This excludes Transjordan (Tuchman, *Bible*, 329*fn*).
13. See map legend in Sachar, 87.
14. Sachar, 98.
15. Sachar, 110–11.
16. Blumberg, 65.
17. Blanche Dugdale, "Weizmann and Balfour," in Weisgal, 134; see also Tuchman, 318.
18. Karsh, *Islamic Imperialism*, 127–29.
19. The McMahon Letter of October 1915, written to Hussein by Sir Henry McMahon, the British high commissioner for Egypt, excluded the region "west of the districts of Damascus, Homs, Hama and Aleppo" (in other words, Palestine). Laqueur and Rubin, 15; Tuchman, *Bible*, 328.
20. Katz, *Battleground*, 46–52.
21. Blumberg, 69–71; Laqueur and Rubin, 17–18.
22. Tuchman, *Bible*, 329–30.
23. Katz, *Lone Wolf*, vol. 1, 574–76; Netanyahu, 61–62.
24. Katz, *Lone Wolf*, vol. 1, 576; Netanyahu, 62.
25. The Haganah was a newly organized Jewish defense force, armed mainly with sticks.
26. Katz, *Lone Wolf*, vol. 1, 586–92.
27. O'Brien, 146.
28. Katz, *Lone Wolf*, vol. 1, 712–18.
29. Blumberg, 81.
30. Sachar, 126.
31. Laqueur and Rubin, 39–41.
32. Sachar, 127.
33. Blumberg, 92.
34. James, vol. 4, 3343.
35. Laqueur and Rubin, 30–36.
36. Sachar, 130.
37. Quoted from Michael Assaf's, "On the Arab Question," in Weisgal, 55.
38. Tuchman, *Bible*, 329*fn*, 349.
39. Karsh, *Islamic Imperialism*, 136–37.
40. Sachar, 112–15.
41. Gilbert, *Israel*, 37.
42. Quoted in Bard, *Myths and Facts*, 24.
43. Tuchman, *Bible*, 349.
44. Quoted from Michael Assaf's "On the Arab Question," in Weisgal, 56–57.
45. Quoted in Gilbert, *Israel*, 38.
46. Gilbert, *Israel*, 40.
47. Laqueur and Rubin, 31.
48. Sachar, 134.
49. Gavison, 81–82.
50. Laqueur, 247–50.
51. Quoted from Michael Assaf's "On the Arab Question," in Weisgal, 56.
52. Gavison, 81.
53. Blumberg, 92.
54. Laqueur, 248.
55. Gilbert, *Israel*, 56–57.
56. Blumberg, 112–13.
57. Morris, 114–15. For the number of dead and Cafferata's reluctant intervention, see Katz, *Lone Wolf*, vol. 2, 1127.
58. Gilbert, *Israel*, 61.
59. Weizmann, vol. 2, 331; Sachar, 174; Rose, 276.
60. Quoted in Weisgal, 299. See also Weizmann, vol. 2, 338–39; Blumberg, 124–25.
61. Blumberg, 125–26, 264.
62. Blumberg, 264–65.
63. Gilbert, *Israel*, 76–80.
64. Sachar, 199–201; Gilbert, *Israel*, 80–81.
65. From "The Statement by Dr. Weizmann made before the Palestine Royal Commission in Jerusalem, on November 25, 1936," reproduced in Weisgal, 304–28.
66. Sachar, 203.
67. O'Brien, 226.
68. Peters, 433–34.
69. Rose, 318.
70. Quoted in Eban, *Witness*, 467.
71. Sachar, 211–13.
72. Sachar, 214–15; Gilbert, *Israel*, 92–93.
73. Sachar, 222.
74. Sachar, 225.
75. Weizmann, vol. 2, 402–3.
76. James, vol. 6, 6133–36; Tuchman, *Bible*, 348.
77. Blumberg, 168.
78. O'Brien, 238 39.
79. Blumberg, 168.
80. Blumberg, 187, 267; Weizmann, vol. 2, 423, 428–29.
81. Blumberg, 268.
82. Litvinoff, 216–17.
83. Laqueur and Rubin, 66–67.
84. Gilbert, *Israel*, 118; O'Brien, 258.
85. Gilbert, 123–25.
86. Blumberg, 207; Weizmann, vol. 2, 441.
87. Blumberg, 209–10.
88. Eban, *Witness*, 133–34.

89. Rose, 461.
90. Weizmann was not against violating the 1939 white paper immigration clauses to help Holocaust refugees, even if this led to armed clashes, but he was against terrorism root and branch.

Chapter 3

1. Kurzman, *Ben-Gurion*, 268.
2. Rose, 418.
3. Blumberg, 209; see also Rose, 419–20; Kurzman, *Ben-Gurion*, 268.
4. Blumberg, 210; see also Gilbert, *Israel*, 139.
5. Kurzman, *Ben-Gurion*, 268; Rose, 420.
6. Ben-Gurion, *Memoirs*, 38.
7. Ben-Gurion, *Memoirs*, 34; Silverstein, 19.
8. Ben-Gurion, *Memoirs*, 39.
9. Ben-Gurion, *Memoirs*, 50–52; Silverstein, 25.
10. Silverstein, 27.
11. Ben-Gurion, *Memoirs*, 54–60.
12. Silverstein, 31–33; Samuels, 57–58; Bar-Zohar, 24–25.
13. Silverstein, 33–35; Samuels, 58–59; Bar-Zohar, 26.
14. Silverstein, 38.
15. Katz, *Lone Wolf*, 1254 (emphasis added).
16. See Article 5 of the Mandate charter in Laqueur and Rubin, 31.
17. Kurzman, *Ben-Gurion*, 178–80; Katz, *Lone Wolf*, 1256–64.
18. Kurzman, *Ben-Gurion*, 188–95; Bar-Zohar, 49.
19. Kurzman, *Ben-Gurion*, 197–98; Bar-Zohar, 51.
20. Kurzman, *Ben-Gurion*, 212–15. See also Begin, 136.
21. Greenfeld, 116.
22. Samuels, 105; Silverstein, 70; Kurzman, *Ben-Gurion*, 222.
23. O'Brien, 242–43; see also Bar-Zohar, 63.
24. Kurzman, *Ben-Gurion*, 228.
25. Gilbert, *Israel*, 119. Many of the "Palestinian" Arabs were actually from Syria, Lebanon and Transjordan, but had come to Palestine to enlist.
26. Sachar, 251.
27. Since it defied Britain's white paper restrictions, clandestine Jewish immigration is often said to have been "illegal." But Article 6 of the Mandate charter obliged the British to "facilitate Jewish immigration" to Palestine. Hence, strictly speaking, it was Britain's anti-immigration white paper policy that was illegal.
28. Gilbert, *Israel*, 125.

29. Silverstein, 77; Kurzman, *Ben-Gurion*, 267.
30. Perlmutter, 177–79; Silver, 70–73; Haber, 162; Begin, 219–21; Seidman, 136–37.
31. From Barnet Litvinoff's epilogue in Blumberg, 271.
32. O'Brien, 259–67; Silver, 61; Ben-Zohar, 88.
33. O'Brien, 268, 271–72.
34. O'Brien, 272–73; Sachar, 279–80.
35. O'Brien, 274–75.
36. O'Brien, 275.
37. Sachar, 281–82. The Jews called the British compound in Jerusalem "Bevingrad" (Meir, 205; Begin, 93).
38. Gilbert, *Israel*, 146–47.
39. Sachar, 282–83; see also O'Brien, 276–77.
40. St. John, 174.
41. Eban, *Witness*, 123. A phone call from Weizmann to the Jewish former French premier, Léon Blum, had helped settle the matter in favor of the Jews (Sachar, 294).
42. Gilbert, *Israel*, 155.
43. Kurzman, *Genesis*, 3–4.
44. Gilbert, *Israel*, 154–55; Karsh, *Conflict*, 29–30; Ben-Gurion, *Personal History*, 65.
45. Gilbert, *Israel*, 157–59, 162–63; Karsh, *Conflict*, 31–33.
46. Goldston, 222–23.
47. Bar-Zohar, 102.
48. Sachar, 297–98.
49. Gilbert, *Israel*, 159, 162.
50. Ibid., 173–74.
51. IDF Archives, War of Independence Collection 88/17, cited in Zionist Organization of America (ZOA), *Deir Yassin*, 5, which in turn cited Millstein, vol. 4, 257.
52. Kurzman, *Genesis*, 139–41.
53. For conflicting loudspeaker reports, see Kurzman, *Genesis*, 142; Bard, *Myths and Facts*, 133; PBS DVD, episode 1; Meir-Levi, *Big Lies*, 18.
54. Kurzman, *Genesis*, 142, 145.
55. Testimony of Yehoshua Gorodenchik (Jabotinsky Archives), cited in ZOA, *Deir Yassin*, 7.
56. Millstein, vol. 4, 266, cited in ZOA, *Deir Yassin*, 8.
57. Kurzman, *Genesis*, 146; ZOA, *Deir Yassin*, 8; Katz, *Battleground*, 18.
58. Bard, *Myths and Facts*, 133–34.
59. Bard, *Myths and Facts*, 134.
60. Bard, *Myths and Facts*, 134–35; Meir-Levi, *Big Lies*, 19.
61. Kurzman, *Genesis*, 148; Bard, *Myths and Facts*, 133–34.
62. See Begin, 162–63; Kurzman, *Genesis*, 148–49.
63. PBS DVD, episode 1; Meir-Levi, 19–20; Bard, *Myths and Facts*, 135.

64. O'Brien, 282.

65. O'Brien, 282; Ben-Gurion, *Personal History*, 73.

66. Gilbert, *Israel*, 184.

67. Kurzman, *Genesis*, 246–47; Sachar, 310–11; Gilbert, 180–82.

68. Gilbert, 186.

69. Israel's Proclamation of Independence, quoted in Laqueur and Rubin, 109.

70. Goldston, 230. Ben-Gurion was aware that the neighboring Arab states intended to intervene as soon as the British left. Prior to the November 29th UN vote, Abba Eban (of whom we shall soon have more to say) met with Azzam Pasha to try to work out a quid pro quo for peace. Eban was told that any Arab leader who pursued such a proposal would be murdered by his people before the day was out (Sachar, 285).

71. O'Brien, 286; Samuels, 140.

72. Gilbert, *Israel*, 160–61.

73. Gilbert, *Israel*, 195–96.

74. Ben-Gurion, *Memoirs*, 88. See Sachar, 301, for Ben-Gurion's territorial strategy.

75. Gilbert, *Israel*, 194.

76. The project was supervised by "Mickey" Marcus, a Jewish veteran of the U.S. army, whom Ben-Gurion had just promoted to general (Israel's first in 2,000 years). Soon afterwards, Marcus was accidentally killed by a Jewish soldier on sentry duty.

77. O'Brien (295–96) has argued that the embargo was an especial blow to the Arabs, since their major supplier, Great Britain, was forced to comply with it under U.S. pressure, while the Israelis had sources of contraband and the ability to smuggle it in. But with the Arabs already well armed, and the Jews scarcely armed at all, it is difficult to imagine any great rejoicing in the Jewish camp.

78. Begin, 168–70.

79. O'Brien, 296–97; Sachar, 329–30; Gilbert, 210–11; Yehuda Lapidot, "The Altalena Affair," Jewish Virtual Library, www.jewishvirtuallibrary.org/jsource/History/Altalena.html (accessed 4/25/11).

80. Silver, 103; Bar-Zohar, 135.

81. Gilbert, *Israel*, 213; Silver, 108; Kurzman, *Ben-Gurion*, 296.

82. Gilbert, *Israel*, 212–13.

83. Seidman, 159–64. (Before the negotiations broke down, it had been agreed — at Begin's insistence — that 20 percent of the weaponry was to go to the Jerusalem front.)

84. For further details on the *Altalena* affair, see Silver, 100–109; Perlmutter, 225–34; Begin, 168–76; and Kurzman, *Ben-Gurion*, 292–96.

85. Sachar, 337; O'Brien, 299–300; Bard, *Myths and Facts*, 39.

86. Karsh, *Conflict*, 74–76.

87. O'Brien, 300.

88. Sachar, 330.

89. Gilbert, *Israel*, 216.

90. O'Brien, 301–2; Sachar, 335.

91. Sachar, 338–39.

92. Kurzman, *Genesis*, 579; Sachar, 339–40.

93. Yadin was an archaeology student. He would later gain fame for excavating Masada.

94. Sachar, 339–46.

95. O'Brien, 304–6; Gilbert, *Israel*, 247.

96. Iraq did not bother to negotiate since it seemed an admission of defeat. Having no common border with Israel, she simply packed up her troops and withdrew.

97. Gilbert, *Israel*, 248.

98. Bard, *Myths and Facts*, 124; Sachar, 336.

99. Kurzman, *Ben-Gurion*, 336; Silverstein, 95.

100. Kurzman, *Ben-Gurion*, 336–39.

101. Samuels, 266–67.

102. Arab refugees, armed and trained by Egypt, who viewed themselves as "martyrs."

103. Kurzman, *Ben-Gurion*, 404–7.

104. Ben-Gurion, *Memoirs*, 209–10; Kurzman, *Ben-Gurion*, 434–36.

105. Samuels, 261.

106. Silverstein, 116.

107. Samuels, 270–71.

Chapter 4

1. Bard, *Myths and Facts*, 46; O'Brien, 363.

2. Avneri, 272. Bard, *Myths and Facts*, 124. Many of the "refugees" are actually more accurately described as "displaced persons," since they did not leave Palestine, but simply relocated to Arab-controlled areas within the former Mandate.

3. Bard, *Myths and Facts*, 137–39. Egyptian President Gamal Abdel Nasser reiterated the point 12 years later with the laconic refrain, "If the refugees return to Israel, Israel will cease to exist" (Bard, *Myths and Facts*, 146).

4. Gilbert, *Israel*, 218.

5. Sachar, 304.

6. Bard, *Myths and Facts*, 129.

7. Gilbert, *Israel*, 161–62, 167.

8. Gilbert, *Israel*, 165–67; Karsh, *Conflict*, 42.

9. Meir-Levi, *History*, 68. See also Bard, *Myths and Facts*, 128.

10. Meir-Levi, *History*, 66–67.

11. Sachar, 308–9, 332–33.

12. Burkett, 140.

13. Bard, *Myths and Facts*, 130–31; Katz, *Battleground*, 17.

14. Atiyah, 183–85; also quoted in Bard, *Myths and Facts*, 131; Katz, *Battleground*, 15.

15. Bard, *Myths and Facts*, 131. See Bard,

Myths and Facts, 130–31 and Katz, *Battleground*, 14–21 for additional examples.

16. Katz, *Battleground*, 18; Bard, *Myths and Facts*, 131.

17. Karsh, *Conflict*, 90; see also Morris, 256.

18. Sachar, 332.

19. Sachar, 332; Bard, *Myths and Facts*, 130; Karsh, *Conflict*, 47; Gilbert, *Israel*, 172–73.

20. Karsh, *Conflict*, 45–50; Bard, *Myths and Facts*, 128–30.

21. Gilbert, *Israel*, 183; Haber, 214.

22. Dershowitz, *Israel*, 83. (For mistreatment of the populace by Arab soldiers, see Bard, *Myths and Facts*, 127.)

23. Gilbert, *Israel*, 171, 174–77; Sachar, 307–8; Karsh, *Conflict*, 45; Bard, *Myths and Facts*, 127.

24. Sachar, 308; Karsh, *Conflict*, 50.

25. Meir-Levi, *Big Lies*, 22.

26. See, for example, Dershowitz, *Israel*, 81.

27. Eban, *Israel* DVD, episode 2.

28. Curtis et al., 59–63.

29. Bard, *Myths and Facts*, 124.

30. Bard, *Myths and Facts*, 138; Morris, 258.

31. Bard, *Myths and Facts*, 140–42.

32. See, for example, Gilbert, *Israel*, 256; Sachar, 441; Morris, 258; Dershowitz, *Israel*, 87–88; Bard, *Myths and Facts*, 141–42; Meir-Levi, *Big Lies*, 10–13.

33. Eban, *Israel* DVD, episode 2.

34. Eban, *Witness*, 15, 29.

35. Ibid., 15.

36. St. John, 46–47, 58–59; Eban, *Witness*, 17.

37. Eban, *Witness*, 18–19, 22–23.

38. Ibid., 30.

39. Ibid., 34–35, 42–43.

40. St. John, 103–7; Eban, *Witness*, 42–44. (Eban had the only copy of the recruitment list and seems to have thought it best not to show it to anyone.)

41. St. John, 143–49, 157.

42. Ibid., 180–85.

43. Ibid., 227–28.

44. St. John, 204; see also Eban, *Witness*, 159.

45. Eban, *Witness*, 193.

46. Ibid., 193–94.

47. Henriques, 185–86.

48. Eban, *Witness*, 197–98, 237.

49. O'Brien, 381–82.

50. St. John, 275.

51. Gilbert, *Israel*, 289–90.

52. According to Sharon, the civilians had hidden within the confines of the seemingly deserted town — their presence unsuspected by the demolition crews (Sharon, 89–90; Sachar, 444). Morris does not find this explanation creditable (Morris, 278–79).

53. O'Brien, 382.

54. Sachar, 482.

55. Eban, *Witness*, 236; St. John, 290.

56. St. John, 293; see also Eban, *Witness*, 249.

57. Eban, *Witness*, 249.

58. Henriques, 189–90.

59. Sachar, 482; Ben-Gurion, *Memoirs*, 202.

60. Henriques, 191–92.

61. Eban, *Witness*, 242.

62. Sachar, 472–75.

63. Bard, *Myths and Facts*, 47.

64. Morris, 284.

65. St. John, 291.

66. Morris, 267; Eban, *Witness*, 245; Sachar, 476.

67. Ben-Gurion made this point to Moshe Sharrett in December 1955 (Morris, 265). Nasser's view, as revealed to an American negotiator in early 1956, was that an accommodation was desirable, but it would require a sizable chunk of the Negev and would likely end in his own assassination (Gilbert, *Israel*, 307–10). Jordan's King Abdullah and three Arab prime ministers had already been assassinated or deposed and executed for taking a soft line on Israel.

68. Eban, *Witness*, 242.

69. Ibid., 242–48.

70. Sachar, 474, 483–84.

71. Eban, *Witness*, 251–52.

72. Ibid., 252.

73. Peres, 106; Gilbert, *Israel*, 312.

74. Sachar, 489; Thomas, 90.

75. Sachar, 490–91; O'Brien, 387; Thomas, 94–95, 98.

76. Eban, *Witness*, 257; Sachar, 492.

77. Dayan, *My Life*, 174.

78. Dayan, *My Life*, 174–75, 187; O'Brien, 387–89.

79. Dayan, *My Life*, 187–89.

80. O'Brien, 389; Slater, *Dayan*, 192; Dayan, *My Life*, 187.

81. Peres, 112.

82. Bar-Zohar, 217–18.

83. Dayan, *My Life*, 195–97; Gilbert, *Israel*, 318–19; Slater, *Warrior Statesman*, 195; Bar-Zohar, 223.

84. Gilbert, *Israel*, 320–21.

85. O'Brien, 389–90.

86. Morris, 296–97.

87. A week earlier, Ben-Gurion had told Eban of a possible accord with France that would produce "sensational results," but added that its consummation was exceedingly unlikely, and gave no details. Nor had Eban received any substantive updates from that time (Eban, *Witness*, 256–58).

88. Eban, *Witness*, 267, 270–71.

89. Ibid., 271–72.

90. Sachar, 505.

91. O'Brien, 393–94; Eban, *Witness*, 275–76.

92. Eban, *Witness*, 276–77; O'Brien, 394.
93. Eban, *Witness*, 277–79; O'Brien, 394–95.
94. Eban, *Witness*, 280–82.
95. Eban, *Witness*, 284; O'Brien, 397.
96. O'Brien, 396.
97. Eban, *Witness*, 294.
98. Ibid., 586.
99. The latter was adapted from his second autobiography, *Personal Witness*.

Chapter 5

1. Judaism's holiest "site" is the "Temple Mount," where Solomon's Temple stood until it was destroyed by the Babylonians in 586 B.C. The Temple was rebuilt 71 years later, but was destroyed again by the Romans in A.D. 70. Surrounding the Temple Mount are massive retaining walls, dating to the reign of Herod the Great (37–4 B.C.). Judaism's holiest extant structure or "shrine" is that section of the western retaining wall that stands closest to where the Temple was located. (In common parlance, the Western Wall is often called the "Wailing Wall"—a term that has taken on derogatory connotations over the centuries and is no longer preferred.)
2. Churchill and Churchill, 141. See also, Dayan, *My Life*, 3.
3. Lau-Lavie, 14–15.
4. Lau-Lavie, 91–92; see also Dayan, *My Life*, 13.
5. Lau-Lavie, 19–20; Slater, *Warrior Statesman*, 18.
6. Van Creveld, 33.
7. The school was founded by the Women's International Zionist Organization in 1926.
8. Slater, *Warrior Statesman*, 30–31.
9. Van Creveld, 52–53; Lau-Lavie, 41–43; Slater, *Warrior Statesman*, 58–62; Dayan, *My Life*, 48–51, 58.
10. As a result of this kibbutz tie, the Palmach became a collectivist army, affiliated with the radically socialist Mapam Party—the political rival of Ben-Gurion's Mapai Party.
11. Lau-Lavie, 44–45.
12. Sachar, 318–19, Gilbert, *Israel*, 192–93.
13. Lau-Lavie, 64–67; Van Creveld, 62–63; Dayan, *My Life*, 77–86. The towns were occupied the following day by a different brigade.
14. Lau-Lavie, 93–95.
15. Dayan, *My Life*, 103.
16. Lau-Lavie, 113.
17. Lau-Lavie, 155–57; Slater, *Warrior Statesman*, 182–83.
18. Lau-Lavie, 163–67; Slater, *Warrior Statesman*, 203–8; Dayan, *My Life*, 206–11.
19. Lau-Lavie, 183.

20. Lau-Lavie, 130. (See chapter 3 for a discussion of the Lavon affair.)
21. Van Creveld, 118; Slater, *Warrior Statesman*, 240–41.
22. Lau-Lavie, 198.
23. Sachar, 445–46.
24. Oren, 19.
25. Sachar, 446–47.
26. Gilbert, *Israel*, 291; Eban, *Witness*, 330.
27. Gilbert, *Israel*, 291.
28. Oren, 15, 19–20; Eban, *Witness*, 329–30.
29. Eban, *Witness*, 330–31.
30. Oren, 24.
31. Morris, 303.
32. Oren, 33–34.
33. Oren, 33–34; Gilbert, *Israel*, 363–64.
34. Gilbert, *Israel*, 353–54; Rabin, 61–63.
35. Oren, 45–46.
36. Ibid., 46–47.
37. Gilbert, *Israel*, 365–66; Sachar, 622.
38. Morris, 304–5.
39. Eban, *Witness*, 354–56; Gilbert, *Israel*, 366; Sachar, 623; Rabin, 68.
40. O'Brien, 409; Sachar, 622–23; Oren, 59.
41. See Gilbert, *Israel*, 333–34.
42. Eban, *Witness*, 357. See also Churchill and Churchill, 30.
43. Sachar, 623–24.
44. O'Brien, 408–10; Rabin, 69–70.
45. Eban, *Witness*, 359–60, 416; Churchill and Churchill, 32.
46. The specific law in question was the 1958 Convention of the Territorial Sea and Contiguous Zone (Bard, *Myths and Facts*, 55).
47. Eban, *Witness*, 404. An example of Egypt's illogic on the straits can be found in Churchill and Churchill, 40–43. Although it fits Eban's description to a T, the Churchills insist (implausibly) that it has "a plausible ring" and makes for "a strong juridical case."
48. Gilbert, *Israel*, 368; see also Oren, 84; Eban, *Witness*, 365–66.
49. Gilbert, *Israel*, 369; Oren, 84.
50. O'Brien, 411; Morris, 306.
51. O'Brien, 411; Sachar, 626.
52. Prittie, 253; O'Brien, 411.
53. Eban, *Witness*. 374–76.
54. Ibid., 379.
55. Ibid., 388. In addition, Dwight Eisenhower had agreed to state that Egypt's blockade was illegal under the 1957 UN agreement (Eban, *Witness*, 385).
56. Eban, *Witness*, 395–96.
57. Churchill and Churchill, 47.
58. Eban, *Witness*, 398–99; Sachar, 630; Rabin, 90–91; Oren, 121–24.
59. Meir, 358–61.
60. Oren, 121; Lau-Lavie, 202–3; Gilbert, *Israel*, 380.
61. Sachar, 632; Lau-Lavie, 203.

62. Oren, 132; O'Brien, 413. See also Prittie, 259–60.

63. Gilbert, *Israel*, 377–78. The three were Britain, Denmark and Canada.

64. Prittie, 259; Gilbert, *Israel*, 377.

65. Slater, *Warrior Statesman*, 246; Lau-Lavie, 200–201.

66. Slater, *Warrior Statesman*, 249; Dayan, *My Life*, 254.

67. Slater, *Warrior Statesman*, 250–51.

68. Dayan, *My Life*, 261, 267; Slater, *Warrior Statesman*, 251, 255.

69. O'Brien, 414.

70. O'Brien, 414; Eban, *Witness*, 405.

71. Eban, *Witness*, 405; O'Brien, 414.

72. Slater, *Warrior Statesman*, 256–59; Van Creveld, 127–28; Gilbert, *Israel*, 380.

73. Slater, *Warrior Statesman*, 259–61.

74. Slater, *Warrior Statesman*, 263–64; Churchill and Churchill, 73–75; Lau-Lavie, 208.

75. O'Brien, 414.

76. Bard, *Myths and Facts*, 55.

77. Sachar, 625; Morris, 309–10.

78. Sachar, 633–34; Churchill and Churchill, 52; Morris, 310.

79. Oren, 170–71.

80. Gilbert, *Israel*, 384; Churchill and Churchill, 82.

81. Sachar, 636; Lau-Lavie, 209.

82. Gilbert, *Israel*, 387; Sachar, 645–47; Slater, *Warrior Statesman*, 268.

83. Sachar, 634–36.

84. Sachar, 641–42; Churchill and Churchill, 115–23.

85. Churchill and Churchill, 164–66.

86. Churchill and Churchill, 167–69.

87. Gilbert, *Israel*, 390–91; Churchill and Churchill, 177–80.

88. Sachar, 638; Van Creveld, 129; Slater, *Warrior Statesman*, 268.

89. See Gilbert, *Israel*, 387; Van Creveld, 132.

90. Gilbert, *Israel*, 385; Eban, *Witness*, 409–10.

91. Gilbert, *Israel*, 385; Eban, *Witness*, 410; Prittie, 266.

92. Oren, 193.

93. Meir, 366; Kort, 79–80; Eban, *Witness*, 200.

94. Slater, *Warrior Statesman*, 272–73. Dayan cited continued enemy resistance as a major reason for his change of heart. He also knew that the UN intended to order a bilateral withdrawal from the canal and "thought it well to have an area from which to withdraw" (Dayan, *My Life*, 294).

95. Eban, *Witness*, 423.

96. Sachar, 655–67; Slater, *Warrior Statesman*, 275–77.

97. PBS DVD, episode 2.

98. Sachar, 658; Oren, 298.

99. Eban, *Witness*, 424–26.

100. Bard, *Myths and Facts*, 59.

101. Prittie, 266; Oren, 195, says they were "butchered by Syrian villagers."

102. Churchill and Churchill, 191.

103. See, for example, Eban, *Witness*, 462.

104. Van Creveld, 128.

105. Slater, *Warrior Statesman*, 265.

106. Van Creveld, 128.

107. Slater, *Warrior Statesman*, 377–78, 385; Meir, 451–52; Dayan, *My Life*, 494.

108. Dayan's old comrade, Shimon Peres, succeeded him as defense minister.

109. The experience led to a third book, entitled *Breakthrough: A Personal Account of the Egypt-Israel Peace Negotiations*.

110. Slater, *Warrior Statesman*, 228–30.

111. Van Creveld, 207–8.

Chapter 6

1. Slater, *Uncrowned Queen*, 73–74. See also Meir, 218.

2. Slater, *Uncrowned Queen*, 71–72; see also Burkett, 127–28.

3. Slater, *Uncrowned Queen*, 73.

4. Meir, 218–19; Burkett, 142.

5. Slater, *Uncrowned Queen*, 75; Meir, 214–19.

6. Eban, *Witness*, 437, 446; O'Brien, 489–90.

7. Eban, *Witness*, 438, 446–50.

8. Ibid., 455.

9. Quoted from the text of UN Security Council Resolution 242.

10. Eban, *Witness*, 457.

11. Eban, *Witness*, 456; Bard, *Myths and Facts*, 67–68.

12. O'Brien, 417.

13. Eban, *Witness*, 456.

14. Ibid., 457–58.

15. Ibid., 458–59.

16. Ibid., 459.

17. Ibid., 459.

18. Among these pragmatists was the movement's founder, the notable Mapai member Eliezer Livneh (Sachar, 709).

19. Gilbert, *Israel*, 402.

20. Eban, *Witness*, 450, 461.

21. Gilbert, *Israel*, 396; Slater, *Warrior Statesman*, 293.

22. Gilbert, *Israel*, 406, 422–23; Sachar, 709–11.

23. Dayan's wing was the old Rafi Party; Allon's was formerly the Ahdut Avoda Party.

24. Slater, *Warrior Statesman*, 309–11; Slater, *Uncrowned Queen*, 173; Eban, *Witness*,

476–77; Gilbert, *Israel*, 408–9; Burkett, 230–31; see also Sachar, 711.

25. Meir, 13.

26. Meir, 71–72; Keller, 32–33; Burkett, 46–47.

27. Slater, *Uncrowned Queen*, 26.

28. Ibid., 31.

29. Slater, *Uncrowned Queen*, 34; Burkett, 66.

30. Burkett, 66–67.

31. Meir, 157–59; Burkett, 90–93.

32. Meir, 184–89. The English-language *Palestine Post* is now the *Jerusalem Post*.

33. Meir, 202–4.

34. Ibid., 214.

35. Peres, 100.

36. Meir, 250–51; Slater, *Uncrowned Queen*, 87–88.

37. Meir, 254. Afterwards, Soviet agents ruthlessly arrested Ivy for her pro–Jewish remarks.

38. Meir, 263–67; Slater, *Uncrowned Queen*, 92–100; Keller, 86–89.

39. Meir, 296; Keller, 90; Slater, *Uncrowned Queen*, 120.

40. Eban, *Witness*, 284.

41. Meir, 336; Slater, *Uncrowned Queen*, 139–42; Burkett, 203–4.

42. Slater, *Uncrowned Queen*, 160; Peres, 99. Dayan bolted Mapai for Ben-Gurion's Rafi Party in 1965.

43. Keller, 102–3; Burkett, 224.

44. Meir, 383; Gilbert, *Israel*, 410.

45. Gilbert, *Israel*, 410; Eban, *Witness*, 482.

46. Meir, 384; Gilbert, *Israel*, 410.

47. Meir, 382.

48. Eban, *Witness*, 487–88.

49. Sachar, 694–95.

50. Reich, 98; Sachar, 695; Eban, *Witness*, 489.

51. Eban, *Witness*, 489–90; Rabin, 176–79.

52. Sachar, 695; Van Creveld, 148; Rabin, 183.

53. DeChancie, 92.

54. Eban, *Witness*, 499–500, 505.

55. Sadat, 219. The quote is from Sadat's autobiography and is not an exact transcription from his speech. Mitchell Bard, however, notes that Sadat's offer of a peace agreement with Israel was not made public (Bard, *Myths and Facts*, 72).

56. Eban, *Witness*, 500; Dayan, *My Life*, 370; Rabin, 192.

57. O'Brien, 509; Eban, *Witness*, 500–503.

58. Meir, 380; Slater, *Uncrowned Queen*, 195.

59. Eban, *Witness*, 500–501.

60. Ibid., 501–3.

61. Bard, *Myths and Facts*, 72.

62. Sachar, 696; Dayan, *My Life*, 370; Rabin, 193.

63. Eban, *Witness*, 501.

64. Meir, 373.

65. Eban, *Witness*, 503–5. Eban thought this decision regrettable. In after years, he argued that if Dayan's plan had succeeded, the surprise attack on Yom Kippur 1973 could not have taken place.

66. Sacher, 696; Kissinger, 201.

67. Sadat, 225–31.

68. Kissinger, 197–99.

69. Kissinger, 201–2 (Kissinger's italics).

70. Only Gideon Rafael, the director-general of Israel's foreign office, seems to have picked up on this (Rabinovich, 14–15; Eban, *Witness*, 507–8; O'Brien, 511).

71. Kissinger, 215–16.

72. Kissinger, 220–21; Eban, *Witness*, 515.

73. The term was applied by Yitzhak Rabin (Rabin, 234; Gilbert, *Israel*, 423).

74. Eban, *Witness*, 465.

75. Sachar, 710.

76. Gilbert, *Israel*, 422; Slater, *Warrior Statesman*, 333. (The interview occurred on May 14, 1973.)

77. Eban, *Witness*, 466.

78. Sachar, 745–46.

79. From Anwar Sadat's interview with Arnaud de Borchgrave, entitled "The Battle Is Now Inevitable," *Newsweek*, April 9, 1973, 44–45; see also Kissinger, 225 (bracketed text added by this author for clarity).

80. Gilbert, *Israel*, 423.

81. Rabinovich, 51; Herzog, 227–28; Kissinger, 460.

82. Herzog, 229; Sachar, 752; Kissinger, 461.

83. Sachar, 748–49.

84. Sachar, 749; Herzog, 227–28.

85. Rabinovich, 50–52.

86. Slater, *Uncrowned Queen*, 235; Burkett, 316.

87. Dayan, *My Life*, 376; Rabinovich, 87; Meir, 426.

88. Meir, 426–27.

89. Gilbert, *Israel*, 429.

90. O'Brien, 522; Herzog, 241–43; Gilbert, *Israel*, 432; Sachar, 759.

91. Gilbert, *Israel*, 429.

92. Gilbert, *Israel*, 434–36.

93. Sachar, 756; Dayan, *My Life*, 393.

94. Slater, *Warrior Statesman*, 354–60; Burkett, 324; Rabinovich, 219–20.

95. Gilbert, *Israel*, 444–45; Sachar, 760–62.

96. Eban, *Witness*, 531; Schiff, 299–303.

97. Gilbert, *Israel*, 440–42.

98. Slater, *Uncrowned Queen*, 244. (This was likely October 9 — see Kissinger, 491–92.)

99. Eban, *Witness*, 533–34; Sachar, 767–68; Rabinovich, 348.

100. See the respective versions given by Eban (*Witness*, 533–35) and O'Brien (525–27).

101. Quoted in Eban, *Witness*, 533–35; see also Kissinger, 493–95, 511–19.

102. Schiff, 304–5.

103. Herzog, 257–61; O'Brien, 524; Gilbert, *Israel*, 443; Sachar, 775–76.

104. Henry Kissinger quoted in PBS DVD, episode 4. In *Years of Upheaval*, 547–51, Kissinger tells the story in more detail (and somewhat differently).

105. Eban, *Witness*, 536–37.

106. Sachar, 781; Herzog, 280; Dayan, *My Life*, 441–42; Burkett, 335.

107. Eban, *Witness*, 538–39; Burkett, 335.

108. Van Creveld, 179.

109. Slater, *Uncrowned Queen*, 262.

110. Meir, 452.

111. Meir, 451–52; see also Rabinovich, 502.

112. Eban, DVD, episode 4.

113. Peres, 99.

114. Slater, *Uncrowned Queen*, 193; Burkett, 247.

115. Slater, *Uncrowned Queen*, 271–72; Burkett, 376–78.

116. Sadat, 215.

117. Kissinger, 226. (Italics added.)

118. Burkett, 378; see also Rabinovich, 12.

Chapter 7

1. O'Brien, 532–35.

2. Eban, *Witness*, 558–59.

3. Sachar, 795; Eban, *Witness*, 558.

4. Sachar, 798.

5. Eban, *Witness*, 557–61.

6. O'Brien, 534–36, 541–43.

7. O'Brien, 544; Reich, 105.

8. Sachar, 817; Gilbert, *Israel*, 468; Rabin, 256, 261.

9. O'Brien, 546.

10. Sachar, 824; O'Brien, 549–50.

11. The embargo had ended with vastly increased oil prices (Sachar, 806–7).

12. Gilbert, *Israel*, 469–70; Reich, 115–17.

13. Eban, *Witness*, 583; Gilbert, *Israel*, 470.

14. O'Brien, 557–58; Gilbert, *Israel*, 475–77.

15. Amdur, 90; Haber, 3–4.

16. Silver, 156.

17. Amdur, 28–29; Haber, 20; Silver, 6.

18. Temko, 24–25.

19. Amdur, 29; Haber, 28–29; Silver, 10.

20. Begin, 22*fn*.

21. Amdur, 31–34. Gilbert, *Israel*, 68.

22. Katz, *Lone Wolf*, 617.

23. Blumberg, 74; Schiff, 8; Sachar, 123, 184.

24. Perlmutter, 48–49, 53–55; Sachar, 184–86; Katz, 919, 930–34, 952–53. The quoted phrase is from Jabotinsky's testimony before the Peel Commission at the House of Lords, February 11, 1937 (Laqueur and Rubin, 53).

25. Article 5 (Laqueur and Rubin, 31) states that "the Mandatory shall be responsible for seeing that no Palestine territory shall be ceded or leased to, or in any way placed under the control of, the Government of any foreign Power." This can only mean that the cession of Transjordan to Emir Abdullah in 1922 was in contravention of the charter. The same, incidentally, may be said of the Golan Heights, which Britain ceded to French Syria in 1923 in exchange for oil-rich lands in what is now the Mosul region of Iraq (CAMERA Staff, "History of the Golan," October, 12, 1995, http://www.camera.org/index.asp?x_context=7&x_issue=27&x_article=204 (accessed 4/26/11).

26. Begin, 30–31.

27. Silver, 14; Katz, 1264.

28. Sachar, 186.

29. Hurwitz, 11; Haber, 39.

30. Amdur, 33; Silver, 17.

31. Katz, 1627–28; Temko, 47–48; Perlmutter, 88; Silver, 19–20; Haber, 50.

32. Temko, 52.

33. Silver, 18.

34. Amdur, 37–39; Silver, 21–26.

35. Begin, 6–7.

36. Silver, 28–29; Temko, 61; Amdur, 42–43.

37. Begin, 11–15.

38. Amdur, 54–55; Haber, 92–93.

39. Perlmutter, 96–97; Haber, 95; O'Brien, 246–47.

40. Begin, 28–29, 36–37.

41. Irgun broadsheet, quoted in Haber, 101.

42. Haber, 107; Silver, 46.

43. Begin, 93.

44. Perlmutter, 159–60; Haber, 110.

45. Begin, 193–94, 209, 238–42, 251–53.

46. Begin, 231–35, 241–43.

47. Begin, 103–5.

48. Begin, 105–8.

49. Perlmutter, 135–36.

50. Begin, 115–16; Haber, 126.

51. Begin, 122–31.

52. Ibid., 145–51.

53. Begin, 228–29; Haber, 167.

54. Begin, 318–19, 325–31.

55. Haber, 176; Hurwitz, 27.

56. Haber, 228. The demand was later scaled back to everything west of the Jordan.

57. Perlmutter, 253.

58. Hurwitz, 55, 65; see also Perlmutter, 11; Seidman, 70, 166.

59. Kurzman, *Ben-Gurion*, 337–38; Silver, 116; see also Temko, 136.

60. Hurwitz, 64.

61. Ehud Olmert (the future prime minister) was among the most outspoken rebels.

62. Perlmutter, 283–84; Hurwitz, 69; Haber, 265–66; Silver, 127–28.

63. Silver, 131.

64. Hurwitz, 71–72; Haber, 272; Silver, 132; Seidman, 174–75.

65. Haber, 273–74, 287–88.

66. Eban, *Witness*, 491.

67. Hurwitz, 82–83.

68. Haber, 290; Perlmutter, 302; Sachar, 741.

69. Silver, 153–54; Hurwitz, 93; Haber, 302–3.

70. Silver, 156–57; Sachar, 834.

71. Sachar, 835; Silver, 157–59; Eban, 584–85.

72. Gilbert, 481–82.

73. O'Brien, 561–65, 567–72.

74. O'Brien, 572–73; Gilbert, 483; Horovitz, 98; Rabin, 319–22.

75. O'Brien, 577–78; Temko, 213.

76. Sachar, 848–49.

77. Silver, 192; PBS DVD.

78. Silver, 183, 193–94.

79. The second, dealing with Palestinian "autonomy" will be discussed in the next chapter.

80. Sachar, 852; Gilbert, *Israel*, 492.

81. Silver, 198.

82. Dayan, *Breakthrough*, 232–34, 245; Kort, 116.

83. Sachar, 855–59; Amdur, 96. The Knesset had approved the text by a vote of 95–18 six days earlier.

84. From the text of Begin's speech, reproduced in Hurwitz, 151.

85. Hurwitz, 135.

86. Ibid., 228–29.

87. Hurwitz, 230–45.

88. i.e., Anwar's wife. Sadat himself had died in October 1981, the tragic victim of a brutal assassination by Islamic extremists.

Chapter 8

1. Rabin, 283.

2. Slater, *Warrior Stateman*, 387.

3. Rabin, 285–87.

4. Sachar, 830; Rabin, 288; Kort, 106.

5. "Yoni" Netanyahu was the elder brother of future prime minister and Likud Party leader, Benjamin Netanyahu.

6. Sachar, 830.

7. Sachar, 830; Reich, 115.

8. Gabriel, 30–33, 39–41.

9. Gabriel, 31; Rubin, 10–11.

10. Rubin, 18–20; Karsh, *Arafat's War*, 27.

11. In the late 1940s, the world was home to millions of refugees. World War II gave rise to many of these millions. The partition of India created millions more. All were rehabilitated within a period of years. But the Arab states refused to resettle Palestinian refugees, even though UNRWA offered them financial incentives to do so. As one UNRWA official explained it: "The Arab nations do not want to solve the refugee problem. They want to keep it as an open sore ... as a weapon against Israel" (quoted in Rubin, 5).

12. Laqueur and Rubin, 7th edition, 117–20; Rubin, 20–22.

13. Rubin, 14–15, 20–22.

14. Karsh, *Arafat's War*, 27–28.

15. Gabriel, 34.

16. Ibid., 39–42.

17. Ibid., 41–42.

18. Bard, *Guide to the Middle East Conflict*, 378–80.

19. Eban, *Witness*, 576.

20. Rubin, 46. The notion was that if international pressure forced Israel to relinquish the West Bank and Gaza, they should go to the PLO, not to Jordan. In this way, Israel's sacrifice would not bring peace, but would be a further step toward her destruction.

21. Gabriel, 39–42.

22. Gabriel, 43. (Regarding the occupants of PLO bus, see Karsh, *Arafat's War*, 30.)

23. Gabriel, 44–47.

24. Rubin, 48.

25. Dayan, *Breakthrough*, 120–21.

26. Gabriel, 56–57.

27. Rubin, 55.

28. Eban, *Witness*, 591–92.

29. Karsh, *Arafat's War*, 50.

30. Alexander and Bogdanor, 84.

31. Eban, *Witness*, 587, 591–92; Sachar, 844–45.

32. Silver, 204; Eban, 598; see also the Israeli government's official policy statement of August 5, 1981, in Laqueur and Rubin, 415–16.

33. O'Brien, 601–2.

34. Dayan, *Breakthrough*, 184–85, 303–4.

35. O'Brien, 608–9.

36. Perlmutter, 366–70; O'Brien, 609–11; Sachar, 879–80.

37. Perlmutter, 365; see also Silver, 218–19.

38. Perlmutter, 326.

39. Eban, *Witness*, 606; O'Brien, 622–23; Perlmutter, 382; Silver, 226.

40. Gabriel, 58; Bard, *Myths and Facts*, 95.

41. O'Brien, 615; Sharon and Chanoff, 432–33, 449.

42. K. Levin, 266; Bard, *Myths and Facts*, 95; Sharon and Chanoff, 444.

43. Silver, 227; Perlmutter, 382; Eban, 607.

44. Perlmutter, 380–83; Eban, *Witness*, 604–5; O'Brien, 617–25; Gilbert, *Israel*, 504.

45. Gabriel, 97–98.

46. Eastern Beirut was controlled by Israel's Christian Maronite allies.

47. Gabriel, 81, 116–18.

48. Gilbert, *Israel*, 508; Gabriel, 159; Sachar, 910. It didn't help that Israel censored the press

while the PLO masterfully seduced them. The PLO's "techniques," says Richard Gabriel, "included granting exclusive interviews ... and providing [journalists] with women and drugs, and sometimes with cash payments" (Gabriel, 125, 135–36, 159).

49. Gabriel, 122–25, 159, 173.

50. Ibid., 85–87, 122–25, 194.

51. Ibid., 159–62.

52. Ibid., 162–64. Tours of the city at the end of the siege revealed highly localized damage — much less than was still evident from the Lebanese Civil War.

53. Though appalling, this figure was deemed unsatisfactory by the international press, which forthwith published exaggerations supplied to it by PLO spokesmen — among them Yasser Arafat's brother, Fahti, the head of the Palestinian Red Crescent (Gabriel, 121, 164–65). It is interesting to note that PLO/Muslim attackers killed twice this number in the attack on Christian Damour in the Lebanese Civil War without the press noticing.

54. Sachar, 911.

55. See Gabriel, 130–31; Sachar, 911–12; Gilbert, *Israel*, 508.

56. Perlmutter, 387.

57. Quoted in Eban, *Witness*, 616.

58. From the Kahan Commission Report, quoted in Laqueur and Rubin, 453.

59. From the Kahan Commission Report, quoted in Silver, 238; Amdur, 105; Temko, 288.

60. Several high-ranking IDF officers resigned over the conduct of the war. The most celebrated was the distinguished brigade commander, Colonel Eli Geva, who offered his resignation rather than lead soldiers into Beirut at the outset of the siege (Gabriel, 184).

61. Nehemiah's original name was Rubitzov. After being turned away by the Jewish Legion in 1917, he changed it to Rabin so that he could reapply with a different examiner (Rabin, 5; Horovitz, 24–25).

62. Horovitz, 26; Slater, *Rabin*, 25.

63. Kort, 22; Horovitz, 24.

64. Kort, 27.

65. Quoted in Kort, 30–31 and in Slater, *Rabin*, 46; see also Rabin, 10.

66. Rabin, 11–12; Kort, 31–32. Moshe Dayan lost an eye that same night.

67. Kort, 11–15, 38; Rabin, 15–18; Slater, *Rabin*, 55–57.

68. Rabin, 17.

69. The passage was reproduced in an appendix of the 1996 edition of Rabin's memoirs (Horovitz, 35–36; Rabin, 383–84).

70. Rabin, 35–36; Kort, 34, 49; Horovitz, 34.

71. Oren, 79–91; Rabin, 66, 73–83; Kort, 67; Slater, *Rabin*, 126–31; Horovitz, 52–53.

72. O'Brien, 494–98.

73. Slater, *Rabin*, 185; Kort, 92; Horovitz, 72–73.

74. Rabin, 311–13; Slater, *Rabin*, 282–83; Horovitz, 94–96.

75. Horovitz, 96.

76. Karsh, *Arafat's War*, 44–45; K. Levin, 269.

77. Rubin, 92–93; K. Levin, 269; Ross, 41.

78. Kurzman, *Rabin*, 405; Horovitz, 113–14; Slater, *Rabin*, 330.

79. Rubin, 94.

80. Kort, 123.

81. Rubin, 86–88.

82. Kort, 123; Kurzman, *Rabin*, 409; Slater, *Rabin*, 338–40.

83. Horovitz, ed., 120–21, 138; Rabin, 356.

84. Gilbert, *Israel*, 537–38.

85. Slater, *Rabin*, 359–61; Kort, 126–27.

86. Horovitz, 129; Slater, *Rabin*, 379–80.

87. Gilbert, *Israel*, 546–47; Sachar, 978–80.

88. Kort, 130–31.

89. Kort, 130–33; Horovitz, 134–35; Slater, *Rabin*, 387–89, 407.

90. Kort, 137–39; Horovitz, 138–43; Sachar, 989–90; Gilbert, *Israel*, 558. Owing to international pressure, Rabin repatriated the deportees the following year.

91. Rubin, 66–73.

92. Ibid., 90–92.

93. Rubin, 109–11, 116, 183; see also Karsh, *Arafat's War*, 51.

94. Rubin, 118–22.

95. Rubin, 134–36; Karsh, *Arafat's War*, 52–53; Sachar, 980–81; Bard, *Myths and Facts*, 142.

96. Rubin, 185–86.

97. Rubin, 178–79.

98. Rabin, afterword, 370; Ross, 89; K. Levin, 324–25.

99. Rubin, 195–96; Kort, 141–42. In fact, the PLO had approved the list of negotiators at Madrid.

100. K. Levin, 325.

101. Peres, 299; Kurzman, *Rabin*, 454–55.

102. Horovitz, 191, 207.

103. Laqueur and Rubin 613; Karsh, *Arafat's War*, 56.

104. Yigal Carmon, "The Story Behind the Handshake" in Kozodoy, 21; Karsh, *Arafat's War*, 56.

105. Karsh, *Arafat's War*, 16. Besides being a terrorist, Yasser Arafat was a habitual liar. The son of a Gazan father and a Jerusalemite mother, he consistently claimed that he was born in Palestine (though the precise location tended to vary). In truth, he was born and raised in Egypt, retaining his Egyptian accent and dialect to his dying day. He frequently re-

counted tales of his exploits during the *Nakba*—Israel's War of Independence — when, in fact, he had spent the entire period in Cairo attending secondary school. A Romanian official who knew him said that "Arafat tells a lie in every sentence" (Karsh, *Arafat's War*, 14–15).

106. Carmon, 22; Karsh, 5; K. Levin, introduction, ix.

107. K. Levin, 344.

108. Karsh, *Arafat's War*, 60–61; Kort, 150; K. Levin, 344.

109. K. Levin, 347, 369.

110. See Kurzman, *Rabin*, 468; Kort, 148–49.

111. Horovitz, 212. Such acts, though exceedingly rare, had occurred before. In 1980, radical Gush Emunim members placed bombs in the cars of two West Bank mayors. Both lost legs in the ensuing explosions. In 1982, IDF reservist Allan Goodman opened fire on innocent Arabs on the Temple Mount, killing 12 and wounding an equal number (Sachar, 894–95).

112. See K. Levin, 363. For casualty figures, see Kort, 149.

113. Kort, 149.

114. Kort, 150; see also Gilbert, *Israel*, 569–70; Horovitz, 152.

115. K. Levin, 362.

116. Ross, 190. In fact, Islamic Jihad and Hamas extremists took credit for the attacks.

117. Karsh, *Arafat's War*, 140.

118. Ross, 198, 205–6; Kort, 154; Gilbert, *Israel*, 583–84; Sachar, 998–99.

119. K. Levin, 387; see also Gilbert, *Israel*, 584.

120. Horovitz, 208, 216–17; Gilbert, *Israel*, 584–85; K. Levin, 363, 388.

121. Levin, 363–64, 388–89.

122. Horovitz, 18–19.

123. Ibid., 19, 21.

124. Ibid., 19–23.

125. Horovitz, 246–56; Kort, 158–62; Kurzman, *Rabin*, 513–15.

126. Rabin, afterward, 341.

127. Kurzman, *Rabin*, 513.

128. Karsh, *Arafat's War*, 57–58.

129. K. Levin, xix.

130. This is the dominant theme of K. Levin's book. The quoted phrase is found on page 386.

131. K. Levin, 324; Karsh, *Arafat's War*, 129.

Chapter 9

1. Bard, *Myths and Facts*, 226; Gold, 286.

2. Bard, *Myths and Facts*, 226; Gold, 2.

3. Gold, 2.

4. Bard, *Myths and Facts*, 227; Sachar, 1037; Gold, 2–3.

5. Nadav Shragai, "Ha'aretz: Review of plans to divide Old City of Jerusalem with PA and PA security forces—facts already on the ground." *Haaretz*, June 18, 2000, http://christianactionforisrael.org/plans.html (accessed 10/4/10). According to Shragai, after obtaining a permit to build a new exit for the underground mosque constructed in Solomon's Stables, the Arab *waqf* had "made a mockery" of Israeli law by bringing "dozens of bulldozers" up to the Temple Mount and bulldozing "6,000 tons of earth" containing priceless artifacts. "Antiquities dating back to a number of periods were tossed on garbage heaps. The Antiquities Authority managed to salvage but a small part of all these treasures." (See also Gilbert, *Israel*, 621.)

6. Hefez and Bloom, 345; Sachar, 1037; Bard, *Myths and Facts*, 199.

7. Bard, *Myths and Facts*, 199.

8. Rabin had initiated these talks without Peres' knowledge in 1992, telling the Syrians that the degree of peace given to Israel would determine the degree of Israel's withdrawal from the Golan Heights. Syria's President Hafez al-Assad had responded that Israel could have "full peace for full withdrawal." The talks had subsequently stalled.

9. Morris, 637.

10. Sachar, 1010; Gilbert, *Israel*, 592.

11. Gilbert, *Israel*, 592–93; Morris, 637–38.

12. Gilbert, *Israel*, 593.

13. Morris, 638; Karsh, *Arafat's War*, 121.

14. K. Levin, 391; Ross, 244–45.

15. Sachar, 1011–12; Gilbert, *Israel*, 593–94; K. Levin, 390.

16. Shindler, 253.

17. K. Levin, p. 394–95; Norman Podhoretz, "Intifada II: Death of an Illusion?" in Kozodoy, 87; Karsh, *Arafat's War*, 100–105.

18. Morris, 638; Gilbert, *Israel*, 594.

19. Sachar, 1014–15; K. Levin, 396–97.

20. K. Levin, 397–98.

21. Ross, 262–63; Sachar, 1016.

22. Sachar, 1016; Morris, 641. Rabin had made the same stipulations in his 1992 election campaign.

23. Sachar, 1016–17; Gilbert, 596; Ross, 264.

24. Gold, 217–18.

25. Gold, 216–19; Karsh, *Arafat's War*, 147–48; Andrea Levin, "The Media's Tunnel Vision," *Middle East Quarterly* 3, no. 4 (December 1996): 3–9, www.meforum.org/article/426 (accessed 4/4/09); K. Levin, 399, 426.

26. Bard, *Myths and Facts*, 229; K. Levin, 400.

27. See Oslo II Accord, Articles XV, XXII and XXI.

28. Quotes are taken from Israel Ministry of Foreign Affairs publication, "Palestinian In-

citement to Violence Since Oslo — A Four-Year Compendium," citing original sources from *Jerusalem Post* (7/28/1996), *New York Times* (8/7/1996) and Israel Radio (6/7/1996), http://www.mfa.gov.il/MFA/Archive/Peace+Process/1997/PALESTINIAN%20INCITEMENT%20TO%20VIOLENCE%20SINCE%20OSLO-%20A%20F (accessed 10/28/08).

29. K. Levin, 399; Gold, 219; Ross, 265.

30. A. Levin. Since 1996, the PA has, uncomplainingly, kept the exit open lest the Arab shops miss out on their tourism boom (Karsh, *Arafat's War,* 150).

31. K. Levin, 399–401; Karsh, *Arafat's War,* 148–49; Gold, 220.

32. Perhaps the most predictable aspect of these talks was that Arafat would agree verbally to mutual concessions, and then, at the last minute, send his obstructionist negotiator, Saeb Ereket, to tell Ross that the PA agreed only with the concessions offered by Israel, and that amendments would be necessary to what the PA was supposed to give in return. See, for example, Ross, 276, 289, 298, 305–6, 311, 312–17.

33. Morris, 644; regarding same-day redeployment, see K. Levin, 402.

34. In some instances, the PA seems to have paid them to do so (K. Levin, 402–3).

35. K. Levin, 403.

36. Ross, 333–35, 362; for the Palestinian population in Zone C, see K. Levin, 387.

37. Sachar, 1020; Ross, 329.

38. The fact that Jews had purchased 75 percent of the Har Homa hillside from Arab owners since 1967, however, renders this assertion dubious. Lest Jews be allowed to point to ownership in other instances, PA justice minister Freih Abu Medein reanimated a defunct Jordanian law making the sale of Arab land to Jews a capital crime. One week later, Palestinian hooligans abducted a 70-year-old Arab realtor who had sold land to Jews previously, and murdered him with a blow to the skull (Gilbert, *Israel,* 600–601).

39. Shindler, 270; Ross, 329ff.

40. It should be noted that the PA and *waqf* did not hesitate to take objectionable, unilateral actions of their own. In April 1997, they usurped the rooms of Jerusalem's Greek Patriarch and incorporated them into the al-Hanake Mosque. Afterwards, they carried out unauthorized construction next to the venerated Church of the Holy Sepulchre causing an internal wall within the latter to collapse (Gold, 215–16).

41. Karsh, *Arafat's War,* 153.

42. Ross, 262, 337–38, 360.

43. Ross, 338; Sachar, 1020. The Oslo Accords called upon Arafat to extradite many of these culprits to Israel, but he had not done so.

44. Note Norman Podhoretz' analogous discussion in regard to the "Tunnel War" in Kozodoy, 90–92 (in which he implicates not just Arafat, but also the entire Arab world). For casualty figures, see Karsh, *Arafat's War,* 153; Sachar, 1020.

45. Ross, 338.

46. Netanyahu's spokesman, Shai Bazak, quoted in Gilbert, *Israel,* 614.

47. Gilbert, *Israel,* 616; Albright is quoted in Ross, 354.

48. Mashaal is presently Hamas' "political leader."

49. Gilbert, *Israel,* 616; Morris, 645; Ross, 357–58.

50. Israel Ministry of Foreign Affairs, "PA Has Failed to Fulfill Its Commitments Under the Hebron Accord — 20-Jul-97," http://www.mfa.gov.il/MFA/Archive/Peace+Process/1997/PA+Has+Failed+to+Fulfill+Its+Commitments+Under+Heb.htm (accessed 10/28/08).

51. Sachar, 1027–28.

52. Sachar, 1031.

53. Reich, 199; K. Levin, 415.

54. Ross, 588–89; Shindler, 276–77.

55. Reich, 196–98; Morris, 655–57; Ross, 626–27; Karsh, *Arafat's War,* 181–82.

56. Bard, *Myths and Facts,* 265–66; Morris, 657. Hezbollah claimed that the farms had been "loaned" to Syria, but constituted sovereign Lebanese territory.

57. Morris, 653–54; Ross, 507–8.

58. Reich, 201; Sachar, 1033; Morris, 658–59; Ross, 650; K. Levin, 421.

59. Sachar, 1027.

60. Karsh, *Arafat's War,* 162, 165–67; see also Bard, *Myths and Facts,* 276–77; Gold, 183–84; Kozodoy, 93.

61. Karsh, 166.

62. Karsh, *Arafat's War,* 169; K. Levin, 422; Shindler, 279.

63. Bard, *Myths and Facts,* 226; Karsh, *Arafat's War,* 170; Ross, 694.

64. Laqueur and Rubin, 7th ed., 552–53; Reich, 202; Karsh, *Arafat's War,* 171.

65. Quoted in Karsh, *Arafat's War,* 171; see also Ross, 705.

66. Karsh, *Arafat's War,* 163–64. For the cantonization claim see "Palestinian Negotiating Team: Remarks and Questions Regarding the Clinton Plan, January 2, 2001," in Laqueur and Rubin, 7th ed., 567–69.

67. Karsh, *Arafat's War,* 166.

68. Bard, *Myths and Facts,* 276–77; Ross, 689. See also "Map Reflecting Actual Proposal at Camp David," in the map section of Ross' book, prior to the prologue.

69. Quoted in Karsh, *Arafat's War,* 50 (emphasis added by this author).

70. Quoted in Peter Bogdanor, "The Devil

State: Chomsky's War Against Israel," in Alexander and Bogdanor, 85.

71. Reich, 204–6.

72. K. Levin, 422–23; Dershowitz, *Israel*, 120–21; Karsh, *Arafat's War*, 172–74, 191.

73. Gold, 3; Reich, 211–12; Karsh, *Arafat's War*, 180–81.

74. Reich, 211–12; K. Levin, 423; Gutmann, 33; Karsh, *Arafat's War*, 178.

75. This was the post–Balfour Declaration influx of 1919–23, which witnessed the arrival of 35,000 Jewish newcomers to the British Mandate.

76. Benziman, 14; Hefez and Bloom, 21.

77. Benziman, 16–19.

78. Finkelstein, 15–16; Hefez and Bloom, 33.

79. Benziman, 20–21.

80. Ibid., 21–24.

81. Sharon and Chanoff, 57.

82. Hefez and Bloom, 9–12; Sharon, 58–61; Benzamin, 27–31; Dan, 11.

83. Hefez and Bloom, 42–43; Sharon and Chanoff, 63–64.

84. Benziman, 29.

85. Finklestein, 26.

86. Hefez and Bloom, 51–55.

87. Hefez and Bloom. 57–58; Sharon and Chanoff, 89–90; Benziman. 53–54.

88. Hefez and Bloom, 58–59; Sharon and Chanoff, 90–91; Benziman, 54–55.

89. Finkelstein, 29–30; Dan, 20; Gilbert, *Israel*, 292.

90. Finklestein, 30; Gilbert, *Israel*, 306.

91. Hefez and Bloom, 63, 69; Benziman, 64–71, 78; Crompton, 41.

92. Benziman, 83–85; Hefez and Bloom, 81; Crompton, 42–43.

93. Benziman, 87.

94. Ibid., 90.

95. Sachar, 642; Hefez and Bloom, xii; Karsh, *Arafat's War*, 213.

96. Sharon and Chanoff, 37–38; Finkelstein, 16; Hefez and Bloom, 36; Crompton, 27.

97. Hefez and Bloom, 109; Finkelstein, 43.

98. Finkelstein, 43; Benziman, 111; Dan, 50, 61.

99. Benziman, 115–16; Hefez and Bloom, 123–6.

100. Rabinovich, 225.

101. Benziman, 144; Rabinovich, 281–83.

102. Hefez and Bloom, 162.

103. Rabinovich, 340–41, 390.

104. Benziman, 173–77; see also Hefez and Bloom, 166–67, 171–75.

105. Hefez and Bloom, 192–94, 197.

106. Benziman, 211–12; Hefez and Bloom, 197–200.

107. Dan, 130.

108. The charge of "reckless disregard,"

which would have gained Sharon up to $50 million in damages, however, was not upheld (Crompton, 68–73; Hefez and Bloom, 263; Dan, 124–25).

109. Hefez and Bloom, 292–96.

110. Hefez and Bloom, 303–4.

111. Dan, 146–47.

112. Dan, 159.

113. Sharon and Chanoff, 6 (in forward by Uri Dan); see also Dan, 178.

114. Gutmann, 35; Bard, *Myths and Facts*, 200; Karsh, *Arafat's War*, 188–89.

115. Gutmann, 35.

116. Gold, 5; Karsh, 191–92.

117. Gold, 5. Sachar (1038) puts the wounded at 164, Reich (208) at 200.

118. Editors, *New York Times*, October 3, 2000, quoted in Gutmann, 32.

119. Bard, *Myths and Facts*, 198; Gilbert, *Israel*, 621; Gold, 5; Karsh, *Arafat's War*, 193.

120. Quoted in Gutmann, 36–37; Karsh, *Arafat's War*, 194.

121. Bard, *Myths and Facts*, 198; see also Hefez and Bloom, 362.

122. Gutmann, 9*ff*; see also, Karsh, *Arafat's War*, 192–93.

123. Gutmann, 17–19; Bard, *Myths and Facts*, 318–19; Honest Reporting, "The Photo that started it all," http://www.honestreporting. com/articles/reports/The_Photo_that_Started_ it_All.asp., shows the actual photograph.

124. Except where otherwise specified, the following is a point-by-point summary of Ricki Hollander's article, "L'Affaire Al Dura: The Saga Continues," *Camera Media Watch* 17, no. 2 (Fall 2008): 7–8, 50. The reader may also consult Gutmann, chapter 2, and Bard, *Myths and Facts*, 204, although these versions were published prior to the Karsenty trials.

125. Tipped off that there would be disturbances, cameramen actually appeared at the junction before the Palestinian demonstrators (Gutman, 45). For details of the IDF investigation and of the media response, see Gutmann, 61–65.

126. Hollander, 7–8, 50.

127. Gutman, 85.

128. The whole story is somewhat more craven: concerned that his reporters would be blamed, incorrectly, for filming the incident, a producer from RTI's competitor, RAI TV, wrote to the PA confirming that RTI had done the filming (Gutman, 92–93; see also Bard, *Myths and Facts*, 312).

129. Gutman, 45–46.

130. Sachar, 1038.

131. The media studiously ignored the gunmen to please the PA (Karsh, *Arafat's War*, 201).

132. Reich, 210–15.

133. Ibid., 215.

134. Hefez and Bloom, 348; Sachar, 1043–44.

135. Ross, 751–53; Sachar, 1041–42; Reich, 215–16; Karsh, *Arafat's War*, 204–6.

136. Hefez and Bloom, 350.

137. Reich, 217.

138. Quoted in Reich, 221.

139. Finkelstein, 91; Dan, 193; Karsh, *Arafat's War*, 214–16; Sachar, 1046–47.

140. Karsh, *Arafat's War*, 217; Hefez and Bloom, 361.

141. Sachar, 1049; Arafat congratulated the bomber's parents (K. Levin, 468).

142. Hefez and Bloom, 365.

143. Gutmann, 152; Karsh, *Arafat's War*, 224. Intimidation of journalists is standard fare in Palestinian-controlled areas. Most reporters "play along" with the "Palestinian narrative" — even to the point of filming staged scenes to get a good picture (Bard, *Myths and Facts*, 311–13).

144. Hefez and Bloom, 367–68; Dan, 189–90; K. Levin, 471.

145. Dan, 194–95.

146. Reich, 227–28; Sachar, 1048–51.

147. K. Levin, 468.

148. Reich, 229; Karsh, *Arafat's War*, 229.

149. Gutmann, 160–61; Sachar, 1053–54; Reich, 231–32.

150. Gutman, 166; Hefez and Bloom, 375–76.

151. In a minimal concession to journalistic responsibility, some reporters noted that the reports couldn't be confirmed — as if this disclaimer was an adequate substitute for checking the facts before leveling such a charge.

152. Bard, *Myths and Facts*, 212–13; see also, Gilbert, *Israel*, 625; Karsh, *Arafat's War*, 233–34; Hefez and Bloom, 376.

153. Sachar, 1055; Hefez and Bloom, 376–77; Karsh, 235.

154. Dan, 206.

155. Hefez and Bloom, 377; Dan, 209–10.

156. Reich, 245–51.

157. Hefez and Bloom, 387, 417; K. Levin, 503.

158. Reich, 255–57.

159. Reich, 257–59; Dan, 218–19, 231–32.

160. Hefez and Bloom, 425–26; Dan, 220.

161. K. Levin, 507.

162. Reich, 260–61. This was the first time Sharon had employed the term "occupation" to describe Israel's presence in the territories.

163. Reich, 264; Hefez and Bloom, 428.

164. Hefez and Bloom, 438–40.

165. Hefez and Bloom, 400–412, 437; Dan, 213–16.

166. Hefez and Bloom, 430. The Geneva initiative called upon Israel to evacuate 98.5 percent of the West Bank, leaving roughly 110,000 settlers unprotected (Sachar, 1067).

167. Dan, 236.

168. Bard, *Survive*, 54.

169. Hefez and Bloom, 430, 439–42, 447–48.

170. Hefez and Bloom, 448–49; Reich, 269.

171. Elliott Abrams, "Hillary Is Wrong About the Settlements," *Wall Street Journal*, June 26, 2009, http://online.wsj.com/article/SB124588743827950599.html (accessed 4/5/10). (Ignoring these facts, U.S. Secretary of State Hillary Clinton reneged on Bush's assurances in 2009, erroneously contending that "no informal or oral enforceable agreements" had been made.)

172. Yassin had been quadriplegic since an athletic accident at age 12.

173. Hefez and Bloom, 450.

174. Sachar, 1070.

175. Hefez and Bloom, 456–57.

176. Hefez and Bloom, 466–67; Sachar, 1074.

177. Quoted in Reich, 2nd ed., 268; Laqueur and Rubin, 7th ed., 595.

178. Bard, *Myths and Facts*, 272–75; Gilbert, *Israel*, 631; Sachar, 1061.

179. Defamers of Israel have put forth outlandish claims, likening the barrier to the Berlin Wall (even though the latter was built to imprison civilians while Israel's security barrier was devised to keep terrorists at bay). Palestinian legislator Hanan Ashrawi declared, "this is not about security. This is about land annexation. It is an apartheid wall. It is a wall that is designed to turn the Palestinian territory into a prison ... preventing the possibility of a territorial [*sic*] contiguous and viable Palestinian state" (Rosemary Church, "Q&A with Jim Clancy," CNN, July 16, 2003, quoted in Dershowitz, *Peace*, 99). A glance at a map of the barrier's intended route, which only peripherally impinges on the West Bank (see, for example, Hefez and Bloom, 475), renders such claims untenable. In November 2003, the United Nations (which had once equated Zionism with racism) condemned the barrier and referred the matter to the International Court of Justice (IJC), whose chief justice hails from China, a nation with a notorious record of human rights violations (Dershowitz, *Peace*, 104). Although it had no jurisdiction in the matter, the ICJ declared the barrier "illegal."

180. Bard, *Myths and Facts*, 2006 ed., 271; see also Sachar, 1061; Gilbert, *Israel*, 631.

181. Mitchell Bard, "Israel's Security Fence," Jewish Virtual Library, July 9, 2009, http://www.jewishvirtuallibrary.org/jsource/Peace/fence.html (accessed 2/21/10).

182. Hefez and Bloom, 468–70; Sachar, 1095–96.

183. Hefez and Bloom, 470.
184. Hefez and Bloom, 471–74; Sachar, 1096.
185. Hefez and Bloom, 474.
186. Hefez & Bloom, 477–83; Sachar, 1111–12. On November 19, 2010, Sharon — still in a coma at age 82 — was moved home from a long-term hospital facility.

Chapter 10

1. Mitchell Bard, *Survive*, 109.
2. Sachar, 1075–76.
3. CAMERA staff, "Timeline and Causes of 'Operation Cast Lead' in Gaza," CAMERA, 2009, http://www.camera.org/index.asp?x_context=7&x_issue=52&x_article=1581 (accessed 4/25/11).
4. Sachar, 1075–76.
5. Sachar, 1114; Gilbert, 638. When Iranian president Mahmoud Ahmadinejad responded to Israel's Gaza withdrawal by calling for Israel to be "wiped off the map," Hamas' "political" chief, Khalid Mashaal, praised him for his "courageous" words (Gilbert, *Israel*, 635).
6. Sachar, 1115; see also Gilbert, *Israel*, 638.
7. Gilbert, *Israel*, 638.
8. Sachar, 1116.
9. Bard, *Survive*, 101, 117–18; Sachar, 1118–19; Gilbert, *Israel*, 641; Reich, 2nd ed., 276–78.
10. Sachar, 1118.
11. Steven Stotsky, "Questioning the Number of Civilian Casualties in Lebanon," CAMERA, September 7, 2006, http://www.camera.org/index.asp?x_print=1&x_context=2&x_outlet=2&x_article=1195 (accessed 9/25/10).
12. AP, "Hezbollah official: 250 militants killed during Lebanon war," *Haaretz*, December 15, 2006, http://www.haaretz.com/news/hezbollah-official-250-militants-killed-during-lebanon-war-1.207308 (accessed 10/4/10).
13. Stotsky, see note 11. (An August 30, 2006, article in the *Kuwait Times* supports the Israeli estimate.)
14. Sabrina Tavernise, "Christians Fleeing Lebanon Denounce Hezbollah," *New York Times*, July 28, 2006, http://www.nytimes.com/2006/07/28/world/middleeast/28refugees.htm (accessed 4/25/11); Washington Times Staff, "Hezbollah's Human Shields," *Washington Times*, July 30, 2006, http://www.washingtontimes.com/news/2006/jul/30/20060730-093558-9976r/ (accessed 4/25/11); Jacob Laskin, "Media Lies and Hezbollah's Human Shields," FrontPageMag.com, August 10, 2006, http://archive.frontpagemag.com/readArticle.aspx?ARTID=3154 (accessed 4/25/11).
15. Sachar, 1124–27; Bard, *Survive*, 111; Reich, 2nd ed., 278.

16. Sachar, 1126.
17. Bard, *Survive*, 27, 37.
18. Gilbert, *Israel*, 645–46.
19. Bard, *Survive*, 13; Reich, 274, 279.
20. Reich, 2nd ed., 286.
21. Mitchell Bard, "The Gaza War: Online Exclusive," Jewish Virtual Library, AICE, January 30, 2009, http://www.jewishvirtuallibrary.org/jsource/myths2/gazawar.html (accessed 1/30/09).
22. Reich, 2nd ed., 290–91.
23. Mitchell Bard, "Fact Sheet #62: The Gaza Blockade," AICE, November 24, 2008, http://www.jewishvirtuallibrary.org/jsource/talking/62_Blockade.html (accessed 4/9/09). Despite the fact that Hamas' allegations were untrue — as confirmed by the Palestinian Authority — they obtained wide currency in the international media, replete with staged photos of women and children holding candlelight vigils in areas of supposed power blackouts (Kaled Abu Toameh, "PA: 'Hamas Is Staging Gaza Blackouts,'" *Jerusalem Post*, November 19, 2008, http://www.jpost.com/MiddleEast/Article.aspx?id=121022, accessed 4/25/11).
24. Gilbert, *Israel*, 644–47; Reich, 2nd ed., 285–86.
25. Regarding statehood by the end of 2008, see Gilbert, *Israel*, 654–55; Reich, 2nd ed., 288–89.
26. While studying at Oriental College in Moscow during the 1970s, Abbas literally earned a Ph.D. in Holocaust denial (Raphael Medoff, "Likely PA Prime Minister a Holocaust-Denier," FrontPageMag.com, February 26, 2003, http://archive.frontpagemag.com/readArticle.aspx?ARTID=19561, accessed 4/25/11). He was implicated in financing the 1972 Munich Massacre. He has been quoted as saying that "Allah loves the martyr" and that "it is not required of Hamas, or of Fatah, or of the Popular Front to recognize Israel" (ZOA, "Mahmoud Abbas Is No Moderate and Deserves No Support," http://www.zoa.org/sitedocuments/pressrelease_view.asp?pressreleaseID=88, accessed 4/25/11). Quotes are taken from the *Wall Street Journal*, January 5, 2005, and PA TV, October 3, 2006). He has denied the fact that a Jewish Temple formerly existed on the Temple Mount, has consistently refused to recognize Israel as a "Jewish" state, and has unwaveringly adhered to the notion of a Palestinian "right of return" (Efraim Karsh, "Arafat Lives," in Kozodoy, 153). In March 2008, he declared that Israel's countermeasures against Hamas in Gaza were "worse than the Holocaust" and that he opposed armed struggle "at this present juncture ... because we cannot succeed in it, but maybe in the future things will change" (Mitchell Bard, "Myth: Palestinian Authority

President Mahmoud Abbas is a Moderate Interested in Compromise," online exclusive, http://www.jewishvirtuallibrary.org/jsource/m yths2/exclusives.html#a139, accessed 4/25/11; JPost Staff, "Abbas: 'Armed Resistance Not Ruled Out.'" *Jerusalem Post*, February 28, 2008, http://www.jpost.com/MiddleEast/Article.asp x?id=93431, accessed 4/25/11; JPost Staff, "Abbas: IDF Action Worse Than the Holocaust." *Jerusalem Post*, March 2, 2008, http://www.jpost.com/Israel/Article.aspx?id=93651, accessed 4/25/11). In the midst of his negotiations with Olmert, he sent a congratulatory letter to the family of Samir Kuntar, who had been released from an Israeli prison in exchange for the corpses of Ehud Goldwasser and Eldad Regev (the two Israeli soldiers abducted by Hezbollah at the outset of the Hezbollah War). Abbas subsequently held an audience with Mr. Kuntar, who was convicted in 1980 of using his rifle butt to dash out the brains of Einat Haran, a four-year-old Israeli girl, and who, subsequent to his release, has been feted as a hero throughout the Arab world where he has announced his intention of carrying out further violent acts against Israel (JPost Staff, "Abbas Congratulates Family of Samir Kuntar," *Jerusalem Post*, July 16, 2008, http://www.jpost.com/MiddleEast/Article.aspx?id=107862, accessed 4/25/11; Associated Press, "Samir Kuntar: I Met with Abbas in Beirut at His Request," *Haaretz*, November 24, 2008, http://www.haaretz.com/news/samir-kuntar-i-met-with-abbas-in-beirut-at-his-request-1.253059, accessed 4/25/11).

27. Ethan Bronner, "Olmert Memoir Cites Near Deal for Mideast Peace," *New York Times*, January 27, 2011, http://www.nytimes.com/2011/01/28/world/midddleeast/28mideast.html (accessed 4/9/11); Haaretz Service, "Olmert: Abbas never responded to my peace offer," *Haaretz*, February 14, 2010, http://www.haaretz.com/news/olmert-abbas-never-responded-to-my-peace-offer-1.263328 (accessed 4/25/11). See also David Horovitz, "Editor's note: Palestinian inflexibility bulldozes Israeli vagueness," *Jerusalem Post*, August 14, 2008, http://www.jpost.com/Opinion/Columnists/Article.aspx?id=111165 (accessed 11/18/08). (Note: It is not clear that Abbas' prestige among Palestinians was sufficient to implement the plan even if he had been agreeable.)

28. Mijal Grinberg and Eli Ashkenazi, "Most Sderot kids exhibit post-traumatic stress symptoms," *Haaretz*, January 17, 2008, http://www.haaretz.com/news/study-most-sderot-kids-exhibit-post-traumatic-stress-symptoms-1.237438 (accessed 4/25/11).

29. From June 17 to December 16, an Egyptian-mediated "cease-fire" was in effect between Israel and Hamas. During this period, Hamas "limited" its rocket and mortar attacks to 329. On the 17th, Hamas unilaterally canceled the "cease-fire." In the next ten days, they fired hundreds of rockets (Bard, "Gaza War," see note 21).

30. Steven Erlanger, "A Gaza War Full of Traps and Trickery," *New York Times*, January 11, 2009, http://www.nytimes.com/2009/01/11/world/middleeast/11hamas.html (accessed 1/19/09).

31. Bard, "Gaza War," see note 21.

32. Erlanger, "Gaza War," see note 30; see also Dershowitz, *Enemies*, 153; Bard, "Gaza War," note 21.

33. Dershowitz, "Israel is well within its rights," *Jerusalem Post*, January, 13, 2009, http://cgis.jpost.com/Blogs/dershowitz/entry/israel_i s_well_within_its (accessed 1/15/09). In one well-publicized instance, Israel was accused of killing as many as 43 innocents in a UN school in Jabaliya, despite being given the school's coordinates and being told that it was to be used as a refuge (January 6). The allegation was widely reported in the media. Three weeks later, however, it was revealed that no Israeli shells had struck the school, and that no one had died there (Patrick Martin, "Account of Israeli Attack doesn't hold up to scrutiny," *Toronto Globe and Mail*, January 29, 2009, http://www.theglobeandmail.com/news/world/africa-mideast/article655111.ece, accessed 4/25/11). Instead, 12 individuals (nine combatants and three civilians) were killed *just beyond* the school grounds when the IDF returned fire from Hamas mortar operators (for 12 fatalities, see David Horovitz, "Counted Out: Belatedly, the IDF enters the life-and-death numbers game," *Jerusalem Post*, February 15, 2009, http://www.jpost.com/Israel/Article.aspx?id=132962, accessed 2/17/09; for mortar operators, see Bard, "Gaza War," note 21). Nine days after the Jabaliya incident, Israeli shellfire damaged a different Gaza UN building, injuring three (January 15). Again Israel was responding to fire that emanated from the direct vicinity of the building. Moreover, Israel immediately sent in fire trucks to help put out the resultant flames (Yaakov Katz and AP, "Shelled UN Building used by Hamas," *Jerusalem Post*, January 15, 2009, http://fr.jpost.com/servlet/Satel lite?cid=1231950855726&pagename=JPost/JPA rticle/ShowFull, accessed 1/15/09). Nevertheless, in the wake of these incidents, UN Secretary-General Ban Ki Moon expressed outrage *at Israel*, without reference to the fact that Hamas had put civilians in harms way.

34. At the time of its report, the IDF had tallied 1,166 Gazan fatalities by name. Apart from the 1,004 cited, 162 adult males could not be

classified definitively as either civilian or combatant. See Stephen Stotsky, "Gaza Casualties: Civilian or Combatant?" CAMERA, updated March 27, 2009, http://www.camera.org/index. asp?x_context=55&x_article=1603 (accessed 12/9/10); IDF, "Majority of Palestinians Killed in Operation Cast Lead: Terror Operatives," March 26, 2009, http://www.mfa.gov.il/MFA/Terrorism-+Obstacle+to+Peace/Hamas+war+against+Israel/Vast_majority_Palestinians_killed_Operation_Cast_Lead_terror_operatives_2 6-Mar-2009.htm, (accessed 4/25/11); David Horovitz, "Counted Out: Belatedly, the IDF enters the life-and-death numbers game," *Jerusalem Post*, February 15, 2009, http://www. jpost.com/Israel/Article.aspx?id=132962 (accessed 2/17/09); Yaakov Katz, "IDF: Civilian deaths less than 25% of total," *Jerusalem Post*, January 14, 2009, http://www.jpost.com/Israel/Article.aspx?id=129314, (accessed 4/25/11).

35. Haaretz Staff, "Hamas admits 600–700 of its men were killed in Cast Lead," *Haaretz*, November 1, 2010, http://www.haaretz.com/news/diplomacy-defense/hamas-admits-600-700-of-its-men-were-killed-in-cast-lead-1.32 3776 (accessed 12/7/10); JPost Staff, "Hamas confirms losses in Cast Lead for first time," *Jerusalem Post*, November 1, 2010, http://www. jpost.com/MiddleEast/Article.aspx?id=193521 (accessed 12/7/10).

36. IDF Spokesperson, "Majority of Palestinians Killed in Operation Cast Lead: Terror Operatives," IDF, March 26, 2009, http://www. mfa.gov.il/MFA/Terrorism-+Obstacle+to+Peace/Hamas+war+against+Israel/Vast_majority_Palestinians_killed_Operation_Cast_Lead_terror_operatives_26-Mar-2009.htm?DisplayMode=print (accessed 12/9/10).

37. CAMERA staff, "Timeline," see note 3.

38. Andrew G. Bostom, "Europe's Rampant Muslim Jew-Hatred, and Absent Jewish 'Islamophobia,'" *American Thinker*, January 9, 2009, http://www.americanthinker.com/2009/01/europes_rampant_muslim_jewhatr.html (accessed 1/9/09); John Leceister, "Fears Mount of Gaza Conflict spill over in Europe," AP, January 6, 2009, http://vladtepesblog.com/?p=4403 (accessed 4/25/11).

39. Abe Foxman, "Gaza goes global," *Jerusalem Post*, January 18, 2009, http://cgis. jpost.com/Blogs/foxman/entry/gaza_goes_global_posted_by (accessed 1/19/09). With their attention focused solely on Israel's alleged insensitivity to civilian casualties in Gaza, the international media scarcely covered these stories. It may be noted, too, that when Palestinian terrorists murdered eight yeshiva students, aged 15 to 26, in Jerusalem in March 2008 and thousands of Gazans celebrated the atrocity in the streets (just as they had done on 9/11), there was no rush to accuse Palestinians of insensitivity (see Donald McIntyre, "Mystery surrounds role of Hamas in Attack on Jerusalem Seminary," *Independent* (London), March 8, 2008, http://www.independent.co.uk/news/world/middle-east/mystery-surrounds-role-of-hamas-in-attack-on-jerusalem-seminary-793156.html (accessed 4/10/09).

40. CAMERA staff, "Timeline," see note 3.

41. Ian Brownlie, Mark Muller, et al., "Israel's bombardment of Gaza is not self-defence — it's a war crime," *Sunday Times* (U.K.), January 11, 2009, http://www.timesonline.co.uk/tol/comment/letters/article5488380.ece (accessed 4/25/11).

42. Open letter to UN Secretary-General Ban Ki-moon, "Find the truth in Gaza," March 16, 2009, http://www.amnesty.org.uk/news_details.asp?NewsID=18109 (accessed 4/25/11).

43. The "weapons analyst" is Marc Garlasco. See HonestReporting Staff, "The Goldstone Report: Rewarding Palestinian Terrorism," http://honestreporting.com/the-goldstone-report-rewarding-palestinian-terror-2/ (accessed 9/2009); John Schwartz, "Rights Group Assailed for Analyst's Nazi Collection," *New York Times*, September 15, 2009, http://www.nytimes.com/20 09/09/15/world/middleeast/15nazi.html (accessed 2/4/11); Jonathan Foreman, "Nazi scandal engulfs Human Rights Watch," *Sunday Times* (U.K.), March 28, 2010, http://www.timesonline.co.uk/tol/news/world/us_and_americas/article7076462.ece (accessed 2/4/11).

44. Richard Goldstone, "Justice in Gaza," *New York Times*, September 17, 2009, http://www.nytimes.com/2009/09/17/opinion/17goldstone.html, (accessed 9/19/09). Asked for his reaction to the report's findings, a spokesman for Israel's foreign ministry replied that it made him nauseous (Haviv Rettig Gur, "Syria, Somalia can't preach morality," *Jerusalem Post*, September 16, 2009, http://www.jpost.com/Israel/Article.aspx?id=154987, accessed 4/25/11).

45. UN Watch Oral Statement Delivered by Colonel Richard Kemp, UN Human Rights Council, 12th Special Session, October 16, 2009, Debate on Goldstone Report.

46. Richard Goldstone, "Reconsidering the Goldstone Report on Israel and war crimes," *Washington Post*, April 1, 2011, http://www.washingtonpost.com/opinions/reconsidering-the-goldstone-report-on-israel-and-war-crimes/2011/04/01/AFg111JC_story.html (accessed 4/5/11).

47. Israel Ministry of Foreign Affairs, "Behind the Headlines: The Israeli Humanitarian Lifeline to Gaza," May 25, 2010, http://www.mfa.gov.il/MFA/About+the+Ministry/Behind+the+Headlines/Israeli_humanitarian_lifeline_Gaza_25-May-2010.htm (accessed 12/23/10).

48. Tobias Buck, "Gaza looks beyond tunnel economy," *Financial Times*, May 24, 2010, http://www.ft.com/cms/s/0/4c51267a-66ca-11df-aeb1-00144feab49a.html#axzz1KZP6vZvi (accessed 4/25/11).

49. Janine Zacharia, "In Gaza, a complex, dysfunctional way of life," *Washington Post*, June 3, 2010, http://www.washingtonpost.com/wp-dyn/content/article/2010/06/02/AR2010060204687.html (accessed 6/13/10).

50. Alan Dershowitz, "Israel obeyed international law: Legally, the Gaza flotilla conflict is an open-and-shut case," *New York Daily News*, June 2, 2010, http://articles.nydailynews.com/2010-06-02/news/29438207_1_gaza-flotilla-blockade-gaza-strip (accessed 6/13/10); Leslie Gelb, "Israel Was Right," *Daily Beast*, May 31, 2010, http://www.thedailybeast.com/blogs-and-stories/2010-05-31/israel-was-right-to-board-the-gaza-flotilla/ (accessed 6/13/10).

51. Barak Ravid and Yuval Azoulay, "Israel: Gaza aid convoy can unload cargo in Ashdod for Inspection," *Haaretz*, May 27, 2010, http://www.haaretz.com/news/diplomacy-defense/israel-gaza-aid-convoy-can-unload-cargo-in-ashdod-for-inspection-1.292560 (accessed 6/13/10).

52. David Horovitz, "Analysis: The flotilla fiasco," *Jerusalem Post*, June 1, 2010, http://www.jpost.com/Israel/Article.aspx?id=177099 (accessed 6/13/10).

53. Israel Ministry of Foreign Affairs, "IDF forces met with pre-planned violence when attempting to board flotilla," May 31, 2010, http://www.mfa.gov.il/MFA/Government/Communiques/2010/Israel_Navy_warns_flotilla_31-May-2010.htm (accessed 4/25/11).

54. Mitchell Bard, "MYTH: 'The flotilla bound for Gaza was on a humanitarian mission,'" Myths and Facts online, http://www.jewishvirtuallibrary.org/jsource/myths2/exclusives.html#a129 (accessed 6/13/10).

55. Isabel Kershner, "Deadly Israeli Raid Draws Condemnation," *New York Times*, May 31, 2010, http://www.nytimes.com/2010/06/01/world/middleeast/01flotilla.html (accessed 4/25/11).

56. Josef Federman, "Gaza blockade eased after deadly raid," Associated Press, June 2, 2010, http://www.theoaklandpress.com/articles/2010/06/02/news/doc4c060178475b6725670496.txt (accessed 6/13/10).

57. Ron Ben Yishai, "A brutal ambush at sea," Ynet News, May 31, 2010, http://www.ynetnews.com/articles/0,7340,L-3896796,00.html (accessed 6/13/10).

58. Israel Ministry of Foreign Affairs, "Summary of equipment and aid aboard the Gaza flotilla," June 7, 2010, http://www.mfa.gov.il/MFA/Government/Communiques/2010/Equipment_aid_Gaza_flotilla_7-Jun-2010.htm (accessed 12/23/10).

59. Itamar Marcus and Nan Jacques Zilberdik, "Three of the four Turks killed on ship sought Martyr's death," *Palestinian Media Watch Bulletin*, June 3, 2010, http://www.palwatch.org/main.aspx?fi=157&doc_id=2367 (accessed 6/13/10).

60. Israel Ministry of Foreign Affairs, "IDF forces met with pre-planned violence," see note 53.

61. Haaretz Service, "Gaza flotilla captain: Activists prepared attack against IDF raid," *Haaretz*, June 11, 2010, http://www.haaretz.com/news/diplomacy-defense/gaza-flotilla-captain-activists-prepared-attack-against-idf-raid-1.295591 (accessed 6/13/10).

62. Yaakov Katz, "IDF: Mercenaries to blame for violence," *Jerusalem Post*, June 4, 2010, http://www.jpost.com/Israel/Article.aspx?id=177452 (accessed 6/13/10).

63. Jerusalem Post Staff and AP, "Netanyahu calls UNHRC flotilla report 'biased, distorted.'" *Jerusalem Post*, September 23, 2010, http://www.jpost.com/Israel/Article.aspx?id=189035 (accessed 12/25/10).

64. Jerusalem Post Staff, "US concerned UNHRC flotilla probe may stop peace talks," *Jerusalem Post*, September 28, 2010, http://www.jpost.com/International/Article.aspx?id=189515 (accessed 12/25/10).

Chapter 11

1. Paraphrased from Berlinski, *A Tour of the Calculus*, 3.

2. Vladimir Jabotinsky, "The Ethics of the Iron Wall," *Jewish Standard* (London), September 5, 1941, http://www.mideastweb.org/Ironwall.htm (accessed 4/19/11).

3. Sachar, 1129.

4. Glenn Kessler, "U.S. praises Netanyahu plan," *Washington Post*, November 26, 2009, http://www.washingtonpost.com/wp-dyn/content/article/2009/11/25/AR2009112500760.html (accessed 12/28/10).

5. JPost.com staff and Associated Press, "Fayyad storms out of New York meeting with Ayalon," *Jerusalem Post*, September 21, 2010, http://www.jpost.com/LandedPages/PrintArticle.aspx?id=188883, (accessed 12/28/10).

6. Joel Lion, "A Freeze on Mideast Politics," *Jewish Week*, October 5, 2010, http://www.thejewishweek.com/news/israel/freeze_mideast_politics (accessed 12/28/10).

7. Haaretz Service and News Agencies, "Netanyahu offers settlement freeze in return for recognition as Jewish State, Palestinians say

no," *Haaretz*, October 11, 2010, http://www.haa retz.com/news/national/netanyahu-offers-set tlement-freeze-in-return-for-recognition-as-jewish-state-palestinians-say-no-1.318447 (accessed 12/28/10).

8. Saeb Erekat, "The returning issue of Palestine's refugees," *Guardian*, December 10, 2010, http://www.guardian.co.uk/comments free/2010/dec/10/israel-palestine-refugee-rig hts (accessed 12/23/10).

9. Natasha Mozgovaya, "U.S. condemns Palestinian claim that Western Wall 'isn't Jewish.'" *Haaretz*, November 30, 2010, http://www. haaretz.com/news/diplomacy-defense/u-s-condemns-palestinian-claim-that-western-wall-isn-t-jewish-1.328098?localLinksEna bled=false (accessed 12/27/10).

10. In spite of Israel's myriad concessions during the Oslo and Road Map years, Palestinian media, schools and mosques have continued to deny Judaism's roots in historical Palestine, to extol the virtues of "martyrdom," and to call for Israel's liquidation. In 2003, at the height of the Al-Aksa *intifada*, a poll found that 59 percent of Palestinians would favor continued terrorism and 80 percent would still demand the "right of return" — i.e., Israel's demographic destruction — even if Israel withdrew completely to the 1949 armistice lines (K. Levin, 495, 508). To this day, official PA maps of "Palestine" (including those in all Palestinian school textbooks) depict the projected Arab state as encompassing the whole of pre–1967 Israel in addition to the West Bank and Gaza

(Bard, *Survive*, 114). The conclusion is obvious: as Michael Oren (Israel's ambassador to the United States) has argued, what Israel's supposed peace partners seek is not a "two-state" solution, but a "two-stage" solution, with the first stage being the establishment of a Palestinian state, and the second being the eradication of Israel (Michael B. Oren, "An End to Israel's Invisibility," *New York Times*, October 13, 2010, http://www.nytimes.com/2010/10/14/opi nion/14oren.html (accessed 4/25/11).

11. Vladimir Jabotinsky, "The Ethics of the Iron Wall," *Jewish Standard* (London), September 5, 1941, http://www.mideastweb.org/Iron wall.htm (accessed 4/19/11).

12. Vladimir Jabotinsky, "The Iron Wall," *Jewish Herald* (South Africa), November 26, 1937, http://www.mideastweb.org/Ironwall. htm (accessed 4/19/11; italics are in the original).

13. Laqueur and Rubin, 7th ed., 119.

14. Article XIII of the Hamas charter, quoted in Laqueur and Rubin, 7th ed., 342.

15. Joel Greenberg, "Palestinian factions Fatah and Hamas formally sign unity accord," *Washington Post*, May 4, 2011, http://www.wash ingtonpost.com/world/palestinian-factions-formally-sign-unity-accord/2011/05/04/AFD 89MmF_story.html (accessed 5/25/11).

16. Itamar Marcus and Nan Jacques Zilberdik, "Palestinian TV children's quizzes teach that there is no Israel," *Palestinian Media Watch Bulletin*, September 2, 2009, http://www.imra. org.il/story.php3?id=45535 (accessed 4/25/11).

Bibliography

Newspapers and Magazines

Financial Times (London)
Guardian (London)
Haaretz (English edition)
Independent (London)
Jerusalem Post
Los Angeles Times
Newsweek
New York Post
New York Times
Sunday Times (London)
Telegraph (U.K.)
Times (London)
Toronto Globe and Mail
Wall Street Journal
Washington Times
Websites
CAMERA.org
CNN.com
ESPN.com
HonestReporting.com
Israel Ministry of Foreign Affairs (www.MFA.gov.il)
The Israel Project (www.theisraelproject.org)
Jewish Virtual Library (www.jewishvirtuallibrary.org)
Mideast Web (www.mideastweb.org)
Palestinian Media Watch (Palwatch.org)
WorldNetDaily (www.wnd.com)

Books and Journal Articles

Alexander, Edward. *The Jewish Wars: Reflections by One of the Belligerents.* Carbondale and Edwardsville: Southern Illinois University Press, 1996.
_____. "No, an Exercise in Jewish Self-Debasement." *Middle East Quarterly* 5, no. 4 (December 1998): 28–30.
Alexander, Edward, and Paul Bogdanor, eds. *The Jewish Divide Over Israel.* New Brunswick, NJ: Transaction Books, 2008.
Amdur, Richard. *Menachem Begin: World Leaders Past and Present.* New York: Chelsea House, 1988.
Asprey, Robert B. *War in the Shadows: The Guerilla in History.* Authors Guild Backprint.com ed. Volume 2. Lincoln, NE: iUniverse, 2002.
Associated Press. *Lightning Out of Israel: The Six-Day War in the Middle East.* Upper Saddle River, NJ: Prentice Hall, 1967.
Avneri, Arieh L. *The Claim of Dispossession.* New Brunswick, NJ: Transaction Books, 1984.
Bard. Mitchell G. *The Complete Idiot's Guide to the Middle East Conflict.* 2nd ed. Indianapolis: Alpha Books, 2003.
_____. *Myths and Facts: A Guide to the Arab-Israeli Conflict.* Chevy Chase, MD: AICE, 2002.
_____. *Myths and Facts: A Guide to the Arab-Israeli Conflict.* Revised ed. Chevy Chase, MD: AICE, 2006. (This edition used only where specifically cited.)
_____. *Will Israel Survive?* New York: Palgrave Macmillan, 2007.
Bar-On, Mordechai. *Never-Ending Conflict: Israeli Military History.* Mechanicsburg, PA: Stackpole Books, 2004.

Bar-Zohar, Michael. *Ben-Gurion, the Armed Prophet.* Englewood Cliffs, NJ: Prentice-Hall, 1968.

Begin, Menachem. *The Revolt.* Jerusalem: Steimatzky's Agency, 1977.

Bein, Alex. *Theodore Herzl.* Translated by Maurice Samuel. Philadelphia: Jewish Publication Society of America, 1942.

Ben-Gurion, David. *Israel: A Personal History.* New York: Funk & Wagnalls, 1971.

_____. *Memoirs.* New York: World Publishing Company, 1970.

Benziman, Uzi. *Sharon: An Israeli Caesar.* New York: Adama Books, 1985.

Berlinski, David. *A Tour of the Calculus.* New York: Vintage Books, 1997.

Blumberg, H. M. *Weizmann: His Life and Times.* New York: St. Martin's, 1975.

Burkett, Elinor. *Golda.* New York: Harper Collins, 2008.

Chouraqui, André. *A Man Alone: The Life of Theodor Herzl.* Jerusalem: Keter Books, 1970.

Churchill, Randolph S., and Winston S. Churchill. *The Six Day War.* Boston: Houghton Mifflin, 1967.

Cohen, Israel. *Theodor Herzl: Founder of Modern Zionism.* New York: Thomas Yoseloff, 1959.

Collins, Larry, and Dominique Lapierre. *O Jerusalem!* New York: Simon & Schuster, Touchstone Books, 1988.

Crompton, Willard. *Ariel Sharon.* New York: Chelsea House, 2007.

Curtis, Michael, Joseph Neyer, Chaim I. Waxman, and Allen Pollack. *The Palestinians: People, History, Politics.* New Brunswick, NJ: Transaction Books, 1975.

Dan, Uri. *Ariel Sharon: An Intimate Portrait.* Translated by Catherine Spencer. New York: Palgrave Macmillan, 2006.

Dayan, Moshe. *Breakthrough: A Personal Account of the Egypt-Israel Peace Negotiations.* New York: Alfred A. Knopf, 1981.

_____. *The Story of My Life.* London: Weidenfeld and Nicolson, 1976.

DeChancie, John. *Gamal Abdel Nasser: World Leaders, Past & Present.* New York: Chelsea House, 1988.

Dershowitz, Alan. *The Case Against Israel's Enemies.* Hoboken, NJ: John Wiley & Sons, 2008.

_____. *The Case for Israel.* Hoboken, NJ: John Wiley & Sons, 2003.

_____. *The Case for Moral Clarity: Israel, Hamas and Gaza.* CAMERA monograph series. Boston: Committee for Accuracy in Middle East Reporting, 2009.

_____. *The Case for Peace.* Hoboken, NJ: John Wiley & Sons, 2005.

Eban, Abba. *Abba Eban: An Autobiography.* New York: Random House, 1977.

_____. *Heritage: Civilization and the Jews.* New York: Summit Books, 1984.

_____. *Israel: A Nation Is Born.* DVD. Educational Broadcasting Corporation, 1992.

_____. *My People: The Story of the Jews.* New York: Berhman House, 1968.

_____. *Personal Witness.* New York: G. P. Putnam's Sons, 1992.

_____. *Voice of Israel.* New York: Horizon Press, 1957.

Elon. Amos. *Herzl.* New York: Holt, Rinehart and Winston, 1975.

Gabriel, Richard A. *Operation Peace for Galilee: The Israeli-PLO War in Lebanon.* New York: Hill and Wang, 1984.

Gavison, Ruth. "The Jews' Right to Statehood: A Defense." *Azure* 15 (Summer 2003): 70–108.

Gilbert, Martin, ed. *The Illustrated Atlas of Jewish Civilization.* New York: Macmillan, 1990.

Gilbert, Martin. *Israel: A History.* Revised and Updated edition. New York: Harper Perenniel, 2008.

Gilder, George. *The Israel Test.* Minneapolis: Richard Vigilante Books, 2009.

Gold, Dore. *The Fight for Jerusalem: Radical Islam, the West, and the Future of the Holy City.* Washington. Regnery, 2007.

Goldston, Robert. *Next Year in Jerusalem.* New York: Fawcett Crest, 1978.

Gordon, Matthew S. *Hafez Al-Assad: World Leaders, Past & Present.* New York and Philadelphia: Chelsea House, 1989.

Greenfeld, Howard. *A Promise Fulfilled.* New York: Greenwillow Books, 2005.

Gutmann, Stephanie. *The Other War: Israelis, Palestinians and the Struggle for*

228   BIBLIOGRAPHY

Media Supremacy. San Francisco: Encounter Books, 2005.

Haber, Eitan. *Menachem Begin: The Legend and the Man.* Translated by Louis Williams. New York: Delacorte, 1978.

Hefez, Nir, and Gadi Bloom. *Ariel Sharon.* Translated by Mitch Ginsberg. New York: Random House, 2006.

Henriques, Robert. *100 Hours to Suez.* New York: Viking Press, 1957.

Herzl, Theodor. *The Complete Diaries of Theodor Herzl.* Edited by Raphael Patai. Translated by Harry Zohn. 5 vols. New York and London: Herzl Press and Thomas Yoseloff, 1960.

_____. *The Diaries of Theodor Herzl.* Edited and translated by Marvin Lowenthal. New York: Universal Library/Grosset & Dunlap, 1962.

_____. *Excerpts from His Diaries.* Selections by Mordecai Newman. Translations by Maurice Samuel and Joseph Lipsky. Jewish Pocket Library. New York: Scopus, 1941.

_____. *The Jewish State.* Minneapolis: Filiquarian, 2006.

Herzog, Chaim. *The Arab-Israeli Wars.* 3rd ed. Updated by Shlomo Gazit. New York: Random House, 2005.

Herodotus. *The History of Herodotus.* Translated by George Rawlinson. 4 vols. New York: Tandy-Thomas, 1909.

Hollander, Ricki. "L'Affaire Al Dura: The Saga Continues." *Camera Media Watch* 17, no. 2 (Fall 2008): 7–8, 50.

Horovitz, David, ed. *Shalom, Friend: The Life and Legacy of Yitzhak Rabin.* New York: Newmarket, 1996.

Hurwitz, Zvi Harry. *Begin: His Life, Words and Deeds.* New York: Geffen, 2004.

Isaacs, Ronald H., and Kerry M. Olitzky. *Critical Documents of Jewish History: A Sourcebook.* Northvale, NJ, and London: Jason Aronson, 1995.

James, Robert Rhodes, ed. *Winston Churchill: His Complete Speeches, 1897–1963.* 8 vols. New York and London: R. R. Bowker, 1974.

Johnson, Paul. *A History of the Jews.* New York: Harper & Row, 1987.

Karsh, Efraim. *The Arab-Israeli Conflict:*

The Palestine Conflict, 1948. Oxford: Osprey, 2002.

_____. *Arafat's War.* New York: Grove, 2003.

_____. *Islamic Imperialism: A History.* New Haven and London: Yale University Press, 2006.

_____. *Palestine Betrayed.* New Haven and London: Yale University Press, 2010.

Katz, Samuel. *Battleground: Fact & Fantasy in Palestine.* New York: Taylor Productions, 2002.

_____. *Days of Fire.* Garden City, NY: Doubleday, 1968.

Katz, Shmuel (Samuel). *Lone Wolf.* 2 vols. New York: Barricade Books, 1996.

Keller, Mollie. *Golda Meir.* New York: Franklin Watts, 1983.

Kissinger, Henry. *Years of Upheaval.* Boston: Little, Brown, 1982.

Kort, Michael G. *Yitzhak Rabin, Israel's Soldier Statesman.* Brookfield, CT: The Millbrook Press, 1998.

Kozodoy, Neal, ed. *The Mideast Peace Process: An Autopsy.* New York: Encounter Books, 2006.

Kurzman, Dan. *Ben-Gurion: Prophet of Fire.* New York: Simon & Schuster, 1983.

_____. *Genesis 1948: The First Arab-Israeli War.* New York: New American Library, Inc., 1970.

_____. *Soldier of Peace: The Life of Yitzhak Rabin.* New York: HarperCollins, 1998.

Laqueur, Walter. *A History of Zionism.* New York: MLF Books, 1972.

Laqueur, Walter, and Barry Rubin, eds. *The Israel-Arab Reader.* 5th ed. New York: Penguin Books, 1995.

_____. *The Israel-Arab Reader.* 7th edition, revised and updated. New York: Penguin Books, 2008. (This edition used only where specifically cited).

Lau-Lavie, Naphtali. *Moshe Dayan, a Biography.* Hartford: Hartmore House, 1968.

Levin, Andrea. "The Media's Tunnel Vision." *Middle East Quarterly* 3, no. 4 (December 1996): 3–9.

Levin, Kenneth. *The Oslo Syndrome: Delusions of a People Under Siege.* Hanover, NH: Smith and Kraus, 2005.

Lewis, Bernard. *What Went Wrong: The*

Clash Between Islam and Modernity in the Middle East. New York: Harper Perenniel, 2002.

Litvinoff, Barnet. *Weizmann, Last of the Patriarchs.* New York: G.P. Putnam's Sons, 1976.

Lloyd George, David. *War Memoirs of David Lloyd George.* 6 vols. Boston: Little, Brown, 1933.

Loftus, John, and Mark Aarons. *The Secret War Against the Jews.* New York: St. Martin's Griffin, 1994.

Marshall, S. L. A. *Sinai Victory.* Nashville, TN: The Battery Press, 1985.

Marshall, Brigadier General S. L. A. *Swift Sword: The Historical Record of Israel's Victory, June, 1967.* With the editors of American Heritage Magazine and United Press International. New York: American Heritage Publishing, 1967.

Matuskey, Gregory, and John P. Hayes. *King Hussein: World Leaders Past & Present.* New York, New Haven and Philadelphia: Chelsea House, 1987.

McNamara, Robert. *In Retrospect: The Tragedy and Lessons of Vietnam.* With Brian VanDeMark. New York: Times Books/Random House, 1995.

Meir, Golda. *My Life.* New York: G. P. Putnam's Sons, 1975.

Meir-Levi, David. *Big Lies.* Los Angeles: Popular Center for Culture, 2005.

_____. *History Upside Down: The Roots of Palestinian Fascism and the Myth of Israeli Aggression.* New York: Encounter Books, 2007.

Miller, Shane. *Desert Fighter: The Story of General Yigael Yadin and the Dead Sea Scrolls.* New York: Hawthorne Books, 1967.

Millstein, Uri. *The War of Independence.* 4 vols. Tel Aviv: Zmora-Bitan, 1991.

Morris, Benny. *Righteous Victims.* New York: Vintage Books, 2001.

Moynihan, Daniel Patrick. *A Dangerous Place.* With Suzanne Weaver. Boston: Little Brown, 1978.

Neff, Donald. *Warriors at Suez: Eisenhower Takes America into the Middle East.* New York: The Linden Press/Simon & Schuster, 1981.

Netanyahu, Benjamin. *A Durable Peace.* New York: Warner Books, 2000.

O'Brien, Conor Cruise. *The Siege.* New York: Simon & Schuster, 1986.

Oren, Michael B. *Six Days of War.* Oxford: Oxford University Press, 2002.

Orwell, George. *Homage to Catalonia.* New York: Harcourt, Brace & World, 1952.

Parkes, James. *A History of the Jewish People.* Middlesex: Penguin Books, 1964.

PBS. *The 50 Years War.* DVD. PBS Home Video, 1999.

Peres, Shimon. *Battling for Peace.* New York: Random House, 1995.

Perlmutter, Amos. *The Life and Times of Menachem Begin.* Garden City, NY: Doubleday, 1987.

Peters. Joan. *From Time Immemorial.* Chicago: JKAP Publications, 1984.

Phillips, Melanie. *The World Turned Upside Down.* New York: Encounter Books, 2010.

Prittie, Terence. *Eshkol: The Man and the Nation.* New York: Pittman, 1969.

Rabin, Yitzhak. *The Rabin Memoirs.* Berkeley: University of California Press, 1996.

Rabinovich, Abraham. *The Yom Kippur War.* New York: Schocken Books, 2004.

Reich, Bernard. *A Brief History of Israel.* New York: Checkmark Books, 2005.

_____. *A Brief History of Israel.* 2nd ed. New York: Checkmark Books, 2008.

Rose. Norman. *Chaim Weizmann.* New York: Penguin Books, 1986.

Ross, Dennis. *The Missing Peace: The Inside Story of the Fight for Middle East Peace.* New York: Farrar, Straus and Giroux, 2004.

Roth, Cecil. *A History of the Jews: From Earliest Times Through the Six Day War.* Revised edition. New York: Schocken Books, 1989.

Rubin, Barry. *Revolution Until Victory? The Politics and History of the PLO.* Cambridge, MA: Harvard University Press, 1994.

Sachar, Howard M. *A History of Israel from the Rise of Zionism to Our Time.* New York: Alfred A. Knopf, 2007.

Sadat. Anwar. *In Search of an Identity: an Autobiography.* New York: HarperCollins, 1978.

Samuels, Gertrude. *B-G: Fighter of Goliaths.* Lincoln, NE: Authors Guild Backprint, 2000.

Schiff, Ze'ev. *A History of the Israeli Army (1870–1974).* Translated and edited by Raphael Rothstein. San Francisco: Straight Arrow Books, 1974.

Schiff, Ze'ev, and Ehud Ya'ari. *Israel's Lebanon War.* Edited and translated by Ina Friedman. New York: Simon & Schuster, 1984.

Seidman, Hillel. *Menachem Begin, His Life and Legacy.* New York: Shengold, 1990.

Shapira, Anita. *Yigal Allon, Native Son: A Biography.* Translated by Evelyn Abel. Philadelphia: University of Pennsylvania Press, 2008.

Sharon, Ariel, and David Chanoff. *Warrior.* New York: Touchstone Books, 2001.

Shindler, Colin. *A History of Modern Israel.* Cambridge: Cambridge University Press, 2008.

Silberman, Neil Asher. *A Prophet from Amongst You: The Life of Yigael Yadin: Soldier, Scholar, and Mythmaker of Modern Israel.* Reading, MA: Addison-Wesley, 1993.

Silver, Eric. *Menachem Begin: The Haunted Prophet.* New York: Random House, 1984.

Silverstein, Herma. *David Ben-Gurion.* New York: Franklin Watts, 1988.

Singer, Isadore. *Russia at the Bar of the American People.* New York & London: Funk and Wagnalls, 1904.

Slater, Robert. *Golda: The Uncrowned Queen of Israel.* New York: Jonathan David Publishers, 1981.

_____. *Warrior Statesman: The Life of Moshe Dayan.* New York: St. Martin's, 1991.

St. John, Robert. *Eban.* Garden City, NY: Doubleday, 1972.

Temko, Ned. *To Win or To Die: A Personal Portrait of Menachem Begin.* New York: William Morrow, 1987.

Teveth, Shabtai. *Moshe Dayan: The Soldier, the Man, the Legend.* London: Quartet Books, 1974.

Thomas, Hugh. *Suez.* New York: Harper & Row, 1967.

Tuchman, Barbara. *Bible and Sword.* New York: Ballantine Books, 1956.

_____. *Practicing History: Selected Essays.* New York: Alfred A. Knopf, 1981.

Van Creveld, Martin. *Moshe Dayan.* London: Weidenfeld & Nicolson, 2004.

Weisgal, Meyer W., ed. *Chaim Weizmann, Statesman and Scientist, Builder of the Jewish Commonwealth.* New York: Dial Press, 1944.

Weizmann, Chaim. *Trial and Error.* 2 vols. Philadelphia: The Jewish Publication Society of America, 1949.

Yadin, Yigael. *Bar-Kochba: The Rediscovery of the Legendary Hero of the Second Jewish Revolt against Rome.* New York: Random House, 1971.

Zionist Organization of America (ZOA). "Deir Yassin: History of a Lie." ZOA Publications, March 9, 1998, http://www.freerepublic.com/focus/religion/674327/posts (accessed 9/25/10).

Index

Numbers in **bold italics** indicate pages with photographs.